"*I LOVED THE BOOK! Why didn't I have this book two months ago! . . . a valuable guide . . . very helpful for the first time traveler in Asia . . . worth packing in the suitcase for a return visit.*"—Editor, **Unique & Exotic Travel Reporter**

"*VERY USEFUL, PERFECTLY ORGANIZED. Finally a guide that combines Asian shopping opportunities with the tips and know-how to really get the best buys.*"—**National Motorist**

"*INFORMATION-PACKED PAGES point out where the best shops are located, how to save time when shopping, and where and when to deal . . . You'll be a smarter travel shopper if you follow the advice of this new book.*"—**AAA World**

"*DETAILED, AND RELEVANT, EVEN ABSORBING in places . . . The authors know their subject thoroughly, and the reader can benefit greatly from their advice and tips. They go a long way to removing any mystery or uneasiness about shopping in Asia by the neophyte.*"—**The Small Press Book Review**

WHAT SEASONED TRAVELERS SAY

"*IMMENSELY USEFUL . . . thanks for sharing the fruits of your incredibly thorough research. You saved me hours of time and put me in touch with the best.*"—**C.N.**, DeKalb, Illinois

"*FABULOUS! I've just returned from my third shopping trip to Southeast Asia in three years. This book, which is now wrinkled, torn, and looking much abused, has been my bible for the past three years. All your suggestions (pre-trip) and information was so great. When I get ready to go again, my 'bible,' even though tattered and torn, will accompany me again! Thanks again for all your wonderful knowledge, and for sharing it!*"—**D.P.**, Havertown, Pennsylvania

"*I LOVE IT. I've read a lot of travel books, and of all the books of this nature, this is the best I've ever read. Especially for first timers, the how-to information is invaluable.*"—**A.K.**, Portland, Oregon

"*THE BEST TRAVEL BOOK I'VE EVER READ. Believe me, I know my travel books!*"—**S.T.**, Washington, DC

"*MANY MANY THANKS for your wonderful, useful travel guide! You have done a tremendous job. It is so complete and precise and full of neat info.*"—**K.H.**, Seattle, Washington

"*FABULOUS BOOK! I just came back from Hong Kong, Thailand, and Singapore and found your book invaluable. Every place you recommended I found wonderful quality shopping. Send me another copy for my friend in Singapore who was fascinated with it.*"—**M.G.**, Escondido, California

"*THIS IS MY FIRST FAN LETTER...you made our trip more special than I can ever say.*"—**N.H.**, New York, New York

THE TREASURES AND PLEASURES OF AUSTRALIA

By Drs. Ron and Caryl Krannich

TRAVEL AND INTERNATIONAL BOOKS

International Jobs Directory
Jobs For People Who Love to Travel
Mayors and Managers in Thailand
Politics of Family Planning Policy in Thailand
Shopping and Traveling in Exotic Asia
Shopping in Exotic Places
Shopping the Exotic South Pacific
Travel Planning on the Internet
Treasures and Pleasures of Australia
Treasures and Pleasures of China
Treasures and Pleasures of Egypt
Treasures and Pleasures of Hong Kong
Treasures and Pleasures of India
Treasures and Pleasures of Indonesia
Treasures and Pleasures of Israel and Jordan
Treasures and Pleasures of Italy
Treasures and Pleasures of Paris and the French Riviera
Treasures and Pleasures of Rio and São Paulo
Treasures and Pleasures of Singapore and Bali
Treasures and Pleasures of Singapore and Malaysia
Treasures and Pleasures of Thailand

BUSINESS AND CAREER BOOKS AND SOFTWARE

101 Dynamite Answers to Interview Questions
101 Secrets of Highly Effective Speakers
201 Dynamite Job Search Letters
Best Jobs For the 21st Century
Change Your Job, Change Your Life
The Complete Guide to International Jobs and Careers
The Complete Guide to Public Employment
The Directory of Federal Jobs and Employers
Discover the Best Jobs For You!
Dynamite Cover Letters
Dynamite Networking For Dynamite Jobs
Dynamite Resumes
Dynamite Salary Negotiations
Dynamite Tele-Search
The Educator's Guide to Alternative Jobs and Careers
Find a Federal Job Fast!
From Air Force Blue to Corporate Gray
From Army Green to Corporate Gray
From Navy Blue to Corporate Gray
Get a Raise in Seven Days
High Impact Resumes and Letters
Interview For Success
Job-Power Source CD-ROM
Jobs and Careers With Nonprofit Organizations
Moving Out of Education
Moving Out of Government
Re-Careering in Turbulent Times
Resumes & Job Search Letters For Transitioning Military Personnel
Savvy Interviewing
Savvy Networker
Savvy Resume Writer
Ultimate Job Source CD-ROM

THE TREASURES AND PLEASURES OF

Australia

BEST OF THE BEST

RON AND CARYL KRANNICH, PH.DS

IMPACT PUBLICATIONS
MANASSAS PARK, VA

THE TREASURES AND PLEASURES OF AUSTRALIA: BEST OF THE BEST

Library of Congress Cataloging-in-Publication Data

Krannich, Ronald L.
    The treasures and pleasures of Australia: best of the best/ Ron and Caryl Krannich.
        p. cm.—(Impact guides)
    Includes bibliographical references and index.
    ISBN 1-57023-060-9
    1. Shopping–Australia–Guidebooks. 2. Australia–Description and travel. 2. Australia–Guidebooks.
I. Krannich, Caryl Rae. II. Title. III. Series.
TX337.A8 K76 2000
380.I'45'0002594–dc21
                                                            00-031893

Publisher: For information, including current and forthcoming publications, authors, press kits, and submission guidelines, visit Impact's Web site: *www.impactpublications.com*

Publicity/Rights: For information on publicity, author interviews, and subsidiary rights, contact Media Relations: Tel. 703-361-7300, Fax 703-335-9486, or *media@impactpublications.com*

Sales/Distribution: For information on distribution or quantity discount rates, call (703-361-7300), Fax (703-335-9486), E-mail (*australia@impactpublications.com*), or write: Sales Department, Impact Publications, 9104 Manassas Drive, Suite N, Manassas Park, VA 20111. Bookstore orders should be directed to our trade distributor: National Book Network, 15200 NBN Way, Blue Ridge Summit, PA 17214, Tel. 1-800-462-6420.

Contents

PART I
Smart Traveling and Shopping

PART II
Great Destinations

CHAPTER 5
Brisbane **125**

CHAPTER 6
Cairns **161**

CHAPTER 7
Darwin **185**

CHAPTER 8
Broome **244**

Liabilities and Warranties

WHILE THE AUTHORS HAVE ATTEMPTED to provide accurate information, please remember that names, addresses, and phone numbers do change and shops, restaurants, and hotels do move, go out of business, or change ownership and management. Such changes are a constant fact of life in ever-changing Australia. We regret any inconvenience such changes may cause to your travel and shopping plans.

Inclusion of shops, restaurants, hotels, and other hospitality providers in this book in no way implies guarantees nor endorsements by either the authors or publisher. The information and recommendations appearing in this book are provided solely for your reference. The honesty and reliability of shops can best be ensured by **you**—always ask the right questions and request proper receipts and documents.

The Treasures and Pleasures of Australia provides numerous tips on how you can best experience a trouble-free adventure. As in any unfamiliar place or situation, and regardless of how trusting strangers may appear, the watch-words are always the same—*"watch your wallet!"* If it's too good to be true, it probably is. Any *"unbelievable deals"* should be treated as such. In Australia, as elsewhere in the world, there simply is no such thing as a free lunch. Everything has a cost. Just make sure you don't pay dearly by making unnecessary shopping mistakes.

Preface

WELCOME TO ANOTHER IMPACT GUIDE that explores the many unique treasures and pleasures of shopping and traveling in one of the world's most fascinating places—Australia. Join us as we explore this country from a very different perspective than found in other travel books. We'll take you on an unforgettable journey that will put you in touch with some of the best quality shops, hotels, and restaurants in the world. If you follow us to the end, you'll discover a whole new dimension to both Australia and travel. Indeed, as the following pages unfold, you'll learn there is a lot more to Australia, and travel in general, than taking tours, visiting popular tourist sites, and acquiring an unwelcome weight gain attendant with new on-the-road dining habits.

Exciting Australia offers a wonderful travel experience for those who know what to look for, where to go, and how to properly travel and shop its many cities and towns. We discovered this more than a decade ago when we first explored Australia's unique treasures and pleasures. The result was a book entitled *Shopping in Exciting Australia and Papua New Guinea*. We have returned several times to further explore this ever-changing and delightful country. We discovered there is a lot more to Australia than sun, surf, hedonism, and extreme

xii   THE TREASURES AND PLEASURES OF AUSTRALIA

travel that often characterizes Australia's travel image. For us, Australia is an important shopping and lifestyle destination that yields wonderful quality arts, crafts, and jewelry as well as great restaurants, hotels, and entertainment. Australia remains one of our favorite destinations. Its people and products continue to enrich our lives.

If you are familiar with our other Impact Guides, you know this will not be another standard travel guide to Australia. Our approach to travel is very different from most guidebooks. We operate from a particular perspective, and we frequently show our attitude rather than just present you with the sterile "travel facts." While we seek good travel value, we're not budget travelers who are interested in taking you along the low road to Australia. We've been there, done that at one stage in our lives. If that's the way you want to go, you'll find lots of guidebooks on budget travel to Australia as well as a whole travel industry geared toward servicing budget travelers and backpackers with everything from hostels to Internet shops. At the same time, we're not obsessed with local history and sightseeing. We get just enough history and sightseeing to make our travels interesting rather than obsessive. Accordingly, we include very little on history and sightseeing because they are not our main focus; we also assume you have that information covered from other resources. We're very focused—we're in search of quality shopping and travel. As such, we're very people-oriented. Through shopping, we meet many interesting people and learn a great deal about the country.

What we really enjoy doing, and think we do it well, is shop. For us, shopping makes for great travel adventure. Indeed, we're street people who love "the chase" and the serendipity that comes with our style of travel. We especially enjoy discovering quality products; meeting local artists and craftspeople; unraveling new travel and shopping rules; making new friendships with local business people; staying in fine places; and dining in the best restaurants where we often meet the talented chefs and visit their fascinating kitchens. In the case of Australia, we want to find the best quality arts, crafts, antiques, jewelry, and apparel as well as discover the best artists and craftspeople. In so doing, we learn a great deal about Australia and its talented population.

The chapters that follow represent a particular perspective on Australia. We purposefully decided to write more than just another travel guide with a few pages on shopping. While some travel guides include a brief and usually dated section on the "whats" and "wheres" of shopping, we saw a need to also explain the "how-tos" of shopping in Australia. Such a book would both educate and guide you through Australia's shopping maze as well as put you in contact with the best of the best in accommodations, restaurants, and sightseeing.

The perspective we develop throughout this book is based on our belief that traveling should be more than just another adventure in eating, sleeping, sightseeing, and taking pictures of unfamiliar places. Whenever possible, we attempt to bring to life the fact that Australia has real people and interesting products that you, the visitor, will find exciting. This is a country of very talented designers, artists, craftspeople, traders, and entrepreneurs. When you leave Australia, you will take with you not only some unique experiences and memories but also quality products that you will certainly appreciate for years to come.

We have not hesitated to make qualitative judgments about the best of the best in Australia. If we just presented you with shopping and traveling information, we would do you a disservice by not sharing our discoveries, both good and bad. While we know that our judgments may not be valid for everyone, we offer them as **reference points** from which you can make your own decisions. Our major emphasis is on quality shopping, dining, accommodations, sightseeing, and entertainment, and in that order. We look for shops which offer excellent quality and styles. If you share our concern for quality shopping, as well as fine restaurants and hotels, you will find many of our recommendations useful to your Australia adventure. Best of all, you'll engage in what has become a favorite pastime for many Australians—lifestyle shopping!

Throughout this book we have included "tried and tested" shopping information. We make judgments based upon our experience—not on judgments or sales pitches from others. Our research was quite simple: we did a great deal of shopping and we looked for quality products. We acquired some fabulous items, and gained valuable knowledge in the process. However, we could not make purchases in every shop nor do we have any guarantee that your experiences will be the same as ours. Shops close, ownership or management changes, and the shop you visit may not be the same as the one we shopped. So use this information as a start, but ask questions and make your own judgments before you buy.

Whatever you do, enjoy Australia. While you need not *"shop 'til you drop,"* at least shop it well and with the confidence that you are getting good quality and value for your money. Don't just limit yourself to small items that will fit into your suitcase. Be adventuresome and consider acquiring larger items that can be safely, conveniently, and inexpensively shipped back home.

As we note in the section on shipping, don't pass up something you love because of shipping concerns. Shipping is something that needs to be *arranged*, which is easy to do in Australia.

We wish you well as you prepare to experience Australia's many treasures and pleasures. The book is designed to be used on the streets of nine destinations. If you **plan** your journey according to the first three chapters and **navigate** our nine major destinations based on the next nine chapters, you should have an absolutely marvelous time. You'll discover some exciting places, acquire some choice items, and return home with many fond memories of a terrific Australian adventure. You, too, may go home fat, happy, and broke as well as experience that unexplained urge to return to Australia next year. If you put this book to use, it will indeed become your best friend—and passport—to the many unique treasures and pleasures of Australia. Enjoy!

Ron and Caryl Krannich
krannich@impactpublications.com

THE TREASURES AND PLEASURES
OF AUSTRALIA

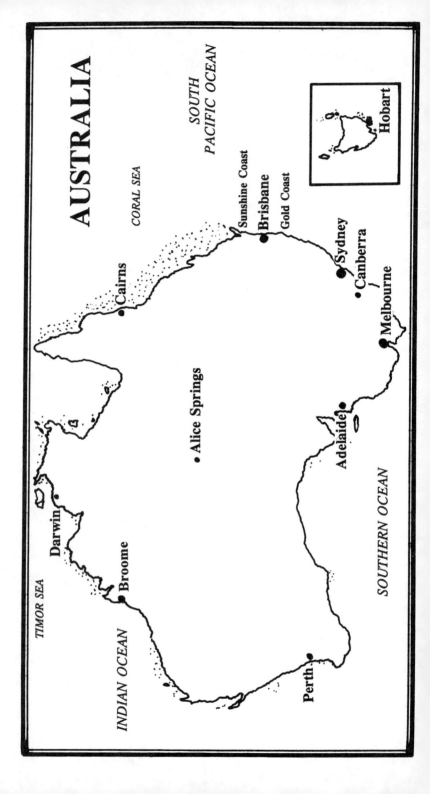

Welcome to Exciting Australia

WELCOME TO ONE OF THE WORLD'S MOST exciting destinations. While far from most major international tourist centers, Australia is near and dear to the hearts of many travelers who have discovered the many treasures and pleasures of this intriguing and thoroughly seductive fun and sun place. Although it is not visited in as large numbers as Italy, France, England, or even Hong Kong, Australia still ranks at the top of most people's lists of "favorite destinations." In fact, Sydney often ranks number one in *Condé Nast Traveler's* annual survey of the world's best cities.

We're not surprised that Sydney and Australia receive such honors and why you, too, may discover this is one of your favorite destinations. Join us as we take you on a journey of many surprises, one that may forever enrich your life. But be forewarned: Australia is the perfect wanderlust destination. A year from now you may have that unexplained urge to return to Australia to explore more of its many treasures and pleasures!

EVERYONE'S FAVORITE DESTINATION

What is it about Australia that makes it such a wonderful place to visit? Try the sunny surf and sand or go deep sea fishing or diving. Catch a great black marlin or explore the world's largest reef. Enjoy a great restaurant overlooking Sydney Opera House and the harbor. Pamper yourself by staying in one of the world's top hotels or resorts. Shop for intriguing Aboriginal art, tribal artifacts from neighboring Papua New Guinea, or unique Australian arts, crafts, jewelry, clothing, and accessories as well as meet the talented artists and craftspeople. Pet a koala bear, feed a kangaroo, or go crocodile and bird watching. Or perhaps explore a rainforest, travel through beautiful wine country, visit delightful craft villages, or head into the desolate Outback for one of the great adventures of a lifetime. If you're a bit less adventuresome, maybe you'll enjoy taking the famous Ghan train journey between Alice Springs and Adelaide, a hot air balloon ride over the Barossa Valley, or a camel ride at sunset along Cable Beach in Broome.

As you'll quickly discover, Australia is many things to many people. Above all, it's a terrific lifestyle destination, a place to lighten up, have fun, and indulge yourself in the many and varied pleasures associated with the best of international travel. It's a country of many surprises, from the very ordinary and familiar to the unusual and exotic. It never fails to stimulate a sense of adventure.

❑ Australia is many things to many people. It's a terrific lifestyle destination. It never fails to stimulate a sense of adventure.

❑ Australia is a huge sparsely populated island primarily urbanized in the southeast.

❑ For many travelers, Sydney remains the world's most attractive city.

❑ Australia is a relatively sophisticated destination with great restaurants, hotels, and resorts; fine shopping and entertainment; varied sightseeing; and a vibrant ethnic, cultural, and artistic life.

An especially lucky country, Australia is blessed with lots of land, sunshine, beaches, friendly people, and things to see and do. Once you arrive and adjust to the relatively long distances between cities and the vast emptiness of its ancient interior, Australia is a very convenient, pleasant, and fun place to get around in and explore. It's literally a huge sparsely populated island primarily urbanized in the southeast which boasts some of the world's most unusual sights and adventures.

If you've never been to Australia, chances are you've heard a great deal about its exciting cities, beautiful beaches, friendly people, and intriguing Outback and Aboriginal population. You've probably seen pictures of Sydney's stunning harbor and Opera House, know something about the Great Barrier Reef, and generally view this place as an inviting fun and sun destination for English-speaking travelers. But there's lots more to Australia than these images!

A NEW AND DIFFERENT AUSTRALIA

If it has been some time since you last visited Australia, chances are you will discover a very different Australia. It has matured a great deal, become more international and cultured, and transformed itself into a major destination for businesspeople and tourists alike. Offering a tourist infrastructure second to none, Australia's treasures and pleasures are numerous and surprising. Much more than the fun and sun image projected in the 1970s and 1980s, it's now a relatively sophisticated destination with great restaurants, hotels, and resorts; fine shopping and entertainment; varied sightseeing; and a vibrant ethnic, cultural, and artistic life.

For many travelers, Sydney remains the world's most attractive city; it's likely to become even more attractive due to the impact of the Summer Olympics 2000. Being "down under" and in close proximity to the world's fastest growing region—Southeast Asia and the Pacific Rim—Australia has become one of our favorite places to visit. We're sure it will also become one of your very favorite destinations.

A QUALITY ADVENTURE
WITH A SHOPPING FACE

As you will quickly discover, *The Treasures and Pleasures of Australia* is not your typical guidebook to Australia nor one on how to do Australia "on the cheap." We make no claims to doing all of Australia for all types of visitors. Like other volumes in our series, Winston Churchill's philosophy on life has helped guide many of our travel choices: *"My needs are very simple—I simply want the best of everything."* In the case of Australia, we've purposefully focused on quality travel experiences with a decided emphasis on shopping for Australian, Aboriginal, and Papuan New Guinea treasures to enhance our home and wardrobes.

Yes, we're talking about putting a shopping face on Australia along with its many other more popular travel faces. This may be surprising to many people, including Australians who do not view their country as a significant shopping destination. But we've discovered a very unique Australia which we want to share with others who know little about this facet of Australia. Indeed, ever since we published the first edition of this book in 1989 as *Shopping in Exciting Australia and Papua New Guinea*, we've discovered quality shopping to be one of the major highlights of traveling to Australia. It's one that is often overlooked by other travel guides as well as many visitors to Australia. This is unfortunate because Australia has a great deal to offer when it comes to shopping, more so than many other countries we have visited. In fact, when we inventory our treasures from all over the world, we've been pleasantly surprised to discover that some of our most cherished purchases came from Australia. Added to Australia's many shopping treasures are numerous quality pleasures from outstanding international hotels and restaurants to exciting sightseeing, outdoor adventures, and entertainment to make for one of the world's greatest travel and shopping adventures.

Assuming you have limited time, wish to experience the best of what Australia has to offer, and seek good value when you travel, we've attempted to highlight what we consider to be the best of Australia's many and varied treasures and pleasures. If you are like us, you'll return home with more than a set of photos, memories, and a temporary weight gain. Being an informed shopper, you'll acquire a treasure-trove of products that represent some of Australia's best artists, craftspeople, and designers, many of whom you may have a chance to meet during your sojourns to Australia's major cities and towns.

UNIQUE TREASURES

Few people think of Australia as a major shopping destination. Indeed, Australia has masterfully created an inviting travel image of a friendly country offering surf, sun, hedonism, and adventure. If one reads the literature and listens to the advertisements, Australia is all about outdoor sports, beaches, fishing, sailing, pubs, the Outback (Australia's desolate interior), underdogs, rugged individualism, and egalitarianism—images reinforced by major international sporting events and *Crocodile Dundee* films and Paul Hogan advertisements. It most recently has begun to project its unique Aboriginal culture and heritage through art, music, and entertainment.

❑ Australia has a great deal to offer when it comes to shopping, more so than many other countries.

❑ Australians, Aboriginals, and neighboring Papua New Guineans are extremely talented and artistic peoples who create some of the finest arts and crafts in the world.

❑ The recession of the early 1990s was both deep and long lasting; it transformed Australia's economy which, in turn, negatively impacted on tourism and shopping.

While there is much truth to such images and stereotypes that entice visitors to the shores of Australia, there is also a great deal of hype and exaggerated claims to fame visitors should take with a smile. This is still a relatively new and provincial nation, lacking a glorious history and homogeneous population, in search of a national identity and an international role that would set it apart from other nations in the Pacific, Asia, Europe, and North America while still acknowledging and incorporating its Aboriginal heritage into a diverse national fabric. Historically a dumping ground for European prisoners, geographically both an Asian and Pacific nation, culturally and linguistically European, and socially and artistically North American, Australians continue in search of the "real" Australian character which would allow them to define who they really are to themselves as well as to the rest of the world. In the meantime, Australians seem preoccupied with enjoying an enviable lifestyle.

There are also many other Australias that deserve equal time. Indeed, we discovered a very different Australia unknown to most travelers—as well as to many local residents—who are primarily oriented toward the Outback, pubs, beaches, reefs, and the city lights. Australians, Aboriginals, and neighboring Papua New Guineans are extremely talented and artistic peoples who create some of the finest arts and crafts in the world, who extend their creative and artistic talents into exciting worlds of fashion, design, and music. In fact, within the past few years, Aboriginal art has come of age and now occupies a prominent place in the Australian and international art worlds. You'll find numerous Aboriginal art galleries, from Melbourne and Sydney to Brisbane and Alice Springs, offering an impressive range of Aboriginal art. At the same time, you'll discover wonderful jewelry designs, colorful fashion, and creative hand-crafted items. The list of unique Australian treasures go on and on. It's a truly surprising list of treasures produced by very talented and independent Australians.

For us, Australia is a prime shopping destination for locally-produced items not widely available outside this country. This is a world of outstanding arts and crafts, intriguing tribal artifacts, creative fashion clothes, unique jewelry, and fabulous contemporary art found in some of the world's most interesting shopping centers, department stores, hotel shopping arcades, small shops, craft centers, markets, and towns. Whatever you do during your stay in Australia, make sure you visit some of the many fine shops and galleries we recommend. Chances are you'll discover several Australian treasures that you will appreciate for many years to come as you put your own shopping face on Australia.

OFFERING NEW CHOICES

Since we first discovered Australia's many shopping treasures
in the late 1980s, Australia has undergone some tough economic times. The recession of the early 1990s, coupled with a
crippling airline strike, was both deep and long lasting; it
transformed Australia's economy which, in turn, negatively
impacted on tourism and shopping. Australia has only recently
come out of the recession that resulted in high unemployment
and fewer shoppers supporting the traditional arts, crafts, and
fashion worlds. As a result, during the past ten years many
shops have gone out of business. Artists and craftspeople who
depended on such shops for their livelihood have seen their
markets shrink considerably. Accordingly, a major fallout took
place within what was a vibrant arts and crafts community only
a few years ago. It will probably be a long time, if ever, before
this community and its profusion of arts and crafts rebound.

In many respects, 1988-1989 were the "Golden Years" for
Australian artists, craftspeople, and shopkeepers who received
a great deal of government and public support. Years of
national and state government subsidies helped promote a
strong and highly visible arts and crafts movement. Today those
subsidies have largely disappeared as the arts and crafts
communities fend for themselves in a relatively weak commercial marketplace. Not enough local buyers can support these
talented communities, and the international market remains
even weaker. What is perhaps most surprising is the fact that
the Australian arts and crafts community was able to achieve
what it did in the late 1980s considering the relatively small
size of the Australian population and limited number of
international buyers. Government subsidies in the forms of
grants and purchases were key to keeping this movement viable.

Despite the trials and tribulations of the arts and crafts, they
remain well and alive in Australia. Quality remains superb and
prices are reasonable. At the same time, Aboriginal art has come
of age and taken center stage as more galleries have opened
throughout Australia offering a wide range of Aboriginal paintings and carvings. So far the government and international
market are supportive of this major art movement.

ENTICING PLEASURES

While the nature of shopping in Australia has changed signifi-
cantly during the past eight years, so have many of Australia's
travel pleasures. The most evident change has been in the food

department. Australian cuisine used to be an oxymoron, and great restaurants where largely nonexistent. Like British food, Australian food was nothing to write home about except for perhaps an occasional shepherd's pie and a few seafood dishes. How times have changed in just a few years! One of the great surprises is the near complete transformation of Australian cuisine in the past ten years. Today Sydney, Melbourne, Adelaide, and other places boast many fine international restaurants and chefs from all over the world. Fueling this trend are the facts that restaurant prices are relatively reasonable and Australians are dining out more than ever before. Indeed, many shop owners lament the fact that Australians seem to be more interested in spending their money in restaurants rather than on shopping! Dining out is definitely "in" these days, and it's largely responsible for the tremendous growth in quality restaurants and dining choices. One of the great highlights of visiting Australia today is sampling its many ethnic restaurants as well as fine dining establishments. Many of these places offer some of the world's most inventive cuisines, most notable for its fusion of European, American, and Asian cuisines. Whatever you do, make sure you sample some of Australia's great restaurants. You may be amazed to discover that dining out is one of the major pleasures of visiting Australia. And to shop and dine in Australia at the same time is simply devine!

Australia also offers a good range of hotels, resorts, and sightseeing experiences. You'll find plenty to see and do wherever you travel in Australia, be it cruising through the Great Barrier Reef, exploring the Barossa Valley, discovering the Outback, or cuddling a Koala bear or feeding a kangaroo. Most places offer at least two or three days of interesting activities to keep most travelers busy. After that you may be hard pressed to find interesting things to do. In fact, our rule of thumb for traveling in Australia is to spend three days in each place with the exceptions of Sydney and Melbourne which probably deserve another day or two. More than five days in any one location may be too long for travelers who like to keep busy. If you the type of traveler who enjoys lying on a beach, by all means spend more time in those places that appeal to your style of travel, especially along the east coast and its nearby islands.

A CONTINENT OF UNIQUE CITIES

Australia is primarily an urban nation clinging to the ocean and nearby hills with two very large cities—Sydney and Melbourne—several intermediate cities, and numerous small towns that dot Australia's colorful coastlines, hills, and Outback. Shopping opportunities abound throughout this vast country of talented artists, craftsmen, and designers consisting of an amalgam of local-born whites, European and Asian immigrants, and Australia's original inhabitants, the black Aboriginals. Visit the shopping centers, hotel shopping arcades, department stores, boutiques, small city shops, and factory outlets to indulge your shopping fancies, but don't forget to also venture into markets, small craft towns, and a few Aboriginal communities. There you will have an opportunity to meet artists and craftsmen as well as discover products closely tied to the cultures and lifestyles of urban artists, eccentric craftsmen dwelling in the hills, and intriguing Aboriginals representing their "Dreamtime" culture in abstract designs on bark, canvas, and wood.

Australia's cities and towns are surprising centers for acquiring some of the world's most interesting and high quality arts, crafts, and fashion clothes. Each city and area has its own unique character and a range of shopping strengths that differ from other cities and areas in Australia. To shop Australia properly, you must visit its many cities and towns as well as have an appreciation for a broad range of unique Australian and imported products, from designer clothes, accessories, and souvenirs to antiques, arts, crafts, artifacts, and home decorative items produced by Australians, Aboriginals, tribal peoples of Papua New Guinea, Asians, and Europeans. Indeed, Australia is a shopper's paradise for a fascinating range of excellent quality products.

Sydney, the country's largest and most cosmopolitan city, is a wonderful place to visit and shop. Nestled along the charming Port Jackson harbor, Sydney boasts a dynamic central business district, adventuresome architecture, fine hotels and restaurants, charming neighborhoods with sidewalk cafés, and numerous cultural, entertainment, and recreational opportunities. Sunny Sydney is a brash, enterprising, fast-paced city which offers some of the best shopping opportunities in all of Australia. It has the country's most interesting shopping centers (Strand Arcade and Queen Victoria Building) and its most exclusive department store (David Jones) and suburban shopping area (Double Bay). If you're looking for clothes, jewelry, antiques, arts, crafts, and souvenirs, the shops and markets of Sydney will not disappoint you. The shopping emphasis here is on clothes, accessories, jewelry, opals, souvenirs, art, crafts, and imported antiques (England) of special appeal to Sydney's cosmopolitan and up-market population as well as to the millions of tourists who come to discover this extremely liveable city. Sydney has something for everyone, from duty-free shopping and imported Italian and French designer clothes and accessories for Japanese tourists to jewelry and fine Australian, Aboriginal, and European art for collectors. Tourists in search of souvenirs will be pleasantly surprised by the numerous choices available in Sydney.

Melbourne, the country's second largest city and elegant competitor to Sydney, is the most European of Australia's cities. It retains much of its old world charm. Its quaint street cars, European architecture, parks, river front, museums, churches, immigrant communities, ethnic restaurants, markets, and shopping centers set this city apart from other places in Australia. The fashion center of Australia, conservative Melbourne is a shopper's paradise for clothes and accessories. Here you will find the latest in Australian designer clothes in downtown and suburban boutiques, department stores, and factory outlets. The arts and crafts are particularly well and alive in Melbourne. Antique and art lovers find many treasures in Melbourne's numerous antique shops, galleries, and markets. The city also is one of the major centers for Aboriginal art. Indeed, some of Australia's best Aboriginal art galleries are found in Melbourne.

Brisbane, capital of the East Coast state of Queensland, surprises many visitors who expected a small and provincial city. This is one of Australia's largest and most cosmopolitan, enterprising, and friendly cities which boasts great weather, a fine performing arts and cultural center, a strong crafts tradition, and the ability to attract millions of visitors to its downtown, suburban, hill, and coastal areas. Walk through its downtown pedestrian mall, explore its colorful suburban communities, or shop in its nearby hill towns and coastal communities and you will quickly discover a Brisbane which offers a wide range of resortwear, designer clothes, antiques, arts, crafts, and Aboriginal art and artifacts.

Adelaide is a pleasant surprise to many visitors who normally end their visit to Australia in Sydney and Melbourne or on the beaches of Queensland. A charming and festive city of beautiful architecture, spacious parks, and an inviting countryside, this is one of Australia's major arts and crafts centers. Shop its downtown pedestrian mall, suburban shops, and craft towns and you will surely leave with some lovely handcrafted items from South Australia.

Alice Springs is Australia's true Outback, a vast, harsh land of sand, heat, and pesky flies. Situated in the Red Centre of the country, Alice Springs is a small but surprising frontier city which plays a major role in opening the Outback of Ayers Rock, desert, wilderness, and Australia's fascinating Aboriginals to thousands of visitors each year. Here the fashion clothes, antiques, arts, and crafts of Brisbane, Sydney, Melbourne, and Adelaide disappear as a whole new shopping experience emerges relating to the Outback environment and culture. Shopping in Alice Springs takes on a different character altogether as you are introduced to the culture of Australia's original inhabitants, the desert Aboriginals, who create some of the world's most unusual art—acrylic sand paintings representing elements of Aboriginal "Dreamtime" stories, woodcarvings, and silk screen fabrics.

Cairns, Australia's gateway city to Papua New Guinea and the South Pacific, offers surprising shopping opportunities for visitors who primarily come here to soak up the sun, explore the Great Barrier Reef, and go sport fishing. A rapidly developing city similar in size to Darwin, the once sleepy Cairns has awakened to the realities of becoming a major tropical resort destination for over one million visitors each year. Boasting new resort hotels, shopping centers, a bustling downtown shopping mall, and nearby craft and resort towns, Cairns is a great place to shop for tribal art from Papua New Guinea, resort wear, contemporary art, and unique handcrafted items. It especially appeals to Japanese tourists who have adopted—although some might say "colonized"—Cairns in recent years and indulge in one of their favorite travel activities—shop for duty-free goods in duty-free shops operated by fellow Japanese!

Darwin, a small and somewhat isolated tropical city at the Top End of the Northern Territory, is a friendly and delightful place to visit. A relatively new city since being destroyed by devastating Cyclone Tracy in 1974, Darwin is famous for its wonderful hinterland that includes the great Kakadu National Park and the Tiwi Islands, Darwin also has a lot to offer shoppers who are interested in Aboriginal art, local crafts, and jewelry. This also is the working headquarters for the world famous and pioneering pearl farming family and exquisite jewelers, the Paspaleys. A city of delightful restaurants, water sports, and a major museum, Darwin also is Australia's gateway city to Southeast Asia. From here you can visit the nearby islands of Indonesia. Spend a couple of days in Darwin and you'll be ready to explore the intriguing Outback and nearby islands of the Northern Territory.

Broome is a another world altogether, an exotic town with a romantic and flamboyant past centered on the fascinating development of Australia's unique pearling industry. It's the stuff of adventure novels—pearl divers, ship wreaks, quirky artists, and camels and crocodiles on the beach. If it weren't so real, someone would probably have invented this place with its colorful personalities and local adventures. Indeed, at times isolated Broome doesn't seem to belong to the rest of Australia. Known for its pearling industry and unique ethnic communities, balmy Broome is one of those great travel discoveries you occasionally stumble upon while on the way to somewhere else. A gateway city to Western Australia and the nearby Kimberley region with is vast, empty, and fascinating territory, Broome is a thoroughly seductive place. Spend a couple of days here exploring its beautiful beaches, fascinating pearl farms, and rugged Outback and you'll wish you had scheduled another week in Broome. But the real surprise in Broome is shopping. For such a small town, Broome is a shopper's paradise. Even if you are not a dedicated shopper, you are likely to have a wonderful time exploring Broome's many jewelry stores that offer pearls and Argyle diamonds as well as visit several interesting art galleries that display some of Australia's most interesting Outback art, especially Aboriginal and contemporary paintings.

Perth and Fremantle dominate Western Australia with their population of over 1.2 million in a state of 1.8 million. Boasting a wonderful climate for year-round sports, these are outdoor and active communities. Friendly and inviting and lacking the congestion of other large Australian cities, Perth a great place to spend a few days exploring the city and nearby towns to the south and east. Shoppers discover a good range of arts, crafts, and jewelry in Perth and its surrounding suburban communities. It also offers excellent restaurants and entertainment venues for all types of travelers.

A SHOPPING EMPHASIS

Much of *The Treasures and Pleasures of Australia* is designed to provide you with the necessary **knowledge and skills** to become an effective shopper. We especially designed the book with two major considerations in mind:

- Focus on quality shopping
- Emphasis on finding unique items

Throughout this book we attempt to identify the **best quality shopping** in Australia. This does not mean we have discovered the cheapest shopping or best bargains, although we have attempted to do so when opportunities for comparative shopping arose within and between communities. Our focus is primarily on shopping for **unique and quality items** that will retain their value in the long run and can be appreciated for years to come. This means many of our recommended shops may initially appear expensive. But they offer top value that you will not find in many other shops. For example, when we discover the unique jewelry designs of Robert Clerc and Percy Marks in Sydney, Makers Mark in Melbourne, or the gorgeous pearl jewelry of Paspaley Pearls in Broome, Darwin, and Sydney, we acknowledge the fact that their work is expensive, but it is very beautiful and unique, so much so that you quickly forget their prices after you acquire and continue to admire their outstanding work. When we examine tribal art from Papua New Guinea, we identify key shops in Sydney, Melbourne, and Cairns that offer good quality items. While more expensive than items found along the Sepik River or in Port Moresby in Papua New Guinea, many of the artifacts found in these shops are older one-of-a-kind pieces you cannot find elsewhere. The same is true for a few art, antique, and home decorative shops we discovered in Brisbane and Adelaide that offer artifacts from Papua New Guinea which were once part of private collections. These items may initially seem expensive, but some are museum quality which cannot be purchased elsewhere at any price; in Paris, London, or New York, where many similar pieces eventually end up because of auctions and dealers, these items would cost five times more.

On the other hand, we also identify what we consider to be the best buys for quality items. For example, while you will find excellent quality Aboriginal bark and acrylic paintings in Brisbane, Sydney, Melbourne, and Adelaide, you can discover similar quality Aboriginal paintings at half of the big city prices in Alice Springs and Darwin. If you are interested in clothes and accessories, some of your best buys are found in the factory outlets of Melbourne where you can buy, for example, a $300 designer sweater for only $100! And your best buys on opals come when you know the differences in the types and quality of opals and look for deep discounts on these stones or shop for antique opal jewelry.

APPROACHING THE SUBJECT

The chapters that follow take you on a whirlwind travel adventure of Australia with a decided emphasis on quality shopping, dining, and sightseeing. We literally put a shopping face on Australia, one that we believe you will thoroughly enjoy as you explore Australia's many other pleasures.

Our **choice of cities** may seem unusual, with some curious absences, to many readers. While we would have preferred to cover all cities in Australia, including Hobart and Canberra as well as more craft towns in the hills and along the coasts of Sydney, Melbourne, and Adelaide, we had to make choices given the time limits and logistics involved. We quickly learned, for example, Canberra and Hobart offered some—but by no means extensive shopping. But these places are not as much in Australia's central shopping loop for clothes, arts, crafts, and Aboriginal arts and artifacts as are cities and towns surrounding Sydney, Melbourne, Adelaide, Brisbane, Cairns, Darwin, Alice Springs, Broome, and Perth.

We've given a great deal of attention to constructing a complete **user-friendly book** that focuses on the shopping process, offers extensive details on the "how," "what," and "where" of shopping, and includes a sufficient level of redundancy to be informative, useful, and usable. The chapters, for example, are organized like one would organize and implement a travel and shopping adventure. Each chapter incorporates sufficient details, including names and addresses, to get you started in some of the best shopping areas and shops in each city or town. We purposefully include what we call a functional level of redundancy, where the same shops appear in both "Where to Shop" and "What to Buy" sections, so the reader can easily cross-reference the important "where" of shopping.

Indexes and table of contents are especially important to us and others who believe a travel book is first and foremost a guide to unfamiliar places. Therefore, our index includes both subjects and shops, with shops printed in bold for ease of reference; the table of contents is elaborated in detail so it, too, can be used as another handy reference index for subjects and products. If, for example, you are interested in "what to buy" or "where to shop" in Melbourne, the best reference will be the table of contents. If you are interested in factory outlets in Melbourne, look under "Factory outlets" in the index. And if you are interested in learning if and where you can find a Coogi knitwear store in Melbourne—just in case you passed up a lovely item in one of their stores in Sydney or Perth—then look under **"Coogi Connection"** in the Melbourne section of the index. By using the table of contents and index together, you can access most any information from this book.

The remainder of this book is divided into two parts and eleven additional chapters which look at both the process and content of shopping in Australia. Part I—**"Smart Traveling and Shopping"**—assists you in preparing for your Australia adventures by focusing on the how-to of traveling and shopping. Chapter 2, **"Know Before You Go,"** takes you through the basics of getting to and enjoying your stay in Australia. It includes advice on when to go, what to pack, required documents, currency, business hours, international and domestic transportation, tipping, tourist offices, and the promises and pitfalls of travel. Chapter 3, **"The Treasures and The Rules,"** examines Australia's major shopping strengths, from art and jewelry to fashion clothes and accessories. It also includes advice on comparative shopping and shipping strategies as well as identifies nine important rules for shopping in Australia.

The nine chapters in Part II—**"Great Destinations"**—examine the how, what, and where of shopping and traveling in nine of Australia's major shopping destinations: Sydney, Melbourne, Brisbane, Cairns, Darwin, Broome, Perth/Fremantle, Adelaide, and Alice Springs. Here we identify major shopping strengths of each city; detail the how, what, and where of shopping; and share information on some of the best hotels, restaurants, and sights for each community and surrounding area.

OUR RECOMMENDATIONS

We hesitate to recommend specific shops, restaurants, hotels, and sights since we know the pitfalls of doing so. Shops that offered excellent products and service during one of our visits, for example, may change ownership, personnel, and policies from one year to another or they may suddenly move to another location or go out of business. In addition, our shopping preferences may not be the same as your preferences. The same is true for restaurants, hotels, and sights: they do change.

Since we put shopping up front in our travels to Australia, our major concern is to outline your Australian shopping options, show you where to locate the best shopping areas, and share some useful shopping strategies that you can use anywhere in Australia, regardless of particular shops we or others may recommend. Armed with this knowledge and some basic shopping skills, you will be better prepared to locate your own shops and determine which ones offer the best products and service in relation to your own shopping and travel goals.

However, we also recognize the "need to know" when shopping in unfamiliar places. Therefore, throughout this book we list the names and locations of various shops we have found to offer good quality products. In some cases we have purchased items in these shops and can also recommend them for service and reliability. But in most cases we surveyed shops to determine the quality of products offered without making purchases. To buy in every shop would be beyond our budget, as well as our home storage capabilities! Whatever you do, treat our names and addresses as **orientation points** from which to identify your own products and shops. If you rely solely on our listings, you will miss out on one of the great adventures of shopping in Australia—discovering your own special shops that offer unique items and exceptional value and service.

The same holds true for our recommendations for hotels, restaurants, sites, and entertainment. We sought out the best of the best in these major "travel pleasure" areas. You should find most of our recommendations useful in organizing your own special Australian adventure.

EXPECT A REWARDING ADVENTURE

Whatever you do, enjoy your Australian adventure as you open yourself to a whole new world of shopping and traveling. We're confident you'll discover some very special treasures and pleasures that will also make Australia one of your favorite destinations.

So arrange your flights and accommodations, pack your credit cards and traveler's checks, and head for one of the Pacific's most delightful destinations. Three to four weeks later you should return home with much more than a set of photos and travel brochures. You will have some wonderful purchases and travel tales that can be enjoyed and relived for a lifetime.

Shopping and traveling Australia only takes time, money, and a sense of adventure. Take the time, be willing to part with some of your money, and open yourself to a whole new world of travel. If you are like us, the treasures and pleasures outlined in this book will introduce you to an exciting world of quality products, friendly people, and interesting places that you might have otherwise missed had you just passed through Australia to eat, sleep, see sites, and take pictures. When you travel our Australia, you are not just another tourist. You are a special kind of international traveler who discovers quality and learns about these places through the people and products that define their cultures.

PART I

Smart Traveling
and Shopping

Know Before You Go

W HAT EXACTLY DO YOU KNOW ABOUT Australia that will help you best prepare for your adventure? While Australia is not on major international routes, nor well known to many outsiders, most first-time visitors have some idea of what to expect. At least they have heard about such cities as Sydney and Melbourne, and perhaps Brisbane and the Great Barrier Reef. Such questions as *"How do I get there?"* and *"What can I expect in terms of local transportation, food, accommodations, weather, and potential problems?"* are concerns for many people planning to make a trip to this unique part of the world.

LOCATION AND GEOGRAPHY

Located south of Indonesia and west of New Zealand, Australia is the world's largest island continent. Approximately the size of the continental United States, over 80 percent of Australia's population clings to the coastal cities and towns that are primarily found in the southeast (Brisbane, Sydney, Canberra, Melbourne, Adelaide, and Hobart) but also in the southwest (Perth/Fremantle); small but important pockets of population are found in the center (Alice Springs), north (Darwin), northeast (Cairns), and northwest (Broome).

Australia is an ancient land of great diversity, contrasts, surprises, and monotony. Its regions, cities, and towns each have their own particular character that sets them apart from the rest of Australia. Projecting an image of an earthy, rugged, friendly, unpretentious, classless, sports-minded, and beach-oriented people, surprising Australia is also a very talented, cultured, creative, artistic, provincial, and sometimes insecure, bureaucratic, contentious, and opinionated nation in search of its own national identity. The people are a diverse mix of transplanted European and Asian immigrants as well as indigenous Aboriginals, many of whom still wander harsh reserved interior lands. Its flora and fauna, including the Great Barrier Reef, rainforests, deserts, canyons, kangaroos, koalas, emu, wallabies, wombats, platypus, and cockatoos, accent the unusual and surprising in Australia. Its vast and varied landscape of hills, mountains, deserts, canyons, and the stark and monotonous Outback often gives way to miles and miles of gorgeous beaches. The ancient traditions of its indigenous peoples reflect the world's longest continuous civilization struggling to survive as a unique people in the 21st century.

❑ Over 80 percent of Australia's population clings to the coastal cities and towns that are primarily found in the southeast.

❑ The people are a diverse mix of transplanted European and Asian immigrants as well as indigenous Aboriginals.

❑ Australia is the world's oldest continent which has been physically isolated from the rest of the world for nearly 60 million years.

❑ Given the seasonal and climatic diversity of Australia, almost any time is a good time to visit this country, depending where you go.

Situated in the Southern Hemisphere, with its nearest neighbors being Papua New Guinea, Indonesia, New Zealand, and Antarctica, Australia is a fascinating geographical anomaly. It is not what you would normally expect to encounter in an Asian or Pacific country. In terms of location, Australia is both Asian and Pacific, but in terms of its geography and people it is neither.

Australia is the world's oldest continent which has been physically isolated from the rest of the world for nearly 60 million years. It's ancient age and isolation are partly responsible for its unique flora, fauna, and unusual looking and heavily worn landscape. Uninviting and uninspiring to many explorers, Australia has always been a frontier country with most people living on its urban and coastal fringes with their faces to the sea and their backs turned on an empty and inhospitable interior.

But Australia also has its moments of beauty, be it the rainforests, beaches, and harbors of the East Coast, Kakadu

National Park in the Northern Territory, the awesome and rugged Kimberley of Western Australia, the Blue Mountains of New South Wales, the Barossa Valley of South Australia, or Sydney's inviting harbor and grand Opera House.

The country is divided into six states (Queensland, New South Wales, Victoria, South Australia, Tasmania, and Western Australia), the Northern Territory, and the National Capital area of Canberra. The majority of the population lives in the southeast region in and around the cities of Brisbane, Sydney, Canberra, Melbourne, and Adelaide. Perth in Western Australia, Alice Springs in the central Outback, and Darwin in the North are relatively isolated cities that have developed their own unique character.

Most tourists visit the East Coast to enjoy the beaches and visit the Great Barrier Reef, one of the great wonders of the world with its massive coral reefs and idyllic islands. They also tend to venture on to Sydney, Canberra, perhaps Melbourne. Visitors determined to see most of the country also venture on to Adelaide, Alice Springs, Darwin, Perth, and Hobart. To see it all, however, takes a great deal of time. But one should try to see as much as possible in Australia because it is a very special place with many exciting sights, inviting cities, wonderful beaches, intriguing shopping, and many great adventure destinations.

CLIMATE AND WHEN TO GO

Australia's climate varies depending on one's location on this continent. The north, northwest, and northeast of Darwin, Broome, Cape York, Cairns, and Townsville are tropical areas with a mixture of hot, humid, and mild temperatures year-round, similar to many parts of the Caribbean and Southeast Asia. The most heavily populated Southeast region, encompassing Brisbane, Sydney, Canberra, Hobart, Melbourne, and Adelaide, has distinct seasons which tend to be very hot in the summer and cool in the winter. While it seldom snows, except in the mountains, the weather can turn bitter cold during the winter in Sydney, Canberra, Melbourne, Adelaide, and Hobart. Perth and Fremantle often boast an enviable year-round sunny and mild Mediterranean climate.

Given the seasonal and climatic diversity of Australia, almost any time is a good time to visit this country, depending where you go. The summer months of November to March, for example, in the center and the north can be very hot—even torrid—and dry. The winter months, June through August, can become bitter cold in the far south. The East Coast usually manages to have decent weather year-round, although it rains a lot there during January and February. In general, the best time to travel to Australia will be the spring and fall, but summer and winter can also be very pleasant times. Since Australia is in the Southern Hemisphere, remember her seasons are just the opposite of those in the Northern Hemisphere. The main summer months are January and February.

WHAT TO PACK AND WEAR

Packing clothes for Australia's various climates can be a problem, especially if you arrive in the midst of Australia's winter. We recommend taking light-weight clothes and packing light in anticipation of filling your bags with purchases along the way. If you will be in Australia during the winter, take a medium-weight jacket, wool sweater, and a pair of gloves. Chances are you might encounter a mild winter. If not, you can always buy another sweater in Australia—preferably one made from the fine Australian wools or an inexpensive import from China—and layer your clothes. We do not recommend taking many heavy bulky clothes, although on a bitter cold day or night you may wish you had! We prefer taking the minimum amount of outer wear and take our chances with the cold winter. The worst thing that can happen is that you must go shopping for warmer clothes. If this happens, the best place to buy inexpensive clothes will be some of the markets and factory outlets in Sydney and Melbourne. Australian-made clothes, especially those found in department stores and shopping centers, tend to be expensive.

Australia is a very casual country. You can wear casual shirts, blouses, and slacks most everywhere. However, fine dining establishments in Sydney and Melbourne expect patrons to dress more formally—coat and tie for men and a dress or suit for women. The same is true if you expect to attend a performance at the Sydney Opera House. You may want to pack accordingly for such occasions. At the same time, many people break these rules by dressing "smart casual" for most occasions.

REQUIRED DOCUMENTS

All travelers to Australia, except those holding Australian or New Zealand passports, require a valid passport and visa or ETA (Electronic Travel Authority) for entry. Both a visa and an ETA are good for stays of up to 90 days with multiple entries permitted for a one year period. Beginning in December 1999, individuals who apply for a visa must pay a US$40 application fee; however, an ETA is free! If you choose to apply for a visa, you must complete a visa application form which is available through Australian embassies, Australian consulate-generals, or on the embassy's Web site: *www.aust.emb.org/tourinst.htm*. If you apply in person at an embassy or consulate-general, the visa can usually be issued on the spot. If you mail the application along with your passport and money (only accepts a cashier's check, money order, or credit card), allow one week for return by courier service or express mail and up to four weeks for return by certified or registered mail.

The good news is that the traditional paper and money visa application process is being gradually replaced by the Electronic Travel Authority (ETA). Indeed, Australia has developed one of the smartest and most efficient ways of handling required documents for visitors by actually making the application process hassle free! The ETA replaces a visa and it is fully electronic. It's good for the same amount of time as a visa—for stays of 90 days, with multiple entries for a period of one year. Unlike a visa, the ETA does not require completing an application form, getting a stamp in your passport, or sending your passport anywhere. Best of all, it's free of charge. Thousands of travel agents, especially in the U.S. and Canada, as well as Australian airlines, can now issue a tourist ETA. Before acquiring a paper application form and going through the hassle and cost of mailing it, check with your travel agent and/or airline about getting an ETA.

Whatever you do, don't forget to secure your visa or ETA in plenty of time before departing for Australia. You cannot gain entry to Australia without both a valid passport and an Australian visa or ETA.

THE PEOPLES

Australia has a relatively diverse population. While most of its 18 million population are white, with European immigrant roots, Australia also has a sizeable black Aboriginal population and a large number of Asian immigrants which adds to this country's interesting and sometimes exotic character.

Most Australians and Asians live in cities and a few Outback communities. Many Aboriginals inhabit the harsh interior, although some, such as the Tiwi, live on Bathurst and Melville islands and the fertile coastal and Arnhem Land areas of the north. A large number of Aboriginals also live in and around urban areas, some of whom have assimilated into the education and economic mainstream of white Australian society and others who live separate and on the economic fringes of society. This population diversity gives Australia a unique character. Darwin, for example, has an interesting mix of whites, Aboriginals, and Asians. It's numerous ethnic restaurants testify to the fact that Darwin's European and Asian immigrants still prefer their ethnic foods. Alice Springs has a large and nomadic Aboriginal population that is most notable in the downtown area or camped along the dry river bed. Many talented urban Aboriginal artists and musicians are found in Sydney, Melbourne, and Adelaide.

Australia's Chinese and Japanese heritage is especially evident in the small pearling town of Broome and in the ethnic enclaves of Sydney and Melbourne. Cairns is a favorite destination for many overseas Japanese visitors.

Australia's diverse European heritage is perhaps best represented in the various villages that comprise greater Melbourne. Its diverse mix of ethnic restaurants, especially Italian, Greek, Chinese, Japanese, Vietnamese, Indian, Thai, and Malaysian, along with inventive fusion cuisine, testify to Melbourne's strong ethnic base.

GETTING THERE

Several international airlines service Australia. You can take international flights into most major cities in Australia—Sydney, Melbourne, Adelaide, Canberra, Brisbane, Cairns, Darwin, and Perth. The national carrier, Qantas, is the major international carrier servicing most large coastal cities in Australia. Its major competitor, Ansett Australia, also flies into many of the same cities as well as links Australia with Southeast Asia. Other major airlines, such as Air New Zealand, United, Continental, Delta, Canadian Airlines, UTA French Airlines, British Air, Cathay Pacific, Japan Airlines, Air India, Lufthansa, KLM, and Singapore Airlines, also fly to Australia.

During our last two visits to Australia, we flew into Sydney on United Airlines nonstop from San Francisco. In fact, we made the round-trip from the U.S. twice and found United's personnel and their dedication to passengers to be "top flight" all the way.

On the first trip to Australia, we flew Connoisseur Class (United's Business Class) and found the service outstanding. From the personnel who made the reservations, the check-in and gate personnel, to the flight attendants, everyone took time to listen and try to accommodate our requests and ensure that we had a pleasant flight.

When after only two days in Sydney we got word that a family member was seriously ill and we needed to change our schedule to fly back to the States from a different departure city and a month earlier than we were ticketed, and to a different U.S. destination than the tickets we were holding, United came through and got us on a flight that was fully booked with only two hours notice.

When we returned to Australia a few weeks later, we flew on United again—this time in Economy Class. We expected to encounter a different level of service, but were pleased to find that the attention to passengers' needs was just as much in evidence as it had been in Connoisseur Class. At the check-in counter, the agent went out of his way—even though there was a line behind us—to accommodate our request for seating that our travel agent had neglected to request. And no, we did not get preferential treatment because we are travel writers. The agent behind the check-in counter had no idea who we were.

When we departed Sydney the second time, we had several more pieces of luggage than we had when we began our trip. We had done more than our share of shopping! A large Aboriginal painting and several ethnographic pieces meant not only additional luggage, but strangely configured pieces as well. Again, United was most efficient at handling the extra baggage and everything came through the long journey home in perfect shape. When we went to retrieve our baggage at Washington Dulles, we found our luggage—including our oversized pieces that had received special handling—were already delivered at the main terminal and waiting for us.

If this is what employee ownership is about, we are all for it. We will be flying the "Friendly Skies" again soon.

Ansett Airlines is Australia's major domestic airline, which also has a few international flights (we've taken their Bali to Darwin flight). It also has regional subsidiaries such as Hazelton, Flight West, Kendell, and Airlines of Tasmania. All of the cities included in this book are serviced by Ansett Airlines.

All of our domestic flights were on Ansett Airlines, one of the nicest surprises during the travels through Australia. We were very impressed with Ansett Airlines and their personnel. It's a very friendly, professional, and take-charge airline. Indeed, this is one of the best airlines we have ever flown. Check-in agents were efficient, but friendly, and flight attendants were first-rate. On one of our flights, for example, an elderly gentleman in the row behind us developed a medical problem. The flight crew quickly responded by moving one of the passengers

seated beside him to another seat, and an Ansett flight attendant sat next to him—checking on him and calming him—for
the remainder of the flight. Aircraft are new and well main-
tained, flights were smooth, and flight schedules were main-
tained. Ansett Airlines also is a full service travel organization
that offers several travel services. Be sure to book and reconfirm
your flights in plenty of time. During certain times of the year,
Ansett Airlines may be fully booked if you wait until the last
minute.

All Australian airlines have some of the most restrictive
cabin luggage restrictions we have encountered anywhere in the
world—one small bag (22 x 15 x 8) not weighting more than 11
pounds. While we are not sure of the reason for such an
extreme restriction, it is the rule nonetheless, and airline personnel can be extremely bureaucratic in enforcing this restriction to the letter. For shoppers who are used to being permitted
by other airlines to carry some of their delicate purchases on
board, these restrictions will require you to pack large purchases
well and send them through with your luggage. Luckily, Australian baggage handlers take good care of luggage.

GETTING AROUND WITH EASE

It is fairly easy to get around Australia. Not only are all of its
major cities and towns serviced by airlines, it also has an
extensive all weather road system linking these communities by
bus, car, and truck. Given limited time, our preference is to fly
between major cities. However, within each city, we use a
combination of public transportation and private car. In large
cities such as Brisbane, Sydney, Melbourne, and Adelaide,
where parking can become a problem, we often use buses and
taxis to get around to the various shopping areas within the
cities. In addition to buses and taxis, light rail systems operate
within the cities of Sydney, Brisbane, and Melbourne (trams).

It is relatively easy to drive in Australia. Maps are good and
roads are usually well marked, although a street with one name
often changes to another name unexpectedly. However, keep in
mind that this is a very big country to drive, and driving in the
Outback can be dangerous should you have a breakdown. For
people with limited time, we recommend flying to the major
cities, using local transportation within the city, and renting a
car to visit outlying areas.

We normally rent a car when we want to shop outside the
central city, such as in hill towns and coastal communities. In
the cases of Darwin, Broome, Cairns, Perth, and Fremantle,

renting a car is very convenient for both getting around in the cities and visiting outlying areas. Alice Springs is such a small town that you can easily walk to all the downtown shops and shopping centers. We do not recommend driving a car in the Outback; breakdowns in the remote Outback can quickly endanger one's life.

You will find several rental car companies in every city. The major rental agencies usually have desks at the airports—Hertz, Avis, Budget, and Thrifty. Less expensive local car rental agencies are located near the airports or in the downtown areas. Renting a car is not cheap, nor need it be expensive. If you shop around, you can find a few car rental agencies that rent cars for A$30 or less a day with 200 to 300 free kilometers—more than enough to cover most shopping areas in, around, and outside most cities.

Australia also has a rail system that links Cairns to Brisbane, Sydney, Canberra, Melbourne, Adelaide, and Perth as well as the famous Ghan line connecting Adelaide with Alice Springs.

❑ Australia has developed one of the smartest and most efficient ways of handling required documents for visitors by actually making the application process hassle free! It's called the ETA.

❑ All Australian airlines have some of the most restrictive cabin luggage restrictions in the world which can present challenges to shoppers who carry many of their treasures on board.

❑ For people with limited time, we recommend flying to the major cities, using local transportation within the city, and renting a car to visit outlying areas.

❑ You will usually get a better exchange rate with traveler's checks than with cash.

SAFETY AND SECURITY

Australia is a relatively safe place to travel. Crime against tourists is relatively infrequent. Driving in Australia is relatively sane, although be cautious when approaching the huge road trains (long multi-car trucks) that barrel down the open highways at top speeds. However, take normal safety precautions wherever you go, from using in-room safes and safe deposit boxes in hotels for valuables to watching your purse and wallet. Since Australians in general tend to be a very friendly and approachable people, don't be afraid to ask for assistance if necessary. Your major problems with safety may be more related to the beaches (be careful of the surf, box jelly fish, and sun), Outback travel (don't travel alone without sufficient gasoline and survival provisions), outdoor and water sports (broken bones and drowning), alcohol and drugs (widespread and easy to engage in excess), and encounters with snakes and crocodiles than meeting unsavory individuals who might take advantage of you and your valuables.

CUSTOMS AT HOME

It's always good to know your country's Customs regulations before leaving home. If, for example, you are a U.S. citizen planning to travel abroad, the United States Customs Service provides several helpful publications which are available free of charge from your nearest U.S. Customs Office (or write P.O. Box 7407, Washington, DC 20044). Several also are available in the "Traveler Information" section of the U.S. Customs Web site, *www.customs.ustreas.gov/travel.htm*:

- *Know Before You Go* (Publication #512): Outlines facts about exemptions, mailing gifts, duty-free articles, as well as prohibited and restricted articles. Original art purchased in Australia should enter the U.S. duty-free as should items over 100 years old with proper documentation. However, most other items, especially jewelry, will be dutiable.

- *International Mail Imports* answers many questions regarding mailing items from foreign countries back to the US. The U.S. Postal Service sends packages to Customs for examination and assessment of duty before they are delivered to the addressee. Some items are free of duty and some are dutiable. The rules have changed on mail imports, so do check on this before you leave the U.S.

- *GSP and the Traveler* itemizes goods from particular countries that can enter the U.S. duty-free. GSP regulations, which are designed to promote the economic development of certain Third World countries, permit many products, especially arts and handicrafts, to enter the United States duty-free, but only if GSP is currently in effect. If not, U.S. citizens will need to pay duty as well as complete a form that would refund the duties once GSP goes into effect again and is made retroactive—one of the U.S. Congresses' annual budgetary rituals that is inconvenient to travelers and costly for taxpayers. Many items purchased in Papua New Guinea may be allowed to enter duty-free when GSP is operating; however, items from PNG purchased in Australia (or any second country) are not allowed duty-free entry. Do check on this before you leave the U.S. so you won't be surprised after you make your purchases in Australia.

U.S. citizens may bring in U.S. $400 worth of goods free of U.S. taxes every 30 days; the next $1,000 is subject to a flat 10% tax. Goods beyond $1,400 are assessed duty at varying rates applied to different classes of goods. Original works of art enter the U.S. duty free. If you are in Sydney and uncertain about U.S. duties on particular items, contact the U.S. Embassy and ask for local U.S. Customs assistance.

CURRENCY AND EXCHANGE RATES

The Australian dollar (A$) consists of 100 cents. Paper bills are printed in different colors and include a unique anti-counterfeit clear seal. They come in denominations of $5, $10, $20, $50, and $100. Australia mints six coins: 5¢, 10¢, 20¢, 50¢, $1, and $2. The exchange rate is relatively stable between the U.S. and Australian dollar: US$1 = A$1.75. For current exchange rates, visit this useful online currency converter: *www.oanda.com*.

Use your own judgment on how much cash or traveler's checks to carry with you. In Australia, you will usually get a better exchange rate with traveler's checks than with cash. Major credit cards are widely accepted in most major cities, hotels, resorts, restaurants, and shops. ATMs are readily available, although they do charge transaction fees. The best place to exchange cash and traveler's checks will be banks. However, if you are carrying American Express or Thomas Cook traveler's checks, you'll find their offices give excellent exchange rates on their checks.

ELECTRICITY, WATER, DRINKS

Electricity in Australia is 240/250 volts, AC 50HZ. If you bring 110 volt appliances with you, be sure to bring a voltage converter. Most hotels use the Australian 3-pin power outlet. Chances are if you have an international set of socket adapters, you have a 2-prong plug that will fit. The third prong is for grounding the appliance. Some hotels can loan you an adapter but many do not have them available or they are in short supply. Our advice: purchase an international travel converter and adapter kit before you leave home which will have the proper adapter plugs for Australia

Tap water is normally safe to drink. You will find most international soft drinks as well as many good teas, beers, and fruit juices in local supermarkets. In most cities you'll find small convenience stores, supermarkets, or take-away eateries that offer a good range of drinks for restocking your hotel's pricey mini-bar.

Health and Insurance

Australia is a very clean and health conscious country, more so than most countries in the world. You need not worry about potential health problems other than lying in the sun too long or being stranded in the Outback! Health care and facilities are excellent should you become ill. We do recommend taking with you a sufficient supply of any special medications you require even though you are likely to find what you need in local pharmacies. Australia is one of the few countries where rabies has never occurred. This is largely due to the very restrictive and vigilant policies against the importation of diseased animals. Expect to have your cabin sprayed as your international flight comes in for a landing. This, too, is indicative of Australia's obsession with keeping its country free of any foreign pests. So far they have been remarkably successful.

Should you have an emergency that requires calling an ambulance, fire, or police, dial 000 for immediate assistance.

It's always a good idea to make sure your personal insurance or travel insurance includes coverage for illness or accident during your stay in Australia. Also, consider evacuation insurance in case serious illness or injuries would require that you be evacuated home through special transportation and health care arrangements. One of the best kept travel secrets for acquiring inexpensive evacuation insurance is to become a member of DAN (Divers Alert Network). In the U.S., call 1-800-446-2671 (The Peter B. Bennett Center, 6 West Colony Place, Durham, NC 27705). Without such insurance, special evacuation arrangements could cost between US$10,000 and US$20,000! If you are into adventure travel and plan to engage in physically challenging activities, health and evacuation insurance should be on your "must do" list before departing for Australia.

Food and Accommodations

Food and accommodations can be expensive in many parts of Australia if you stay at deluxe hotels and resorts and dine in top restaurants. A deluxe hotel, for example, can cost A$400 or more a night in Sydney. However, budget conscious travelers will discover that Australia also has a good range of medium and inexpensive accommodations. Most hotels provide coffee and tea making facilities in guestrooms as well as an iron and ironing board. Local tourist offices can assist you in selecting accommodations that best fit your budget.

You will find plenty to eat and drink in Australia. Most cities have excellent restaurants and take-away food shops offering a good range of ethnic, but by no means inexpensive, foods. The real surprise in Australia are the many modern Australian and fusion cuisine restaurants that manage to turn out some of the world's most inventive dishes. Combining the best of European and Asian cooking with some of Australia's special seafoods (especially barramundi) and meats (kangaroo, emu, camel, and crocodile), many of Australia's chefs have followed the European culinary tradition of developing popular followings and opening their own signature eateries. Capuccino café culture and al fresco dining are definitely "in".

Dining in Australia is anything but dull these days! Indeed, you could easily spend a few weeks in Australia on a culinary tour of its cities and towns. For now, shopping and dining are two great travel sports in Australia you can easily combine by following the recommendations in this book.

BUSINESS HOURS

Most businesses remain open 9am-5pm, Monday through Friday. Shopping hours are normally 9am-5:30pm, Monday through Friday, and 9am-12noon on Saturday. Most downtown and suburban shopping centers and shops remain open until 9pm on either Thursday or Friday night, depending on the particular city. Most retail shopping comes to a halt at 12noon on Saturday as well as all day Sunday.

Two exceptions to this weekend closing rule are the arts and crafts shops and weekend markets. Artists and craftspeople operate shops seven days a week. Markets will generally be open Saturday or Sunday, or both days. Knowing this, it's a good idea to do all your other shopping during the week, keep Thursday or Friday nights open for suburban shopping, and concentrate on shopping for arts and crafts on the weekends. Indeed, Australia's weekend market culture is so widespread—a form of entertainment that combines shopping with dining, socializing, and people-watching—that you will have difficulty covering the many markets that open on the weekends. You'll need to be selective in choosing which markets to visit both in the cities and countryside. Craft towns and wineries also are very popular shopping destinations on weekends.

ANTICIPATED COSTS

The cost of travel to Australia has actually declined during the past decade. With increased competition on international air routes to Australia (Qantas no longer monopolizes these routes), the cost of international airfare has substantially decreased during the past few years. For example, at certain times of the year, you can now fly round-trip from Los Angeles to Sydney for around US$800 whereas ten years ago this same routing cost more than US$1,300.

Depending on your style of travel, Australia can be a relatively inexpensive or a very expensive destination. Back-packers, for example, have their own network of accommodations, restaurants, and transportation that makes Australia a relatively inexpensive travel destination. It's also a great jumping-off point for traveling to even more inexpensive Southeast Asia, especially Indonesia, Malaysia, Thailand, Vietnam, and Myanmar.

However, if you follow our many "best of the best"recommendations, you'll find Australia no more or less expensive than other major countries that offer quality travel and shopping. Cities such as Sydney and Melbourne are similar to Los Angeles and Chicago or Toronto and Vancouver. You should expect the top hotels and restaurants to be relatively expensive. And you also should expect them to be top quality, offering the very best Australia has to greet its guests.

TIPPING

Australians have a well deserved international reputation for not being good tippers—the real tightwad travelers! Indeed, many Australians have an aversion to tipping; they simply don't tip at home nor abroad. Nor have businesses institutionalized tipping by including service charges on hotel and restaurant bills. In general, you are not expected to give tips. Given generous minimum wage laws and the high cost of labor in Australia, most service workers are well paid for their labor. However, as more visitors come to Australia and tip service workers, the practice of giving gratuities is becoming more acceptable. Since tipping is not a general custom in Australia, it's up to you whether to give or not give tips. This does not mean you should not tip in Australia. Tips are appreciated, but they should serve as rewards for a job well done rather than given automatically as a cultural habit, which is really the original intent to tipping practices. Airport porters, taxi drivers, and hairdressers do not expect to receive tips, but you may want to tip for exceptional service. If you receive excellent service in a restaurant, consider leaving a 10 percent tip.

PROMISES AND POTENTIAL PITFALLS

Traveling and shopping in Australia is relatively easy if you approach it right. We find Australia very clean, comfortable, and convenient to get around; health and sanitation standards are some of the best in the world; the people are generally friendly and helpful; many Australians display an interesting character—a creative, innovative, analytical, independent, and entrepreneurial *"give it a go"* streak; the sights are both interesting and unusual; and the shopping is often marvelous. It's such an easy country to navigate that one sometimes forgets that this is not home. It's only when you see the unusual landscape, encounter the Aboriginals, drive on the left side of the road, or have difficulty with some of the Australian English words and phrases that you feel you are in a foreign country after all:

Australian English	American English
French dressing	Italian dressing
ground floor	first floor
entree	appetizer
main course	entree
sauce	catsup
jumper	sweater
Manchester	linen

As you'll quickly discover when ordering your entree and main course in restaurants, you'll need to speak some Australian in order to be understood, or at least prevent misunderstanding.

The downside of Australia is very minor considering all its positives. Except for a few sections of Sydney, the interior countryside is not particularly attractive; most cities are architecturally unattractive, although they are becoming more interesting; street signs are often missing or streets change their names unexpectedly; large companies, businesses, and officials tend to be overly bureaucratic and obsessed with rules and regulations rather than with getting things done; except among Asian immigrants, Australian service and the work ethnic leave much to be desired; products and services tend to be overpriced; many Australians have an irritating habit—in part due to their insularity—of overstating that they are or they possess the "biggest" and "best" in comparison to other cities and countries; the sight and plight of Australia's Aboriginals as well as public debates on Asian immigrants and Papua New Guinea that challenge the dominant image of an easy going, caring, tolerant, and classless Australia.

Tourist Offices and Web Sites

The national Australian Tourist Commission as well as most state tourist offices provide a wealth of information and assistance for independent travelers. Even the smallest towns tend to have a tourist office which dispenses information and advice to travelers. Before leaving for Australia, you should visit the official Web site of the Australian Tourist Commission:

www.australia.com

Also check various state and city Web sites for information prior to arrival. The following commercial sites will provide useful information on several Australian destinations:

www.citysearch.com.au
www.waiviata.com.au/Australia

When visiting particular cities, be sure to stop at the local tourist offices which we identify in each of the city chapters. These offices provide free maps, brochures, and travel guides as well as answer questions. They will also book tours and accommodations. Organized to both promote local travel vendors and assist travelers with local travel plans, these offices can be very helpful in making local travel arrangements. If, for example, you'll looking for a specialty tour of the area, they can assist you in identifying your alternatives and making the necessary phone calls to make reservations. In many respects, these offices take on the information and advice functions of travel agencies.

Since Australia is a highly "wired" country, you will discover many Web sites (use standard search engines) dealing with various aspects of Australia. We identify a few of the most useful sites as well as include Web addresses of several shops, hotels, and attractions in each of our nine destination chapters.

If you need to use the Internet while traveling, you'll find numerous Internet centers that provide relatively inexpensive Web access (A$1 for 10 minutes). Many of these Internet stores are located near high usage tourist centers—budget accommodations and restaurants frequented by young travelers.

The Treasures and
The Rules

AUSTRALIA OFFERS A WIDE VARIETY OF SHOP-
ping choices from the latest in fashion clothes and
accessories to exquisite jewelry, contemporary art, and
Australian, Aboriginal, and tribal arts and crafts. Australia's major shopping strengths are in the areas of arts, crafts,
clothes, jewelry, antiques, and souvenirs. The arts and crafts—
both Australian and Aboriginal—are some of the best quality
and most unique items we have found anywhere in the world.
The Aboriginal art is especially striking and expressive of
Australia's ancient and indigenous culture. Australian clothes
are unique in two aspects: for the use of lovely Australian wools
and the large number of Australian designers creating fashionable garments, from formal wear to resort wear. Jewelry made
from Australian opals, South Sea pearls, and Argyle diamonds,
as well as uniquely crafted gold and silver jewelry, are especially
attractive purchases in Australia.

WHAT TO BUY

Many travelers do not think of Australia as a shopper's paradise. This stereotype is true only if you equate a shopping

paradise with bargain prices and an abundance of shops selling the latest in electronic gadgetry. Australia is not Hong Kong, but there is no need for apologies on her part either. Australia has plenty to keep most shoppers happy and ready to return to her shores for yet another shopping experience.

With the exception of factory outlet shopping for local-made clothes and accessories in Sydney and Melbourne, few things in Australia are good buys for individuals who expect to find bargain prices. Lacking inexpensive products, shops in Australia tend to offer many unique and high quality handcrafted products. Therefore, *a good buy in Australia is something you love that you can not find elsewhere*. These might include, for example, a lovely handcrafted item not available outside Adelaide; a one-of-a-kind antique chest; an opulent opal with a glorious play of colors; a string of beautiful Broome pearls; a wonderful designer dress; an Aboriginal acrylic dot painting or carving; or a *tambuan* (woven ceremonial figure) from neighboring Papua New Guinea. Such good buys will each become wonderful continuing reminders of the great time you had on your trip to the "wonder down under".

Gems and Jewelry

It is nearly impossible to think of Australian gems and jewelry without thinking about opals, pearls, and Argyle diamonds. And you certainly can't be in any city in Australia for long without being bombarded with the outlets selling unset opals, opal jewelry, and opal decorating accessories as well as offering films showing the opal mining process and an on-the-spot demonstration of the opal cutting and polishing process.

If you are used to seeing the milky white opals most frequently sold in shops in the U.S., you are in for a surprise in the shops of Australia. The "white" or "milk" opals are mined in Coober Pedy in South Australia. This is by far the largest opal mine field in Australia and that is why you primarily see the White Opal in stores overseas. However, the scarcer—and hence more valuable—opals tend to have far more color and beauty. These are known as the Boulder Opal and the Black Opal. The Boulder Opal has an overall white background but splashed with a play of colors that in both range and intensity are much greater than the colors seen in the White Opal. The Black Opal, as its name suggests, is formed by a background that appears black or dark gray/blue, and also displays a range of vibrant colors across its face.

The price of opals varies with a number of factors besides the obvious one of size. There are three different types of opals and the most valuable is a solid opal. If you are making a purchase of an opal as an investment you probably won't consider any other type. However, if you want the beauty of an opal but without paying as high a price as you would pay for the solid opal, you may consider buying a doublet or a triplet. A doublet is made by glueing thin slices or veneers of precious opal to a "common" opal backing with a black epoxy resin. The dark backing intensifies the colors of the opal making the stone appear to have better color. The triplet is made by adding a clear cap of quartz, perspex or glass to the top of a doublet and all else being equal is usually the least expensive of the three types. Each type of opal has its niche in filling various consumer's needs. You may decide to buy a solid opal for yourself and a doublet or a triplet as a gift for a relative back home. The important thing is that you are aware of the differences and make your purchase carefully so that you do not pay solid opal prices only to get home and find you purchased a doublet!

Another thing to look for when purchasing an opal is the play of color. The extent and overall completeness of color adds to the value of the stone. The number of colors as well as the actual colors also play a part in determining an opal's value. The highest valued opal includes all the colors of the spectrum—especially red and violet/ purple which are rare.

The opal is not crystalline like other gems, but a hydrated silica. Although its hardness (about 5½ to 7 on MOH's hardness scale) is about the same as an emerald, it is a more delicate stone. Before you buy, check to make sure your opal is free from cracks and flaws—major flaws can be seen with the naked eye. An opal with a crack or flawline is more susceptible to breaking if you should hit it against something by accident. An opal that is set in a surrounding bezel is less vulnerable to breaking than one that is in a prong setting; however, it is more difficult to spot a doublet or triplet in a bezel setting.

Be sure to carry your passport and airline ticket with you when shopping for opals or any gold or silver jewelry. You can

❑ With the exception of factory outlet shopping, few things in Australia are good buys for individuals who expect to find bargain prices.

❑ The "white" or "milk" opals are mined in Coober Pedy in South Australia which has the largest opal mine field in the country.

❑ Be sure to carry your passport and airline ticket when shopping for opals or any gold or silver jewelry. You can purchase on a tax-free basis because as an overseas visitor you are exempt from the GST tax.

❑ Pearls constitute a relatively new retail industry in Australia as well as a fascinating story of adventure and intrigue.

purchase on a tax-free basis because as an overseas visitor you do not have to pay Australian GST tax. This Goods and Services Tax is essentially a value-added tax and is already included in the price of the goods. With your passport and airline departure ticket in hand you can often save up to 30% on the marked price of the goods. The actual amount varies from one store to another. In most of the duty-free shops the tax savings is about 30% but in various jewelry stores the percentage varies from about 8% to 30%. There is no duty on opals because they come from Australia, so since you are buying tax-free rather than duty-free, you can take the item with you. If you are buying jewelry that has been imported and has duty-free status, you will be required to pick up your purchase at the airport as you depart the country.

The outlets for opal jewelry—both jewelry stores and "duty-free"—shops abound all over Australia. While the largest cities have the greatest number of outlets for opal jewelry, you will find opal shops in every city. Opal pioneers, such as **Quilpie Opals**, have shops in several cities. **Percy Marks** in Sydney offers exquisite opal jewelry.

Diamonds may not seem to be uniquely Australian, but Australia has its own special diamonds—Argyle diamonds. Although there are the classic whites we're all familiar with, Argyle's are found in an incredible range of colors: deep cognac, champagne, light yellows, peach, beige, green, blue and exotic pinks. Pink has become synonymous with Argyle—one of the most beautiful varieties of natural colored diamonds and rarely found anywhere else in the world—it is both rare and expensive. So rare are the Argyle pinks that at a sale in Geneva, all 82 stones varying from rose to burgundy, were snapped up by one dealer. Argyle diamonds are even laser inscribed with a code visible under magnification as a mark of authenticity.

Australia, especially in the Broome and Darwin areas, produces some of the world's finest **pearls**. As we will see in the chapters on Broome, Darwin, and Perth, this is a relatively new retail industry in Australia as well as a fascinating story of adventure and intrigue. For gorgeous pearl jewelry, be sure to visit Australia's premier pearler and jeweler—**Paspaley**—which has retail shops in Broome, Darwin, and Sydney. You also should visit **Linneys** in both Broome and Perth (Sabiaco), which is responsible for revolutionizing Australia's retail pearl industry. Better still, go directly to the source, the small town of Broome and immerse yourself in the culture of pearl farming as well as visit the many retail pearl and jewelry shops, including Paspaley and Linneys, that dominate commerce in Broome.

If you are interested in viewing or buying pearls, Argyle

diamonds, and opals, in Sydney try **Percy Marks** and **Hardy Brothers**; in Adelaide and Melbourne stop at **Costello's**; and in Perth (Sabiaco) visit **Linneys**.

There are outstanding jewelers working in gold and silver who are crafting **jewelry** in **unique Australian designs**. Master jeweler **Robert Clerc** in Sydney (G11 Queen Victoria Building), for example, offers many innovative designs in gold, from Aboriginal themes to special Egyptian collections.

A wonderful surprise for most first-time visitors to Australia are the handicrafts found in and around the major cities. The range and quality of handicrafts found in other product areas is also available in **craft jewelry**. In fact, the work is often so lovely and so professionally crafted that it almost seems a misnomer to consider it a handicraft, but that really is the category to which it belongs. From handcrafted gold or silver items to ceramic or textile fashioned earrings, brooches, bracelets and bolo ties these pieces are truly works of art. Although you will find good quality jewelry represented in most of the shops that show handicrafts, no doubt the overall best quality of the craft jewelry is to be found at **Makers Mark** in Melbourne and Sydney. This innovative shop represents the jewelry designs of Australia's top artisans.

DESIGNER CLOTHES AND ACCESSORIES

One of Australia's major shopping strengths are its fashion clothes. While you will find some imported clothes and boutiques from such noted designers as Diane Freis and Laura Ashley, most fashion clothes are creations of Australian designers. Hundreds of creative fashion designers, primarily based in Melbourne and Sydney but also found in Adelaide, Brisbane, and Canberra, turn out uniquely designed clothes ranging from high fashion to resort wear and using Australian wools, cottons, and imported silks and polyesters.

Australian fashion design is very much a cottage industry related to local artistic and entrepreneurial traditions. Noted designers such as Collette Dinnigan, John Cavill, Lou Wiseman, Jenny Kee, Liz Davenport, Jill Fitzsimon, Walter Kristensen, Adele Palmer, Angela Padula, Ken Done, Rob Paynter, Teena Varigos, Stunning, Lizzie Collins, Carla Zampatti, Shephards, and Anthea Crawford, create some truly unique fashion clothes that largely define the world of Australian high fashion at home and abroad. While many of these designers have their own boutiques in Melbourne, Sydney, and elsewhere, others sell their creations through department stores, clothing stores, and factory outlets. Other Australian designers produce a medium range of clothing which appeals to a larger and less affluent audience of clothing and department store buyers: Country Road, Sportsgirl, Rodney Clark, R. M. Williams, Morrisons, and Brian Rochford. Especially in Melbourne and Sydney, you'll find lots of trendy boutiques and clothing stores that appeal to young people.

Shopping for Australian designed clothes is a shopping adventure in and of itself. You discover young struggling designers in Melbourne; acquaint yourself with fashionable boutiques in shopping centers, hotel shopping arcades, and department stores; and learn about one of Australia's most creative and artistic cottage industries which is beginning to make its mark on the international fashion scene. Most of the major designers are well represented in the boutiques and department stores of Melbourne, Sydney, and Adelaide. Sydney's fashion centers are Double Bay, Strand Arcade, and the Queen Victoria Building. In Melbourne one must visit the many shops in the 100 block of Collins Street, Toorak Road and Chapel Street in South Yarra, and numerous factory outlets to discover why Melbourne is indeed known as Australia's fashion center. In Adelaide the shops along King William and Unley Roads constitute this city's fashion center.

Australian clothes can be expensive, so don't expect to do bargain shopping for uniquely designed clothes. The best deals are found during sales or at factory outlets. Garments produced in limited designs and quantities, such as fine wool knits requiring extensive hand work, are also good buys compared to similar quality garments found in the boutiques of Europe. Some Australian designers and clothing stores, such as Carla Zampatti, Country Road, and Shepherds have boutiques and shops abroad in such places as New York City and Washington, DC. If you are in these areas before arriving in Australia, you may want to sample their creations and compare prices.

AUSTRALIANA

Merchandise we characterize as Australiana, ranges from marvelous puzzles made in part from precious metals and stones beautifully displayed in suede lined leather boxes to printed T-shirts sporting local animals, scenery, or Aboriginal designs. Hence, Australiana products run the gamut from relatively inexpensive items that make great gifts for friends back home to really exquisite pieces with price tags to match.

Some small shops tend to stock only Australiana, and most department stores will have a section devoted to Australiana goods. Most of these shops feature Aboriginal arts and crafts. Boomerangs and didgeridoos are available although these are of a different quality than those discussed under traditional Aborigine arts. Although they are often made by Aborigines, the boomerangs are generally smaller than the traditional boomerangs, are the returning type boomerang, and sport anything from a drawing of a kangaroo to a picture of the Sydney bridge.

Cuddly stuffed animals of all sizes are available depicting the unique animals of Australia. Koalas are a favorite with many, while others may prefer a kangaroo, platypus or opossum. While a stuffed furry animal may be great for the kids, adults may prefer the beautiful bronze animals. These lovely animals —available in other metals as well—depict unique animals from the frill neck lizard to the platypus.

Placemats and coasters feature Aboriginal designs, native animals and birds, as well as local scenes. There are soaps, bath oils and drawer liners—all with the scent of Australian native flowers. If you want to try growing your own flowers, packaged seeds of native flowers are available. Old-fashioned Australian health remedies and goods such as eucalyptus and ti tree oil and Billy tea can be bought as can notecards, stationery and gift wrap in Australian designs.

Leather wallets stamped with local designs, neckties with tasteful small kangaroo designs, scarves with local motifs are all available alongside sterling silver jewelry and spoons as well as fun and fashion jewelry. Some shops carry Australiana gear— often referred to as citified outback clothing. Drizabone coats, Akubra hats, Snowy River hats, serious slouch hats or swagman humorous hats, moleskin pants, shearer's shirts and wool jumpers—everything Australian you've ever seen in the movies—is on sale for you to buy and take home.

Although they're not easy to carry home, one of our favorite Australiana products are the wood frame animals covered with sheepskin that children can ride. Most glide back and forth rather than rock, but if you're shipping other things back home anyway, these make great gifts for the kids on your list.

HANDCRAFTED PRODUCTS

Australia produces marvelous arts and crafts. Both the quantity and the quality are excellent. Craftspeople work in almost any medium and the outcome ranges from just cute or interesting to superb. The preponderance of work seems to be in **ceramics and pottery**. All size pieces are available from small vases that can easily be packed in a suitcase to large pieces or sets of dishes that would need to be shipped. Designs range from country-cute to sophisticated modernistic pieces.

You'll also find many beautiful **wood crafts** in Australia. Bowls, vases, and covered boxes of some of the most beautiful burl woods you have ever seen. One of our favorite styles combined a small wood covered box in interesting shapes set off by one or two lovely silver spiders—and we never thought we would use "lovely" to describe a spider! Even the bowls were beautiful in their simplicity of style contrasting with the interesting grains of the wood itself. We even found some lovely baby rattles and teething rings being made out of special Australian woods.

There are wonderful selections of **jewelry** handcrafted by talented artisans. Craftspeople are working in gold and silver as well as copper fashioning beautiful contemporary styled earrings, pins, rings, necklaces and bracelets. Whether they have worked in the metal alone or combined metal with semi-precious stones, many of the designs are stunning. There are also artisans who are combining metal and ceramics to produce some unique and attractive jewelry.

Many artists are working in **stained glass** and producing everything from pieces to hang in front of windows to lamps. Some are small enough to pack easily and carry home in a suitcase.

Fiber artists are producing an array of marvelous **textiles**. Silk, cotton and of course, the great wools that Australia is famous for can all be found being worked by the craftspeople into beautiful garments as well as works of art for home decorating. Whether woven or handprinted fabrics, these are special works of art.

Many craftspeople also work in **metals**—silver alloys and copper alloys were especially prevalent for fashioning into plates, bowls or even clocks as well as the popular fountains. Everywhere you look you will find marvelous works of art being made by the craftspeople of Australia. Much of what you will see is museum quality work. Expect to be pleasantly surprised by the profusion and quality of the work you will encounter. Even if you have never been interested in arts and crafts before, we predict that the Australians will win you over.

ABORIGINAL ART

One of the most intriguing aspects of visiting Australia is to learn about its Aboriginal heritage, meet Aboriginal artists, and shop for Aboriginal art. Indeed, you could easily devote most of your trip to Aboriginal Australia by touring Aboriginal communities, visiting museums with Aboriginal art collections, and shop at the many commercial galleries that represent Australia's leading Aboriginal artists. In so doing, you'll learn a great deal about an ancient people and their traditions. It's a fascinating journey into one of the most unique aspects of Australia.

A little background on this tradition is in order. The original Australians, the Aborigines, have experienced a history somewhat like the American Indians. As the early inhabitants of the land and without undue competition for its resources, they were free to wander unrestrained by things like cities or roads and fences. Everything they needed they were able to take from the earth, yet without destroying the balance of nature that would allow earth and man to live in harmony. Once "civilization" arrived on the scene however, things began to change. Little by little the space left for the Aboriginals was taken over by agriculture or herding or given over to cities and towns. Traversing the "*songlines*" was no longer always possible. The old existence was gone and yet many could not or chose not to adapt to the new ways of life that were absorbing the countryside. After a somewhat turbulent period, the Australians have come to accept the Aboriginal way of life, though different, as one that should be protected and preserved. That is fortunate for those shoppers who have an interest in collecting ethnic art and artifacts from various parts of the world. It is unlikely that the traveler will find for sale any truly antique pieces of Aboriginal art—most of that fragile work that has survived is already in museums or in private collections. Occasionally it appears at major antique auctions in Sydney. However, there are some truly beautiful pieces that are being produced today.

Perhaps the art that most first-time travelers to Australia are most familiar with are the **bark paintings** which are primarily produced in Arnhem Land area of in the Northern Territory (near Darwin and the Kakadu National Park). Some of these are still painted in the traditional way using bark fibers rather than a brush to apply the colors. Other Aboriginal artists use a brush. The colors are usually a combination of ochre, black and white, but yellow is often included. The X-ray style that is often used depicts the major organs inside the animal's body. The bark paintings are most attractive as decorative pieces if they are put on top of a frame or encased in a frame of Lucite against a black or ochre backdrop. If you like the bark paintings but aren't sure how to best display one, look around at what some of the better shops are doing to display the ones they have on sale. You may decide to purchase one from a less expensive source and take it home and have your local framer help you suitably display your bark painting. You can also find bark baskets produced in a similar way to the paintings. These baskets can be especially attractive if dried flowers are displayed in them. We found the very best quality bark paintings, with prices to match, in galleries in Sydney. However, we found some very good quality bark paintings at a fraction of the price in Darwin. You will be able to find some bark paintings in all the major cities, especially Melbourne. However, more and more artists now use bark paper for paintings. It is easier to transport back home. In fact, we saw fewer bark paintings on our most recent visit to Australia.

More contemporary and a bit easier to carry home with you are the Papunya paintings produced northwest of Alice Springs. Called **sand paintings**, don't expect anything like the sand paintings of the Southwest American Indians. They are more accurately called **acrylic dot paintings**. Acrylic based paints are applied to canvas and most are heavily comprised of dots to form the pattern. Although you will see many of these already framed, most are not yet framed or can be taken out of the frame and rolled carefully and placed in a tube for ease of carrying home. Small paintings in tubes can be placed in a suitcase or hand-carried on the plane. We had a large painting—approximately 4x6'—rolled and put in a strong PVC tube. It came back in the cargo hold of the plane as checked luggage and arrived in perfect condition.

Acrylic dot paintings use the patterns of the ancient sand paintings and tell stories to the Aborigine. Central Australian Aborigines traditionally drew in sand the stories of the dreaming—the time when, according to Aboriginal belief, the world and all it contains came into being. These intricate patterns disappeared with the wind and the rain. But the stories and the designs were passed by memory from one generation to the next. Outsiders are often told the basics of the stories behind a particular painting, but don't expect to ever be told the full meaning. You'll find the largest selection of acrylic paintings at the best prices in Alice Springs. That should come as no surprise since such paintings are produced in that area. However, you will find examples of this work in all the major cities, especially Melbourne and Sydney.

You will also see **carved wood animals, bowls,** and **boomerangs**. The animals and bowls include wood burned designs. This type of design is made by the Aborigines of central Australia and a good variety at good prices can be found in Alice Springs. The boomerangs are often painted with the designs of the Dreamtime, and have a decidedly different look about them than the touristy ones found in the Australiana shops. They also tend to be larger in size. You will also see woodcarved animals painted in black, white, yellow or ochre as well as the *pukamani* or **burial poles**. These items come from the Tiwi people of Melville and Bathurst islands and the best buys are found in Darwin or can be purchased at their source if you take the tour offered by Tiwi Tours.

Good quality Aboriginal art can be very expensive, with some paintings selling for more than A$50,000 (works by Emily or Clifford Possum). We saw beautiful bark paintings in Sydney that ranged in price from A$3000 to A$5000. We decided we could live without one and kept looking. In Darwin we finally found one we liked as well as the ones in Sydney for only A$300. No doubt the expensive ones in Sydney were by artists with more established reputations. You will have to decide whether you are buying for investment and are willing (and able) to pay the price for the noted artists or whether you simply want a piece you love to decorate your home.

You can also find Aboriginal prints on silk and cotton scarves in many shops. Most of these are not actually made by Aboriginal artists. If this makes a difference to you be sure to ask if it is not marked on the item. Another interesting item you are sure to see are the ostrich eggs with Aboriginal designs painted on them. These may seem a bit delicate to pack in your luggage, but many shops indicate they can pack them well for travel.

Aboriginal art is now a big business, although still contro-versial, business in Australia. You will find several top quality Aboriginal art galleries in the major cities. The best are found in Sydney (**Coo-ee Aboriginal Art, Jinta Desert Art Aborigi-nal Art Gallery, Aboriginal and Tribal Art Centre,** and **Hogarth Galleries Aboriginal Art Centre**); Melbourne (**Aboriginal Gallery of Dreamings, Aboriginal and Pacific Art Gallery,** and **Aboriginal Desert Art Gallery**); Alice Springs (**Australian Aboriginal Dreamtime Gallery, The Original Dreamtime Gallery, Papunya Tula Artists, Aboriginal Art and Culture Centre,** and **Aboriginal Desert Art Gallery**); Darwin (**Aboriginal Fine Arts, Raintree Aboriginal Fine Arts,** and **Framed**); and Adelaide (**Tandanya Retail Shop** and **Dacou Gallery**).

TRIBAL ART FROM PNG

It may seem strange to some to find a segment in the Australian goods section devoted to artifacts from Papua New Guinea. But if you have an interest in PNG artifacts, you will want to know what you are likely to find in Australia since this is one of the prime locations to buy PNG art. If, for example, you are interested in museum quality or old pieces of PNG art, head as soon as possible for Australia. Old PNG artifacts are rarely seen outside museums or private collections in PNG. Those pieces that are still in villages have most likely been declared "National Cultural Property"; whether they have been declared so or not, it is illegal to export old pieces without permission of the National Museum in Port Moresby.

Because of Australia's proximity and close association with PNG many valuable old pieces were taken out of Papua New Guinea to Australia many years ago. At times a collector loses interest in part of his collection or when an individual dies the benefactors of her estate may not have an interest in keeping these specialized items. In either case, the items are likely to wind up for sale in an antique furniture or art gallery. We came across shops in both Brisbane and Adelaide that happened to have some unique old PNG pieces for sale. However, this could happen in any city. So if you have an interest in these items be on the lookout as you travel around Australia.

We also found many shops selling more recent acquisitions from PNG. Almost every city has shops that specialize in PNG art. The best shops are found in Sydney (**New Guinea Arts**, **Caspian Gallery**, **Oceanic Art Gallery**, and **Asian and Primitive Art Gallery**), Cairns (**Gallery Primitive**), and Melbourne (**Aboriginal and Pacific Art Gallery**).

ARTS AND ANTIQUES

Australia is a paradise for fine art and antique lovers. Sydney, Melbourne, and Brisbane abound with art and antique shops that offer everything from oils, watercolors, and lithographs to Australian and European furniture and collectibles. You could literally spend weeks in Australia just shopping for art and antiques.

Australia's fine art market is booming and prices can be very high. You will find numerous galleries in Sydney, Melbourne, and Brisbane offering works of local portrait and landscape artists who capture the unique Australian character and colored landscape. Many of the small towns within a few hours drive of these and other cities offer excellent selections of Australian art. Indeed, no visit to Australia for Australian art would be complete without focusing your shopping on many of these towns.

One of the curious aspects of the antique business in Australia is its regular resupply of antiques from Europe. Since Australia is still a relatively new country whose antiques are seldom more than 100 years old, many antique shops must regularly import containers of antiques from England and France to satisfy the insatiable appetite for period furniture and collectibles.

You will find the largest concentration of antique shops along Queen Street in Sydney, High Street and Malvern Road in Melbourne, Latrobe Terrace in Paddington of Brisbane, and numerous suburbs that surround these and other cities. Don't forget to also visit small craft towns which have numerous antique shops offering all kinds of unique items discovered in the attics and basements of Australians living in the hills and Outback.

TAKE KEY SHOPPING INFORMATION

Depending on what you plan to buy, you should take all the necessary information you need to make informed shopping decisions. After all, you don't want to end up purchasing an opal watch in Sydney for US$500 and then discover you can get the same item back home for US$400. Put this information in a separate envelope. If you are looking for home furnishings, include with your "wish list" room measurements to help you determine if particular items will fit into your home. You might take photographs with you of particular rooms you hope to furnish.

❑ Take with you measurements and photographs of rooms that could become candidates for home decorative items.

❑ Be sure to take information on any particular clothes, accessories, or jewelry (sizes, colors, comparative prices) with you to look for or have made when in Australia.

❑ Do comparative shopping before arriving in Australia.

If you plan to shop for clothes, your homework should include taking an inventory of your closets and identifying particular colors, fabrics, and designs you wish to acquire to complement and enlarge your present wardrobe. Keep in mind that good quality clothes and accessories made in Australia can be very expensive. And top quality imported designer-label clothes and accessories (mainly from Italy and France) will probably be more expensive than similar items found in department stores and boutiques back home. If you are from the U.S., you should look at comparable selections found at the top department stores, such as Saks Fifth Avenue, Neiman Marcus, Macy's, and Nordstrom. This means visiting their designer-label and couture sections for comparable quality and prices.

DO COMPARATIVE SHOPPING

You should do comparison shopping before you leave home. Once you arrive in Australia, the only comparisons you can make are between various shops you encounter in Sydney, Melbourne, and other cities. You'll never know if you are getting a good deal unless you have done your homework beforehand.

Unless you know the comparable value of goods back home, you won't recognize a bargain when it stares you in the face. Since few things are bargains in Australia, chances are you will be looking for unique items made in Australia or Papua New Guinea that are not readily available elsewhere. This is especially true in the cases of clothing, accessories, jewelry, arts, crafts, and antiques. Take, for example, Aboriginal arts and crafts. Top quality Aboriginal acrylic paintings are found in a few art galleries in Sydney, Melbourne, and Alice Springs. Prices can vary considerably from one gallery to another, from a A$60 print to a A$50,000 oil. Therefore, you are well advised to visit several of the major galleries to compare various works of art, artists, and prices.

The first step in doing comparative shopping is determining exactly what you want and need. Make lists. As you compile your list, spend some time "window shopping" in the local stores, examining catalogs, and telephoning for information.

KEEP TRACK OF RECEIPTS

It's important to keep track of all of your purchases for making an accurate Customs declaration. Since it's so easy to misplace receipts, you might want to organize your receipts using a form similar to the following example. Staple a sheet or two of notebook or accountant's paper to the front of a large manila envelope and number down the left side of the page. Draw one or two vertical columns down the right side. Each evening sort through that day's purchases, write a description including style and color of the purchase on the accompanying receipt, and enter that item on your receipt record. Record the receipt so later you'll know exactly which item belongs to the receipt.

CUSTOMS DECLARATION RECORD FORM

	Receipt #	Item	Price (A$)	Price (US$)
1.	422158	Opal watch	$500.00	$400.00
2.				
3.				
4.				

Put the receipts in the manila envelope and pack the purchases away. If you're missing a receipt, make a note of it beside the appropriate entry.

SHOP BY THE RULES

One of the great pleasures of visiting Australia is its interesting shopping. It's unlike shopping you will encounter elsewhere. Australian jewelry, from opals and Argyle diamonds to gorgeous South Sea pearls to finely crafted gold pendants, especially appeal to visitors. The Australians, Aboriginals, and Papuan New Guineans also are rightly known for producing unique arts and crafts that make excellent home decorative items.

As you begin shopping in Australia, keep these basic "rules" in mind:

1. **Don't expect to bargain much or receive large discounts.** Very little bargaining takes place in Australian shops or even in markets. Most shops have fixed prices and expect customers to pay accordingly. The best deals are during sale periods or at factory outlets that advertise 30-70% discounts. However, should you be purchasing a large ticket item, such as jewelry or a painting, it doesn't hurt to ask for a discount; you might be pleasantly

surprised to discover that violating this rule indeed gets you a discount! But do so in a very subtle manner: *"Is it possible to do any better on this price?"* After all, anything is possible, right? We occasionally get 5-10 percent discounts by asking in such a manner.

2. **Use your credit cards whenever possible.** Shops everywhere accept major credit cards. It's always good to charge a purchase just in case you later have a problem with authenticity or shipping. Your credit card company may be able to assist you in resolving such problems. Credit card purchases usually receive the best exchange rates.

3. **Be sure to comparative shop for many items.** Many shops carry similar items and prices can vary considerably from one shop to another on opals, jewelry, clothes, and accessories. Comparative shopping is less effective in the case of Australian, Aboriginal, and Papuan New Guinean arts and crafts since many of these are unique one-of-a-kind items. Nonetheless, be sure to survey your shopping options by visiting various galleries offering such products. You'll quickly get some idea as to how to best value such items.

4. **Be sure to ask for assistance and background information.** One of the great pleasures of shopping in Australia is learning about various products and producers. Since you may be unfamiliar with many items, especially Australian and Aboriginal art, be sure to ask questions about the various selections. Shopkeepers tend to be very friendly and informative. They can quickly educate you about their products and artists. If you are interested in antiques, Australian arts and crafts, Aboriginal art, and arts and crafts from Papua New Guinea, you'll be in for a real treat as merchants share their knowledge with you about the backgrounds of such items. In some cases you may have an opportunity to meet the artists and craftspeople. In so doing, you will probably gain a new appreciation for "Made in Australia" products as well as the many cultures of this fascinating country.

5. **Remember to ask about duty-free prices.** Be sure to ask about duty-free prices when purchasing gems and jewelry. As a tourist, you qualify for duty-free prices. Show your passport and visa when making such a purchase. The tax

will be deducted at the time of the purchase. Some merchants consider this to be their "discount".

6. **Expect shops to arrange packing and shipping.** Don't be afraid to purchase large or delicate items that you may not want to take with you. Most shops have experience in packing and shipping. However, if you decide to have items shipped, it's always a good idea to get a receipt stating who is doing what and take a picture of the items being shipped. We always take photos just in case we might have a problem with a shipment, which is rare.

7. **Take your purchases with you as part of your carry-on or check-through luggage.** While shipping from Australia is relatively easy to arrange, it also can be very expensive. Australian postal rates, as well as sea and air freight rates, tend to be very expensive. We usually try to take our purchases with us whether they be small or large. In preparation, we usually limit ourselves to one check-through piece of luggage on our flight to Australia. For the two of us, this allows us three more check-through pieces of luggage on our international flight back home. On a recent trip, we returned home with five check-through prices; three were oversize. We paid excess baggage fees of US$110. Had we air freighted our purchases, we would have incurred more than US$2,000 in shipping charges. Our advice: take very little luggage with you on your way to Australia in anticipation of accumulating purchases along the way that you will want to take with you. You'll save a great deal of time and money by planning in this manner. If you purchase an item that can be checked through as luggage, ask the shop to pack the item well so it can be checked through with your airline as a piece of luggage. Most shops can do this or they can arrange for excellent packing that will protect delicate purchases.

8. **Be careful about patronizing "duty-free" shops.** Most so-called duty-free shops are specifically set up to cater to Japanese tourists who tend to get exploited by fellow Japanese in these "shoppers' paradises." Like similar shops found elsewhere in the world, they are often run by Japanese who steer bus loads of Japanese tourists to their shops. Not surprising, most of the products found in these places are high quality designer-label items imported from Italy and France (clothes, accessories, jewelry) or the ubiquitous Australian opals, souvenirs, and sweaters.

Often the prices in these places are much higher than elsewhere, even though they may offer special 10 percent discount coupons or other special offers (a free opal) to get you to visit their shops. As you will quickly discover, the shops are set up by Japanese for Japanese. English is not widely spoken in many of these places! Expect you may pay 10 to 30 percent above retail in such shops.

9. **Be very careful when buying opals, diamonds, and pearls.** If you're unfamiliar with Australian stones, pearls, and jewelry, you can easily make some expensive shopping mistakes. As we noted in our earlier discussion of gems and jewelry on pages 36-39, opals come in many forms and price ranges, from souvenir quality doublets and triplets to exquisite Black and Boulder opals. The same is true for Argyle diamonds and South Sea Pearls. Patronize some of Australia's top quality jewelry shops, such as Percy Marks (Sydney), Paspaley (Sydney, Darwin, Broom), Linneys (Perth and Broome), and Costello's (Perth and Melbourne) that will educate you on the differences in quality and prices. Souvenir, jewelry, and duty-free shops crowded with Japanese tourists are not good places to get such an education.

SHIPPING WITH EASE

You should not pass up buying lovely items because you feel reluctant to ship them home. Indeed, some travelers only buy items that will fit into their suitcase because they are not sure how to ship larger items home. But you can easily ship from Australia and expect to receive your goods in good condition within 6-8 weeks. We seldom let shipping considerations affect our buying decisions. For us, *shipping is one of those things that must be arranged*. You have numerous shipping alternatives, from hiring a professional shipping company to hand carrying your goods on board the plane. Shipping may or may not be costly, depending on how much you plan to ship and by which means.

Before leaving home, you should identify the best point of entry for goods returning home by air or sea. Once you are in Australia, you generally have five shipping alternatives:

- Take everything with you.
- Do your own packing and shipping through the local post office (for small packages only).

- Have each shop ship your purchases.
- Arrange to have one shop consolidate all of your purchases into a single shipment.
- Hire a local shipper to make all arrangements.

Taking everything with you is fine if you don't have much and you don't mind absorbing excess baggage charges. If you are overweight, ask about the difference between "Excess Baggage" and "Unaccompanied Baggage". Excess baggage is very expensive while unaccompanied baggage is less expensive, although by no means cheap.

If items are small enough and we don't mind waiting six to eight weeks, we may send them through the local post office by parcel post; depending on the weight, sometimes air mail is relatively inexpensive through local post offices.

Doing your own packing and shipping may be cheaper, but it is a pain and thus no savings in the long run. You waste valuable time waiting in lines and trying to figure out the local rules and regulations concerning permits, packing, materials, sizes, and weights.

On the other hand, most major shops are skilled at shipping goods for customers. They often pack the items free and only charge you for the actual postage or freight. Many of these shops use excellent shippers who are known for reasonable charges, good packing, and reliability. For example, if you decide to have jewelry custom-made, the jewelry shop will most likely arrange to have your purchase sent to you within three days by using the reliable international courier DHL. If you choose to have a shop ship for you, insist on a receipt specifying they will ship the item. Also, stress the importance of packing the item well to avoid possible damage. If they cannot insure the item against breakage or loss, do not ship through them. Invariably a version of Murphy's Law operates when shipping: *"If it is not insured and has the potential to break or get lost, it will surely break or get lost!"* At this point, seek some alternative means of shipping. If you are shipping only one or two items, it is best to let a reputable shop take care of your shipping.

If you have several large purchases—at least one cubic meter —consider using local shippers since it is cheaper and safer to consolidate many separate purchases into one shipment which is well packed and insured. Sea freight charges are usually figured by volume or the container. There is a minimum charge —usually you will pay for at least one cubic meter whether you are shipping that much or less. Air freight is calculated using both weight and volume and usually there is no minimum. You pay only for the actual amount you ship. One normally does not air freight large, heavy items, but for a small light shipment, air freight could actually cost you less and you'll get your items much faster. When using air freight, use an established and reliable airline. In the case of sea freight, choose a local company which has an excellent reputation among expatriates for shipping goods. It is relatively easy to get this information. Consult the Yellow Pages under the heading "Shipping" or "Removers". In each city you will find numerous shippers listed, many with familiar names. However, you will be taking pot luck if you randomly choose one from this list. Instead, you should do some quick research. Ask your hotel concierge or front desk personnel about reliable shippers. For small shipments, try to have charges computed both ways—for sea and for air freight. Sea shipments incur port charges that can further add to your charges. If you have figures for both means of shipping, you can make an informed choice.

We have tried all five shipping alternatives with various results. Indeed, we tend to use these alternatives in combination. For example, we take everything we can with us until we reach the point where the inconvenience and cost of excess baggage requires some other shipping arrangements. In Australia, we consolidate our shipments with one key shop early in our trip and have shipments from other cities sent to that shop for consolidation. The ideal consolidation point for sea shipments is Sydney.

When you use a shipper, be sure to examine alternative shipping arrangements and prices. The type of delivery you specify at your end can make a significant difference in the overall shipping price. If you don't specify the type of delivery you want, you may be charged the all-inclusive first-class rate. For example, if you choose door-to-door delivery with unpacking services, you will pay a premium to have your shipment clear Customs, moved through the port, transported to your door, and unpacked by local movers. On the other hand, it is cheaper for you to designate port to port. When the shipment arrives, you arrange for a broker to clear the shipment through Customs and arrange for transport to your home. You do your own unpacking and dispose of the trash. It will take a little more of your time to make the arrangements and unpack.

We simply cannot over-stress the importance of finding and establishing a personal relationship with a good local shipper who will provide you with services which may go beyond your immediate shipping needs. A good local shipping contact will enable you to continue shopping in Australia even after returning home!

Great
Destinations

4

Sydney

F OR MANY WORLD TRAVELERS, IT DOESN'T GET better than Sydney. Selected by *Condé Nast Traveler* in 1996 as the number one travel destination in the world, designated three years in a row as the world's most livable city, and elected to host the 2000 Summer Olympics, Sydney is truly one of the world's great places to visit—and live, if time permits. Residents of Melbourne might try to convince you that Melbourne is better than Sydney, but don't believe them. It's in a league of its own—a trend setter in its own right—and thus does not warrant such parochial comparisons. Energetic and trendy, Sydney is where the action is. If you have very limited time in Australia, you must do Sydney for at least three days; a week would be much better. You won't be disappointed in spending more time here than in other Australian cities. Sydney is simply a great city. You'll soon discover why so many people fall in love with such a big city as you indulge in its many treasures and pleasures.

If you like vibrant big cities, delightful weather, lovely harbor views, diverse sights, friendly people, fine hotels and restaurants, wonderful shopping, and great night life—along with beautiful sand, sea, and surf—you may fall in love with Sydney. It seems to have it all, a sort of lifestyle city. Here's Australia's largest city with a metropolitan population of 3.8

million. Spread over a 50 kilometer area, metropolitan Sydney is where one can live the good life beside beautiful beaches that seem to stretch forever along the emerald South Pacific Ocean. Indeed, many Australian's believe Sydney may well be the best place to live in the world. And so may you!

In physical appearance, Sydney is to Australia what Seattle and San Francisco is to the United States. Sydney's lifestyle, however, resembles that of Los Angeles and Southern California. It's one of the world's most pleasant, cosmopolitan, and liveable cities. Unlike many other big cities, energetic Sydney feels good to be in. It invites you to enjoy its many pleasures, and just play, play, and play. And all you need is a little time— and lots of money, money, money!

Visit Sydney and you will certainly come away with a wonderful collection of Australian memories based on touring the harbor, visiting the museums and historical sites, enjoying its many beaches, prowling its pubs, sampling its terrific restaurants, meeting its friendly people, and shopping its many arcades and neighborhoods. Sydney is a traveler's delight. It's a wonderful place to spend several days to indulge your shopping, traveling, gastronomic, and hedonistic fancies.

❑ Sydney is truly one of the world's great places to visit– and live, if time permits. You'll probably quickly become attached to this city.

❑ Sydney shoppers increasingly engage in *lifestyle shopping*– combine shopping with dining, sightseeing, entertainment, and maybe even a stop at the spa.

❑ Double Bay, sometimes jokingly referred to as "Double Pay", is Australia's version of Hollywood's Rodeo Drive.

❑ Sydney can be very expensive, comparable to New York City, but by no means as expensive as Tokyo, Hong Kong, London, or Paris. Don't expect to find many bargains here.

GETTING TO KNOW YOU

Sydney is a five-star city. It has everything a traveler would want, and then some. If sightseeing is your travel passion, Sydney will keep you occupied for at least three days with its many old buildings, museums, and parks; you can even engage in adventuresome sightseeing by climbing the Sydney Harbor Bridge! If restaurants and nightlife are your passions, get ready for some real treats. Sydney's restaurants and inventive chefs are second to none. Entertainment, from classy opera and theater to trendy rock and jazz bars, are found in abundance and they continue to proliferate. Cruises and beach activities abound in Sydney and its outlying areas. Best of all, Sydney is a relatively easy city to get to know and love.

But it's shopping, good quality shopping, that more and more occupies visitors' time in Sydney. While shopping is not normally considered to be one of Australia's major attractions, it has become a favorite pastime for many visitors, including local residents, who increasingly engage in **lifestyle shopping**—combine shopping with dining, sightseeing, entertainment, and maybe even a stop at the spa.

Sydney is a shopper's paradise. It offers a full range of both imported and Australian-made products presented in a wide variety of exciting shopping settings. You'll find the latest in Australian and European designer fashion in Australia's most exclusive suburb—**Double Bay**—as well as along its major upscale shopping streets in the heart of downtown Sydney, especially Castlereagh and Elizabeth Streets.

Double Bay is Australia's version of Hollywood's Rodeo Drive, disdained by many Australians for its ostensible elitist and snobbish character. It's where car and people-watching is as much fun as shopping for quality goods and dining in chic restaurants and cafes.

Or visit the beautiful and majestic **Queen Victoria Building** to leisurely browse through over 200 shops offering everything from the latest designer fashion to Australiana as well as enjoy its many restaurants and food stalls. Nearby stands the smaller but elegant old **Strand Arcade**, still offering nice selections of Australian designer-fashion and uniquely designed jewelry, as well as the upscale **David Jones Department Store**. Just a few blocks away are the upscale **Chifley Plaza** and **Centerpoint Shopping Centre**.

And don't forget to spend some time in the arts and crafts shops of the quaint, historical, and picturesque area called **The Rocks**. Here you can stroll the streets, browse the shops, attend the popular weekend market, climb the stairs, dine the restaurants, and carouse the pubs—all accompanied by majestic views of the Sydney Harbour Bridge, Opera House, and Circular Quay.

If your tastes include trendy arts, crafts, and clothing, or you have an eye for good quality antiques and fine arts, you will discover many interesting shops lining the streets and lanes of **Paddington** (Oxford Street), **Woollahra** (Queen Street), and **Mosman** (Military Road).

For those wishing to combine shopping with a social experience, there's the **Marketplace at Harbourside** (Darling Harbour) as well as **factory outlets** (especially Sully Hills area) and numerous antique and weekend **markets** such as Paddington Bazaar (corner of Oxford and Newcombe Streets in Paddington), Paddy's Market (Ross Street in Glebe), Balmain

Market (Arling Street and Curtis Road in Balmain), The Rocks Market (Upper George Street in The Rocks), and numerous **auctions** taking place throughout the metropolitan area (see the Saturday edition of the *Sydney Morning Herald* for a listing of upcoming auctions for the week).

Whatever your shopping choices, you will be delighted with the many and varied shopping opportunities offered in Sydney. Only Melbourne can offer a comparable shopping environment and volume of shopping experiences.

Like so much of Australia, you should come to Sydney to experience its delights rather than expect to discover its bargains. Similar to other large metropolitan areas in the world, Sydney can be very expensive, comparable, for example, to New York City, but by no means as expensive as Tokyo, Hong Kong, London, or Paris. Accommodations can be expensive, with most deluxe hotels costing more than A$300 a day. Food is surprisingly reasonable compared to other large cities. Shopping can also be expensive, especially for clothes. But **bargains** can be found at sales and in factory outlet shops. If you come from a country with high import duties on luxury goods, such as New Zealand, Sydney's duty-free shops do offer bargains.

The best buy in Sydney is public transportation (*www.syd neybuses.nsw.gov.au*). Taxis, buses, CityRail, and car rentals are still reasonable compared to other cities in the world. Our recommendation is to spend your money on local transportation to browse shops for unique items you cannot find in other Australian cities nor back home. Truly unique items in Sydney are arts and crafts, antiques, gems (opals and Argyle diamonds), jewelry, and Australian-designed fashion clothes. You will find many international designer goods, especially European clothing and accessories, but you are likely to find the same products with better selections and prices in major cities elsewhere in the world, including back home.

Sydney is an especially vibrant, friendly, and cosmopolitan city. The streets are busy with workers and shoppers hurrying from one area to another. Believed by many Australians to have the most beautiful harbor in the world, Sydney's delightful harbor is pretty and pleasant, but by no means better than the majestic harbors of Hong Kong, Rio, and Acapulco—or even San Francisco. There's plenty to do in Sydney, be it shopping, touring the harbor, visiting the beaches, taking day trips to the outlying areas, visiting the many museums and historical sites, dining in restaurants with beautiful views of the city and harbor, taking in theatrical performances, or visiting its many pubs and entertainment spots.

Sydney is a cosmopolitan and cultured city that is very easy to get to know and a wonderful place to visit—and live. The transportation system is excellent, and the weather often cooperates to make this city one of the prime destinations in all of Australia as well as in the Southern Hemisphere. Sydney is the good life, with a booming economy, a delightful natural setting, an attractive skyline, pleasant streets and shopping arcades, and a competitive-spirited chauvinism that delights in putting down supposedly straight-laced Melbourne in comparison to friendly Sydney. Sydney is what many Australians and visitors aspire to—having the best of everything and living the good life. This is a city where one should work a little, shop some, and play a lot. Spend a week here and you will want to come back to living the good life, Sydney-style!

THE STREETS OF SYDNEY

The city of Sydney is centered in the protected harbor of Port Jackson. Viewed best from the North Shore or the southwest pylon of the Sydney Harbour Bridge, it's a striking downtown area. From the central business district—marked by the Sydney Harbour Bridge, The Rocks, Opera House, Circular Quay, and several high-rise office buildings and hotels to the north, and punctuated by narrow streets darkened by glittering high-rise commercial buildings and elegant shopping arcades to the south—Sydney's skyline flattens out into numerous residential suburbs sprawling north, south, east, and west. The beaches and upscale residential communities are located to the northeast (Balmoral, Manly, and Palm Beach), west (Balmain), and east (Double Bay, Watson Bay, and Bondi). Nondescript, working-class suburbs sprawl to the west for nearly 40 kilometers.

Most of Sydney's quality shopping is confined to the city center, eastern suburbs, and north shore. These are also the areas for visiting Sydney's major historical sites, museums, and beaches and for enjoying harbor tours, restaurants, and entertainment, or just walking around the loveliest areas of this great city.

GETTING ORIENTED

The best way to get oriented to this city is to acquire a good map of the area. Unfortunately, most free tourist maps of the city only cover the central business district; they leave out much of the eastern and northern sections of the metropolitan area.

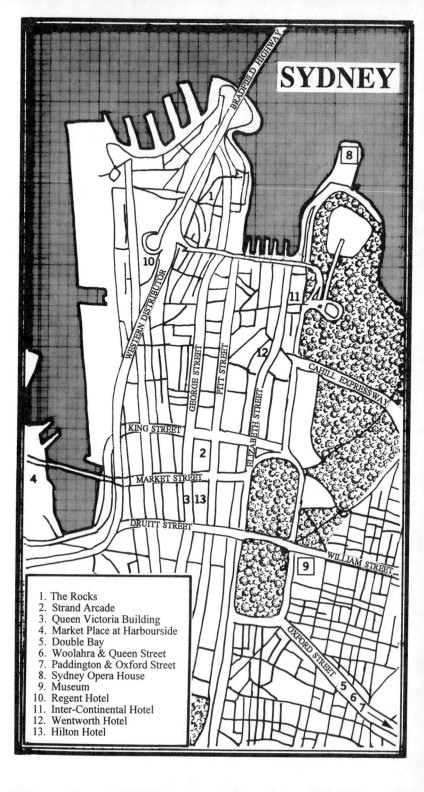

SYDNEY

1. The Rocks
2. Strand Arcade
3. Queen Victoria Building
4. Market Place at Harbourside
5. Double Bay
6. Woolahra & Queen Street
7. Paddington & Oxford Street
8. Sydney Opera House
9. Museum
10. Regent Hotel
11. Inter-Continental Hotel
12. Wentworth Hotel
13. Hilton Hotel

Most major bookstores, such as the **Travel Bookshop** (175 Liverpool Street) and **Dymocks Booksellers** (424-426 George Street), carry detailed maps on Sydney and outlying areas.

One of the first stops you should make in Sydney is the centrally located **Sydney Visitor Centre** (106 George Street, The Rocks, Tel. 9255-1788, open daily 9am-6pm). This center is jam-packed with maps and free literature on Sydney and the surrounding area. The personnel behind the counters can be very helpful on everything from restaurants and entertainment to tours. They will make hotel and tour bookings. You'll also find tourist information booths at the Airport, bus terminal, Circular Quay, Martin Place, Darling Harbour, and the Pitt Street Mall. You also can call the **Sydney Information Line** (recorded message, Tel. 9911-7700) and the **Tourist Information Service** (Tel. 9669-5111) for information on accommodations, entertainment, tours, and shopping. The Sydney Visitor Centre, as well as your hotel concierge desk and some shops, may have free copies of the latest editions of the following useful guides to Sydney's sightseeing tours, shopping, restaurants, and entertainment:

This Week in Sydney
The Rocks Restaurant and Hotel Guide
The Rocks Shopping Guide
Sydney Airport Arrivals Guide
Sydney Guest Guide
Sydney Harbour Connection
Sydney Mapguide
Sydney Tourist Guide
Sydney Visitors Guide
Where Magazine

While Sydney is Australia's largest city and metropolitan area, it's a relatively easy city to get around. The downtown area—called simply **The City**—is relatively compact. It's easy to walk to most shopping arcades and department stores within 10-20 minutes. The main shopping area in The City is bounded by **George and Elizabeth Streets**, which run North and South, and by **Hunter and Park Streets**, which run East and West. Walking these streets, you find the major shopping arcades and department stores in Sydney, such as the Queen Victoria Building, Strand Arcade, Chifley Plaza, Sydney Central Plaza, Centrepoint, MLC Centre, Skygarden, and the David Jones and Grace Bros department stores.

Just to the north of the city and immediately northwest of Circular Quay—Sydney's Harbor Terminal—is **The Rocks**. The main shopping area here is found along Argyle, Playfair, and George Streets. This is another compact walking area which offers a large variety of shops, pubs, restaurants, hotels, historical sites, and gorgeous views of the harbor, bridge, and Opera House.

To the west of the city are the popular shopping areas of Double Bay, Woollahra, and Paddington. The exclusive shopping suburb of **Double Bay** can be reached by ferry, bus, or taxi. The 20-minute taxi ride from The City also passes by Paddington and Woollahra. Another relatively small and compact shopping area great for walking, Double Bay is bounded by three main shopping streets—Knox, Cross, and Bay.

Woollahra and Paddington are just a few minutes from Double Bay. These two shopping areas are linked together at the intersection of Queen Street (in Woollahra) and Oxford Street (in Paddington). The major shops—mainly art and antique—in **Woollahra** are found along Queen Street and in a few streets and lanes to the north, just off Queen Street near the intersection with Oxford Street. You can easily walk this section of Queen Street within 5 to 10 minutes, spending perhaps an hour browsing through the more interesting looking arts and crafts shops.

The **Paddington** area is less compact and more inconvenient for walking. Beginning at the Queen Street intersection, the Paddington shopping area stretches nearly three kilometers west, along Oxford Street past Victoria Barracks to Taylor Square. While most shops are found on the north side of Oxford Street, be sure to also explore the small streets and lanes to the north of Oxford Street, especially near the eastern section of Paddington. You will find many shops along such streets and lanes as Jersey Road, Taylor Street, Elizabeth Street, and William Street. Larger shops, such as Hogath Galleries at 7 Walker Lane (top of Brown Street), are tucked away on such streets. You will need to spend some time walking these areas.

Harbourside at Darling Harbour is Sydney's trendy harborfront entertainment, dining, and shopping area. Located southwest of The City, adjacent to Chinatown, this area is within easy walking distance from the downtown area via Market and King streets. A monorail system also services this area.

❑ The best buy in Sydney is public transportation.

❑ Most quality shopping is confined to the city center, eastern suburbs, and north shore.

❑ One of the first stops you should make is the Sydney Visitor Center in The Rocks. It's jam-packed with maps and free literature on the city and surrounding area.

❑ Sydney is a relatively easy city to get around. The central business district and The Rocks are relatively compact walking areas with lots of great shops and restaurants.

Neutral Bay and Mosman on the North Shore and Manly to the northeast are within short driving distances from The City. **Manly** is a popular beach with an interesting Saturday beachfront market, a pedestrian shopping mall, trendy cafes, and the popular Oceanworld. You can reach Manly by taking a 30-minute ferry ride or a 15-minute JetCat ride (from Circular Quay). Alternatively, you can take a bus or taxi or drive yourself there via the Sydney Harbour Bridge, Military Road (Neutral Bay and Mosman), Spit Road, and Sydney Road.

The **Neutral Bay and Mosman** shopping areas are located along Military Road, with the majority of shops concentrated near the intersection of Military and Spit Roads in Mosman. The best way to reach this area is by bus, taxi, or car. You may wish to rent a car for the day to visit this shopping area as well as Manly and several beach towns and the Hawkesbury region to the north, or head for the Blue Mountains to the west.

Other shopping areas include **Chinatown** to the immediate south of The City and east of the Marketplace at Harbourside (at Darlinghurst Harbour); **Balmain** to the West with its trendy bars, restaurants, and shops; **Birkenhead Point** (in Drummoyne) six kilometers west of the city; and several suburban communities with local shopping arcades. While these areas offer some unique shopping opportunities, you may wish to include them only if time permits. Although they are regularly serviced by bus, rail, and taxi, most of these areas are not convenient for visitors.

WHAT AND WHERE TO BUY

Sydney has everything. All you need is money, walking shoes, and enthusiasm for shopping. If you want the latest in imported fashion or electronic gadgetry, Sydney has it. But be prepared to pay premium prices. Imported goods are not a good buy except for such nationals as New Zealanders and Japanese who must pay even higher prices in their countries.

In Sydney we seek the **unique**—designs and products we cannot find elsewhere in Australia nor abroad. And Sydney has plenty of these designs and products to keep you busy shopping for several days!

OPALS

You'll find hundreds of shops throughout Sydney offering beautiful opals at duty-free prices. One of the largest concentrations of such shops is found along upper **Pitt Street** near

Circular Quay. These are "Duty-Free Shops" which primarily advertise opals, but they also sell the usual duty-free fare of liquor, cameras, candies, perfumes, designer fashion goods, jewelry, and watches as well as typical Australiana, such as Aboriginal arts and crafts, stuffed koalas and kangaroos, fur coats, and sheepskin jackets. Many of these shops are especially organized for Japanese and other Asian tourists who prefer shopping at duty-free emporiums; many are staffed with Japanese personnel who primarily speak Japanese. The shops offer both unset and set opals at prices ranging from A$10 to A$20,000. Other shops selling opals are found in and around all of the major shopping arcades in the downtown section and The Rocks. Many shops selling Australiana also sell souvenir-quality opal jewelry (doublets and triplets).

To get the best buys, you will need to shop around to learn about opals and compare quality and prices. Several shops provide informative brochures on buying various opals. A number of factors determine value and hence cost:

- **Know whether you are buying a solid opal, a doublet, or a triplet**. The most expensive would be a solid opal, free of any apparent cracks or flaws, with overall complete play of color. The best solid opals display the full color spectrum including red and violet/purple.

- **The stone should be free of cracks and flaws.** Opals are a porous stone and have a greater tendency to break than other stones of similar hardness—5½ to 7 on MOH's scale. They are more likely to break if there is an evident flaw line or occlusion.

- **Prices vary considerably based on the extent and overall completeness of color**. The actual colors and number of colors also determine value. The highest value has all colors of the spectrum, especially red and purple which are rare.

- **The cheapest opals are the triplets and doublets**. A triplet consists of three thin layers of opal glued together to look like a solid opal. Triplets are usually white or have very little color; they may have small flaw lines visible to the naked eye. Doublets consist of two thin layers of opal glued together. Triplets and doublets are usually considered tourist souvenirs or a tourist "rip-off" if sold as a solid opal. Inspect opals carefully so you don't pay solid opal prices for doublets and triplets!

The opal business in Sydney is extremely competitive, so be sure to ask questions about the quality of stones as well as differences in prices. Make sure the quoted prices include the standard 30 tax-free discount you should receive as an overseas visitor. Many of the shops will provide you with free transportation to their shop upon request. Refer to pages 36-38 for an expanded discussion about Australian opals.

Some of the largest and most reputable opal dealers in Sydney include:

❑ **Percy Marks:** *The Regent Sydney, 199 George Street, Tel. 7247-1322; 60-70 Elizabeth Street, Tel. 9233-1355; and The Hotel Inter-Continental, 117 Macquarie Street, Tel. 9251-3481. The Rocks, Tel. 9247-8860. www.percym.com.au.* Oldest jeweler in New South Wales. Excellent quality opals.

❑ **Flame Opals:** *119 George Street, The Rocks, Tel. 9247-3446.* One of Sydney's oldest and largest dealers.

❑ **Gemtec:** *51 Pitt Street, Tel. 9251-1599.* A long-time favorite of visitors to Sydney. A large operation.

❑ **Centrepoint Opal Cave:** *Shop G06 Gallery Level, Centrepoint Tower, 100 Market Street, Tel. 9231-4211.*

❑ **Australian Opal House:** *Shop 2/20 Victoria Wal, Queen Victoria Building, 455 George Street, Tel. 9261-3193.*

❑ **House of Giulians:** *Corner George and Bridge Streets, Tel. 9252-2051. www.giulians.com.au.*

❑ **Rocks Opal Mine:** *Clocktower Square, Corner Argyle and Harrington Streets, The Rocks, Tel. 9247-4974.*

❑ **Opal Fields:** *115 George Street, The Rocks, Tel. 9247-6800.* Also at the Queen Victoria Building, Harbourside Darling Harbour, and Millennium Hotel.

❑ **Opal Beauty:** *Shop 39, 2nd Floor, Queen Victoria Building, George Street; Shops 4 and 5, The Rocks Centre, Argyle Street, The Rocks; and Rockhounds, 141 George Street, The Rocks, Tel. 9241-5101.*

❑ **Australian Opal Cutters:** *Suite 10, Level 4, National Building, 250 Pitt Street, Tel. 9261-2442. www.opalinfo. com.au.*

❑ **Berta Opals:** *Unit 7, 2-12 Pyrmont Bridge Road, Pyrmont, Tel. 9552-6388 (2 minute walk from Harbourside Monorail Station).*

JEWELRY

You will find numerous jewelry shops throughout Sydney offering exquisite gems and jewelry. While most of these shops also offer opals, they sell a larger spectrum of jewelry than shops specializing in duty-free goods or Australiana. You will find, for example, Argyle diamonds from Western Australia as well as imported precious and semi-precious stones (amethyst, carnelian, agates, rubies, sapphires) set in a variety of designs. A few shops offer excellent South Seas pearls produced in Western Australia as well as Tahiti. Many of the best jewelers are located in and around the major hotels (The Regent and Inter-Continental), shopping arcades (Strand, Queen Victoria Building, Centrepoint, Chifley Plaza), and in Double Bay.

While much of the jewelry is dutied or taxed, as a foreign visitor you may be able to avoid both and find some pieces crafted in unique Australian styles and settings which you cannot find elsewhere in the world. Some of the most well established, reputable, and quality jewelers in Sydney include:

❑ **Percy Marks:** *The Regent Sydney, 199 George Street, Tel. 7247-1322; 60-70 Elizabeth Street, Tel. 9233-1355; The Hotel Inter-Continental, 117 Macquarie Street, Tel. 9251-3481; and Australian Diamonds and Pearls, 75½ George Street, The Rocks, Tel. 9247-8860. www.percym.com.au.* A personal favorite, this jeweler has terrific quality and designs. Select an exquisite piece of jewelry from one of their stores or select a stone and have it made into a one-of-a-kind design made especially for you. Ships worldwide.

❑ **Paspaley Pearls:** *142 King Street, Tel. 9232-7633. www. paspaleypearls.com.* Offers top quality South Seas pearls from their farms in Broome and Darwin. Produces wonderful jewelry designs that competes well with top jewelry designers in Paris, London, and New York.

❑ **Robert Clerc:** *Shop G11, Queen Victoria Building, Tel. 9267-8274.* A master Swiss jeweler known for his unique gold designs and special signature collections (Aboriginal and Egyptian).

❑ **Tiffany & Co.**: *Chifley Plaza, 2 Chifley Square. Tel. 9235-1777.* The jewelry may be imported from the U.S., but it's what you expect from Tiffany—simply exquisite.

❑ **Bvlgari**: *91 Market Street, Tel. 9267-8866.* Beautiful classic Italian jewelry for men and women.

❑ **House of Giulians**: *Corner George and Bridge Streets, Tel. 9252-2051. www.giulians.com.au.* Excellent quality opal, pearl, and diamond jewelry.

❑ **Perri Jewellers**: *Shop 708, MLC Centre, King and Castlereagh Streets, Tel. 9231-1088.* A long-time favorite.

❑ **Hardy Brothers**: *Ground Level, Skygarden, 77 Castlereagh Street, Tel. 9232-2422.* Well established and a long-time favorite of locals and visitors alike.

❑ **Rox Gems and Jewellery**: *Shop 31, Strand Arcade, Pitt Street Mall, Tel. 9232-7828.*

❑ **Australia's Precious Metals Mint**: *Corner York and Druitt Streets, Tel. 9267-7481.* Part of the popular Perth Mint. Offers rings, pendants, and bracelets made from Argyle diamonds, Broome pearls, and Australian opals.

TAPESTRIES AND RUGS

You will find a few specialty shops which produce unique tapestries and rugs using Australian and New Zealand wools. These shops specialize in doing custom designs for customers throughout the world. You can select from current stocks or commission your own tapestry or rug for your favorite room. Be sure to take pictures and room measurements as well as any drawings you wish to incorporate in a tapestry or rug. All of these shops are experienced in shipping goods overseas. Five such shops are found in various locations in Sydney:

❑ **Kaminski Gallery**: *21 Nurses Walk, The Rocks, Tel. 9247-2418.* Produces beautifully handwoven tapestries with lots of colorful designs and unique themes.

❑ **Tapestry Craft**: *32 York Street, Tel. 9299-8588.* Australia's largest needlecraft store. Includes cross-stitch embroidery, tapestry, and accessories.

❑ **Robyn Cosgrove Rugs:** *18 Transvaal Avenue, Double Bay, Tel. 9328-7692.* Nice quality Turkish rugs. Many unique designs.

❑ **Caspian Gallery:** *469 Oxford Street, Paddington. Tel. 9331-4260.* Includes an excellent collection of tribal rugs in the midst for this noted Aboriginal, Indonesian, and Papuan New Guinea art and antique gallery.

❑ **Nomadic Rug Traders:** *125 Harris Street, Pyrmont, Tel. 9660-3753.* Specializes in old Oriental rugs, textiles, and tribal art.

ABORIGINAL, PNG, AND SOUTHEAST ASIAN ARTS AND CRAFTS

In many respects, shops in this category are some of the most interesting in all of Australia. They offer items that reflect the unique cultures found in Australia and neighboring countries. Several shops throughout Sydney specialize in the collection of arts and crafts produced by various Aboriginal tribes as well as tribal groups from neighboring Papua New Guinea and several Southeast Asian countries, especially Indonesia and Malaysia. Some shops only specialize in Aboriginal, PNG, or Southeast Asian arts and crafts whereas others include tribal arts and crafts from all of these groups and areas. The quality of these shops varies considerably, from shops offering lots of mass produced tourist souvenirs to those offering quality art pieces appropriate for serious collectors and museums.

Many shops mix Aboriginal arts and crafts with such Australiana as stuffed koala bears and kangaroos, opals (primarily doublets and triplets), T-shirts, Akubra hats, and sheepskin products. You can expect to find some Aboriginal arts and crafts, especially bark paintings, didgeridoos, and boomerangs, in most Australiana shops. But don't expect to find good quality Aboriginal arts and crafts in these shops; most are tourist grade since such shops are essentially souvenir and handicraft shops.

Some of the best quality shops specializing in Aboriginal arts and crafts are found in the The Rocks, Paddington, and the Queen Victoria Building. These shops in particular offer good quality Aboriginal arts and crafts appropriate for serious collectors:

❑ **Hogarth Galleries Aboriginal Art Centre:** *7 Walker Lane (top of Brown Street), Paddington, Tel. 9360-6839. Closed*

Sunday and Monday. Hard to find in this small back lane.
Take Shadford and Liverpool streets off of Oxford Street
to get to Walker Lane. Also operates the Aboriginal Art
Centre in The Rocks and the Aboriginal Art Shop at the
drive-up level of the Opera House. Regularly sponsors
exhibitions at Paddington gallery.

❏ **Coo-ee Aboriginal Art:** *98 Oxford Street, Paddington, Tel.
9332-1544.* Don't be turned off by all the touristy Australiana on the ground level; the good stuff is in the basement and upstairs. Be sure to go to the lower level for
good quality Aboriginal bark paintings, acrylic paintings,
and sculptures. Upstairs you will find quality fine arts,
prints, and fabrics as well as an exhibition gallery. One of
Australia's leading galleries for promoting Aboriginal art
both at home and abroad. Take a very good look here
because there is more to the shop than surface appearances.

❏ **Aboriginal and Tribal Art Centre:** *Level 1, 117 George
Street, Tel. 9247-9625.* Looks nondescript from the narrow
street-level entrance. But go upstairs to this expansive and
colorful gallery. Includes a good collection of Aboriginal
paintings (both bark and acrylic) and carvings as well as
some art from Papua New Guinea. Belongs to the Hogarth Galleries network of quality shops.

❏ **Jinta Desert Art Aboriginal Art Gallery:** *154-156
Clarence Street, Tel. 9290-3639.* Primarily displays acrylic
paintings of major Aboriginal artists. Carries many of the
top early Aboriginal artists such as Clifford Possum and
Billy Stockman. Also includes some Tiwi wood sculptures.
Until you get to the major galleries in Melbourne, this is
one of the best Aboriginal galleries in Australia. Also
operates similar galleries in both Melbourne (Aboriginal
Art Galleries of Australia) and Alice Springs (Aboriginal
Desert Art Gallery).

❏ **Aboriginal and Pacific Art:** *Dymocks Building, 8th Floor,
428 George Street, Tel. 9223-5900.* Located directly across
the hall from New Guinea Arts, this relatively new gallery
specializes in one-of-a-kind collector's pieces, especially
baskets, sticks, animals, prints, and paintings from
Arnhem Land. Very expensive and at times quirky—not
everything is on display, so you may have to ask lots of
questions to find out what's really available!

❑ **Djamu Gallery Shop:** *Customs House, Alfred Street, Circular Quay, Tel. 9908-4644.* Operated by the Australian Museum. Includes several Aboriginal (Tiwi figures, baskets, cards, didgeridoos, textiles) and PNG (masks, carvings) artifacts. Includes probably the best collection of books on Aboriginal and PNG art found in Australia.

A few shops specialize in arts and crafts from Papua New Guinea, Indonesia, and the South Pacific. If you have an interest in such arts and crafts, visit these shops for an overview of what is available in Sydney:

❑ **New Guinea Arts:** *Dymocks Building, 8ᵗʰ Floor, 428 George Street, Tel. 9232-4737; and Queen Victoria Building, Level 2, Shop 16, 455 George Street, Tel. 9267-5134.* The best shop for relatively inexpensive arts and crafts from Papua New Guinea. Jam-packed with a wide range of carvings and masks from Papua New Guinea as well as some Aboriginal artifacts. Excellent service, including packing and shipping. Operated as a nonprofit organization that provides assistance to the tribal peoples of PNG.

❑ **Caspian Gallery:** *469 Oxford Street, Paddington. Tel. 9331-4260.* Specializes in Aboriginal, Indonesian, and Papuan New Guinea art as well as tribal rugs. Beautifully displayed one-of-a-kind collector's pieces in a historic home. One of the best shops in all of Asia and the Pacific. Owned and operated by noted expert and collector Bill Evans who is a fountain of information on such intriguing and exotic art.

❑ **Oceanic Art Gallery:** *76 Queens Street, Woollahra, Tel. 9327-6010.* Housed in the same building with two other galleries—Peter Lane Gallery and Au Lion Des Neiges. Wonderful collection of quality art from PNG. Offers many collector pieces.

❑ **Asian and Primitive Art Gallery:** *43 Williams Street, Paddington, Tel. 9331-7073. www.citysearch.com.au.* Small corner shop (may be moving soon) with an excellent collection of top quality pieces acquired through auctions and collectors—Aboriginal, Papuan New Guinea, Indonesia, Thai, and Myanmar. The place to see really good quality old Aboriginal pieces—not the typical tourist quality arts and crafts found in most Australian shops.

Australian Arts and Crafts

Numerous shops offering quality contemporary Australian arts and crafts are found in The Rocks, Paddington, The Strand Arcade, and Queen Victoria Building. You'll find delightful items produced by some of the best craftsmen from New South Wales as well as from all over Australia. These shops are filled with some of the best arts and crafts in Australia. You will find good buys on glass, leather, textiles, clothing, wood carvings, ceramics, jewelry, and metal work.

In contrast to the 5½-day work week of many other shops in Australia, most of these shops are open seven days a week. For best quality and selections, we highly recommend the following shops, most of which are located at The Rocks:

❑ **Makers Mark**: *Chifley Plaza, Chifley Square, Tel. 9231-6800. www.makersmark.com.au.* Terrific contemporary arts and crafts produced by some of Australia's master crafts-people. Look for beautiful handcrafted jewelry, wood crafts, glassware, and leather purses. Very expensive but very nice.

❑ **Gannon House Gallery**: *45 Argyle Street, The Rocks, Tel. 9251-4474. www.ozemail.com/au/~gannonhs.* One of our favorite shops with a good eye for quality. Terrific selections of Australian arts and crafts displayed in eight rooms. Includes everything from ceramics, paintings, and wood crafts to Aboriginal didgeridoos and boomerangs. Great collection of wood-turned bowls. Good prices. Works directly with artists.

❑ **Raglan Gallery**: *5-7 Raglan Street, Manly, Tel. 9977-0906.* Well worth a special trip to Manly just to visit this shop. Take the delightful ferry ride to Manly and discover one of Australia's nicest arts and crafts shops. Specializes in excellent quality ceramic and glass art as well as paintings and some Aboriginal art (dot acrylic and bark paintings, Tiwi poles). Offers many unique pieces. Tasteful selections by owner Jan Karras who also exhibits abroad.

❑ **Australian Craftworks**: *127 George Street, The Rocks, Tel. 9247-7156.* Located in the historic "Old Police Station." Offers excellent selections of top quality Australian crafts. Explore several rooms of this unique two-storey building for some of the best is wood, glass, ceramics, jewelry, and Aboriginal arts. Includes the colorful ceramic works of

Kathrin McMiles. Also offers clothes, handbags, belts, cards, candles, T-shirts, didgeridoos, and boomerangs.

❏ **Quadrivium:** *Queen Victoria Building, 2-50 Gallery Level South, 455 George Street, Tel. 9264-8222. www.citysearch. com/au/syd/quadrivium.* One of QVB's surprising shops. Represents a unique concept that simultaneous displays the decorative and fine arts. This large gallery displays the best of contemporary Australian art and design—studio glass, ceramics, jewelry, and object design. Represents Australia's leading artists and designers. Also includes a section on contemporary and traditional Asian art and Aboriginal art from Utopia.

❏ **Craftspace Gallery:** *Part of the Centre for Contemporary Crafts. Includes three shops at three different locations: Customs House, 31 Alfred Street, Circular Quay, Tel. 9247-7318; 88 George Street, The Rocks, Tel. 9247-7984; and 6-8 Scott Street, Pyrmont, Tel. 9552-4431.* Includes one-of-a-kind glassware, ceramics, textiles, wood, metal, mixed media, scarves/wraps, and contemporary jewelry.

❏ **Object Galleries:** *Third Floor, Customs House, 31 Alfred Street, Circle Quay, Tel. 9247-9127. www.object.com.au.* Part of the Centre for Contemporary Crafts. Showcases the best of new Australia craft and design work.

❏ **Australian Image & Telopea Gallery:** *Shop 2 Metcalfe Arcade, 80-84 George Street, The Rocks, Tel. 9241-1673.* Nice quality handicrafts—ceramics, glass, pottery, sweaters, jewelry, cups, and scarves. A 60-member cooperative with a large selection of attractive handicrafts produced by members of the Society of Arts and Crafts of NSW.

❏ **Best of Australiana:** *Level 2, Shop 1, Queen Victoria Building, Tel. 9261-2249.* Offers excellent quality crafts, from table ware and hand blown glass to ceramics, designer jewelry, and woodcraft. Represents major craftsmen.

The weekends are favorite times to browse through crafts markets in and around the Sydney area. Indeed, you can easily spend Saturday and Sunday just browsing the Sydney and suburban markets. Some of the most popular such markets include:

❑ **Rocks Market:** *Held every Saturday and Sunday at the Bridge end of George Street and along Playfair Street, open 10am-5pm, Tel. 9255-1717.* Includes more than 150 stalls offering a nice range of arts, crafts, jewelry, gifts, furniture, and collectibles. One of Sydney's better quality markets—not the typical flea market with lots of cheap junk. Vendors are carefully screened by a committee to ensure a good product mix as well as top quality products.

❑ **Paddington Bazaar:** *Centered at St. John's churchyard, Oxford and Newcombe Streets, open 10am-5pm on Saturday, Tel. 9331-2646 or 1902-260-622 (Bazaar info line; charges 50¢ a minute). http://surf.to/paddington.* Also known as Paddington Market and St. John's Churchyard Bazaar. This festive weekend market includes lots of small stalls offering a wide range of arts, crafts, clothes, T-shirts, tribal jewelry, toys, books, music, paintings, sculptures, knick-knacks, and old wares along with street entertainment.

❑ **Paddy's Markets:** *Two markets: **Paddy's Flemington**, along Parramatta Road, Flemington, open Friday 10am-4:30pm and Sunday 9am-4:30pm; and **Paddy's Haymarket**, corner of Thomas and Hay Streets (next to Chinatown), Haymarket, open Friday, Saturday, and Sunday 9am-4:30pm.* Includes hundreds of small indoor stalls operated by budding entrepreneurs offering a wide range of arts, crafts, clothes, toys, posters, CDs, luggage, sunglasses, books, and souvenirs as well as a food section. Includes lots of cheap junk that may be fun shopping for some visitors but a waste of time for others who are looking for unique quality items.

❑ **Balmain Markets:** *Corner Darling Street and Curtis Road, Balmain, open 8:30am-4pm on Saturday.* Located on the grounds of an historical church, this popular market includes 150 stalls offering handicrafts, antiques, clothing, and books. Also includes an international food hall.

❑ **Manly Arts & Crafts Market:** *Sydney Road and Market Lane Road (just off the Corso next to the beach), Manly. Open 10am-5pm Saturday, Sunday and public holidays. Tel. 9482-2741. www.markets.sydney.net (also includes information on craft shows and pagan fairs in Manly).* Offers a good range of arts and crafts, handmade clothes, paintings, jewelry, ornaments, sculpture, music, gift items, and souvenirs.

Also includes a Gourmet Court with a wide range of foods, many of which are attractively packaged.

You will also find a monthly (first Sunday of each month) arts and crafts fair in Hornsby as well as arts and crafts shops and markets in towns outside Sydney. Areas such as the Blue Mountains, Berrima, Hunter Valley, and Mudgee are noted craft centers. If you wish to visit and shop in these outlying areas, contact the Sydney Visitors Centre in The Rocks for more information.

Fine Arts, Antiques, and Collectibles

Treasure hunters and lovers of fine arts and antiques will find numerous shops and centers offering a variety of Australian, European, and Asian pieces. Indeed, Sydney is one of Australia's most important centers for fine arts, antiques and collectibles. You can easily spend several days "antiquing" in Sydney and its surrounding suburbs. Shops along **Queen Street in Woollahra** and **William Street in Paddington** bulge with fine Australian, European, and Asian antiques. Art galleries are found throughout the metropolitan area. Several antique centers and markets offer a wide variety of fine arts, antiques, and bric-a-brac to satisfy most connoisseurs of such selective shopping.

A good way to get oriented to the art and antique scene in and around Sydney is to pick up copies of various publications reviewing as well as advertising the latest collections of arts and antiques which are available in various shops, bookstores, and newsstands. In particular, look for the widely distributed *Antiques in New South Wales*. Published every five months, this free 100+ page newspaper/ magazine is available in many arts and antique shops. It's filled with articles and ads from Sydney's major art and antique shops. Also, look for two useful fliers (directories with maps):

Guide and Map to Art Galleries in Eastern Suburbs and Inner City

Guide and Map to Antique Dealers and Books Dealers in Eastern Suburbs and Inner City

Published by the Paddington Art Gallery (Tel. 9332-1840), both of these useful fliers are available in several shops.

Sydney's antique business is organized into antique fairs, shops, markets, and auction rooms. Many antique shops—

especially small stalls in antique centers or emporiums—offer
"collectibles" (old wares and bric-a-brac) of all sorts, from
antique jewelry to brass lanterns, and in all price ranges. While
the best antique shops tend to be individual shops, you'll also
find several good dealers in these four antique centers:

❏ **Woollahra Antique Centre:** *160 Oxford Street, Woollahra,
open daily 10am-6pm, Tel. 9327-8840.* Includes 50 antique
dealers offering quality furniture glassware, porcelain,
jewelry, silver, clocks, watches, and books. Includes a
popular coffee shop.

❏ **Sydney Antique Market:** *531 South Dowling Street, Surry
Hills, open daily 10am-6pm, Tel. 9332-2691. www.sydant
cent.com.au.* Claims to be Australia's oldest and largest
antique center with more than 70 dealers offering a wide
range of furniture, silver, porcelain, glass, rugs, jewelry,
dolls, clocks, watches, pens, bottles, toys, kitchenware,
and books.

❏ **Flinders Antique Centre:** *113-117 Parramatta Road,
Camperdown, open daily 10am-6pm, Tel. 9516-1212.* Offers
14,000 square feet of 19th and 20th century furniture and
collectibles as well as many architectural pieces including
statues, fountains, and marble fire places.

❏ **Camperdown Mews Antique Centre:** *210, 212-220
Parramatta Road, Camperdown, Tel. 9550-5554.* This relatively new antique center includes many respected dealers
offering everything from furniture and decorative arts to
jewelry, objets d'arts, and collectibles.

❏ **Great Australian Antique Market:** *62 Parramatta Road,
Glebe, Tel. 9660-0814, open daily 10am-6pm.* Includes 25
deals offering a large range of French, English, and Deco
furniture, from desks to clocks and objets d'art.

If you are interested in antique auctions —including the sale
of antique cars—be sure to look at the auction section in the
Saturday edition of *The Sydney Morning Star* or contact the
Sotheby's office to learn about their monthly specialty fine arts
and antiques auctions.

Antique shops offering excellent quality furniture and home
decorative items are particularly concentrated along Queen
Street and Jersey Road in Woollahra, just northeast of Oxford
Street in Paddington. This is the area for serious and sophisti-

cated antique dealers who nicely display their goods for discerning buyers. Several quality shops specialize in 18th and 19th century French and English furniture as well as 20th century Australian furniture. Other shops along Queen Street offer fine collections of Oriental arts, antiques, and furniture. We especially like the "Three Galleries" at 76 Queen Street which literally consist of three art and antique shops (open Monday to Saturday 11am-5pm) offering an interesting range of South Pacific and Asian antiques: **Peter Lane Gallery** (Tel. 9362-0115), **Au Lion des Neiges** (Tel. 9362-0115), and **Oceanic Art Gallery** (Tel. 9327-6010).

Other shops in Sydney specializing in arts and antiques are dispersed throughout the metropolitan area.

You will find several other antique shops within a 15 minute walk of Queen Street. Go to the corner of Queen and Oxford streets and proceed west along Oxford Street going toward The City. You will find the largest concentration of small antique shops offering all types of interesting collectibles—rare and affordable antique jewelry, silverware, glassware, porcelain, old books, furniture, and antique memorabilia—in **Woollahra Antiques Centre** at 160 Oxford Street (Tel. 9327-8840). Directly opposite Centennial Park, this is one of Sydney's best antique market-emporiums housing 50 antique shops. Be sure to look for **William Street**, a narrow one-way street just off of Oxford Street, where you will find a few additional antique shops. Also look for a few quality antique shops along Hargrave (**Antiques on Hargrave/House of Desks Antiques**, 108-110 Hargrave Street, Tel. 9363-3663) and Paddington Streets.

You will find many art and antique shops outside the Woollahra and Paddington areas, but few areas are as concentrated as these two. The next largest center for arts and antiques would be the **Neutral Bay-Mosman area** on the North Shore—a 15-minute drive from The City and The Rocks areas via the Sydney Harbour Bridge. Head for Military Road, which stretches several kilometers from Neutral Bay to Mosman. You'll find several art, antique, and collectible shops in the area, especially near the intersection of Military and Spit Roads. You may want to start at the **Mosman Antique Centre** at 700 Military Road (Tel. 968-1319) which has 34 dealers offering English and Continental furniture and decorative pieces, Art Deco, jewelry, china, oil lamps, original prints, and lots of collectibles.

Other art, antique, and collectible shops are found throughout the metropolitan area and in small towns of New South Wales in less concentrated areas than Woollahra, Paddington, and Mosman. In The City you will find in the Queen Victoria

Building at 455 George Street (**Bundi Fine Antiques**, Shop 10-12, Level 2, Tel. 9261-2210); and The Strand Arcade (**Margo Richards**, Shop 76, First Level Gallery, Tel. 9232-3870).

Double Bay has two of the most unique art and antique shops in the metropolitan area:

❑ **Russian Empire Trading Company:** *14 Transvaal Avenue, Double Bay, Tel. 9363-9887. Open Monday to Saturday 10am-5pm.* A very interesting and unusual shop. Offers a wonderful collection of unusual antiques from the Old Russian and Soviet Empires. Includes 19th century Baltic farmhouse furniture, toys, icons, ikat textiles from Central Asia, wedding chests, dough bowls, and numerous provincial items. Only such shop we encountered in Australia.

❑ **Four Winds Gallery:** *Shop 11 Bay Village, 28-34 Cross Street, Double Bay, Tel. 9328-7951. Open daily 10am-5pm.* Offers a very nice collection of American Indian paintings, sculptures, and jewelry.

Several other shops are found in the suburban areas of Double Bay (Bay and Cross streets), Rose Bay (Dover Road), Surry Hills (Riley and South Dowling roads), Camperdown (Parramatta Road), Newtown (King Street), Glebe (Glebe Point and St. Johns Road), Huntsville (Ormonde Parade), Balmain (Darling and Beattie streets and Balmain Road), Haberfield (Dalhousie Street), Drummoyne (Lyons Road), Beescroft (Wongala Crs.), Hornsby (Pacific Highway, St. Leonard, and Gordon), Newcastle (King and Wood streets), Avoca Beach (Avoca Drive), Hamilton (Beaumont Street), Morisset (Dora Street), Windsor (George Street), Kurrajong (Old Bells Road), and the Blue Mountains (Great Western Highway, Lawson; Station Street and Railway Parade, Wentworth).

Art galleries offering fine Australian, European, and North American oils, prints, and water colors are also found throughout the metropolitan area. For a quick introduction into art, visit these key Web sites:

Art Hop	*www.lincnet.com.au/OZART*
Art Gallery of NSW	*www.artgallery.nsw.gov.au*
Museum of	
Contemporary Art	*www.mca.com.au*
Soho Gallery	*www.sohogalleeries.net*
State of the Art	*www.startart.com.au*

The largest number of fine art galleries are concentrated in the The Rocks, Paddington, Woollahra, Darlinghurst, Double Bay, and The City areas. In The Rocks, look for these two large and pricey art galleries that promote single artists/ owners:

❑ **Billich Gallery**: *100 George Street, The Rocks, open daily 11am-7pm, Tel. 9252-1481.* Displays the towering contemporary paintings of noted Australian artist Charles Billich. Includes originals, limited-edition prints, and sculptures. A very large gallery devoted to the excessive promotion of this award-winning celebrity artist.

❑ **Ken Done Gallery**: *1-5 Hickson Road, The Rocks, open daily, 10am-5:30pm, Tel. 9247-2840.* Showcases the colorful original paintings and prints of popular artist/ designer Ken Done.

Other local artists with their own galleries in the Queen Victoria Building at 455 George Street include **Eva Hannah Gallery** (Level 2, Shop 43-45, *www.evahannahgallery.com.au*) and **Heaven and Earth** (Level 2, Shop 23, Tel. 9267-5030—artists Samantha Wortelhock and Damien Naughton).

The largest fine art gallery in the central business district is **Gallery Link International** (Wentworth Hotel, 61 Phillip Street, Tel. 9223-1700). It represents the works of several leading Australian artists, such as Elizabeth Durack, Dennis Baker, Kevin Best, Sandro Noccentini, Pro Hart, and Walangari Karntawarra.

As we noted earlier, a few shops, such as **Coo-ee Aboriginal Art** (98 Oxford Street, Paddington, Tel. 9332-1544), **Jinta Desert Art Gallery** (154-156 Clarence Street, Tel. 9290-3639), **Hogarth Galleries Aboriginal Art Centre** (7 Walker Lake (top of Brown Street, Paddington, Tel. 9360-6839), and **Aboriginal and Tribal Art Centre** (Level 1, 117 George Street, Tel. 9247-9625), specialize in Aboriginal paintings.

Depending on the time of the year you visit Sydney, you may be able to attend one or two annual art and antique fairs, such as the annual Sydney Antiques Fair which is held in the winter months. Ask shopkeepers about upcoming fairs and special exhibits. If you drive through some of the small towns in New South Wales, especially around the Blue Mountain area, you may find all kinds of treasures that have accumulated in the attics and backyards of local residents. Indeed, looking for art, antiques, and collectibles in Sydney and its environs may well become one of the most memorable experiences of your Australian shopping adventure!

FASHION AND SPORTSWEAR

Sydney is one of Australia's two major centers for fashion and sportswear production and distribution. All of Australia's major designers are represented in Sydney's department stores and boutiques. Several Sydney-based fashion designers operate their own boutiques in and around The Strand Arcade and Double Bay area. You will also find, especially in the Sully Hill area, some factory outlets—but by no means as plentiful as in Melbourne—offering designer labels at substantial savings. Exclusive couture shops, high fashion and up-market boutiques, and medium-range clothing stores are all well represented in Sydney. Imported clothes are also widely available in shops throughout Sydney, but especially in the exclusive boutiques of Double Bay and the shopping arcades in The City. Shopping for such designer clothes and sportswear may become one of the major shopping highlights during your stay in Sydney.

If you wander through the women's and men's sections of such major department stores as **David Jones** (corner of Market, Elizabeth, and Castlereagh Streets, Tel. 9266-5544) and **Grace Bros** (corner of Pitt and Market Streets, in the new Sydney Central Plaza, Tel. 9238-9111), you will find fashion and sportswear under the labels of major Australian designers.

If you are interested in some unique fashion, sportswear, and accessory designs produced by innovative Sydney designers, be sure to visit the shops in The Strand Arcade, Centrepoint, MLC Centre (visit **Belinda**), Sky Garden Shopping Centre, Queen Victoria Building, and Chifley Plaza.

Castlereagh Street is the center for brand name European clothes and accessories: **Gucci**, **Gianfranco Ferre**, **Ferragamo**, **Prada**, **DKNY**, **Hermes**, and **Alfred Dunhill**.

Chifley Plaza includes the innovative **Oroton** accessory designs and the popular **R. M. Williams** bush outfitters alongside **Adele Weiss**, **Zambelli**, **MaxMara**, **Tengdahl**, **Oxford**, **Pierucci**, and **Bruno Magli**.

The **Queen Victoria Building** also houses several boutiques of leading Australian designers as well as international brand names. Indeed, you will find 65 women's and men's fashion shops here. For local designers, look for **Anthea Crawford**, **Brian Rochford**, **Liz Davenport**, **Monsoon**, **Shepherds**, **Country Road**, **Purely Australian**, and **Don Art and Design**.

Centrepoint is another major fashion center in The City. Connected to David Jones and Grace Brothers department stores, this center has over 60 women's and men's fashion shops offering clothes, footwear, and accessories which cater to both mid-range and up-market clientele. Many of these shops

333

are branches of shops found in the Queen Victoria Building, The Strand Arcade, and other shopping centers throughout the city. This center houses **Bee Fashions**, **Cue**, **David Lawrence**, **Fashion Warehouse**, **Georges of Sydney**, **Liz Davenport**, **Laura Ashley**, **Maggie T**, **Papoucci**, and **Toroni**.

The upscale **MLC Centre** (corner of King and Castlereagh Streets, Martin Place) offers several international fashion brands on Level 7: **Posh**, **Georg Jensen**, **Cartier**, **Gucci**, **Hunting World**, and **Salvatore Ferragamo**.

The venerable **Gowings** (corner of Market and George Streets, Tel. 9264-6321 and 319 George Street, Wynyard, Tel. 9262-1281, *www.gowings.com.au*) has been in operation for more than 130 years offering everything for men and boys as well as outdoor and adventure equipment.

The Rocks also has several unique fashion and sportswear shops you may be interested in browsing through. One of the best shops that showcases 215 Australian artists and designers, including the popular Coogi knitwear, is **Dorian Scott** (105 George Street, Tel. 9221-8145). **Country Road** (The Argyle Department Store, 18-24 Argyle Street, Tel. 9251-7299) represents one of the most respected Australian fashion names for contemporary men's and women's clothes and accessories. For hats of all styles as well as coats, boots, parkas, vests, scarves, and belts, visit **The Rocks Hatters** (81 George Street, Tel. 9252-3525). For colorful Australian designer clothing and knitwear, visit **Artwear** (77½ George Street, Tel. 9247-3668). **Done Art and Design** (123-125 George Street, Tel. 9251-6099) showcases the popular resortwear, swimwear, childrenswear, and homeware of artists Ken Done and designer Judy Done. **Brian Rochford** (1st Floor, The Argyle Department Store, 18-24 Argyle Street, Tel. 9252-2553) also offers bright and colorful swimwear and resortwear by one of Australia's award-winning designers.

The **Double Bay** area houses the most exclusive fashion and sportswear shops in Sydney. Bay, Cross, and Knox streets are lined with fashionable boutiques offering clothes from A$20 to A$10,000. Look for **Belinda** at 8 Transvaal Avenue, **Morrissey** at 2 Guilfoyle Avenue, and **Saba** at 39 Bay Street. The **Ritz-Carlton Promenade**, **The Georges Centre**, and **Bay Village** house several nice shops. For leather, hat, and scarf accessories, visit **D'Aliccia** (Shop 1, Cosmopolitan Centre, Knox Street).

FACTORY OUTLET CLOTHING AND ACCESSORIES

While Melbourne is the center of buying clothing and accessories at **factory outlets**, Sydney has its own factory outlets offering discontinued, end-of-line stock, seconds, samples, and overruns of name-brand men's, women's, and children's clothes, shoes, and accessories at savings from 30 to 70 percent. Most of these outlets are scattered throughout the metropolitan area, but many are concentrated in and around the **Surry Hills, Parramatta, Chatsworth, Redfern**, and **Campertown** areas.

Factory outlet shopping in Sydney is best done by the well informed who know where to go, what to buy, and how to shop. Some factory outlets are open by appointment only whereas others are open to the general public during regular business hours. Our recommendation is to purchase a copy of *Bargain Shopper's Guide to Sydney* (A$9.95) which is available at most bookstores and newsstands or can be ordered directly from the publisher: Universal Magazines, Unit 5-6 Byfield Street, North Ryde, NSW 2113, Australia.

The most convenient way to shop these outlets is to join a local shopping tour. Try **Shopping Spree Tours** (P.O. Box 361, Darlinghurst, NSW 2010, Tel. 9360-6220, Fax 9332-2641, or e-mail tours@shopping-tours.com.au or visit their Web site: *www.shopping-tours.com.au*).

AUSTRALIANA, SOUVENIRS, AND GIFTS

Sydney's shops are big on offering a large range of Australiana, souvenirs, and gifts to visitors. The quality ranges from tourist junk to some very fine arts, crafts, and jewelry classified as Australiana. Every major shopping area will have one or more shops specializing in knickknacks they term "Australiana".

One of the best places in all of Australia to purchase good quality Australiana is **The Rocks** area of Sydney. Several shops here offer good quality and selections of Australiana. **The Didjeridu Shop** (Shop 36, The Rocks Centre, 12-26 Playfair Street, Tel. 9251-2294), for example, has an excellent selection of boomerangs, clothes, musical instruments, and books on Australia. Next door is the **Platypus Gallery** (Shop 36, Tel. 9241-1590) offers a nice selection of Australiana products with emphasis on unique Australian timbers and handmade artefacts (puzzles, wind chimes, wood carved pieces, stuffed animals, puppets, scarves, coasters, placemats). In the nearby Metcalfe Arcade you will find the **Lambswool Trader** (80/84 George Street, Tel. 9247-9174) offering quality leather and sheepskin goods and related souvenirs. **Gannon House Gallery** (45 Argyle Street, The Rocks, Tel. 9251-4474. *www.ozemail.com/au/~gannonhs*) remains one of our very favorite shops for excellent quality arts, crafts, and Australiana. You are bound to find some unique gift items here. We also like **Dorian Scott** (105

George Street, The Rocks, Tel. 9221-8145; also has shops at the Hotel Intercontinental, Macquarie Street, Tel. 9246-1818 and Sydney International Airport, Tel. 9317-2881) with its nice selection of Australia fashion, jewelry, crafts, hats, Coogi clothes, wool shawls, and prints.

Other shopping areas are filled with Australiana and souvenir shops. In Gallery Two of the Queen Victoria Building, for example, look for **Best of Australiana** (41), **Ashi's Treasures of Australia** (44), **Blue Gum Designs** (47), **Bushmans Gift** (31), **Crocodile Stop**, and **QVB Souvenirs** (5-7).

In Paddington, be sure to visit the ground level of **Coo-ee** (98 Oxford Street, Tel. 9332-1544) for a good collection of Australiana which primarily represents Aboriginal arts and crafts (boomerangs, didgeridoos, music, and books). The shop transforms itself into a major gallery for quality Aboriginal art, but only if you venture upstairs or into the basement!

The **Marketplace** at Harbourside is another major area with numerous small shops and pushcarts catering to tourists with all types and qualities of Australiana, souvenirs, and gifts.

LEATHER CLOTHES AND HATS

If you are looking for some "citified outback clothes," you're in luck in Sydney. Try the **Goodwood Saddlery** (237-239 Broadway, Tel. 9660-6788) for famous brands in Australian Outback clothing (Akubra, Driza-Bone, and R. M. Williams) as well as Australian stock saddles. **Thomas Cook Boot and Clothing Company** (129 Pitt Street, near Martin Place, Tel. 9232-3334, and 790 George Street, Haymarket, near Central Station, Tel. 9212-6616—*www.thomascookclothing.com.au*) offers a good range of classic Australian Outback and Adventure clothing. The local branch of **R. M. Williams** (Chifley Plaza, 2 Chifley Square, Tel. 9233-5608) sells leather clothes, especially Driza-Bone oilskin rain coats and riding jackets, moleskin pants, kangaroo-hide belts, and Akubra hats—everything you ever needed to look like Crocodile Dundee or the Man from Snowy River or attend those hoe-downs and bush dances you have been waiting for!

Both **The Rocks Hatters** (81 George Street, The Rocks, Tel. 9252-3525) and the **Strand Hatters** (Shop 8, Strand Arcade, 412 George Street, Tel. 9231-6884) offer a fun selection of hats. The **Rocks Hatters** has all types of hats (felt, straw, canvas, legionnaire caps, suede bush, grazier) as well as coats, boots, photojournalist's vest, parkas, scarves, belts, Driza-Bone hats, and Thomas Cook adventurewear. The popular **Strand Hatters** is very focused on hats. Indeed, it offers

Australia's largest range of hats which can be expertly fitted, steamed, shaped, and feathered, if you wish.

DUTY-FREE GOODS

Sydney has the largest concentration of duty-free shops in the country. They are especially popular with Japanese and New Zealand tourists who feel they are getting a bargain on everything from opals to liquor. However, you'll have to judge for yourself whether these places are worth shopping.

The majority of duty-free shops are found in and around the Pitt Street area in downtown Sydney. The two most popular duty-free shops are **Downtown Duty Free** (Strand Arcade, basement level, 412 George Street, Tel. 9233-3166; also at 105 Pitt Street, Tel. 9221-4444) and **Angus and Coote** (496 George Street, Hilton Hotel, Tel. 9267-1363).

BOOKS

You'll find books everywhere in Sydney, from large chain stores to small used and antique book stores. Two of the largest book stores include **Dymock's** (424-430 George Street, Tel. 9235-0155), and **Ariel Booksellers** (42 Oxford Street, Paddington, Tel. 9332-4581).

MAJOR SHOPPING AREAS

Sydney offers a wide variety of shopping settings. This energetic city is always on the move with new and controversial office and shopping complexes either being planned or under construction. From The Rocks along the harbor to the expansive Harbourside development in Darling Harbour, Sydney's commercial development is increasingly moving to the southern part of the city and into the suburbs.

The best shopping in terms of quality and convenience will be found in the shopping arcades, neighborhood shops, and markets of **The Rocks** (The Rocks Centre, Argyle Department Store, Clocktower Square, Metcalfe Arcade, and George, Argyle, and Playfair Streets); **The City**, or central business district (Queen Victoria Building, Strand Arcade, Pitt Street Mall, Skygarden, Centrepoint, MLC Centre, Chifley Plaza, Martin Place, and George, Pitt, King, and Castlereagh Streets); **Darling Harbour** (Marketplace at Harbourside); **Double Bay** (Knox, Cross, and Bay Streets); **Woollahra** (Queen Street); **Paddington** (Oxford and William Streets); **North Shore** (Neutral

Bay and Mosman); and **Glebe** and **Balmain** (southwest and west of the city center). Such oceanfront communities as **Manly** (southeast) and **Bondi** (north shore) also offer some unique shopping opportunities.

We have not included several additional suburban areas which also offer shopping opportunities, because these areas primarily function as shopping centers for local residents. Most of these areas have few unique items to offer visitors. Sydney's bustling Chinatown, for example, is not included because it offers nothing uniquely Australian to visitors. Go there for some good Oriental restaurants or the adjacent Paddy's Market on Saturday and Sunday.

THE ROCKS

The Rocks, nestled just south of the Sydney Harbour Bridge and west of the Sydney Opera House and Circular Quay, is Sydney's most historical area and one of Australia's most successful urban renewal projects. This harborside village and hilly commercial area is Sydney's oldest commercial and maritime quarter. It includes lots of interesting shops, restaurants, and hotels adjacent to the harbor and the Sydney Opera House.

The Rocks is rich in history and urban folklore. This is where the first settlers—an unwitting gang of nearly 1,000 prisoners—landed in 1788. It's where much of Sydney's colorful commercial, maritime, and bawdy history developed. It's where over 100 citizens died of the bubonic plague in 1890; where high levels of crime, prostitution, and disease as well as occasional fires characterized what was a slum area until the 1930s when the Sydney Harbour Bridge sliced through the area for ostensible "urban renewal" purposes. But neither fires nor the bridge project could renew this area in the direction of the positive urban renewal that took place in the 1970s. Completely transformed in recent years to become one of Sydney's beautiful and charming tourist attractions and shopping destinations, The Rocks is a "must" stop for anyone visiting Sydney.

The Rocks is one of the most charming, quaint, and colorful shopping areas in all of Australia. Stroll down its cobblestone streets, climb the stairs connecting shops and streets, take a leisurely walk along the charming harbor that bounds this area, duck into a popular pub or two, or dine in one of its fine restaurants and you will be in for a most delightful day of sightseeing and shopping at The Rocks.

You also may want to stay at one of The Rocks' fine hotels, such as The Regent, Park Hyatt Sydney, Observatory Hotel, Pier One Parkroyal, or Old Sydney Park Royal. These hotels are very convenient in relation to the major shops and attractions in The Rocks and The City proper.

Although The Rocks has a reputation among locals for being a "touristy area," it has not succumbed to becoming a tacky tourist trap; it has many pockets of class. The Rocks is one of our favorite shopping areas in all of Australia. We really like the ambience of this area with its pleasant mix of shops, restaurants, bars, and hotels that draw bustling crowds in the evenings and on weekends. But most important of all, this area boasts numerous quality shops showcasing some of Australia's finest arts and crafts. Because of the arts and crafts shops, much of The Rocks is open seven days a week. If you are like us, you will want to visit this area more than once during your stay in Sydney. At night the area is alive with people enjoying the harbor views and dining at the many fine local restaurants. It's a great place for "lifestyle shopping."

Major shopping at The Rocks is centered in and around George, Argyle, Hickson, and Playfair Streets as well as in four shopping centers: The Rocks Centre, Argyle Department Store, Clocktower Square, Metcalfe Arcade. **George Street** in The Rocks begins just north of the Regent Hotel. This street is filled with shops, pubs, and restaurants. It is lined with horse drawn carts and carriages to take you around The Rocks and surrounding areas. You'll find three of Sydney's best arts and crafts shops—**Gannon House Gallery** (45 Argyle Street, The Rocks, Tel. 9251-4474), **Australian Craftswork** (127 George Street), and **Craftspace Gallery** and **Object** (88 George Street). For anyone interested in Australian arts and crafts, these are three "must visit" shops in Sydney. The quality of arts and crafts in these shops is superb. Also, stop at the **Bottom of the Harbour Antiques** (104 George Street, Tel. 9246-8107) for a unique collection of nautical antiques, and **Dorian Scott** (105 George Street, Tel. 9221-8145) for good quality Australian fashion design and Australiana. The **Aboriginal and Tribal Art Centre** (117 George Street, Tel. 9247-9625) offers good quality Aboriginal arts and crafts, including paintings and carvings. One of Sydney's largest art galleries, which displays the works of a single artist, also is located along this street, **Billich Gallery** (100 George Street).

Along adjacent **Argyle Street** you will find a few shops, especially in the Clocktower Square and the Argyle Department Stores. Many of the shops here offer lots of arts, crafts, and clothes.

Hickson Road houses the works of one of Australia's most famous artists and designers, Ken Done, in the expansive **Ken Done Gallery** (1 Hickson Road).

The **Argyle Department Store** (formerly the Argyle Centre and also referred to as Argyle Store) has numerous shops selling everything from koalas to candles. Browse through the three stories of shops and you will certainly find something you will treasure. At ground level you will find shops offering quality Australiana, such as **The Didjeridu Shop** and **Platypus Gallery**.

Along adjacent **Playfair Street** and **Nurses Walk** you'll find several distinctive shops offering arts and crafts. Be sure to visit this area on weekends when it becomes part of the popular Rocks Market (Saturday and Sunday, 10am-5pm). Just down the street, off George Street, is the **Metcalfe Arcade** found in the historical Metcalfe Stores building. Several shops on the First Level sell unique arts, crafts, and Australiana. Stop by to see the samples and unique work being done in Australian and New Zealand wools. Nearby is a delightful arts and crafts shop operated by volunteers: **Australian Image and Telopea Galleries** which is operated by the Society of Arts and Crafts of New South Wales (Shop 2). **The Candle Factory**, **Lambs-wool Trader**, and **Bead Bar** are well stocked with arts, crafts, jewelry, and Australian items.

While visiting The Rocks, you may wish to dine at one of the harborside restaurants. The historical Campbells Storehouse has several good restaurants with nice views of the harbor. One of Sydney's best Chinese restaurants, Imperial Peking, is found in this complex alongside the popular Wolfie's Grill, Waterfront, and Italian Village Restaurants. The restaurants with the best view of the harbor are the Quay and Doyles Seafood located just across from the restaurants fronting Campbells Storehouse. Be sure to make reservations since most of these popular restaurants are heavily booked for both lunch and dinner.

If you like history, you'll want to stop at the Visitors Centre, Cadmen Cottage, Observatory Park, and Garrison Church—all within short walking distance of each other. For one of the best views of Sydney Harbor and the Opera House and a review of the history of bridge building, climb the stairs and walk out to the southeast pylon of the Sydney Harbour Bridge, where you will climb 200 stairs to get a beautiful view of this area. Take your camera for some wonderful shots of the harbor. For a truly adventuresome once-in-a-lifetime walk and climb, consider joining the popular and truly unforgettable BridgeClimb tour (Tel. 9252-0077, *www.bridgeclimb.com*) which is a thrilling three-hour climb and walk via catwalks, ladders, and arches on top of the Sydney Harbour Bridge.

THE STRAND ARCADE (CITY)

Here is one of Sydney's most elegant historical shopping areas located in the heart of the city's commercial district between Pitt Street Mall and George Street. First built in 1892, this beautiful four-storey Victorian building houses over 50 shops. Once one of Sydney's most upscale and exclusive shopping centers, it has been eclipsed by newer and more exclusive shopping arcades, such as Chifley Plaza, Centrepoint, MLC Center, and the Queen Victoria Building, in recent years. Nonetheless, The Strand Arcade is still a classy place to visit; it's best noted for its unique architecture and ambience as well as includes several nice boutiques, jewelry stores, cafes, and take-away restaurants. This is where you can purchase the latest in Australian fashion; design your own jewelry; get your shoes repaired and clothes altered; buy gifts and accessories; order wedding invitations and a wedding dress; get a tooth filled; buy freshly roasted coffee and a bouquet of flowers; acquire a unique Australian hat; and shop for duty-free goods. This is also where many of the rich and famous visit—where such international celebrities as David Bowie, Lauren Bacall, Tina Turner, Sophia Loren, and Cher have been known to stop when in Sydney. It's a very pleasant and friendly shopping area—one you may return to several times during your visit. The best shops are found on the ground level. For example, look for **Opal Treasures**, **Strand Jewellers**, and **Masterpiece Jewellery** for nice quality jewelry; **The Strand Hatters** for lots of unique hats; and **Victoria and Albert** for good quality antiques. The first level has several boutiques, jewelry stores, and cafes. **Dinosaur Designs**, with its distinctive orange, black, and white vases and bowls, has a shop here. The basement level houses the **Downtown Duty-Free** shop.

QUEEN VICTORIA BUILDING (CITY)

Located directly across from the aging Hilton Hotel and Royal Arcade, bounded by George, Market, York, and Druitt Streets, and linked to the Town Hall, Railway Station, and Grace Brothers Department Store, the Queen Victoria Building (QVB—*www.qvb.com.au*) houses one of Australia's largest, most elegant, and colorful up-market shopping centers. Similar in character to The Strand Arcade, but on a much grander scale, this is a gorgeous building with a sandstone and domed exterior resembling a Byzantine Palace. Noted for its spacious interior with elegant arches, intricate and colorful tiled floors, and beautiful stained glass, the Queen Victoria Building is an outstanding example of Victorian architecture. It's Australia's most distinctive shopping arcade.

While the Queen Victoria Building is a premier shopping center, you may want to spend some time here for sightseeing purposes. The history and architecture of this building are fascinating. Indeed, you may want to combine your sightseeing with shopping and dining at this unique building.

First constructed as the Queen Victoria Market Building in 1898 and lovingly preserved, converted, and modernized for the convenience of shoppers, browsers, and diners alike from 1983 to 1986 by the Malaysian Ipoh Limited business group, the Queen Victoria Building is filled with over 200 shops, cafes, and restaurants. It's a great place for trendy shoppers who are into "lifestyle shopping." It's a place where you can easily spend half a day strolling the four long levels connected by stairs, escalators, and elevators; browsing through nice boutiques; educating yourself about arts, crafts, Australiana, and opals; selecting a perfect gift; stopping for a cup of cappuccino or having a full course lunch or dinner; or watching the unique Royal Automata Clock on the top floor on the hour present six famous events from British history, including the beheading of King Charles I! Also, look for several other unique presentations and art works, such as the Imperial Jade Carriage made with 300 tons of raw jade (Market Street end of Gallery Two), the Queen Victoria Statue, and the unique Foucalt Pendulum (*www.physics. usyd.edu.au*).

The Queen Victoria Building is jam-packed with boutiques, jewelry, gift, souvenir, art, antique, beauty, kids, and service shops as well as numerous take-away eateries, cafes, and restaurants. Most shops are open daily from 9am to 6pm, although the shops on Gallery One and Two open at 10am; on Sundays and holidays, shops are open from 11am to 5pm.

The quickest way to orient yourself to this expansive arcade is to pick up the **free guidebook** which is available from the central Information Desk. It includes maps of each floor as well as lists shops by category and location. For example, the Lower Ground Floor and Gallery One are largely devoted to fashion, jewelry shops, and cafes. Gallery Two largely houses art, craft, antique, Australiana, and opal shops. At the same time, you can take a **guided tour** of this historic building which departs at 11:30am and 2:30pm. Contact the Tour Desk on the Ground Floor or call (Tel. 9264-9209) the Tour Manager for more information.

For womenswear on the lower ground floor and Gallery One, look for **Liz Davenport, Anthea Crawford, Brian Rochford, David Lawrence, Monsoon, Nelson Leong, Esprit, Portmans, Saba Knitwear, Shepherds,** and **Vivian Chan Shaw.** For menswear, look for **Oxford Shop, Joe Bananas, Polo Ralph Lauren, Baubridge and Kay,** and **Urban Edge.** For both menswear and womenswear, visit the famous **Country Road** as well as **Canterbury of Sydney, Clothes of the Outback, Done Art & Design, Purely Australian, Jag,** and **Studio One.**

The Gallery Two Level includes several nice art, antique, craft, and Australiana shops: **New Guinea Primitive Arts** (small branch shop of **New Guinea Arts** which is located nearby in the Dymocks Building), **Bunda Fine Antiques, Eva Hannah Gallery, Heaven and Earth Art Gallery, Quadrivium**, and **Best of Australiana**. Several jewelry shops specialize in opals: **Australian Opal House, Opal Beauty, Opal Fields, and Earths Natural Wonders**. For gifts and Australiana, check out **Ashi's Treasures of Australia, Ayres Rock Souvenir, Blue Gum Designs, QVB Souvenirs**, and **The Best of Australiana**.

One of the highlights of visiting the Queen Victoria Building is watching the unique Royal Automata Clock (located at the Druitt Street end of Gallery Two) on the hour, from 10am to 9pm, present its historical tales. Crowds normally gather on the hour and delight in this presentation. Also, you will find numerous cafes, restaurants, and take-away food stalls serving everything from health foods and fresh juices to pasta and seafood. Several good take-away food stalls—with tables and benches nearby—are found on the bottom floor near the entrance to the underground passageway connecting the Queen Victoria Building with the Grace Brothers Department Store.

OTHER MAJOR CITY SHOPPING ARCADES

The downtown commercial area—bounded by Bridge, George, Castlereagh, and Market streets and intersected by Pitt and King Streets as well as Martin Place—houses several large and small shopping arcades and department stores in addition to the elegant Strand Arcade and the Queen Victoria Building. Within the past few years, several shopping arcades in the downtown area have gone upscale with many quality fashion boutiques and jewelry stores as well as large food courts to service the noon-time shoppers who spill into the streets from nearby office buildings. The names and locations of these multi-level arcades can be confusing since one shopping complex tends to feed into another and thus all of them appear to merge into one large shopping complex along Pitt and George streets. The best way to shop this area is to head for the **Pitt Street Mall**, **Martin Place**, and **Chifley Square** areas. These are pedestrian shopping areas which are fed by adjacent office and shopping complexes. The majority of shopping arcades are in or around Pitt Street Mall.

In addition to the Queen Victoria Building and The Strand Arcade, the major shopping arcades in the downtown area (The City) include:

❑ **Chifley Plaza:** *2 Chifley Square, Tel. 9221-4500. Open weekdays 10am-6pm, Saturday 10am-5pm, and closed Sunday. www.chifleyplaza.com.au.* One of Sydney's most elegant shopping centers for top quality fashion, jewelry, crafts, and gifts. This granite and glass shopping and service arcade could be mistaken for a bank. Look for these famous brand names: **Bruno Magli, Crabtree & Evelyn, MaxMara, Zambelli Menswear,** and **Tiffany & Co.** Also includes one of Australia's very best arts and crafts centers, **Makers Mark,** which alone is worth a visit here. Also includes famous Australian leather shops **Oroton** (handbags) and **R. M. Williams** (clothes) and Australian fashions and accessories at **Adele Weiss, Tengdahl, Oxford,** and **Pierucci.** In addition to several sevices (flower, cleaners, travel, optical, hair, pharmacy, dental), Chifley Plaza also includes a few restaurants (Matsukaza Japanese Restaurant is one of the city's best) and cafes as well as a small food court.

❑ **Centerpoint Shopping Centre:** *Located at Pitt Street Mall and surrounding the landmark Sydney (AMP) Tower, Sydney's tallest structure. Tel. 9231-1000. Open Monday through Wednesday, 9am-6pm; Thursday, 9am-8pm; Friday, 9am-6pm; Saturday, 9am-5pm; and Sunday, 11am-4pm. www. centrepoint.com.au.* Includes four floors of over 170 specialty shops, cafes, and fast-food counters offering local and international fashion labels, jewelry, gifts, and more. For jewelry, visit **Angus & Coote, George Jensen, Jorgen Jensen, Opal Cave,** and **Raymond's Jewelry;** women's fashion shops include **David Lawrence, Georges of Sydney, Laura Ashley, Liz Davenport, Maggie T,** and **Papoucci.** For fashion accessories, try the nice leather selections at **Oroton.** You won't go hungry here with over 30 cafes, restaurants, and take-away food stalls, (lower level and facing Pitt Street Mall), including McDonald's, Burger King, and Wendys.

❑ **MLC Centre:** *Corner of King and Castlereagh Streets at Martin Place.* This large and recently renovated shopping complex offers numerous up-market shops and boutiques as well as a popular food court (try the wonderful Doner Kabab Roll at Ala Turko for A$5!). Includes three floors (Level 6 at King Street, Level 7 at Castlereagh Street, and Level 8) of international brand name clothes and accessories, Australian fashion, jewelers, and cafes and restaurants. Be sure to visit the shops on Level 7, especially the award-winning **Perri Jewellers** (Tel. 9231-1088) and the **Belinda** boutique (presents both international and local fashion designers, Tel. 9233-0781). You'll also find international name brand shops here such as **Jensen, Cartier, Gucci, Hunting World,** and **Salvatore Ferragamo.**

❑ **Sydney Central Plaza:** *Pitt Street Mall, at the corner of Pitt and Market Streets, Tel. 9238-9111. Open Monday through Saturday, 9am-6pm; Thursday 9am-9pm; and Sunday 11am-5pm.* Basically houses the recently refurbished and more chic **Grace Bros** department store as well as the **Disney Store** (lower ground floor) and several specialty retail shops, cafes, bars, and food stores (Cornucopia–Food in Abundance) under a five-storey atrium. Grace Bros has never looked so good!

❑ **Skygarden:** *77 Castlereagh Street (between Pitt Street Mall and Castlereagh Street), Tel. 9231-1811, www.skygarden.com. au.* Includes over 60 stores on 7 levels offering designer fashions, gifts, and homewares as well as an international food court. Relatively new and luxurious shopping and dining complex. Level 2 includes several galleries displaying the work of Australian artists and Aboriginal artwork and artefacts. For jewelry, be sure to stop at one of Sydney's best jewelers, **Hardy Brothers** (Tel. 9232-2422).

Also, look for a few other shopping arcades in this area, such as **Piccadilly** (one block south of Pitt Street Mall—*www.picca dillyretail.net.au*), **Martin Place** (between Castlereagh and Elizabeth Streets just north of King Street), **Town Hall Arcade** (40 shops underground, at Darling Harbour and Kent Streets, just outside the Queen Victoria Building), and the **AMP Tower** (near the intersection of Market and Pitt Streets). The old **Royal Arcade** at the Hilton Hotel (across of the Queen Victoria Building) has seen better times.

UPSCALE SHOPPING STREETS

Sydney's most exclusive shopping streets, which are in close proximity to the Pitt Street Mall, Martin Place, and Chifley Square areas, are King and Castlereagh Streets. **King Street** includes the very exclusive Australian pearler and jeweler **Paspaley** (142 King Street, Tel. 9232-7633, *www.paspaley pearls.com*). If you love pearls, you'll fall in love with this shop. Also look for **Chanel** on King Street. Just around the corner you'll find several international brand name fashion clothes and accessory shops along Castlereagh Street, such as **Louis Vuitton, Loewe, Gucci, Gianfranco Ferre, Salvatore Ferragamo, Prada, Georg Jensen, DKNY, Hermes,** and **Alfred Dunhill**. This street also leads to Level 7 of the upscale MLC Centre where you will find **Hunting World** and **Belinda**.

HARBOURSIDE SHOPPING CENTRE
(DARLING HARBOUR)

Darling Harbour represents Sydney's and Australia's most ambitious urban redevelopment project—and it seems to work after several years of development and redevelopment. Once a disused rail yard, it is an attempt to create an integrated cultural, entertainment, commercial, and shopping complex on the city's historical Darling Harbour located southwest of the city center and adjacent to Chinatown. Developed around a much larger concept of waterfront shopping than the failed Pier 1 and Birkenhead Point, Darling Harbour is nearly identical in appearance and structure to Baltimore, Maryland's (USA) harborside development—but on a much grander scale and with great success. Nestled in Darling Harbour and surrounded by the Sydney Aquarium, Sega World, Panasonic IMAX Theatre, Chinese Garden of Friendship, Powerhouse Museum, National Maritime Museum, Convention Centre, and luxury hotels, the nearly refurbished Harbourside Shopping Centre with over 150 retail stores and restaurnats has become a popular shopping areas for local residents.

The popularity of Harbourside Shopping Centre is probably due more to the ambience of its architecture and harborside setting than to any special shopping opportunities found here. Harbourside Shopping Centre is clearly a social event for local residents; shopping is its side show. Young people, especially families, love to come here to enjoy the atmosphere of people, restaurants, shopping, sightseeing, and the water views. If you have been to similar developments in the United States (Baltimore and Norfolk), you know what to expect. This is a nice place to go for a relaxing day of strolling, browsing, eating, sightseeing, and evening entertainment. Harbourside Shopping Centre is filled with small shops and pushcarts selling gift items, souvenirs, Australiana, and clothes. Many are small branches of larger stores in The City. However, Harbourside's greatest strength is its large number of restaurants, food stalls, and surrounding sites for family entertainment. We like this area but not because of its shopping. Shopping opportunities are much better elsewhere in Sydney. Our recommendation: go here for the full range of tourist attractions and do some shopping at the same time. Look for such shops as **Gavala Aboriginal Art Centre** (Shop 377, Level 2, Tel. 9212-7232—this is Sydney's only Aboriginal owned retail center and fine art gallery which also sponsors demonstrations), for lots of gift items, and the **Cotton Store** with its educational program on the Australian cotton industry and 100% Australian cotton fashion labels. Harbourside is a pleasant change from some of

the indoor shopping malls found in downtown Sydney. It's easy
to get to this area by walking west from the city center along
Market Street. Taxis, buses, and a monorail system service this
area.

DOUBLE BAY

Double Bay, a wealthy suburb located eight kilometers east of
the city center, is one of Sydney's most exclusive shopping
areas. It's a shopping village with a nice ambience—tree lined
streets, smart boutiques, galleries, exquisite jewelry shops,
antique and glassware shops, elegant restaurants, and sidewalk
cafes. It's the place where Australia's rich and famous find their
social identity along Knox, Bay, and Cross Streets as well as see
the latest fashions from London, Paris, and Rome. It's where
you will find the largest concentration of Rolls Royces, Mercedes, Jaguars, BMWs, Porches, and Range Rovers competing
for parking spaces or just cruising the streets to see and be seen.
It's the area toward which the not so rich and famous Australians enjoy expressing their deep-seated class and egalitarian
attitudes. They joke by calling this area "Double Pay" rather
than "Double Bay" because of its pricy nature. They take
pleasure in noting that after 200 years of egalitarian history,
there are still snobbish and pretentious people in Australia—and many can be found in Double Bay.

For all this local nonsense aimed at bringing the people and
places of Double Bay down a social notch or two, Double Bay
remains one of the best places to shop in Australia. You can
easily spend a half day here browsing through shops and
stopping for coffee, tea, or lunch. It has a nice ambience, more
in line with a Carmel, California than with its more frequent
comparison to Rodeo Drive in Hollywood, California.

Despite what you may hear about the "expensive"nature of
shopping in Double Bay, the prices are not that different from
other quality shopping areas. The major difference is that this
area offers a large concentration of high quality products and
custom services you may have difficulty finding elsewhere in
Sydney. After all, that's exactly why people with good tastes
and an eye toward quality like to do their shopping in Double
Bay. Many of Australia's super rich and famous by-pass this
area altogether as they jet off to London, Paris, and Rome to do
what they consider to be "real quality" shopping.

And despite what locals may tell you, we do not find this
area to be at all snobbish or pretentious. It's just a pleasant
"lifestyle shopping" area. Indeed, the opposite is more apparent.
You can easily spend half a day shopping here. You'll want to
browse through the numerous shops and stop for a cup of
coffee or tea or have lunch. Start with the shops at the east end

of the Cosmopolitan Centre on Knox Street, near New South Head Road, and work your way along both sides of this street as well as along the adjacent Cross and Bay Streets. This is the heart of the Double Bay shopping area. You'll find dozens of small boutiques selling the latest in Australian designed and imported fashion clothes, shoes, and accessories.

Double Bay is pleasant place to just stroll down the streets and stop in shops and shopping arcades that look interesting. Be sure to browse through **The Georges Centre** and adjacent **Ritz-Carlton Promenade** along Cross Street, **Bay Village**, and ths small cottages along **Transvaal Avenue**. We especially like the **Russian Empire Trading Company** (Russian antiques, and icons; 14 Transvaal Avenue, Tel. 9363-9887) and **Robyne Cosgrove Rugs** (quality Oriental rugs; 18 Transvaal Avenue, Tel. 9328-7692) along Transvaal Avenue; **Inro Designs** (Shop 4, Harris Arcade, 12 Cross Street, Tel. 9363-2947) a very small but noted shop for nice costume jewelry and stylishly designed clothes, including Indian sarees; **Belinda** (8 Transvaal Avenue), **Morrissey** (2 Guilfoyle Avenue), and **Saba** (39 Bay Street) for designer label fashion; **Jan Logan** (36 Cross Street, Tel. 9363-2529) and **L'Artigiano** (Shop 12, Bay Village, 28/34 Cross Street, Tel. 9363-9146) for fine jewelry; **Four Winds Gallery** (Bay Village, 28 Cross Street, Tel. 9328-7951) for American Indian jewelry and art work; **D'Aliccia Handbags and Accessories** (Shop 1, 15 Knox Street, Tel. 9327-5765) for a nice selection of reasonably priced belts, purses, and hats; and **Art and Frame International** (2 Cross Street, Tel. 9327-3309) for paintings by local artists. For a quick lunch—if you get there before the noon crowds arrive—try Luigi Brothers Delicatessen-Café (372 New South Head Road).

WOOLLAHRA AND QUEEN STREET

The suburb of Woollahra is also located east of the city center, adjacent to Paddington and near Double Bay. If you love antique furniture, Woollahra is the place to go. This is Sydney's major up-market antique center. Shops along Queen Street in Woollahra sell a large variety of excellent quality and expensive 18th and 19th century European and Australian antique furniture and home decorative pieces. A few shops specialize in Asian furniture and collectibles. Additional antique shops are found along Jersey Road in Woollahra.

It's best to start your antique shopping adventure in the 100 block of Queen Street and work your way South until you come to Jersey Road and Oxford Street in Paddington. You can easily spend two hours browsing through the many shops along Queen Street and Jersey Road. Look for such shops as **Gaslight Antiques** (106 Queen Street), **Hamish Clark Antiques** (94

Queen Street), **Art of Wine and Food Antiques** (80 Queen Street), **Lynette Cunningham Asian Art** (80 Queen Road), **Anne Schofield Antiques** (36 Queen Street), and **Peter Lane Gallery**, **Oceanic Art Gallery**, and **Au Lion des Neiges** (76 Queen Street). Once you reach Oxford Road, you begin entering another major shopping area, the historical Paddington.

Paddington is one of Sydney's best known historical and cultural areas. Stretching several blocks north from Oxford Street between Queen Street in the east to Glenmore Road in the west. The shops and homes in this area have retained their traditional 19th century architecture which you may or may not find attractive. This area is noted for its mix of antique, secondhand, Australiana, and arts and crafts shops; avant garde galleries; boutiques offering outrageous clothes; and trendy restaurants. The area especially comes alive on weekends when the famous Paddington Market on Oxford Street draws large crowds of weekend shoppers who browse along Oxford and the adjacent streets of Paddington and Woollahra.

You may find Paddington somewhat overrated and run down. It's a very mixed area where you will find few good quality shops, especially after shopping in Double Bay and Woollahra. The area looks and feels like it is in transition. The walk along Oxford Street is long, and quality shops are few and far between. You will find a few good shops along the side streets, such as William, Walker, Hargrave, and Glenmore.

Nonetheless, if you persist in walking the length of Oxford Road and exploring adjacent streets, you will discover several excellent shops that will make the trip to Paddington well worthwhile. But be forewarned that you will have to walk some long distances. In particular, look for these shops: **Caspian Gallery** (469 Oxford Street, Tel. 9331-4260) for top quality Aboriginal and Melanesian art and tribal rugs; **Coo-ee Aboriginal Art** (98 Oxford Street, Tel. 9332-1544) for original works of Aboriginal art as well as Australiana; **Hogarth Galleries** (7 Walker Lane, top of Brown Street, Tel. 9360-7069) for good quality Aboriginal paintings, prints, and carvings; **Asian and Primitive Art Gallery** (43 Williams Street, Tel. 9331-7073) for top quality Aboriginal, Papuan New Guinea, and Southeast Asian artifacts. Be sure to explore Hargrave and Williams Streets which have numerous good quality antique shops, such as **House of Desks Antiques**, Antiques on Hargrave, 108-110 Hargrave Street, Tel. 9363-3663, and arts and craft galleries, such as **Ceramic Art Gallery** (35 William Street, Tel. 9361-5286), **Savill Galleries** (156 Hargrave Street, Tel. 9327-8311) and **Sherman Galleries**

(1 Hargrave Street, Tel. 9360-5566).

Paddington also is home to **Woollahra Galleries** (160 Oxford Street), one of Sydney's more popular antique centers with over 50 antique shops. It also has a popular weekend market. If you are in Sydney on a Saturday and your shopping interests include arts, crafts, clothing, and secondhand markets, be sure to stop by **Paddington Bazaar** (St. John's churchyard, Oxford and Newcombe Streets, open 10am-5pm on Saturday, Tel. 9331-2646) to browse through the many stalls selling a wide variety of arts, crafts, clothes, and jewelry. The market breathes a great deal of life into the shops lining the streets of Paddington and Woollahra on Saturday.

THE NORTH SHORE—NEUTRAL BAY AND MOSMAN

Few tourists ever venture north across the Sydney Harbour Bridge to explore additional shopping opportunities. A major shopping area you should consider, time permitting, is the North Shore area between Neutral Bay and Mosman along Military Road. Numerous art, antique, home decorative, clothing, and jewelry stores as well as ethnic restaurants line both sides of this road. The majority of shops are concentrated at the east end of Military Road near the intersection of Spit Road in Mosman.

MANLY

Manly, a popular seaside town, is approximately 15 minutes north of Mosman by car. If you are already in Neutral Bay and Mosman, you may want to go a little further on to Manly. Shopping opportunities here are limited to the typical tourist kitsch found at beachside resorts—T-shirts, souvenirs, and beachwear. However, if you are looking for unique arts and crafts, we highly recommend one shop in Manly—**Raglan Gallery** (5-7 Raglan Street, Tel. 9977-0906) for its fine collection of quality ceramics, pottery, and paintings. Manly also has a popular beach front arts and crafts market—**The Manly Arts and Crafts Market** (Sydney Road and Market Lane Road, just off the Corso next to the beach, open 10am-5pm Saturday, Sunday and public holidays, Tel. 9482-2741).

DEPARTMENT STORES

If you are in the market for an upscale department store selling every conceivable Australian and imported item, you're in luck. Sydney's two major department stores—**David Jones** and **Grace Bros**—are located in the heart of the city, along George,

Market, Pitt, Castlereagh, and Elizabeth Streets. Both are connected to Centrepoint by walkways; Grace Bros is also connected to the Queen Victoria Building by an underground walkway at the corner of George and King streets.

Grace Bros (*www.gracebros.com.au*) is bounded by George and Market streets as well as the Strand Arcade and the Pitt Street Mall. Newly renovated and now in its new chic home—the Sydney Central Plaza at the corner of Pitt and Market Streets (Tel. 9238-9111)—this massive store sells everything from ladies fashions to housewares. Grace Bros is open Monday through Saturday, 9am-6pm; Thursday 9am-9pm; and Sunday, 11am-5pm.

David Jones (*www.davidjones.com.au*), Sydney's version of Harrod's and Australia's oldest department store, has two stores which are both connected to Centrepoint at Market Street. Beautifully appointed, these are Sydney's premier stores for clothes, jewelry, and home furnishings. David Jones has similar hours to Grace Bros.

Don't miss the popular food centers at both Grace Bros and David Jones.

WEEKEND MARKETS

As noted earlier in our discussion of arts and crafts, you will find several weekend markets in the Sydney metropolitan area selling everything from fresh fruits, vegetables, flowers, and junk to quality arts and crafts. Most of these markets are open from 10am to 5pm Saturday and Sunday. The five most interesting weekend markets are The Rocks Market, Paddington Bazaar, Paddy's Markets, Balmain Market, and Manly Arts and Crafts Market. The Rocks Market is the best quality market. The other markets are less selective and thus often have the look and feel of one big flea market where you may or may not be able to do serious shopping. Please see our earlier discussion on pages 18-19 for details on each of these markets as well as visit this Web site for information primarily related to markets, craft shows, and pagan fairs in Manly: ***www.markets.sydney.net***.

HOTEL SHOPPING ARCADES

Hotel shopping arcades in Sydney are comparatively small compared to many large cities in the region, such as Hong Kong, Singapore, Bangkok, and Jakarta. Most deluxe hotels will have a few shops selling jewelry, fashion clothes, and souvenirs. For example, **Percy Marks** at both The Regent of Sydney Hotel (199 George Street, Tel. 9247-1322) and the Inter-Continental Hotel (117 Macquarie Street, Tel. 9251-3481) offers some of

Australia's top quality diamond, opal, and gold jewelry. The **Gallery Link International** at the Wentworth Hotel (61 Phillip Street, Tel. 9223-1700) offers quality fine art from some of Australia's leading artists.

The four largest hotel shopping arcades are found at the Wentworth, Regent of Sydney, Inter-Continental, and Hilton International—all located in the center of the city within easy walking distance of most shopping centers, department shorts, and shops.

BEST OF THE BEST

JEWELRY AND OPALS

- ❑ **Percy Marks:** *The Regent Sydney, 199 George Street, Tel. 7247-1322; 60-70 Elizabeth Street, Tel. 9233-1355; The Hotel Inter-Continental, 117 Macquarie Street, Tel. 9251-3481; and Australian Diamonds and Pearls, 75½ George Street, The Rocks. Tel. 9247-8860. www.percym.com.au.* The oldest jeweler in New South Wales with excellent quality opals, diamonds, and gold jewelry. Terrific quality and designs. Select from their exquisite stock or have their designers create a one-of-a-kind piece especially for you!

- ❑ **Paspaley Pearls:** *142 King Street, Tel. 9232-7633. www.paspaleypearls.com.* Terrific quality South Seas pearls from the famous Paspaley pearl farms in Broome and Darwin. Exquisite designs from some of the world's leading designers.

- ❑ **Robert Clerc:** *Shop G11, Queen Victoria Building, Tel. 9267-8274.* A master Swiss jeweler known for his unique gold designs and special signature collections (Aboriginal and Egyptian).

- ❑ **Makers Mark:** *Chifley Plaza, Chifley Square, Tel. 9231-6800. www.makersmark.com.au.* This top end Australian arts and crafts shop is famous for its outstanding quality handcrafted jewelry produced by many of the country's leading jewelry designers.

- ❑ **Flame Opals:** *119 George Street, The Rocks, Tel. 9247-3446.* One of Sydney's oldest and largest dealers.

- ❑ **House of Giulians:** *Corner George and Bridge Streets, Tel. 9252-2051. www.giulians.com.au.* Excellent quality opal, pearl, and diamond jewelry.

❏ **Perri Jewellers:** *Shop 708, MLC Centre, King and Castlereagh Streets, Tel. 9231-1088.* A long-time favorite.

❏ **Hardy Brothers:** *Ground Level, Skygarden, 77 Castlereagh Street, Tel. 9232-2422.* A long-time favorite.

TAPESTRIES AND RUGS

❏ **Kaminski Gallery:** *21 Nurses Walk, The Rocks, Tel. 9247-2418.* Produces beautifully handwoven tapestries with lots of colorful designs and unique themes.

❏ **Robyn Cosgrove Rugs:** *18 Transvaal Avenue, Double Bay, Tel. 9328-7692.* Nice quality Turkish rugs. Many unique designs.

❏ **Caspian Gallery:** *469 Oxford Street, Paddington. Tel. 9331-4260.* Includes an excellent collection of tribal rugs in what is otherwise one of Australia's top Aboriginal, Indonesian, and Papuan New Guinea galleries.

PACIFIC AND SOUTHEAST ASIAN ARTS

❏ **New Guinea Arts:** *Dymocks Building, 8ᵗʰ Floor, 428 George Street, Tel. 9232-4737; and Queen Victoria Building, Level 2, Shop 16, 455 George Street, Tel. 9267-5134.* The best shop for relatively inexpensive arts and crafts from Papua New Guinea. Jam-packed with a wide range of carvings and masks from Papua New Guinea as well as some Aboriginal artifacts. Excellent service, including packing and shipping. Operated as a nonprofit organization that provides assistance to the tribal peoples of PNG.

❏ **Caspian Gallery:** *469 Oxford Street, Paddington. Tel. 9331-4260.* Specializes in Aboriginal, Indonesian, and Papuan New Guinea art as well as tribal rugs. Beautifully displayed one-of-a-kind collector's pieces in a historic home. One of the best shops in all of Asia and the Pacific. Owned and operated by noted expert and collector Bill Evans who is a fountain of information on such intriguing and exotic art.

❏ **Oceanic Art Gallery:** *76 Queens Street, Woollahra, Tel. 9327-6010.* Housed in the same building with two other galleries—Peter Lane Gallery and Au Lion Des Neiges. Wonderful collection of quality art from PNG. Offers many outstanding collector pieces.

❑ **Asian and Primitive Art Gallery:** *43 Williams Street, Paddington, Tel. 9331-7073. www.citysearch.com.au.* Small corner shop with an excellent collection of top quality pieces collected from auctions and collectors—Aboriginal, Papuan New Guinea, Indonesia, Thai, and Myanmar. The place to see really good quality old Aboriginal pieces—not the typical tourist quality arts and crafts found in most Australian shops.

ABORIGINAL ARTS AND CRAFTS

❑ **Coo-ee Aboriginal Art:** *98 Oxford Street, Paddington, Tel. 9332-1544.* Don't be turned off by all the touristy Australiana on the ground level; the good stuff is in the basement and upstairs. Be sure to go to the lower level for good quality Aboriginal bark paintings, acrylic paintings, and sculptures. Upstairs you will find quality fine arts, prints, and fabrics as well as an exhibition gallery. One of Australia's leading galleries for promoting Aboriginal art both at home and abroad. Take a very good look here because there is more to the shop than surface appearances.

❑ **Jinta Desert Art Aboriginal Art Gallery:** *154-156 Clarence Street, Tel. 9290-3639.* Primarily displays acrylic paintings of major Aboriginal artists. Carries many of the top early Aboriginal artists such as Clifford Possum and Billy Stockman. Also includes some Tiwi wood sculptures. Until you get to the major galleries in Melbourne, this is one of the best Aboriginal galleries in Australia. Also operates similar galleries in both Melbourne (Aboriginal Art Galleries of Australia) and Alice Springs (Aboriginal Desert Art Gallery).

❑ **Aboriginal and Tribal Art Centre:** *Level 1, 117 George Street, Tel. 9247-9625.* Looks nondescript from the narrow street-level entrance. But go upstairs to this expansive and colorful gallery. Includes a good collection of Aboriginal paintings (both bark and acrylic) and carvings as well as some art from Papua New Guinea. Belongs to the Hogarth Galleries network of quality shops.

❑ **Hogarth Galleries Aboriginal Art Centre:** *7 Walker Lane (top of Brown Street), Paddington, Tel. 9360-6839. Closed Sunday and Monday.* Hard to find in this small back lane. Take Shadford and Liverpool streets off of Oxford Street to get to Walker Lane. Also operates the Aboriginal Art Centre in The Rocks and the Aboriginal Art Shop at the drive-up level of the Opera House. Regularly sponsors exhibitions at Paddington gallery.

❑ **Aboriginal and Pacific Art:** *Dymocks Building, 8th Floor, 428 George Street, Tel. 9223-5900.* Located directly across the hall from New Guinea Arts, this relatively new gallery specializes in one-of-a-kind collector's pieces, especially baskets, sticks, animals, prints, and paintings from Arnhem Land. Very expensive and at times quirky—not everything is on display, so you may have to ask lots of questions to find out what's really available!

AUSTRALIAN ARTS AND CRAFTS

❑ **Makers Mark:** *Chifley Plaza, Chifley Square, Tel. 9231-6800. www.makersmark.com.au.* Terrific contemporary arts and crafts produced by some of Australia's master crafts-people. Look for beautiful handcrafted jewelry, wood crafts, glassware, and leather purses. Very expensive but very nice.

❑ **Gannon House Gallery:** *45 Argyle Street, The Rocks, Tel. 9251-4474. www.ozemail.com/au/~gannonhs.* One of our favorite shops with a good eye for quality. Terrific selections of Australian arts and crafts displayed in eight rooms. Includes everything from ceramics, paintings, and wood crafts to Aboriginal didgeridoos and boomerangs. Great collection of wood-turned bowls. Good prices. Works directly with artists.

❑ **Raglan Gallery:** *5-7 Raglan Street, Manly, Tel. 9977-0906.* Well worth a special trip to Manly just to visit this shop. Take the delightful ferry ride to Manly and discover one of Australia's nicest arts and crafts shops. Specializes in excellent quality ceramic and glass art as well as paintings and some Aboriginal art (dot acrylic and bark paintings, Tiwi poles). Offers many unique pieces. Tasteful selections by owner Jan Karras who also exhibits abroad.

❑ **Australian Craftworks:** *127 George Street, The Rocks, Tel. 9247-7156.* Located in the historic "Old Police Station." Offers excellent selections of top quality Australian crafts. Explore several rooms of this unique two-storey building for some of the best in wood, glass, ceramics, jewelry, and Aboriginal arts. Includes the colorful ceramic works of Kathrin McMiles. Also offers clothes, handbags, belts, cards, candles, T-shirts, didgeridoos, and boomerangs.

❑ **Quadrivium:** *Queen Victoria Building, 2-50 Gallery Level South, 455 George Street, Tel. 9264-8222. www.citysearch. com/au/syd/quadrivium.* One of QVB's surprising shops. Represents a unique concept that simultaneously displays the decorative and fine arts. This large gallery displays the best of contemporary Australian art and design—studio glass, ceramics, jewelry, and object design. Represents Australia's leading artists and designers. Also includes a section on contemporary and traditional Asian art and Aboriginal art from Utopia.

WEEKEND ARTS AND CRAFTS MARKETS

❑ **Rocks Market:** *Held every Saturday and Sunday at the Bridge end of George Street and along Playfair Street, open 10am-5pm, Tel. 9255-1717.* Includes more than 150 stalls offering a nice range of arts, crafts, jewelry, gifts, furniture, and collectibles. One of Sydney's better quality markets—not the typical flea market with lots of cheap junk. Vendors are carefully screened by a selection committee to ensure a good product mix as well as top quality products.

❑ **Manly Arts & Crafts Market:** *Sydney Road and Market Lane Road (just off the Corso next to the beach), Manly. Open 10am-5pm Saturday, Sunday and public holidays. Tel. 9482-2741. www.markets.sydney.net (also includes information on craft shows and pagan fairs in Manly).* Offers a good range of arts and crafts, handmade clothes, paintings, jewelry, ornaments, sculpture, music, gift items, and souvenirs. Also includes a Gourmet Court with a wide range of foods, many of which are attractively packaged.

❑ **Paddington Bazaar:** *Centered at St. John's churchyard, Oxford and Newcombe Streets, open 10am-5pm on Saturday, Tel. 9331-2646 or 1902-260-622 (Bazaar info line; charges 50¢ a minute). http://surf.to/paddington.* Also known as Paddington Market and St. John's Churchyard Bazaar. This festive weekend market includes lots of stalls offering a wide range of arts, crafts, clothes, T-shirts, tribal jewelry, toys, books, music, paintings, sculptures, knick-knacks, and old wares along with street entertainment.

FINE ARTS, ANTIQUES, AND COLLECTIBLES

❑ **Woollahra Antique Centre:** *160 Oxford Street, Woollahra, open daily 10am-6pm, Tel. 9327-8840.* Includes 50 antique dealers offering quality furniture glassware, porcelain, jewelry, silver, clocks, watches, and books. Includes a popular coffee shop.

❑ **Sydney Antique Market:** *531 South Dowling Street, Surry Hills, open daily 10am-6pm, Tel. 9332-2691. www.sydant cent.com.au.* Claims to be Australia's oldest and largest antique center with more than 70 dealers offering a wide range of furniture, silver, porcelain, glass, rugs, jewelry, dolls, clocks, watches, pens, bottles, toys, kitchenware, and books.

❑ **Three Galleries:** *76 Queen Street.* Consists of three art and antique shops (open Monday to Saturday 11am-5pm) offering an interesting range of South Pacific and Asian antiques: **Peter Lane Gallery** (Tel. 9362-0115), **Au Lion des Neiges** (Tel. 9362-0115), and **Oceanic Art Gallery** (Tel. 9327-6010).

❑ **Russian Empire Trading Company:** *14 Transvaal Avenue, Double Bay, Tel. 9363-9887. Open Monday to Saturday 10am-5pm.* A very interesting and unusual shop. Offers a wonderful collection of unusual antiques from the Old Russian and Soviet Empires. Includes 19th century Baltic farmhouse furniture, toys, icons, ikat textiles from Central Asia, wedding chests, dough bowls, and numerous provincial items. Only such shop in Australia.

❑ **Gallery Link International:** *Wentworth Hotel, 61 Phillip Street, Tel. 9223-1700.* It represents the works of several leading Australian artists, such as Elizabeth Durack, Dennis Baker, Kevin Best, Sandro Noccentini, Pro Hart, and Walangari Karntawarra.

FASHION AND SPORTSWEAR

❑ **Dorian Scott:** *105 George Street, The Rocks, Tel. 9221-8145; Hotel Intercontinental, Macquarie Street, Tel. 9246-1818; and Sydney International Airport, Tel. 9317-2881.* Showcases 215 Australian artists and designers, including the popular Coogi knitwear.

❑ **Done Art and Design:** *123-125 George Street, The Rocks, Tel. 9251-6099.* Showcases the popular resort wear, swim-wear, childrenswear, and homeware of artists Ken Done and designer Judy Done.

❑ **Brian Rochford:** *1st Floor, The Argyle Department Store, 18-24 Argyle Street, The Rocks, Tel. 9252-2553.* Offers bright and colorful swimwear and resortwear by one of Australia's award-winning designers.

AUSTRALIANA, SOUVENIRS, AND GIFTS

❑ **Gannon House Gallery:** *45 Argyle Street, The Rocks, Tel. 9251-4474. www.ozemail.com/au/~gannonhs).* One of our very favorite shops for excellent quality arts, crafts, and Australiana. You are bound to find some unique gift items here.

❑ **Best of Australiana:** *Level 2, Shop 1, Queen Victoria Building, Tel. 9261-2249.* Offers excellent quality crafts, from table ware and hand blown glass to ceramics, designer jewelry, and woodcraft. Represents major craftsmen.

❑ **Lambswool Trader:** *80/84 George Street, Metcalfe Arcade, The Rocks, Tel. 9247-9174.* Offers quality leather and sheepskin goods and related souvenirs. If you're looking for a last-minute gift item, you're bound to find something here.

❑ **The Didjeridu Shop:** *Shop 36, The Rocks Centre, The Rocks, 12-26 Playfair Street, Tel. 9251-2294.* Offers an excellent selection of boomerangs, clothes, musical instruments, and books on Australia.

LEATHER CLOTHES AND HATS

❑ **Thomas Cook Boot and Clothing Company:** *129 Pitt Street, near Martin Place, Tel. 9232-3334, and 790 George Street, Haymarket, near Central Station, Tel. 9212-6616—www.thomascookclothing.com.au.* Offers a good range of classic Australian Outback and Adventure clothing.

❑ **R. M. Williams:** *Chifley Plaza, 2 Chifley Square, Tel. 9233-5608.* Sells leather clothes, especially Driza-Bone oilskin rain coats and riding jackets, moleskin pants, kangaroo-hide belts, and Akubra hats—everything you ever needed to look like Crocodile Dundee or the Man from Snowy River or attend those hoe-downs and bush dances you have been waiting for!

❑ **Strand Hatters:** *Shop 8, Stand Arcade, 412 George Street, Tel. 9231-6884.* Specializes in uniquely designed hats.

Offers Australia's largest range of hats which can be expertly fitted, steamed, shaped, and feathered, if you wish.

❑ **The Rocks Hatters:** *81 George Street, The Rocks, Tel. 9252-3525.* Offers all types of hats (felt, straw, canvas, legionnaire caps, suede bush, grazier) as well as coats, boots, photojournalists vest, parkas, scarves, belts, Driza-Bone hats, and Thomas Cook adventurewear.

ACCOMMODATIONS

Sydney offers a good range of accommodations, from five-star deluxe to budget. Within the past few years, bed-and-breakfasts have become more and more popular within the city. Like many other large international cities, accommodations in Sydney tend to be expensive.

The best hotels, with good views of the harbor and close proximity to major sightseeing, restaurants, shops, and entertainment, are found in the Rocks and adjacent Circular Quay area. Less expensive accommodations tend to be found in the Kings Cross area. Sydney's "best of the best" include the following:

❑ **The Regent Sydney**: *199 George Street, Sydney NSW 2000, Australia, Tel. (61 2) 9238-0000, Fax (61 2) 9251-2851.* Located at the heart of the business district and the historic Rocks entertainment and shopping district, the newly renovated (1999) Regent Sydney is blessed with a great location for both business and leisure travelers and provides luxury, service, and great views of either the city or the spectacular Sydney harbor, the Opera House and Harbour Bridge. A frequent winner of travel industry and readers' poll awards, The Regent is our personal favorite in Sydney. Its 531 rooms include executive rooms and suites. All rooms feature fax connections, voice mail message service, electronic safe, and mini-bar. The desks are executive size and provide space to get work accomplished, and there is enough light that the guest can even read in bed in these rooms! Bathrooms are equipped with a full range of personal amenities. Complimentary services include in-room tea and coffee making facilities; fax machine; newspaper; early arrival/departures tea, coffee, muffins and pastry in the lobby. The Club Floor provides private check-in/check-out; full Club Lounge service; complimentary buffet breakfast; all day snacks; complimentary beverages and hors d'oeuvres; pressing; local calls and the first two hours use of the Business Center meeting room.

Kable's, the hotel's premier restaurant, enjoys a reputation for fine food and is patronized by hotel guests and Sydney residents alike. The wine bar at the entrance to Kable's is a comfortable place to sample Australia's best boutique wines. The combination of fresh flavors provides a dining experience that rates among Australia's best. Winner of many culinary honors, Kable's menu changes frequently. The Bar, incorporated into the spacious lobby, is perfect for refreshments and light snacks. The Café serves light meals all day and into the late evening. The hotel shop on Level 3 offers Australian souvenirs, and the wonderful shopping and entertainment in the historic Rocks is right outside your front door. Spa and Fitness Center; Business Center; Meeting and Banquet Facilities. ·

❏ **Inter-Continental Sydney**: *117 Macquarie Street, Sydney NSW 2000, Australia, Tel. (61 2) 9230-0200, Fax (61 2) 9240-1240. Web site: www.interconti.com.* Just steps from Sydney Harbour, the Opera House and the Royal Botanic Gardens, Hotel Inter-Continental restored Sydney's Treasury Building before opening in 1985, and incorporated it into the hotel. The Cortile, with its skylights, vaulted sandstone arcades, and white marble floors was once the Treasury's open central courtyard and now serves as the hotel's reception area and lobby. The Cortile provides a general meeting place where light meals and cocktails are served throughout the day and evening. An attached 31-storey modern tower houses 498 guestrooms and suites–including the Australia suite, which with its glorious view of the harbor and opera house and opulent decor accented with a baby grand piano, is enough to make you weep—with joy if you are staying in it, and from regret if you are not! All guestrooms have a safe, coffee and tea making facilities, and mini-bar. Club Inter-Continental provides extras such as valet service and private Club Lounge with its own business center, meeting room, and complimentary breakfast, tea, coffee and cocktails. Club guests also enjoy a "meet and greet" service where hotel staff welcome them at the airport and transfer them to the hotel in a Mercedes limousine. Business rooms are available—designed for the working traveler featuring ergonomic desk chairs and state-of-the-art work stations.

Restaurants include One One Seven where the chef specializes in matching Australian wines with new Australian cuisine. For casual dining, Café Opera presents a wide selection of international dishes. Sketches Bar & Bistro allows diners to design pasta dishes of their choice, and 30 Something, serves wood-fired pizzas accompanied by spectacular views from the thirty-first floor. Health Club; Business Center; Meeting and Banquet Facilities.

❑ **The Observatory Hotel**: *89-113 Kent Street, Millers Point, Sydney NSW 2000, Australia, Tel. (61 2) 9256-2222, Fax (61 2) 9256-2233.* Located at the edge of The Rocks, and only a 5-minute walk from the central business district, a complimentary city limousine service is available to guests between 7am and 10am Monday thru Friday. The Observatory Hotel, one of the Orient-Express Group, is luxuriously furnished with Australian antiques, oil paintings and tapestries. Service is warm and friendly, as might be expected in a small, boutique style hotel. However, a full range of services and facilities are provided. The 100 spacious and comfortable rooms and suites have all the amenities expected in a deluxe hotel. Rooms have four telephones and fax facilities, CD player and individual videos, tea and coffee-making facilities, mini-bar and safe. The luxury marble bathrooms feature oversized tubs, heated towel racks and large vanities with double sinks, and separate shower and toilet enclosures. Colonial style sash windows and period balconies afford views of Observatory Hill and Walsh Bay. Galileo, the main restaurant, serves modern Australian cuisine with Italian influences. The Orient features simple dishes and Australian cuisine. The Health and Leisure Club features a 20-meter pool, mirrored by a ceiling of fibre optic lights designed to recreate the constellations of the Southern Hemisphere. Business and Conference Facilities.

❑ **Park Hyatt Sydney**: *7 Hickson Road, The Rocks, Sydney NSW 2000, Australia, Tel. (61 2) 9241-1234, Fax (61 2) 9256-1555.* Located on Sydney Harbour in the famed entertainment and shopping area, The Rocks, with spectacular views of the harbor and Opera House and under the Harbour Bridge, it is convenient to the central business district. Only four stories with guestrooms on the top three levels, The Park Hyatt has a warm, intimate feel while providing the full range of expected services. There is no traditional reception desk. Instead, check-in is available on each level for an extra personal touch. Elegant Australian, European and Oriental influences are apparent in the public areas as well as the guestrooms. The 158 guestrooms (which include 32 executive suites, 3 premier suites, a diplomatic suite and the governor suite) feature remote controlled curtains, VCR and CD player, 3 phones and 2 lines, and a voice mail message service. Tea and coffee making facilities, mini-bar and safe. The marble baths have a separate shower and tub as well as a separate dressing area. The vanity table with mirror and hairdryer outside the bathroom is a real plus. Fax machines are in all suites and portable fax units are available for superior and deluxe guestrooms. The restaurants feature real dining value: great food, reasonable prices, and a harbor view. No. 7 at The Park features contemporary Sydney cuisine with an outdoor terrace overlooking the harbor. Verandah at the Park features relaxed and casual dining for breakfast, lunch, afternoon tea, dinner and supper with an outdoor terrace overlooking Sydney Harbour. The Bar features a fireplace, cocktails and drinks in a warm traditional atmosphere. Fitness Center; Business Center; Meeting and Banquet Facilities.

❑ **The Ritz-Carlton Sydney**: *93 Macquarie Street, Sydney NSW 2000, Australia, Tel. (61 2) 9252-4600, Fax (61 2) 9252-4286, Toll-free in U.S. 800-241-3333.* A short walk from the Sydney Opera House and central business district, The Ritz-Carlton is a luxury boutique style hotel but offering the amenities and services expected from much larger properties. A frequent winner of travel industry and readers' poll awards, its 105 spacious guestrooms are first class. Beyond a small foyer, guests enter a beautifully appointed drawing room lobby accented with 18th and 19th century paintings. A fireplace lends ambience to the setting. A European style is apparent in the decor of the guestrooms as well as the public areas. A safe, mini-bar and tea and coffee making facilities in every room; many rooms have French doors which open onto a small balcony from which you can stand and view the harbor. Large marble bathrooms with double sinks, separate bathtub and shower, and private toilet enclosure. The Ritz-Carlton Club offers additional amenities and the services of a Club Concierge. Complimentary food and beverages are available throughout the day on the Club floor. The Dining Room features Australian cuisine and includes a choice of vegetarian selections. The Bar serves lunch, afternoon tea and a post-opera menu. Fitness Center; Business Center; Meeting Facilities.

❑ **The Ritz-Carlton Double Bay**: *33 Cross Street, Double Bay NSW 2028, Sydney, Australia, Tel. (61 2) 9362-4455, Fax (61 2) 9362-4744. Toll-free from U.S. 800-241-3333.* Located ten minutes from the central business district in the upscale harborside suburb of Double Bay near lively cafes and exclusive boutiques. 140 spacious guestrooms overlook the harbor, bay, or courtyard. Guestrooms are decorated in European style. In-room safe, mini-bar and tea and coffee making facilities. Large marble bathrooms feature double sinks, and separate bathtub, shower and toilet enclosures. Club floor. The same services and amenities as Ritz-Carlton Sydney. The Saltwater Grill serves dinner—seafood and desserts are their specialities. The Lobby Lounge serves breakfast, a buffet lunch and afternoon tea. Fitness Center; Business Center; Meeting Facilities.

❏ **Old Sydney Parkroyal**: *55 George Street, Sydney NSW 2000, Australia, Tel. (61 2) 9252-0524, Fax (61 2) 9251-2093.* Parkroyal is the premier line of the SPHC Group. Although not as luxurious as the deluxe hotels described above, it offers comfortable accommodation with good value, and in this instance, a location that is hard to beat. The Old Sydney Parkroyal is a boutique style hotel situated in the center of The Rocks historic district with entertainment and shopping venues right outside the front door and convenient to the central business district. Step into the lobby and you will notice the warm ochre colors of the eight story atrium as well as the ambience of the fireplace. 174 comfortable rooms are designed to utilize space efficiently and many rooms have views of the Harbour Bridge and Sydney Opera House. Mini-bar and tea and coffee making facilities in guestrooms. Service is attentive and accompanied with a smile. A special touch is added by equipping guests with their own personalized pet, a goldfish named Wanda (we suspect there are a lot of Wandas found in this hotel). A fish bowl with a curious swimming Wanda is placed in guestrooms as a companion along with a small amount of fish flakes and feeding instructions. The Playfair Terrace Restaurant serves a buffet breakfast and a la carte dining. Rooftop pool, sauna and spa with a great harbor view; Business services desk; Meeting Facilities.

❏ **Sheraton on the Park**: *61 Elizabeth Street, Sydney NSW 2000, Australia, Tel. (61 2) 9286-6000, Fax (61 2) 9286-6608).* Located in Sydney's retail and business district, guests have access to city attractions. Its 557 rooms are stylish and contemporary in design. In-room safe and mini-bar in guestrooms. Executive Club offers extra services. Gekko, the signature restaurant, offers modern Australian cuisine; Botanica Brasserie presents all-day elegant dining offering buffet or menu selections, and The Conservatory offers casual dining including light meals. Health Club; Business Center; Meeting Facilities.

❑ **Renaissance Sydney Hotel**: *30 Pitt Street, Sydney NSW 2000, Australia, Tel. (61 2) 9372-2233, Fax (61 2) 9251-1122.* Located at the Circular Quay at the harbor, the hotel sits in the heart of the financial district and the Circular Quay Ferry terminal and historic Rocks district are right outside the doorstep. The Renaissance Sydney has 581 spacious guestrooms, including 35 suites. Rooms have daylight block out shutters, in-room safe and mini-bar. The Renaissance Club floors offer extra services. Crayons Restaurant, Raphael's Wine Bar (award winner) and the Macquarie Lounge offer a range of dining. Fitness Center; Business Center; Meeting Facilities.

Several new properties have just opened in time for the Olympics 2000. The very best include **Pier One Parkroyal** at The Rocks (Tel. 61-2-8298-9964; Fax 61-2-8298-9964); **The Kirketon** in Darlinghurst (Tel. 61-2-9332-2011; Fax 61-2-9332-2499); **Rushcutters Harbourside** next to the Rushcutters Bay Park just east of Kings Cross (Tel. 61-2-8353-8988; Fax 61-2-8353-8999); and **The Westin** at Martin Place in The City (Tel. 61-2-8223-1111; Fax 61-2-8223-1222).

RESTAURANTS

Australian restaurants and cuisine have come of age during the past decade. The wide range of cuisines as well as outstanding restaurants available in this city reflect Sydney's changing cosmopolitan character. The real treat in Sydney are the many restaurants that serve modern Australian cuisine or what is best termed fusion cuisine. Blending elements of Australian, European, and Asian cooking, many of the dishes served in what we've classified as Modern Australian restaurants are truly unforgettable. Indeed, dining in such restaurants is often an exciting adventure in new cuisine—once in a lifetime dishes served from the kitchens of Sydney's many inventive chefs. Dining out in Sydney is often an adventure in eating!

In addition to finding numerous Modern Australian, Italian, and French restaurants in Sydney, you'll encounter numerous ethnic restaurants (Chinese, Thai, Indonesian, Vietnamese, Greek, Lebanese, Indian) as well as most major international fast food chains. For some of the best and least expensive food, try the many food courts and take-away stalls that are found throughout the city, especially in the major shopping centers such as the Queen Victoria Building and the MLC Centre.

Sydney's best restaurants tend to be disproportionately found in The Rocks area as well as in Sydney's top hotels. Most of the best restaurants are operated by noted international chefs who produce some of Australia's most inventive dishes and creative menus. While most restaurants are licensed to serve alcohol, some are still BYOB restaurants. Being popular dining spots, reservations are essential in most of Sydney's major restaurants.

One of the pleasant aspects of dining in Sydney is that many restaurants and cafes are outdoors or they offer indoor and outdoor dining options. Given Sydney's often sunny and pleasant climate, dining al fresco is a real treat, especially when it's along the waterfront in The Rocks or Darling Harbour.

MODERN AUSTRALIAN

❑ **Kables:** *The Regent Sydney, 199 George Street, Tel. 9238-0000. Open for breakfast, lunch, and dinner: 6:30-11:30am (daily), 11:30am-3pm (Monday-Friday), and 6:30pm-12 midnight (Monday-Saturday).* Newly reopened (August 1999) as part of the A$50 million hotel renovation, this remains one of Sydney's top restaurants for casual but fine dining in a vibrant setting. Divided into five sections (Wine Bar, three open dining areas, and a Private Dining Room), this richly appointed restaurant with an extensive, imaginative menu serves outstanding seafood and lamb dishes. Features a unique buffet bar, with many Saturday night specials. The huge kitchen, which boasts 80 chefs with their own bakery, chocolate factory, and ice cream-ery to service the hotel's many food outlets and banquets, is an bustling city unto itself. Call ahead to see if you can get a table in the kitchen—one of the most amazing and memorable dining experiences in Australia! Excellent service. Very expensive.

❑ **Quay:** *Overseas Passenger Terminal, Circular Quay West, Tel. 9251-5600.* Located in the location of the former popular Bilson's restaurant which closed in 1999, the Quay is equally excellent for seafood. Boasts a wonderful view of the harbor. This smart causal restaurant offers an extensive menu and an excellent wine list. Reservations essential. Very expensive.

❑ **Rockpool:** *107 George Street, The Rocks, Tel. 9252-1888.* Closed Sundays. For over five years, Rockpool has remained one of Sydney's smartest and most popular restaurants representing creative new Australian cuisine.

Located in the heart of The Rocks, this upscale chrome, glass, and white linen restaurant offers a very extensive and inventive menu which includes an interesting fusion of Middle Eastern, Mediterranean, Chinese, and Thai cuisines. Very expensive. Reservations essential.

❑ **Bennelong:** *Sydney Opera House, Tel. 9250-7548. Closed Sunday.* Terrific location overlooking Sydney Harbour. Not your ordinary theater restaurant. A surprisingly good restaurant. Serves excellent seafood and numerous inventive French to Australian dishes. Popular with theatergoers who stop here for a light meal before attending a performance at the Opera House. Reservations essential.

❑ **Catalina Rose Bay:** *Lyne Park off New South Head Road, Balmoral, Tel. 9371-0555.* This beautifully appointed and very popular restaurant offers some of Sydney's most inventive dishes, from pot roasted Kangaroo Island chicken to hazelnut souffle. Nice views of the harbor.

❑ **Tetsuya's:** *729 Darling Street, Rozelle, Tel. 9555-1017.* Dinner reservations essential (often weeks in advance) for this award-winning restaurant. Inventive cuisine of noted chef Tetsuya Wakuda combines Western and Japanese cooking. One of the areas very best restaurants. It's easier to get in for lunch. Closed Sunday and Monday and no dinner on Saturday.

❑ **MG Garage Restaurant:** *490 Crown Street, Surry Hills, Tel. 9383-9383. Closed Sunday and for lunch on Saturday.* Noted chef Janni Kyritsis of Bennelong fame does it again with his inventive menu and wonderful modern Australian dishes. This upscale and rather chic restaurant is one of the "in" places for diners in the know. Reservations essential. Expensive.

❑ **The Verandah at the Park:** *Park Hyatt Sydney, 7 Hichson Road, The Rocks, Tel. 9241-1234.* Very pleasant restaurant looking out at the Sydney Opera House and quay. Offers a brasserie-style menu and casual dining for breakfast, lunch, afternoon tea, and dinner. Includes an outdoor terrace overlooking the Sydney Harbour.

❑ **Wolfie's Restaurant Grill:** *17-21 Circular Quay West, The Rocks, Tel. 9241-5577.* Noted for its prime grain fed beef dishes produced in the restaurant's high-tech chargrill kitchen. Serves an impressive range of salads. Great views of the harbor. Can dine inside or outside.

❑ **Reds Restaurant:** *12 Argyle Street, The Rocks, Tel. 9247-1011. Open daily for dinner.* This award-winning restaurant directed by Chef Jeff Turnbull serves numerous inventive dishes. Try the chargrilled Angus Beef Scotch fillet and West Australian marron stirfried with chilli, garlic, lemongrass, and bok choy.

SEAFOOD

❑ **Golden Century Seafood Restaurant:** *393-399 Sussex Street, Haymarket, Tel. 9212-3901. Open daily, 12noon-4am.* This award-winning restaurant is renowned for its excellent fresh seafood, such as king crab, lobster, and abalone. Try the mudcrab with ginger and shallots.

❑ **MCA Fish Café:** *Museum of Contemporary Art, 140 George Street, The Rocks, Tel. 9241-4253. Closed Sunday.* Very popular for lunch (Sunday through Friday), this small café offers both indoor and outdoor dining with a nice view of the Opera House and Circular Quay. Serves only fresh line-caught fish. Try the deep-fried ocean perch and grilled harpuka. Reservations highly recommended.

❑ **Doyle's at the Quay:** *Lower Level, Overseas Passenger Terminal, Circular Quay West, Tel. 9252-3400.* Almost an Australian institution, the Doyle family has been dishing out great seafood since 1885. Offers excellent fresh seafood at one of the best locations on the harbor.

❑ **Waterfront Restaurant:** *27 Circular Quay West, The Rocks, Tel. 9247-3666.* This popular seafood restaurant faces the Sydney Harbour and Opera House. Open daily for lunch and dinner.

❑ **Jordons:** *197 Harbourside Festival Marketplace, Darling Harbour, Tel. 9281-3711.* Located along the waterfront at Darling Harbour, this popular restaurant is noted for the Jordons Seafood Platter. Nice views of the city skyline. Both indoor and outdoor dining. Open daily for lunch and dinner.

❑ **Pier:** *594 New South Head Road, Rose Bay, Tel. 9327-6561.* Wonderful harbor views from this popular seafood restaurant. Noted for its Tasmanian salmon and pot roasted John Dory.

ITALIAN

❑ **Bel Mondo:** *Level 3, The Argyle, 18-24 Argyle Street, The Rocks, Tel. 9241-3700. Open daily, 12noon-3pm and 6-10pm.* Somewhat hard to find—may have to ask for directions several times since it's tucked away on top of The Argyle. This chic Italian restaurant, operated by the talented chef Stefano Manfredi, serves excellent dishes with wonderful views of the Sydney Harbour (reserve a window table since 80 percent of tables have no view). Includes an antipasto/wine bar.

❑ **Italian Village:** *7 Circular Quay West, The Rocks, Tel. 9246-6111.* This popular outdoor dining spot offers an excellent view of the Sydney Opera House. Serves regional Italian cuisine.

❑ **La Mensa:** *257 Oxford Street, Paddington, Tel. 9332-2963.* A great place to stop for lunch when in the Paddington area. This smart combination café and deli has been an instant hit since it opened in 1995. Operated by Stefano Manfredi of the popular and upscale Bel Mondo in The Rocks. Serves excellent soups, salads, and pastas. Includes a small but charming outdoor (court) dining area. It's first come first served, so get there early before the crowds descend on this popular eatery!

FRENCH

❑ **Claude's:** *10 Oxford Street, Woollahra, Tel. 9331-2325. Dinner only. Closed Sunday and Monday.* Reservations essential in this very small and popular French restaurant operated by Chef Tim Pak Poy. Try the smoked salmon and crayfish dishes. BYOB.

❑ **Banc:** *53 Martin Place, Haymarket, Tel. 9233-5300. Closed Sunday. No lunch on Saturday.* This well appointed restaurant offers some of the city's finest cuisine. Try the stuffed roast guinea fowl and the wonderful desserts.

GERMAN

❑ **Lowenbrau Keller:** *Corner of Argyle and Playfair Streets, The Rocks, Tel. 9247-7785.* Great location in the heart of The Rocks. Serves delicious German dishes, such as bratwurst, spit roasts, and strudels. Offers a daily Bavarian luncheon buffet. A traditional Oom Pah Pah band plays at night.

SOUTHEAST ASIAN

❑ **Sailor Thai:** *106 George Street, The Rocks, Tel. 9251-2466.*
Located in a historic building in the heart of The Rocks.
This is one of Sydney's very best Thai restaurants.
Everything here is good. Has an upper and lower dining
levels. The upper level (Sailors Thai Canteen) is along
George Street and is more casual with its single long
stainless steel communal table. To get to the lower level,
where dining is more intimate, take the stairs to the right
of the building and enter the dining room on the left.

JAPANESE

❑ **Unkai Restaurant and Sushi Bar:** *ANA Hotel Sydney,
Level 36, 176 Cumberland Street, The Rocks, Tel. 9250-6123.*
Terrific view of the harbor accompanies this fine Japanese
restaurant. Offers three tatami rooms. Sushi bar located
next to Unkai also has its own tatami room.

ENJOYING YOUR STAY

You'll find lots to see and do in Sydney in addition to shopping,
dining, and pampering yourself at one of Sydney's top hotels.
In fact, you can easily spend a few days in Sydney just sightseeing in the city and surrounding suburbs. The city boasts several
excellent museums as well as numerous historical sites worth
visiting.

You'll find a great deal of literature for conducting your own
tour of the city, including detailed maps, at the Sydney Visitors
Centre in The Rocks. However, should you wish to join a tour,
the Centre has information on various tours and will help you
book a tour. One of the best ways to see Sydney on your own
is to purchase a three-day **SydneyPass** for unlimited travel by
bus, train, or ferry for $75 (five-day passes cost $100 and 7 day
passes cost $120). You can purchase this pass through tourist
agents or from the driver on any Explorer or Airport bus.

The red **Sydney Explorer** bus is a great way to see the
highlights of the city. If you purchase a SydneyPass, you can
use it on the Sydney Explorer. If not, you can purchase a
separate day ticket for $30 to use only on the Sydney Explorer.
The Sydney Explorer consists of a 28 kilometer circular route
that stops at 24 different places that represent Sydney's top
sightseeing attractions. It stops every 17 minutes from 9am to
7pm at these 24 location:

1. Sydney Cover/Circular Quay
2. Sydney Opera House
3. Royal Botanic Gardens/Museum of Sydney
4. State Library of NWS/Sydney Mint Museum
5. Mrs Macquaries Chair
6. Art Gallery of NSW
7. Hard Rock Café
8. Kings Cross
9. Macleay Street
10. Elizabeth Bay House
11. Potts Point
12. Woolloomooloo Bay
13. Wynard Station
14. Queen Victoria Building
15. Australian Museum
16. Central Station
17. Chinatown
18. Start City
19. Darling Harbour
20. Chinese Garden
21. Darling Walk
22. Sydney Aquarium
23. Campbells Cove
24. The Sydney Visitor Centre

Here are some of our favorite picks which should make your stay in Sydney very special and enjoyable.

MUSEUMS

❑ **Art Gallery of New South Wales:** *Art Gallery Road, The Domain, Tel. 9225-1744 (information) or 9225-1790 (what's on line). Open daily, 10am-5pm.* Includes an outstanding collection of Australian, Aboriginal, Asian, and European Art. The Yiribana Gallery includes a comprehensive collection of Aboriginal art. The gallery shop includes a good selection of art books.

❑ **Australian Museum:** *6 College Street, Tel. 9360-6000. Open daily, 9:30am-5pm.* Includes natural and Aboriginal history displays. While primarily a natural museum, its innovative cultural exhibits, such as Viewpoints and the Interpretive Theatre Program, are especially interesting and popular. Very good shop with books and gifts.

❑ **Australian National Maritime Museum:** *Darling Harbour, Tel. 9552-7777. Open daily 9:30am-5pm.* Offers an interesting collection of maritime artifacts, from surfboards to racing yachts and ships, including a World War II destroyer, a Russian submarine, and an Australian pearling lugger. Includes six galleries documenting Australia's maritime history. Many interactive displays.

❑ **Powerhouse Museum:** *500 Harris Street, Ultimo, at Darling Harbour. Tel. 9217-0444. Open daily, 10am-5pm.* An applied arts and sciences museum, this is Sydney's largest museum with numerous interactive displays. Includes everything from costumes and jewelry to steam engines and airplanes. Many interactive displays.

❑ **Museum of Contemporary Art:** *Circular Quay West, Tel. 9592-4033. Open daily, 11am-6pm.* Includes a permanent collection of modern arts. Exhibits changing contemporary art shows and includes films and lectures. Includes a great shop and restaurant.

❑ **Museum of Sydney:** *Corner of Bridge and Phillip Streets. Tel. 9251-4611.* One of Sydney's most interesting and innovative museums. Chronicles the fascinating history of colonial Sydney (1788-1850). Located on the site of the first Government House in Sydney. Boasts an excellent café and museum shop for gifts.

❑ **Sydney Jewish Museum:** *Darlinghurst Road and Burton Street, Darlinghurst, Tel. 9360-7999. Open Monday through Thrusday, 10am-4pm; Friday, 10am-2pm; and Sunday, 11am-5pm.* Chronicles the history of Jewish settlement in Australia as well as the historical plight of the Jews in Europe and the founding of Israel.

VIEWS OF CITY AND HARBOR

❑ **AMP Tower Centrepoint:** *100 Market Street, top of Centrepoint Shopping Centre at Pitt Street Mall, Tel. 9231-1000. Open Sunday through Friday, 9am-10:30pm and Saturday, 9am-11:30pm. $10 admission fee which includes a free tour.* This is Sydney's tallest structure (250 meters) which provides a panoramic view of the city. On a clear day, you can see as far as the Blue Mountains (50 miles). Also includes a restaurant at the top, the Sky Lounge, for a unique dining experience.

❑ **Sydney Harbour Bridge:** *S. East Pylon, Sydney Harbour Bridge, Tel. 9247-3408. Open daily, 10am-5pm.* Climb the Pylon Lookout to visit a small museum on the bridge construction and to get a terrific panoramic view of the harbor and Opera House. Adventuresome visitors take the unique and very popular three-hour, 1500 meter tour to the very top of the bridge with the BridgeClimb group (Tel. 9252-0077, *www.bridgeclimb.com*—advanced bookings, a few weeks in advance, are essential).

HARBOUR CRUISES

❑ **Captain Cook Cruises:** *Circular Quay and Darling Harbour, Tel. 9206-1111.* Twelve boats operate 20 scheduled cruises daily from Circular Quay and Darling Harbour. The most popular tour is the Sydney Harbour Explorer cruise which focuses on five major harborside attractions: The Rocks, Sydney Opera House, Watson's Bay, Taronga Zoo, and Darling Harbor.

❑ **Blue Line Cruises:** *Tel. 9552-2722.* The famous Sydney Showboats make regularly scheduled daily cruises: Harboursight cruises (10:30am, 2:30pm, 5:15pm); Jazz Luncheon Cruises (12:30pm); Twilight Dinner Cruise (5:15pm); and Showboat Spectacular dinner cruise and show (7:30pm).

HISTORIC BUILDINGS

❑ **Sydney Opera House:** *Bennelong Point, at Circular Quay, Tel. 9250-7250.* An easily recognizable symbol of Australia with its roof of sails. Take a guided one-hour tour (Backstage Tour for $20 and Front of House Tour for $10) to get a good understanding of the controversial origins and significance of this fascinating structure. Includes four restaurants and cafes as well as shops on the lower level. Tours, which run from 9:15am-4pm, may be suspended during rehearsal or performance periods.

❑ **Queen Victoria Building:** *George, York, Market, and Druitt Streets. Tel. 9264-9209 (Tour Desk). Open 24 hours a day. www.qvb.com.au.* This beautifully restored old sandstone Victorian building is one of Australia's landmark architectural achievements. Now an upscale shopping complex with over 200 shops and restaurants, it's well worth taking a guided tour to understand its architecture and fascinating history. See our previous discussion of this building in the "Where to Shop" section on pages 89-91.

❑ **Elizabeth Bay House:** *7 Onslow Avenue, Elizabeth Bay, Tel. 9358-2344. Open Tuesday to Sunday, 10am-4:30pm.* Constructed in 1835 as an English neoclassical style home, this is one of Australia's most elegant old mansions that captures the lifestyle of 19th century colonial days.

❏ **Hyde Park Barracks:** *Macquarie Street (top of King Street), Tel. 9223-8922. Open daily, 10am-5pm.* Showcases how male convicts lived in Sydney from 1819 to 1848. Visit the Greenway gallery for exhibits on Australian history, ideas, and culture.

❏ **Cadmans Cottage:** *110 George Street, The Rocks.* Sydney's oldest building. Currently houses the Sydney Harbour National Park Information Centre.

❏ **Vaucluse House:** *Wentworth Road, Vaucluse, Tel. 9388-7922. Open Tuesday to Sunday.* Located on Sydney Harbour, this famous house is part of a 19th century estate of William Charles Wentworth. Interesting gardens.

PARKS, GARDENS, ZOOS

❏ **Royal Botanic Gardens:** *Opera House. Tel. 9773-4646. Open daily, 9am-5pm.* Take a train (trackless) tour through these magnificent gardens. Great views of the harbor and Opera House. Trains leave every 20 minutes from each stop. Be sure to visit the Government House (completed in 1845) with its interesting States Rooms (open 10am-4pm, Tel. 9931-5222).

❏ **Chinese Garden:** *Darling Harbour, Tel. 9281-6863. Open daily, 9:30am-5:30.* Pleasant and tranquil "Garden of Friendship" next to Darling Harbour represents the important role the Chinese have played in Australian history. Incorporates winding pathways, mountains, forests, bridges, lakes, waterfalls, and pavilions.

❏ **Taronga Zoo:** *Sydney Harbour (north shore), Bradleys Head Road, Mosman, Tel. 9969-2777. Open daily, 9am-5pm. Admission fees.* A convenient 12-minute ferry ride from Circular Quay. One of the world's most interesting zoos with a spectacular showcase of unique and exotic Australian animals and reptiles—koalas, kangaroos, dingoes, Tasmanian Devils, platypus, echidnas, and kookaburras. Special features include Koala Encounters, Kodak Free Flight Bird Shows, and McDonald's Gorilla Forest.

❏ **Sydney Aquarium:** *Darling Harbour, Tel. 9262-2300 Open daily, 9:30am-10pm.* This large and spectacular aquarium displays live coral and numerous tropical fishes.

ENTERTAINMENT

Sydney is a fun city with a great deal going on in the evenings, from ballet, opera, dance, and theatrical performances to casinos, bars, pubs, and nightclubs. It appeals to all cultural tastes, from high to low. For high culture, check out the current ballet, dance, and opera performances at the **Sydney Opera House** (Tel. 9250-7777). This is the center for the performing arts in Sydney. Its ballet, theater, and concert halls are in regular use by the Australian Ballet Company, Sydney Dance Company, Australian Opera Company, Sydney Symphony Orchestra, and the Australian Chamber Orchestra. Also, check out the dance performances at the **Aboriginal Islander Dance Theatre** (Tel. 9252-0199) and the **Sydney Dance Company** (Tel. 9221-4811). Theatrical performances are regularly scheduled at **The Wharf Theatre** (Tel. 9250-1777); **Lyric Theatre** (Tel. 9777-9150); **Her Majesty's Theatre** (Tel. 9212-3411); and **Capitol Theatre** (Tel. 9320-9122).

If you're into jazz clubs, gambling, bars, pubs, and the seamier sides of nightlife, Sydney will not disappoint you. The **Kings Cross** area is still Sydney's red light district and its center for the sleazy side of Sydney's entertainment complex with its many raunchy bars, massage parlors, and burlesque shows. However, Kings Cross also is a center for many excellent cafes and restaurants. Try the **Bourbon and Beefsteak Bar** for a less frenzied experience in this area.

Sydney's large gay community tends to hang out at night along Oxford Street. **The Albury Hotel** (6 Oxford Street, Tel. 9361-6555) and **The Grand Pacific Blue Room** on Oxford Street are especially popular.

Gamblers head for the Las Vegas-style **Sydney Casino** (20-80 Pyrmont Street, Pyrmont, Tel. 9777-9150) which is open 24-hours a day.

Jazz clubs have become very popular in Sydney. For some of the best Australian and overseas jazz performances, head for **The Basement** (29 Reiby Place, Circular Quay, Tel. 9251-2797); **Kinselas** (383 Bourke Street, Darlinghurst, Tel. 9331-3299); and **Strawberry Hills Hotel** (453 Elizabeth Street, Surry Hills, Tel. 9698-2997).

Pubs are especially popular in The Rocks. Try **The Fortune of War** (137 George Street, Tel. 9247-2714), one of Sydney's oldest pubs. Also, stop at the **Irish Mercantile Hotel** (25 George Street, Tel. 9246-3570) and **Harts Pub** (Corner of Gloucester and Essex Streets, Tel. 9250-6022).

The nightclub scene is well represented at **The Craig Brewery** (225 Harbourside, Darling Harbour, Tel. 9281-3922), **RIVA** (Sheraton on the Park, 138 Castlereagh Street, Tel.

9286-6666), and **Hotel CBD** (75 York Street).

To find out what's currently going on in Sydney in the entertainment and nightlife departments, be sure to check out the "Metro" section of the Friday edition of the *Sydney Morning Herald*.

BEYOND SYDNEY

If time permits, you may want to take day or overnight trips to several places outside Sydney. If you enjoy beaches and water sports, head for the famous **Bondi** beach, 25 kilometers to the southeast of the city. **Manly**, 25 kilometers northeast of the city, is another beach resort with fine hotels, restaurants, pedestrian shopping mall, and a colorful weekend arts and crafts market. You can easily reach these places by car, bus, taxi, or ferry.

Other popular areas to visit outside Sydney include:

- Parramatta
- Hawkesbury River
- Blue Mountains
- Central Coast (Old Sydney Town)
- Hunter Valley (vineyards)
- Southern Highlands
- Royal National Park
- Snowy Mountains
- Canberra (the national capital)

You can **rent a car** (Avis, Tel. 9353-9000; Thrifty, Tel. 9331-1385; Dollar, Tel. 9223-1444; Ascot, Tel. 9332-3777; Bayswater, Tel. 9360-3622) to drive to all of these places or take a guided tour with one of many tour companies operating from Sydney. For more information on these and other sites, as well as to book tours, contact the various tourist information desks:

❑ **Sydney Visitors Centre:** 106 George Street, The Rocks, Tel. 9255-1788.

❑ **Sydney Visitors and Information Booth:** Martin Place, City, Tel. 9235-2424.

❑ **Countrylink—New South Wales Travel Centre:** 11-31 York Street, Tel. 02/13-2077.

❑ **Manly Visitors Information Bureau:** Ocean Beach, South Steye, Manly, Tel. 9977-1088.

❏ **Parramatta Tourist Information Bureau:** Corner Market and Church Streets, Parramatta, Tel. 9630-3703.

❏ **Visitors Centre Palm Grove:** Darling Harbour (under Freeway), Tel. 9286-0111.

5

Brisbane

W ELCOME TO AUSTRALIA'S CENTER FOR SUN surf, and hedonism—Australia's version of Florida, the Caribbean, and the French Riviera with a flashy dash of Las Vegas! Discover beautiful beaches, along with the world famous Great Barrier Reef, all within a few hours drive from downtown Brisbane. A very popular destination, nearly 60% of all visitors to Australia come here to relax, surf, fish, shop, dine, gamble, and party. From bustling cities and quaint towns to noisy beach resorts and idyllic islands, this area offers many travel surprises and shopping delights.

A CITY AND ITS HINTERLAND

Brisbane, Australia's third largest city, is strategically located along the east coast in the southern section of Queensland State, Australia's second largest state and most rapidly growing economy. A bustling city of 1.5 million, Brisbane boasts an enviable hinterland of beautiful beaches and mountains stretching for hundreds of miles to the north and south. Known as the Sunshine Capital, for its attractive east coast and sunny recreational climate, Brisbane also is the gateway city to the country's most rapidly developing region. The city and its hinterland are magnets for some of the country's most spectacular commercial investments, real estate developments, tourist attractions, and recreational opportunities. Above all, Brisbane and its surrounding areas are a shopper's delight!

SURPRISING BRISBANE

Brisbane is an unusually pleasant, casual, sophisticated, cosmopolitan, progressive, entrepreneurial, and delightfully livable city. It comes as a surprise to many visitors who primarily pass through this city on their way to Queensland's three great sun and surf playgrounds to the north and south—the Great Barrier Reef, Sunshine Coast, and Gold Coast.

Brisbane is a city with a unique entrepreneurial flair for taking big risks that frequently result in big payoffs. In recent years this city has experienced a level of economic development and dynamism that would be the envy of many cities throughout the world. Its impressive skyline of recently constructed high-rise commercial buildings and numerous first-class and deluxe hotels testify to the fact that Brisbane is on the move as the premier financial and business center for Queensland. Its expansive Cultural Centre, resting on the south bank of the lazy Brisbane River, emphasizes Brisbane's commitment to preserving culture and promoting the finest in arts and entertainment for its citizenry and guests. Its ability to host the Commonwealth Games in 1982 and the World Expo in 1988 as well as attract the world's largest gathering of conventioneers in 1991—50,000 Lions International Congress delegates—clearly demonstrates its cosmopolitan and international character. With the opening of its new International Airport in 1995, Brisbane now boasts the second busiest airport in Australia— after Sydney. And its numerous shopping malls and arcades in close proximity to the city center, as well as quaint arts and crafts towns to the north of the city, offer visitors an excellent mix of travel and shopping opportunities normally associated with cities much larger than Brisbane.

MORE THAN SUN, SURF, AND HEDONISM

Queensland is best known as Australia's seaside recreational capital. For years visitors have flocked to the East Coast to enjoy some of the world's finest beaches and water sports. From

Port Douglas in the north to Coolangatta in the south, the East Coast has grown into a mecca for deep sea fishing, reef walking, scuba diving, boating, and beach bumming. It is to Australia what Miami Beach, Ft. Lauderdale, and Daytona Beach are to the United States—minus the urban problems and traffic congestion. It is Australia's version of the French Riviera and Costa del Sol all rolled into one. Gambling gives it a touch of Las Vegas or Monaco.

Serving as the capital for the State of Queensland, Brisbane for years was content at playing the roles of state bureaucrat, banker, and broker as thousands of Australian and international tourists merely passed through the city on their way to the towns and beach resorts dotting the gorgeous coastline. But no longer do visitors just pass through this terminus to the coast. During the past decade Brisbane transformed itself into a major tourist attraction offering excellent shopping, sightseeing, entertainment, cultural, and recreational opportunities. It's a city worthy of a trip alone to enjoy its many and varied pleasures or at least a two-day stopover in transit to the popular beach and island reef resorts to the north and south. If you love to shop, this city will both surprise and delight you with its pleasant shopping malls, arcades, department stores, and markets offering everything from the latest in fashion to unique Australiana and tribal arts and crafts.

GETTING TO KNOW YOU

Here's a city you will quickly learn to like and feel at ease in navigating. Juxtaposing the old and the new, Brisbane is bright, brash, and assertive. From the moment you step off the airplane into its sunny climate, you will feel at home in this city. Nestled along the meandering Brisbane River, spread over charming hills, and sprouting new buildings left and right, this is a big city with a friendly, inviting, small town atmosphere.

For such a large city, Brisbane is very convenient to shop. Its relatively compact downtown area, centered around a pleasant and vibrant pedestrian mall—Queen Street Mall—houses the city's major shopping arcades, department stores, specialty shops, commercial buildings, and hotels. All are within easy walking distance of one another as well as in close proximity to the city's showpiece for art and culture just across the river in South Brisbane, the Cultural Centre. The public transportation system converges both above and below ground at Brisbane's largest downtown shopping center, The Myer Centre. Major suburban shopping areas of interest to visitors, such as Paddington, Milton, and Fortitude Valley, are within three kilometers of downtown Brisbane, an easy five- to ten-minute bus or taxi ride. Other suburban shopping malls of primary interest to locals, such as Toowong Village and Westfield Indooroopilly Shoppingtown, are conveniently reached by regular bus service or via the rapid Citytrain system.

While Brisbane's shopping is not as sophisticated nor diverse as shopping in Sydney or Melbourne, you will nonetheless find plenty of unique, fun, and adventuresome shopping opportunities here. You will discover, for example, some of Australia's best beachwear in Brisbane as well as fashionable clothes designed by some of Brisbane's and Australia's leading designers. You will not find the haute couture of Sydney's Double Bay or Melbourne's Toorak Village shops, but you will discover some fine fashion shops in Brisbane's Rowes Arcade, Wintergarden, Broadway on the Mall, The Pavillion, and Tattersalls Arcade. Brisbane may not have Sydney's Queen Victoria Building nor Melbourne's Myer Department Store, but it has the specialty shops of The Myer Centre along with a unique entertainment and market center (called Top's) perched on its two top floors. If you like art, antiques, and furniture, you'll want to head to nearby Paddington and Milton. If you are interested in tribal arts and crafts, you will be pleasantly surprised to find a few shops that offer unique collections of items not found elsewhere in Australia. If you're into factory outlet and discount shopping, Brisbane has its own collection of outlets at Stones Corner which is only six kilometers south of the city center. And if your interests include Australian arts and crafts, you will enjoy taking a one-day trip to the pleasant craft towns in the hills north of Brisbane.

❑ Brisbane is a city with a unique entrepreneurial flair for taking big risks. It's the premier financial and business center for Queensland.

❑ Brisbane is to Australia what Miami Beach, Ft. Lauderdale, and Daytona Beach are to the United States–minus the urban problems and traffic congestion.

❑ This is a very convenient city to shop. Its relatively compact downtown area houses most of the city's major shopping arcades, department stores, specialty shops, commercial buildings, and hotels.

❑ Brisbane's impressive high-speed rail service, Citytrain, is most convenient for traveling to the outer suburbs as well as linking to the Gold Coast Railway.

Best of all, you will get to know this city very quickly. You can easily walk its streets, climb its hills, and cruise its river. The local tourist associations can assist you with literature and advice on all aspects of visiting Brisbane, from arranging tours outside the city to navigating its rail and bus systems. If you are just passing through this city on your way to the beach resorts, you may well want to return to Brisbane to enjoy its many urban and suburban pleasures.

THE STREETS OF BRISBANE

The city of Brisbane is located on both the north and south sides of the meandering Brisbane River. However, you will find most shopping opportunities centered on the north side in downtown Brisbane as well as in the suburbs of Paddington, Milton, Spring Hill, and Fortitude Valley.

Downtown Brisbane is a relatively compact area where shops and shopping centers are concentrated within easy walking distance of each other. In fact, in contrast to most other Australian cities, shopping in Brisbane tends to be highly concentrated around numerous shopping centers that feed into a compact downtown pedestrian mall. The major shopping area is bordered by George, Elizabeth, Edward, and Ann Streets. Here you will find Brisbane's major department stores, shopping arcades, specialty shops, hotels, restaurants, banks, and an information booth and tourist offices ready to handle all your travel and shopping questions. Within this area, Queen Street Mall is the major center for shopping. Located between Edward and George Streets, this pleasant pedestrian mall is a shopper's paradise. You will enjoy strolling down its wide traffic-free walkway, browsing through the many shops and arcades that front on the mall, eating at one of the many indoor or outdoor restaurants and small eateries, or just watching the steady flow of shoppers from 8:15am to 9pm each weekday, and from 8:15am to 5:30pm on weekdays. Adjacent George, Elizabeth, Adelaide, Ann, Albert, and Edward Streets yield numerous additional shops and arcades to make this downtown area Brisbane's shopping mecca. If "shopping for luck" is one of your travel pleasures, head for the nearby riverfront **New Conrad Treasury Casino** (130 William Street) where they will be more than happy to take your money!

Plan to walk the major shopping streets of downtown Brisbane. Since all the department stores, shopping arcades, and specialty shops are in such close proximity to one another, you can easily cover the downtown area on foot. You will find plenty of taxis and buses stopping along these streets, but you only need such transportation when leaving downtown for suburban shopping areas.

Outside the downtown area—within five minutes by taxi,

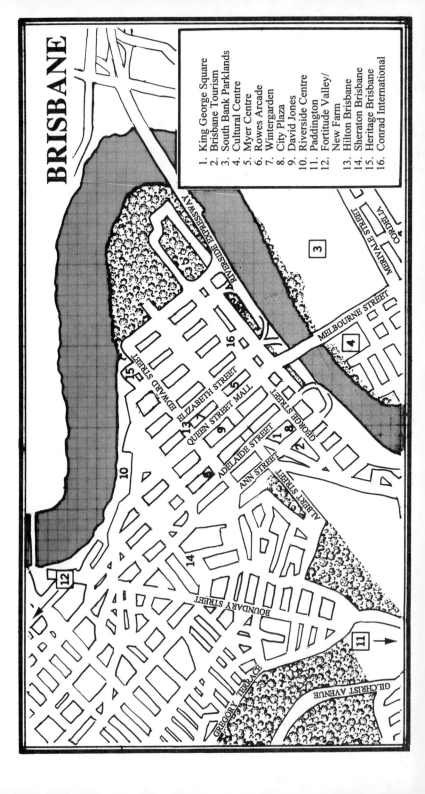

BRISBANE

1. King George Square
2. Brisbane Tourism
3. South Bank Parklands
4. Cultural Centre
5. Myer Centre
6. Rowes Arcade
7. Wintergarden
8. City Plaza
9. David Jones
10. Riverside Centre
11. Paddington
12. Fortitude Valley/
    New Farm
13. Hilton Brisbane
14. Sheraton Brisbane
15. Heritage Brisbane
16. Conrad International

car, or bus—you will find several suburban shopping streets and centers. **Paddington Circle**, a commercial designation for an area encompassing the main streets of suburban Paddington (Given Terrace and Latrobe Terrace) and Red Hill (Musgrave Road), is one of Brisbane's major suburban shopping and historical areas. Consisting of numerous restored cottages, quaint specialty shops, markets, and shopping centers, Paddington Circle is to Brisbane what Toorak Road and High Street are to Melbourne and what Paddington's Oxford Street is to Sydney. The streets are lined with specialty shops selling everything from high fashion clothes to gifts, fine art, and antiques.

The best way to get to Paddington Circle from downtown Brisbane is to take a taxi or a number 144 bus from Adelaide Street to Caxton Given Terrace, Caxton Street, and Latrobe Terrace or a number 146 or 172 bus from Adelaide Street to Musgrave Road in Red Hill. Better still, you may want to rent a car for the day so you have the convenience of driving from one section of this area to another. A good plan would be to rent a car for the day. Drive to Paddington Circle in the morning, preferably during the weekday since Paddington Circle can be very crowded on weekends. Arrive around 10am and spend three hours shopping the main streets of this area. Use the car in the afternoon to explore other suburban areas, such as nearby Milton, Spring Hill, and Fortitude Valley. Since it is easy to drive in Brisbane, you will find the car to be very convenient for shopping in these areas. The city's impressive high-speed rail service, Citytrain, is most convenient for traveling to the outer suburbs as well as linking to the Gold Coast Railway.

One reason we recommend renting a car is that the Paddington Circle area is not easy to walk. You can find buses along the main streets and an occasional taxi or you can call a taxi from a shop. But going from Paddington into Red Hill can be inconvenient. This whole area is spread out over one very long street which runs from Caxton Street in the south to Given Terrace and Latrobe Terrace in the north and along a small street to the east, Musgrave Road. If you plan to walk this area, be sure you have a good pair of walking shoes and a great deal of time and perseverance. This is a very hilly area. The streets running north progressively go up hill. And the east-west streets linking Red Hill's Musgrave Road to Paddington's main street go up and down steep grades.

If you do not have a car, we recommend that you begin shopping this area by taking a bus or taxi to the top of the hill at Latrobe Terrace. Get off at the bus stop on Latrobe Terrace, opposite Gilday Street or shop number 43 on Latrobe Terrace, just before Latrobe Terrace turns into MacGregor Terrace. From here you will be walking down hill as you explore the many shops on both sides of Latrobe Terrace which also becomes Given Terrace. This is a long walk, so expect to spend a good two to three hours walking the length of the street. In many sections of this street you will find few shops, but other sections will have several shops next to each other.

To go from Given Terrace in Paddington to Musgrave Road in Red Hill is a major walking effort. Take George Street from Given Terrace to walk east to Musgrave Road. Despite what your map might indicate, this is more than just a little walk. It may take you 30 minutes as you huff and puff up steep inclines to get to the intersection of Great George Street and Musgrave Road. Depending on how much you like exercise, you may elect to take a taxi from Paddington to Red Hill. Start at the intersection of Great George Street and Musgrave Road so you will be walking downhill along Musgrave Road.

Just south of Paddington is the up and coming area of **Milton**. Boasting its own mini-Eiffel Tower and centered around Park Road and Douglas Street, this is a lively area of cafes, restaurants, galleries, and furniture stores. The Savoire Faire complex (20 Park Road) includes upmarket designer boutiques and restaurants. A design center is located along Douglas Street.

Riverside Centre, located to the north of the city center and on the west bank of the Brisbane River, includes some shops and a popular Sunday market. A long walk from the central city, this area is best reached by taxi or bus.

South Bank Parklands, which is the old world's fair site (Expo '88) along the river in South Brisbane, has been converted into a trendy entertainment, dining, and shopping center with a lively weekend market. Located near the Queensland Cultural Center (consisting of the Queensland Art Gallery and Queensland Museum) and the Brisbane Convention and Exhibition Centre, South Bank Parklands is worth visiting when exploring South Brisbane.

The adjacent suburban areas of **Spring Hill** and **Fortitude Valley** are located north and northeast of the city center. Spring Valley has a few good hotels, shops, and restaurants. Fortitude Valley, once Brisbane's infamous red light district, is a center for bohemian culture. It's home to numerous cafes and ethnic restaurants. Fortitude Valley also is noted for its colorful Chinatown Mall, a replica of an Imperial Chinese Village. Located within one kilometer of downtown Brisbane, you can easily get to these two areas by taking a bus or taxi.

Time permitting, you may want to spend a day or two exploring shopping opportunities outside Brisbane. Three major areas, each offering distinct shopping opportunities, are within a few hours drive of downtown Brisbane: the craft towns of Maleny, Montville, and Mapleton in the northeastern hill country; the Sunshine Coast, from Coloundra in the south to Noosa Heads in the north; and the Gold Coast in and around Surfers Paradise in the south.

We especially recommend renting a car for the day and taking the scenic drive north to the **craft towns of Maleny, Montville, and Mapleton** and then returning to Brisbane by way of the Sunshine Coast. Take Bruce Highway north of Brisbane for about 50 kilometers and turn left onto Old Bruce Highway at the sign for Beerburrum. The road will take you into some lovely hill country. You will initially pass by a few craft shops. The first major craft town you will come to is the small town of Maleny. Here you will find a few very nice art, craft, and antique shops. Returning to the main highway, take a left and drive on to Montville, approximately 15 kilometers north of Maleny. Here you will discover a large concentration of nice quality arts, crafts, and antique shops as well as a few delightful restaurants that make this trip well worth while. From Montville, continue north for another five kilometers until you come to the small town of Mapleton. Not much here compared to Montville, but the drive is nice.

From Mapleton go east a few kilometers until you come to the main highway at Nambour which will take you back to Brisbane if you go south or to the Sunshine Coast if you go east or northeast. The major **Sunshine Coast** town is Noosa Heads, a 45-minute drive northeast of Mapleton. Along the way you will pass through Yandina—noted for its Ginger Factory—Eumundi, and Noosaville. Noosa Heads is a typical beachside resort with lots of sun and surf. You will find several shops near the beach along Hastings Street selling beachwear as well as a shopping center (Specialty Shopping) attached to the Sheraton Hotel. Other than that, this is not a noted shopping area. Go here primarily to see the beachside resorts and the lovely beaches. From Noosa Heads, drive south along the David Low Highway on your way back to Brisbane. You will see many lovely beaches along the way from Noosa Heads to Caloundra —but little or no shopping worth stopping for. After Caloundra it's back to the interior Bruce Highway for a less interesting return drive to Brisbane. Since the whole trip from Brisbane into the craft towns and on to the Sunshine Coast will take a full day, be sure to leave Brisbane by 8am so you will have plenty of time to enjoy the areas. If you shop the towns and keep moving quickly from one area to another, you should return to Brisbane by 6pm.

To the south of Brisbane is the famous **Gold Coast**, a one to two-hour drive from downtown Brisbane. This is Queensland's Miami Beach with numerous high-rise condominiums, beachfront resorts, and shops. Most commercial and recreational activities center around the booming city of Surfers Paradise. Here you will find numerous shops and chic boutiques selling everything from beachwear and Australiana to fine jewelry, art, and clothes. Many shops from Sydney and Melbourne have branch shops in Surfers Paradise. The best way to shop this area is to head for Cavill Mall and adjacent Cavill Avenue, Elkhorn Avenue, Orchard Avenue, and the Esplanade. Two of the best shopping centers are Raptis Plaza and Paradise Centre. Be sure to visit Surfers Paradise Beach Front Markets on Friday nights (5:30-10pm).

WHAT TO BUY

OPALS AND JEWELRY

Like other cities in Australia, Brisbane has its own stores offering a wide selection of opals and jewelry. Most of these shops are concentrated in the downtown section in and around Queen Street Mall. Shops offering a wide selection of fine opals include **Paragon Jewellery** (Level 2, Wintergarden, Queen Street Mall, Tel. 3229-3848); **Quilpie Opals** (Lennons Plaza, 68 Queen Street, Tel. 3221-7369); and **Jewellery and Gem Jungle** (Shop 56B, Level E, The Myer Centre, Tel. 3229-8366).

FINE ARTS AND ANTIQUES

Brisbane and its surrounding area have several art and antique shops offering very good quality oils, prints, lithographs, and European and Australian antiques. We recommend that you start your fine art and antique shopping by visiting the art gallery and museum at the **Queensland Cultural Centre**, on the south bank of the Brisbane River directly opposite the downtown area. Their art and historical collections will give you a good overview of the artistic talent and history of Queensland. The Cultural Centre also has an excellent shop offering a good collection of books on all facets of Australian arts, crafts, and culture. Also stop at the **City Hall Art Gallery and Museum** (Ground Floor, Brisbane City Hall, Tel. 3403-4355, open daily

10am-5pm) to see changing exhibitions of paintings and sculptures of Queensland artists.

You will discover art and antique shops throughout the greater Brisbane area. Unlike Sydney's Paddington and Queens Street or Melbourne's High street, Brisbane's art and antique shops are not concentrated in one particular section of the city or suburbs. In Brisbane you must know what shops are located where and then travel from one shop to another in different parts of the city and suburbs.

In downtown Brisbane, look for **Australian Perspectives Gallery and Coffee Shop** (169 Mary Street) and **The Verlie Just Town Gallery and Japan Room** (Edward and Queen Streets). In nearby Milton, look for **Cintra Galleries** (40 Park Road). In Fortitude Valley, stop by **Philip Bacon Galleries** (2 Arthur Street, Tel. 3358-3555). Bowen Hills is home to the **Galloway Galleries and Fine Arts Centre** (34 Brookes Street).

Outside the downtown area you will find several art and antique shops in nearby suburbs of Paddington, Red Hill, Milton, Spring Hill, Fortitude Valley, New Farm, Bardon, Milton, Clayfield, Annerley, Hawthorn, Sherwood, Windsor, Taringa, Mt. Gravatt, and Greenslopes all located within a few minutes drive from downtown Brisbane. And don't forget to visit the small towns of Maleny and Montville to the north of Brisbane. Montville is the most interesting and important center for arts and antiques. If you are a dedicated art and antique collector, then a one-day excursion to Montville should be a "must" on your travel and shopping agenda.

You will find several excellent quality **art shops in Paddington,** especially in the northern Latrobe Terrace section of Paddington. **Artissima** (139 Latrobe Terrace, open Wednesday through Sunday, 10-5pm) offers wild paintings of Italian artist Polles. **Agent 29** (31 Latrobe Terrace, Tel. 3367-1822) is a concept shop which represents the works of several local painters and sculptors.

The **art, antique, and furniture shops of Paddington** are primarily concentrated under one roof at the **Paddington Antique Centre** (167 Latrobe Terrace, corner of Collingwood Street, open daily 10am-5pm, Tel. 3369-8458), Brisbane's second largest antique center. Here you will find nearly 60 dealers offering a wide range of collectibles. Browse through its narrow pathways and you may discover a unique piece of porcelain, glass, jewelry, Australiana, toys, dolls, and furniture. If you are interested in good quality teak furniture, both indoor and outdoor, be sure to visit **Far Pavilions** (285 Given Terrace, corner of Haywood, Tel. 3368-3361). This shop offers unique pieces of furniture made from old house timbers.

Fortitude Valley and **New Farm**, suburbs adjacent to downtown Brisbane, have a few art and antique shops worth visiting. Fortitude Valley's antique center, **Wickham Street Antique Galleries** (400 Wickham Street—on the road to the airport), has one of the best collections of Victorian and Georgian antique furniture, jewelry, and collectibles.

Clayfield, a suburb located five kilometers north of downtown Brisbane along Sandgate Road, is home for one of Brisbane's largest antique centers. Here you will want to visit the **Brisbane Antique Market** (791 Sandgate Road, Tel. 3262-1444). Located near the airport and open seven days a week, this antique emporium displays the offerings of 40 dealers.

Woolloongabba Village also offers several good antique shops. Look for the **Contemporary Art and Design Centre Gallery** (33 Logan Road, Tel. 3392-0333). You'll find several antique shops along Logan Road: **Wallrock Antiques**, **Juliette Antiques**, **John Cuffe Antiques**, **Roger Hose Antiques**, and **James, Murray and Thomson**.

You will find a few art and antique centers and shops in other suburbs within five to ten minutes from downtown Brisbane:

❏ **Cordelia Street Antique and Art Centre:** *Corner Cordelia and Glenelg Streets, South Brisbane, open Wednesday to Sunday, 10am-5pm, Tel. 3844-8514.*

❏ **Southside Antiques Centre:** *484 Ipswich Road, Annerley, open Monday to Friday, 10am-4pm, and Saturday and Sunday 10am-5pm, Tel. 3892-1299.*

❏ **Scotts New Farm Antique Centre:** *85 Commercial Road, Newstead, open Monday to Friday, 10am-5pm, and Saturday and Sunday, 9am-5pm, Tel. 3852-2352.*

❏ **Chelsea Antiques and Decorative Art Centre:** *32 Vernon Terrace, Tenneriffe Wharf, Newstead, open daily, 10am-5pm, Tel. 3852-2750.*

Fine arts and antiques are well and alive in the hills of Maleny and Montville. Rent a car for the day to make this two hour drive from downtown Brisbane. You will discover one of Australia's most rewarding country art and antique centers. The small town of **Maleny** has three art and antique shops well worth visiting:

❑ **Back in Time:** *29 Maple Street, Tel. 5494-3099.* Nice shop offering antique tableware, tools, silver, and prints.

❑ **Bold in Gold:** *43 Maple Street, Tel. 5499-9299.* In addition to its wonderful jewelry designs, this shop represents 12 artists. A top quality operation.

❑ **Mitchell Gallery:** *50 Maple Street, 5499-9144.* Includes two galleries representing 60 local, national, and international artists. Terrific gallery offering nice quality paintings and many unusual works of art.

Nearby **Montville** is a treasure-trove of fine art and antique shops. Many of the art galleries have gone up-market, representing top quality local, national, and international artists. It's easy to find all the shops in Montville since they are spread over a one-kilometer stretch of Main Street, the highway that passes through the center of town. Coming in from Maleny, you will initially see a pottery factory on your right and a few cottages on your left selling arts and crafts. As you go further into town you will find the major concentration of fine art and antique shops along the left side of the road as well as across the street in an area called The Village Green. Here you will find **Rainbird Gallery and Sculpture Garden** (Tel. 5442-9211) and the **Montville Art Gallery,** two top quality art galleries operated by Pages' Fine Art Galleries (also has two galleries in Noosa Head—Hastings Street Gallery and Beachside Gallery). They represent quality paintings produced by some of Australia's leading artists. Also look for **Tony Gill Galleries** (146 Main Street, Tel. 5442-9228, *www.tonygillgalleries.com.au*) which represents the paintings and sculptures of 50-60 artists as well as has regular exhibitions. At the very end of Main Street, as you leave town, look for the geodesa dome on the left—**The Dome Galleries**—which houses two galleries which are a mixture of arts and crafts: **Ardleigh** (upstairs) and **Gallery D** (downstairs).

You will find several antique shops along Main Street in Montville selling everything from European and Australian furniture to African artifacts and antiques. If you like antique furniture, colonial wares, and estate jewelry, be sure to visit **Montville Antiques** (Tel. 5442-9400). For a selection of African arts and antiques, stop at **An African Dream** (1 Main Street).

AUSTRALIAN ARTS AND CRAFTS

Like many other Australian cities, Brisbane is a center for many Australian artists and craftsmen who produce exquisite arts and crafts found in numerous shops and galleries throughout the Brisbane area. Both the city and the state of Queensland actively promote the arts and crafts through the Queensland Cultural Centre, the City Hall Art Gallery and Museum, and the Crafts Council of Queensland.

Other than visiting the Queensland Cultural Centre and the City Hall Art Gallery and Museum, you will find few arts and crafts shops in downtown Brisbane. Most are located in and around the Queen Street Mall and The Myer Centre. Two of the best shops are **Collectables** (Shop 20, Brisbane Arcade, Queen Street, Tel. 3221-9717), with its nice collection of glass and colorful ceramics, and **Presenting Australia** (Wintergarden, Queen Street Mall) with its collection of Australiana, sweaters, didgeridoos, and boomerangs.

For good quality arts and crafts, be sure to check out the weekend arts and crafts markets, especially the **Cat's Tango Riverside Markets** at the Riverside Centre (123 Eagle Street), which is open Sunday 8am-4pm, and the **Lantern Market** (Friday, 5-10pm) and **Crafts Village** (Saturday 10am-5pm and Sunday 9am-5pm) at South Bank Parklands in South Brisbane.

One of the largest concentrations of arts and crafts shops is found outside the Greater Brisbane area, especially in and around the small hill towns of **Maleny** and **Montville** north of Brisbane. Along the main streets of these two towns, you will find many craft shops selling a wide selection of items produced by Queensland craftsmen. Maleny is especially noted for individual artists who live and work in the community; in fact, you'll have a better opportunity to meet artists in Maleny than in Montville. In **Maleny** a "must stop" is **Peace of Green** (32 Maple Street, Tel. 5499-3111), which represents the works of 23 local professional artists: glass, wood, fabric art, pottery, furniture, stone, leather, leadlight, and handmade paper. Another one of our favorites is **Bold in Gold** (Rainforest Plaza, 43 Maple Street, Tel. 5499-9299) with its wonderful collection of handcrafted jewelry (award-winning designs), paintings, hand blown glass, sculptures, woodcraft, leather, ceramics, and unique rainforest clay pieces (forest and frog scenes) by popular artist Lindsey Mair; this also is good shop in which to make contact with local artists. For a unique collection of handmade clothes and accessories (jackets, blouses, and hats; will make to order) by Dutch artist/designer Johanna van Genderen, visit

Johanna's at Maleny (37 Maple Street, Tel. 5499-9233). If
you are in Maleny on Sunday, be sure to visits the **Maleny
Handcrafts Market** (1 Bunya Street, Tel. 5494-2883) from
9am to 2pm.

Montville is one of the largest arts and crafts centers in the
state of Queensland. Approaching the town from Maleny, you
will initially come to a pottery factory on your right (**Montville
Pottery and Eatery**, Tel. 5442-9204) and country craft shops
on the left (**The Herb Garden**, Tel. 5442-9190). As you go
further along Main Street you will find several arts and crafts
shops on the left (west side of road) selling everything from
traditional country crafts to imported arts and crafts. Look for
Blackforest Hill Clock Centre (Tel. 5442-9409) for a large
collection of handcarved cuckoo and grandfather clocks;
Montville Woods (Tel. 5442-9398) for woodcrafts; **Not Just
Dolls** (Tel. 5442-9577) for limited editions of dolls, accessories,
miniatures, cards, and gift items. At the northern end of town
(easy to miss as you exit the town), look for **The Dome
Galleries** on the left which houses two galleries (**Ardleigh** and
Gallery D) offering a unique mix of arts and crafts, including
glass (includes the Pantano glass blowing studio on site),
woodcraft, silver, and ceramics.

ABORIGINAL AND PNG ARTS AND CRAFTS

While Brisbane is not considered to be a major center for
acquiring quality Aboriginal arts and crafts, it does have an
excellent collection on exhibit at the **Queensland Cultural
Centre**. Two shops in the Centre offer Aboriginal arts, crafts,
and books. The first shop is located just outside the Aboriginal
exhibit. You will find several Aboriginal souvenirs here, including postcards, stationery, placemats, coasters, acrylic paintings,
didgeridoos, and clap sticks. Another shop is located on the
ground floor adjacent to the art gallery. This shop has Brisbane's best collection of books on Aboriginal arts and crafts.

Although the best shopping for Aboriginal arts and crafts is
found in Darwin, Alice Springs, Melbourne, and Sydney, you
will find a few shops in Brisbane offering limited selections of
bark paintings, didgeridoos, clap sticks, boomerangs, weapons,
placemats, coasters, music, and books. A popular tourist quality
shop run by Aboriginals is the **Queensland Aboriginal
Creations** (135 George Street, Tel. 3224-5730).

Our favorite shop for quality international decorative arts
and crafts is Ian Thomson's **Decorators Gallery** (525 Boundary Street, Spring Hill, Tel. 3832-9500). It's the ideal place for

collectors, decorators, and gift seekers alike. You'll find arts and crafts from over 30 countries, including Korean chests, Japanese kimonos, Indian carvings and paintings, Thai and Burmese figurines and tapestries, Louvre Museum replicas, Egyptian jewelry as well as tribal arts from Papua New Guinea, Africa, and Indonesia. You may be surprised in finding top quality art from Papua New Guinea here. Ian Thomson often purchases many fine PNG art pieces from Australian collections. If your timing is right, you may discover some real quality arts and crafts here amongst his many other interesting furniture and decorative pieces.

Asian Connection (6 Edmonstone Street, West End, Tel. 844-0566) is a huge cluttered (look in the rafters, too) warehouse jam-packed with artifacts, Javanese furniture, textiles, Indian rugs, Batak bowls, Lombok boxes, chairs, beds, objets d'art, and handicrafts from Papua New Guinea and Indonesia. Truly an eclectic mix, you may find something interesting here. Much of the collection might be best termed "airport art" or "handicrafts" rather than "antiques" since most of the pieces are relatively new and inexpensive. Also sells T-shirts.

CLOTHES AND ACCESSORIES

While Brisbane does have a few local designers, most clothes are brought into Brisbane shops from Melbourne and Sydney or imported from abroad. Several shops stock popular Australian designer labels, such as Ken Done. You will also find in Brisbane branches of popular clothing stores and designer boutiques which are primarily based in Melbourne, Sydney, and Adelaide: Carla Zampatti, Liz Davenport, Maggie Shepherd, Country Road, Cherry Lane, Designer Savings, Jeanswest, Just Jeans, R. M. Williams, and Settlers & Co.

Although Brisbane is not a noted fashion center, you will find plenty of shopping for fashionable clothes in this city. Brisbane's major clothing strength, however, is its good quality **sports** and **beachwear**, especially distinctively designed swimsuits and clothes using **tropical weight cotton fabrics**, which are not available in many other Australian cities.

Most clothing stores and boutiques in downtown Brisbane are found in and around the Queen Street Mall: Brisbane Arcade, Wintergarden, Broadway on the Mall, Elizabeth Arcade, Tattersalls, Rowes Arcade, Queen Adelaide Building, The Myer Centre, David Jones Department Store, and Myer in the City department store. Several shops at **Wintergarden** carry international and Australian fashion labels such as Gianni

Versace, Giorgio Armani, Monde, Hugo Boss, Liz Davenport, Carla Zampatti, Covers, and Oroton. Shops offering the closest thing to haute couture are found in the small but elegant **Rowes Arcade**. Here is where many of Brisbane's rich and famous—and those with both good taste and plenty of money—come to shop. You'll find several upmarket designer apparel and jewelry stores here. The **Savoire Faire** complex in Milton also includes several upmarket designer boutiques.

Brisbane's famous sportswear and beachwear will be found in the downtown department stores (Myers and David Jones) and shopping arcades (The Myer Centre, Wintergarden, Broadway on the Mall) as well as in many shops along the Sunshine Coast (Noosa Heads) and Gold Coast (Surfers Paradise). You will find unique patterns and designs made from nice lightweight cotton fabrics.

WOOLS, FURS, AND LEATHER PRODUCTS

You will find a few shops offering wools, furs, and leather products. The best places to shop for such items are the shops in The Myer Centre and Wintergarden (**R. M. Williams** and **Oroton**).

HOUSEHOLD FURNISHINGS AND ACCESSORIES

A few shops in and around Brisbane offer good selections of home furnishings and accessories for individuals interested in home decorating. Ian Thomson's **Decorators Gallery** (525 Boundary Street, Spring Hill, Tel. 3832-9500) has an excellent collection of quality arts, antiques, and furniture with an eye towards tasteful home furnishings. Look for his special collections of Asian and South Pacific arts. The **Design Centre** on Douglas Street in **Milton**, as well as adjacent furniture and accessory shops, is well worth visiting. Many of the art and antique shops in **Paddington** (Latrobe Terrace) are popular with home decorators and designers.

AUSTRALIANA, SOUVENIRS, AND GIFTS

Like other cities in Australia, Brisbane has its share of Australiana, souvenir, and gift shops offering everything from tourist kitsch to quality arts and crafts. T-shirts and stuffed koala bears are popular items offered by many such shops. Look for several such shops in or near downtown Brisbane: **National Trust Gift**

Shop (The Mansions, 40 George Street, Tel. 3221-1887); **Emporium of Fine Goods** (at the Heritage, Botanic Gardens, 39 Edward Street, Tel. 3229-5477); **Collectables** (Shop 20, Brisbane Arcade, Queen Street, Tel. 3221-9717) for nice glass and colorful ceramics and tableware; and **Presenting Australia** (Wintergarden, Queen Street Mall) for Australiana, sweaters, didgeridoos, and boomerangs.

Also, be sure to visit the weekend markets, especially the **South Bank Crafts Village** (Friday, 5pm-10pm and Saturday and Sunday, 9am-5pm), **Riverside Markets** (Eagle Street, Sunday 7am-4pm), **Brunswick Street** (Saturday, 9am-3pm), **Eagle Street Pier** (Sunday, 8am-4pm), and **Cleveland Markets** (Sunday, 9am-5pm).

You'll find lots of quality gift items in the art and craft towns of Maleny and Montville. We especially like the delightful selections at **Bold in Gold** (Rainforest Plaza, 43 Maple Street, Maleny, Tel. 5499-9299) and **Johanna's of Maleny** (37 Maple Street, Maleny, Tel. 5499-9233). In fact, if you're traveling to these towns, you may want to wait until you visit their shops before making such purchases in Brisbane.

The beach resort cities of **Noosa Heads** on the Sunshine Coast and **Surfers Paradise** on the Gold Coast have numerous shops selling Australiana, souvenirs, and gifts, with a heavy emphasis on T-shirts and beachwear.

WHERE TO SHOP

The pattern of shopping in Brisbane is very similar to that found in other Australian cities. You will find the typical pedestrian mall located in the heart of the central business district. This is where most of Brisbane's shopping action is centered around numerous shopping arcades, department stores, and specialty shops. Within only a few minutes of the downtown area you will come to several suburban shopping areas. Some of these areas cater to tourists but most are popular with locals who live in the suburbs. Further outside the city you will discover arts and crafts towns as well as large and small resort towns along the Sunshine Coast to the north and the Gold Coast to the south.

SHOPPING APPROACH

We recommend that you begin your shopping in downtown Brisbane along the Queen Street Mall. A compact, high density

area, you can easily spend a good day or two exploring the
many arcades and shops along this and adjacent streets. All the
shops in the downtown area are within easy walking distance.
After completing your downtown shopping, head for a few
nearby suburban areas, especially Paddington, Red Hill, Milton,
Spring Hill, Fortitude Valley, and New Farm—all within a five
to 10-minute bus or taxi ride from the city center. If you want
to see where the locals shop, take a bus to visit the eight major
suburban shopping centers. If you plan to go out of town to
shop in the arts and crafts towns or visit the Sunshine Coast
and Gold Coast, it's best to rent a car and drive to these areas.

While you can easily shop Brisbane on your own, many
bargain shoppers join **Brisbane Warehouse Shopping Tours**
(Tel. 3821-0438). This group takes bus tours to Brisbane's
major discount shops and wholesalers which include clothing,
jewelry, linen, shoe, and gift outlets.

DOWNTOWN SHOPPING MALL, ARCADES, SHOPS

Brisbane's major shopping is centered in and around the **Queen
Street Mall**. A pleasant pedestrian mall running between
Edward and George Streets, this is a shopper's paradise jam-
packed with arcades, department stores, boutiques, restaurants,
food courts, hotels, banks, and entertainment centers. Open
from 8:15am to 5:30pm each day, Queen Street Mall should be
your very first shopping destination. Here you will find Brisbane's major shopping arcades which provide ample opportunities to engage in "lifestyle shopping":

- ❑ **The Myer Centre and Top's:** Completed in 1988, the
  Myer Centre is Brisbane's largest and most popular
  shopping center. Located on Queen Street Mall as well as
  along Elizabeth and Albert Streets, The Myer Centre is
  attached to Brisbane's largest and most elegant department store—Myer on the Mall—as well as includes a
  unique recreation and food center on its top two floors
  appropriately called "The Top's." The Myer Centre
  consists of over 230 specialty shops, 8 theaters, and
  numerous fast food establishments. In addition to the
  unique fantasy and leisure center on the top two floors,
  The Myer Centre also boasts Australia's largest underground bus interchange on the bottom floor. From here
  you can connect with buses to other parts of the city and
  to several suburban areas. The specialty shops run the
  gamut from fashion clothes and accessories to jewelry and

housewares shops. Several of Australia's major clothing stores (**Country Road, Laura Ashley**, and **Canterbury**) have branch stores in this complex. Look for numerous shops selling shoes, handbags, and leather goods as well as jewelry, Australiana, gifts, and home decorative items. The Myer Centre also has an excellent food court at the Ground Level. You'll find McDonald's and Pizza Hut on the Albert Street Level.

❑ **Wintergarden:** This used to be Brisbane's top shopping center until The Myer Centre opened in 1988. Completed in 1982 and expanded in 1986, Wintergarden is considered Brisbane's major fashion center. You will find numerous famous international and Australian label men's and women's apparel and accessory shops in this complex, such as **Giorgio Armani, Monde, Gianni Versace, Hugo Boss, Liz Davenport, Carla Zampatti, Covers, R. M. Williams**, and **Oroton**. Located on the Queen Street Mall and attached to the Hilton Hotel on Elizabeth Street, this is a three-level shopping complex housing 123 specialty stores, boutiques, and restaurants. Wintergarden has similar types of shops as found in The Myer Centre—clothes, accessories, jewelry, and gift. If you're looking for Australiana, **Everything Australian** should have what you want. For jewelry, including nice opal watches, earrings, pendants, and necklaces, be sure to visit **Paragon Jewellery** (Level 2, Tel. 3229-3848).

❑ **Rowes Arcade:** Compared to The Myer Centre and Wintergarden, this is a very small but extremely elegant shopping arcade. Located at 235 Edward Street, Rowes Arcade has entrances on both Edward and Adelaide Streets as well as from the Post Office Square. A nicely restored building with stained glass, mosaic tiles, and cedar paneling, here is where many of Brisbane's rich and famous choose to shop for clothes and accessories. Two levels of shops offer some of Australia's finest quality clothes and accessories.

❑ **Broadway on the Mall:** Located across from Wintergarden, this relatively new mall with over 30 women's, men's, and children's fashion shops as well as several jewelry and gift shops. Includes a food court, cafes, and restaurants.

❑ **Brisbane Arcade:** Located next door to Broadway on the Mall, this arcade of 50 shop reminds one of the Strand Arcade in Sydney with two levels of quality boutiques, jewelry stores, gift shops, and restaurants. One of Brisbane's nicest glass and ceramics shops in located here— **Collectables**.

You will discover several additional shopping arcades in and around Queen Street Mall. Most are small arcades filled with all types of specialty shops and boutiques offering a large range of goods. Look for these arcades in downtown Brisbane:

❑ **Elizabeth Arcade:** Located across from Myer Centre on Elizabeth Street, Includes 24 shops and restaurants.

❑ **Tattersalls Arcade:** Located on Queen Street Mall with entry via Edward Street, this small arcade includes several clothing, shoe, and stationery shops along with a florist, cleaners, and beauty salon.

❑ **City Plaza Shopping Centre**: Located behind City Hall and with entrances from Ann, George, and Adelaide Streets. Has 57 specialty shops offering everything from fashion, jewelry, gifts, and kitchenware to candy. Includes coffee and snack shops.

❑ **T&G Arcade:** Across the street from The Myer Centre and on the corner of Queen and Albert Streets. Entrances on both Queen Street Mall and Albert street. Includes 21 specialty shops offering men's and women's fashion clothes, accessories, jewelry, gifts, and flowers.

❑ **Post Office Square:** Opposite Anzac Square and between Adelaide and Queen Streets. Has several specialty shops along with coffee shops and delicatessens. Heavily trafficked by downtown workers.

❑ **The Pavilion:** On the corner of Queen and Albert Streets. Two levels of shops selling clothes and accessories, sheepskin and leather goods, and Australiana.

❑ **The Mansions:** Located at 40 George Street at the corner of Margaret Street. An elegantly restored building with only four shops. Look for antiques, prints, books, and the **National Trust Gift Shop**.

❑ **City Centre Arcade:** Small shopping arcade on Adelaide street, between Albert and Edward Streets.

❑ **Piccadily Arcade:** Small shopping arcade on Adelaide Street, between Wharf and Creek Streets.

❑ **Riverside Centre:** Brisbane's waterfront commercial development with restaurants and shops. Best to shop here on Sunday when its weekend market is open.

❑ **Savoire Faire:** Located at 20 Park Road nearby Milton, this upmarket shopping and dining complex is noted for its designer boutiques and fashion.

Outside these major shopping centers you will also find many interesting shops along the streets in downtown Brisbane. You'll find several upscale fashion boutiques across from The Myer Centre on Elizabeth Street. You also will find an interesting Aboriginal art and craft shop along George Street: **Queensland Aboriginal Creations** (135 George Street, Tel. 3224-5730). It specializes in Australian gifts and art by Aboriginal and Torres Strait Islander artists and craftspeople (hand painted fabrics, woodcarvings, ceramics, didgeridoos, boomerangs, artifacts, books, and tapes). If you focus on exploring George, Elizabeth, Queen, Adelaide, Albert, and Edward Streets, you will discover numerous interesting shops offering everything from fashion clothes to sporting goods.

DEPARTMENT STORES

Brisbane's three major department stores are located on the Queen Street Mall. **Myer in the City** is Brisbane's most elegant department store. The second largest Myer department store in the country—next to the enormous Myer Department Store in Melbourne—Myer in the City anchors The Myer Centre. Spacious, modern, and inviting, this five-level store offers everything from the latest fashion clothes and travel goods to Australian gifts and souvenirs. Before exploring this store it's best to stop at the Information Centre on Level Q (Queen Street Level) to pick up a brochure and map of the store.

David Jones Department Store is also located on the Queen Street Mall. This is another elegant branch of the David Jones Department Store chain. This store offers good quality men's and women's clothes as well as the usual assortment of household goods.

Coles Department Store is located two doors north of David Jones Department Store on the Queen Street Mall. This is Australia's answer to America's Kmart and F. W. Woolworth. An older and congested store, shop here for inexpensive items from toys to toiletries. Coles also has a grocery section.

QUEENSLAND CULTURAL CENTRE
AND THE SOUTHSIDE

While South Brisbane offers few shopping opportunities, you should at least spend a couple of hours touring the impressive **Queensland Cultural Centre** and browsing through a few nearby shops. From downtown Brisbane you can easily get to the Centre by walking across the Victoria Bridge at Queen Street. Resting on the banks of the Brisbane River, the Cultural Centre houses a museum, art gallery, and performing arts center. It's a big complex well worth visiting early during your stay in Brisbane. Art and antique lovers who browse through the Centre will get some idea of possible shopping choices in the area. The museum, for example, has an excellent collection of arts and crafts from Papua New Guinea and the South Pacific Islands as well as memorabilia on the history of Queensland. The art gallery has permanent as well as traveling exhibits. You will find an excellent collection of Aboriginal art and paintings by many of Australia's famous artists.

While visiting the Cultural Centre, don't forget to stop at the Centre's two shops. Just outside the Aboriginal art exhibit you will find a small shop selling Aboriginal arts and crafts, including postcards, stationery, placemats, coasters, didgeri-doos, acrylic paintings, and clap sticks; most items are of tourist quality. The second shop is located on the ground floor adjacent to the fine arts gallery. This shop primarily sells art books and posters. We found this shop to have one of the best selections of books on Aboriginal arts and crafts as well as on Australian artists.

You will find a few art and antique shops in South Brisbane within a five minute walk from the Cultural Centre. The **Cordelia Street Antique and Art Centre** (corner of Cordelia and Glenelg Streets, Tel. 3844-8514) offers a large assortment of antiques and collectibles, including gold and silver jewelry. **Asian Connection** (6 Edmondstone Street, West End, Tel. 3844-0566), includes Brisbane's largest collection of arts and crafts from Papua New Guinea and Indonesia.

PADDINGTON

A five minute bus or taxi ride from downtown Brisbane (#144, 147, 172), the historical Paddington area is filled with galleries, antique shops, arts and crafts stores, boutiques, home decorative shops, and restaurants and cafes. This area has changed considerably in the past few years (new regulations required the owners to live on premises) as many shops have closed and new ones have opened, especially art galleries and framers.

Paddington's main street—which changes its name three times from Caxton Street to Given Terrace to Latrobe Terrace —is a long and hilly walk. Since most of the shops are concentrated along the Latrobe Terrace section of this street, you may want to start your shopping here. If you don't have a car, we suggest you begin your shopping excursion at the top of the hill near the corner of Gilday Street and Latrobe Terrace. A bus stops here. From here you can walk south—and downhill— along Latrobe Terrace. You will want to explore the shops on both sides of the street.

Several shops are worth visiting in Paddington. We especially like **Artissima** (133 Latrobe Terrace, Tel. 3368-3244, open Wednesday to Sunday, 10am-5pm) for colorful paintings by Polles, Venetian glass, wood tables, and prints; Agent 29 (31 Latrobe Terrace, Tel. 3321-7511) for an interesting mix of local art and sculpture, glass, ceramics, furniture, and tribal art; **Paddington Antique Centre** (167 Latrobe Terrace, Tel. 3369-8088) for antiques and collectibles; and **Second Hand Jewelry** (169 Labrobe Terrace) for silver, gold, and pearl jewelry; home decorative items. One of our favorite shops in this area is **Far Pavilions** (285 Given Terrace, Tel. 3368-3361) with its unique furniture (made from old house timbers), home accessories, and gift items. A good Italian restaurant in this area is **Alberto's** (245 Given Terrace, Tel. 3368-1611).

The adjacent Red Hill area also has a few arts, crafts, and clothing shops worth visiting, especially in the 90s section of Musgrave Road.

MILTON

Located a few minutes west of the downtown area, Milton is a trendy area for cafes, restaurants, galleries, and boutiques. You can't miss it since its symbol is a mini-Eiffel Tower. Most of the shopping and dining is centered along two major streets—Park Road and Douglas Street. Upscale shopping and dining is centered in the **Savoire Faire** complex (20 Park Road).

FORTITUDE VALLEY, NEW FARM, NEWSTEAD, RIVERSIDE CENTRE

Four of Brisbane's major suburban shopping areas are located within five minutes from the central business district. Fortitude Valley, New Farm, Newstead, and Riverside Centre are located adjacent to each other on the north side of the city. **Fortitude Valley** is well known for **Potters' Gallery** (483 Brunswick Street). Housed in an old historic church, Potters' Gallery is the gallery shop of The Queensland Potters' Association. It offers the largest collection of handcrafted pottery in Queensland. Potters' Gallery includes two galleries—one selling members' pottery and another with exhibits of guest potters which changes every three weeks. Art galleries, such as **Philip Bacon Galleries** (2 Arthur Street, Tel. 3358-3555) represent many of Australia's leading artists, such as Boyd, Daws, Crooke, Friend, Fullbrook, Nolan, Sawrye, and Whiteley. Fortitude Valley also houses the colorful **Chinatown Mall**, a replica of an Imperial Chinese Village, bordered by Brunswick, Wickham, and Ann Streets. In addition to offering excellent Oriental restaurants, Chinatown Mall also has a market where you can purchase numerous handcrafted items, gifts, and souvenirs from vendor stalls. Also look for **Wickham Street Antique Galleries** at 400 Wickham Street for a good selection of Victorian and Georgian antique furniture, jewelry, and collectibles.

New Farm is famous for the colorful **Paddy's Markets** (corner of Macquarie and Florence Streets), a five acre five-story covered shopping complex with numerous stalls selling everything from furniture to ribbons. Open seven days a week, Paddy's Markets hosts a weekend Flea Market.

Newstead is home to **Pierrot Arts and Craft Centre** (251 Arthur Street), a market offering one the largest collections of Australian arts and crafts in the Brisbane area.

Riverside Centre is Brisbane's major riverside development housing offices, restaurants, and shops. While still part of the city of Brisbane, Riverside Centre is located on the banks of the Brisbane River adjacent to Fortitude Valley and New Farm. The best time to visit here is on Sunday when Riverside Centre becomes a popular outdoor market selling local arts and crafts.

SUBURBAN AND DISCOUNT SHOPPING

If you're interested in seeing where the locals shop, you may want to visit several of Brisbane's suburban shopping centers, such as **Toowong Village** and **Westfield Indooroopilly Shoppingtown**. However, most visitors do not find these places particularly interesting.

Brisbane has is own bargain shopping center. Located 6 miles south of the city center, you may want to head for **Stones Corner** (Logan and Old Cleveland Roads) which includes several discount outlet shops. You'll find such Australian fashion and homeware brand names as Country Road, Sportsgirl, and Table Eight. Most of these shops include seconds or discontinued seasonal items.

WEEKEND MARKETS

Brisbane has several weekend markets which primarily offer arts and crafts. Several are located within the city but many also can be found in suburban areas. The most popular ones include:

❑ **South Bank Crafts Village:** Located in South Brisbane in the South Bank Parklands (old Expo 88 center) complex. Open Friday, 5pm-10pm (Lantern Market) and Sunday and Sunday, 9am-5pm (Crafts Village).

❑ **Riverside Markets:** Also known as the Cat's Tango Riverside Markets. Located on Eagle Street, just northeast of the city center. Open Sunday 7am-4pm

❑ **Brunswick Street:** Located in Fortitude Valley. Saturday, 9am-3pm.

❑ **Eagle Street Pier:** Located along the river, directly east of Queen Street Mall. Open Sunday, 8am-4pm.

❑ **Cleveland Markets:** Open Sunday, 9am-5pm.

NORTHERN CRAFT TOWNS

Within a two to three hour drive northeast of Brisbane are several small hill towns offering some of the best arts and crafts in Queensland: Maleny, Montville, and Mapleton. They also are fun small towns to visit. A few of the shops can be found online: *www.maleny.net.au/sunwe/retail/index.html*. Take Bruce Highway north of Brisbane for approximately 50 kilometers and turn left at the sign for Beerburrum which is the Old Bruce Highway. You will initially go through the small town of Landsborough and continue on Maleny Road to the first major craft town of Maleny.

Maleny has a few good antique, arts and crafts, a nd clothing shops. Our favorites here include:

❑ **Bold in Gold:** *43 Maple Street, Tel. 5499-9299.* Wonderful shop offering a terrific collection of handcrafted jewelry (award-winning designs by Swiss designer Zita Stadelmann Gsell), paintings, hand blown glass, sculptures, woodcraft, leather, ceramics, and unique rainforest clay pieces (forest and frog scenes) by popular clay artist Lindsey Mair. This also is good shop to make contact with local artists who display their works in this and other shops in Maleny and Montville. A top quality operation.

❑ **Johanna's of Maleny:** *37 Maple Street, Tel. 5499-9233.* Offers a unique collection of handmade clothes and accessories (jackets, blouses, and hats; will make to order) by Dutch artist/designer Johanna van Genderen,

❑ **Peace of Green:** *32 Maple Street, Tel. 5499-3111.* Represents the works of 23 local professional artists: glass, wood, fabric art, pottery, furniture, stone, leather, leadlight, and handmade paper.

❑ **Back in Time:** *29 Maple Street, Tel. 5494-3099.* Nice shop offering antique tableware, tools, silver, and prints.

❑ **Mitchell Gallery:** *50 Maple Street, 5499-9144.* Includes two galleries representing 60 local, national, and international artists with over 400 works in stock. Terrific gallery offering nice quality paintings and many unusual works of art.

❑ **Maleny Handcrafts Market:** *1 Bunya Street, Tel. 5494-2883. Open Sunday from 9am to 2pm.*

Montville is the largest arts and crafts town in this area. Indeed, you can easily spend half a day browsing through its many interesting shops which offer fine arts, crafts, and antiques. All of the shops are located on the one main street that runs through this charming little town. Some of our favorites here include:

❑ **Rainbird Gallery and Sculpture Garden** and the **Montville Art Gallery:** *Main Street, Tel. 5442-9211.* Two top quality art galleries (across the street from each other)

operated by Pages' Fine Art Galleries. Represents quality paintings and sculptures (outdoors) produced by some of Australia's leading artists. The famous Montville Art Gallery has been rebuilt since it was destroyed by fire in 1995.

❑ **Tony Gill Galleries:** *146 Main Street, Tel. 5442-9228. www.tonygillgalleries.com.au.* Represents the paintings and sculptures of 50-60 artists as well as has regular exhibitions. Nice quality and more up-market than most galleries found in this area.

❑ **The Dome Galleries:** Located at the very end of Main Street, as you leave town (look for the geodesa dome on the left). Houses two galleries (**Ardleigh** and **Gallery D**) which offer a unique mix of arts and crafts, including glass (includes the Pantano glass blowing studio on site), woodcraft, silver, and ceramics.

❑ **Montville Antiques:** *Tel. 5442-9400.* Offers antique furniture, colonial wares, porcelain, silver, and estate jewelry.

❑ **Blackforest Hill Clock Centre:** *Tel. 5442-9409.* Includes a large and unique collection of handcarved cuckoo clocks, grandfather clocks, and German arts and crafts.

❑ **Not Just Dolls:** *Tel. 5442-9577.* Offers limited editions of dolls, accessories, miniatures, cards, and gift items.

SUNSHINE AND GOLD COASTS

The Sunshine Coast and Gold Coast are Brisbane's two major sun and surf resort areas. Located within two hours drive north and south of Brisbane respectively, these are two major destinations for visitors who come to this part of Queensland. The **Sunshine Coast** is the smaller and quieter of these two resort areas. Centered at the peninsular town of Noosa Heads, a 40-minute drive northeast of the arts and crafts hill town of Montville, this area has a few shops selling the usual type of beach resort goods—clothes, swimwear, T-shirts, and souvenirs. Most shops are located along **Hastings Street** and in two local shopping centers—**Bay Village** and **Specialty Shopping**. We found few distinctive shops in this area—mainly the usual beach resort-type shops. **Specialty Shopping**, a shopping

center attached to the Sheraton Hotel, includes 31 shops and
restaurants offering clothes, gifts, books, and jewelry. If you're
interested in good quality paintings and sculptures, be sure to
visit **Hastings Street Gallery** (Sheraton Nossa Resort, 14
Hastings Street, Tel. 4474-9140) and **Beachside Gallery** (1st
Floor, 9 Hastings Street, Tel. 4474-5422) which are part of
Pages' Fine Art Galleries of Montville.

The **Gold Coast** is the major resort area in Queensland.
Centered at the town of Surfers Paradise, this is a booming
resort area of deluxe hotels, elegant restaurants, condominiums,
and shopping centers. You will find several typical beach resort-
type clothing and souvenir shops as well as nice quality arts,
crafts, and jewelry stores catering to the upmarket clientele that
stay at Surfers Paradise. Indeed, several shops in Sydney and
Melbourne have opened branch shops here in Surfers Paradise.
Most of the shops are found in and around the major shopping
centers and commercial streets of Surfers Paradise: **Centrepoint Arcade**, **Centre Arcade**, **Dolphin Arcade**, **The Market
Shopping Complex**, **Holiday City Galleria**, **Orchard
Avenue**, and **Elkhorn Avenue**.

BEST OF THE BEST

Brisbane has a few excellent shops that warrant special attention, especially if you have limited time to shop:

OPALS AND JEWELRY

❑ **Paragon Jewellery:** *Level 2, Wintergarden, Queen Street,
Mall, Tel. 3229-3848.* Offers a nice selection of opal
jewelry, from rings, pendants, and necklaces to opal face
watches.

ARTS, ANTIQUES, AND FURNITURE

❑ **Decorators Gallery:** *525 Boundary Street, Spring Hill, Tel.
3832-9500.* This remains one of our favorite shops in all
of Australia, one of first stops in Brisbane. In fact, several
of our most prized Australian treasures have come from
this shop. Essentially a decorator's gallery with strong
emphasis on quality Asian antiques and tribal arts and
crafts, the very informative owner/collector Ian Thomson
always seems to have unique pieces acquired through
private collections or auctions.

❑ **Far Pavilions:** *285 Given Terrace, corner of Haywood, Tel. 3368-3361.* Stocks a very nice collection of unique furniture handcrafted from old house timbers. Also includes many accessory and gift items.

❑ **Asian Connection:** *6 Edmonstone Street, West End, Tel. 3844-0566.* Here's the ultimate cluttered warehouse/emporium that is jam-packed to the rafters with arts, crafts, textiles, and furniture from Papua New Guinea, Indonesia, and India. Take your time browsing. This place can be overwhelming at first because of its large inventory. After a half hour or so, you may end up with an interesting handicraft or home decorative item.

ABORIGINAL ARTS AND CRAFTS

❑ **Queensland Aboriginal Creations:** *135 George Street, Tel. 3224-5730.* Operated by Aboriginals, this small shop includes an interesting collection of bark paintings, didgeridoos, boomerangs, clap sticks, books, and music. More oriented toward tourists in search of souvenirs than to serious collectors of Aboriginal art.

While Brisbane has a few interesting art galleries, art and craft shops, and markets, the largest and best are found in the northern craft towns of **Maleny and Montville**. We already featured on pages 150-152 several of the major shops and galleries, such as **Bold in Gold** and **Mitchell Gallery** in Maleny and **Tony Gill Galleries**, **Rainbird Gallery and Sculpture Garden**, and **Montville Art Gallery** in Montville.

ACCOMMODATIONS

Brisbane offers a wide range of accommodations for all types of budgets and travel styles. Its best hotels include:

❑ **The Heritage Brisbane:** *Edward Street, Brisbane, Qld 4001, Australia, Tel. (61 7) 3221-1999, Fax (61 7) 3221-6895. Website: www.theheritage.com.au.* A member of *The Leading Hotels of the World*, and winner of industry awards, The Heritage houses 232 deluxe rooms and 20 suites—each with panoramic views of the river. Works of art provide an ambience suggestive of a stately home. The spacious guestrooms are equipped with all the amenities expected in a luxury hotel. Large, well-lighted bathrooms have a TV and even a separate luggage room. The staff's attention to detail is the hotel's greatest asset. The Brasserie on the River offers buffet or a la carte dining or enjoy afternoon tea in traditional style. Siggi's, the Heritage's signature restaurant, won the 1999 National Award for "Best Fine Dining Restaurant in Australia". Kabuki serves Japanese cuisine with a flair and offers sushi cooking classes. Fitness Facilities; Business Services; Conference and Banquet Facilities.

❑ **Conrad International Treasury Brisbane**: *130 William Street, Brisbane, Qld 4000, Australia, Tel. (61 7) 3306-8888, Fax (61 7) 3306-8880.* The hotel is located in what was once the Lands Administration Building—a beautiful sandstone structure featuring Edwardian Baroque architecture. The Conrad International Casino, a block away, occupies the historic Treasury Building. The modern rooms—most with balconies—are complimented by antique furnishings. All the expected amenities, plus more, are offered in these luxurious rooms. The bathrooms offer every convenience. Ryans on the Park offers contemporary fresh cuisine and the award winning Marco Polo specializes in fusion cuisine—a blend of Asian and European flavors and dishes. Located in the Casino, Café 21 is open 24 hours for coffee and dessert or an a la carte meal. Health Facilities; Business Center; Meeting and Banquet Facilities.

❑ **Hilton Brisbane**: *190 Elizabeth Street, Brisbane, Qld 4000, Australia, Tel. (61 7) 3234-2000, Fax (61 7) 3231-3199.* Centrally located in the heart of the city overlooking Queen Street Mall, The Hilton features an eye-catching curved design and the largest atrium in the Southern Hemisphere—83 meters high and topped by a spectacular glass dome. All guestroom levels open onto the atrium giving a sense of spaciousness and light. 320 rooms, including 5 suites, offer first-class luxury accommodations. Three floors of Executive Rooms offer extra services and amenities. Victoria's, the hotel's signature restaurant, offers a sophisticated setting while the informal Atrium Café offers daily breakfast and lunch buffet in a bistro setting. Wintergarden Shopping Centre on the first three floors of the hotel. Fitness Facilities; Business Facilities; Convention and Banquet Facilities.

❑ **Sheraton Brisbane Hotel & Towers**: *249 Turbot Street, Brisbane, Qld 4000, Australia, Tel. (61 7) 3835-3535, Fax (61 7) 3835-4960.* Although this high-rise hotel is located above a major commuter rail station, it offers surprisingly quiet accommodations. The lobby is complimented by marble, brass and natural wood finishes made light and open by a skylit atrium. The 410 guestrooms include 18 suites. Both the guestrooms and baths are deluxe and provide all the expected amenities. Towers Rooms and Suites offer additional luxury and services. 3 restaurants and 3 lounges provide entertainment. Fitness Center; Business Center; Meeting Rooms and Banquet Facilities.

RESTAURANTS

Brisbane can be a gourmet's delight with its fresh seafood, beef, lamb, poultry, and pork dishes complimented by fresh tropical fruits and award-winning local wines. Look for lots of restaurants serving "Modern Australian Cuisine." While Brisbane's downtown shopping arcades are jam-packed with the usual mix of cafes, food courts, and restaurants, you'll also find many excellent restaurants in the city, the suburbs, Montville, and the coastal resorts. Some of this area's best restaurants include:

❑ **Siggi's at the Heritage:** *Heritage Hotel, Edward and Margaret Streets, Brisbane, Tel. 3221-4555. Reservations essential. Closed Sunday and Monday.* This award-winning restaurant (1999 National Award for "Best Fine Dining Restaurant in Australia") is the place for outstanding cuisine. Try the tasting menu on Wednesday and Thursday evenings. Changing menu with lots of excellent lamb dishes and desserts.

❑ **Michael's Riverside Restaurant:** *Riverside Centre, 123 Eagle Street, Tel. 3832-5522. Open lunch, Sunday-Friday and dinner, Monday-Saturday.* A long-time favorite, this award-winning restaurant includes wonderful views of the river. Offers modern Italian cuisine in a casual atmosphere. Excellent seafood, pastas, and meats. Offers Australia's most extensive cellar.

❑ **Il Centro:** *Eagle Street Pier, 1 Eagle Street, Tel. 3221-6090. Open daily except for lunch on Saturday.* Offers both indoor and outdoor dining with an excellent river view. Serves many fine Italian dishes, from ravioli to lasagna. Try their excellent desserts.

❑ **The Shingles Inn:** *254 Edward Street, Brisbane, Tel. 3221-9039. Closed Sunday.* Another long-time favorite, this aging restaurant offers wonderful homemade cakes and pastries as well as popular pavlova and lemon meringue pie.

❑ **Baguett Bar Café:** *150 Racecourse Road, Ascot, Tel. 3268-6168.* This bright eclectic bar and café serves excellent Mediterranean dishes. Try the wonderful prawn and risotto dishes. The bar also functions as a local art gallery.

❑ **Summit Restaurant:** *Mount Coot-tha Lookout, Sir Samuel Griffith Drive, Tel. 3369-9922. Open daily for lunch, dinner, and high tea. Café open daily, 7am-11pm.* Located 7 kilometers from the city center, this popular hill-top café and restaurant offers breathtaking views of Brisbane and Moreton Bay. Serves excellent char-grilled lamb and a unique cream of macadamia nut soup.

❑ **About Face:** *252 Kelvin Grove Road, Kelvin Grove, Tel. 3356-8605. Reservations essential.* Located 10 minutes from the city center, this innovative restaurant serves many unique modern Australian dishes that combine Asian, French, and Australian cooking into some fascinating new combinations. Be sure to try the great desserts.

❑ **Tables of Toowong:** *85 Miskin Street, Toowong, Tel. 3371-4558. Reservations essential. Closed Sunday and Monday.* Located 15 minutes from the city center, this imaginative restaurant serves excellent modern Australian dishes which combine Asia, French, and Australian menus and techniques. Try the tasting menu ("Just Dishes") of inventive appetizer-size portions of signature dishes.

❑ **Pier 9 Oyster Bar and Seafood Grill:** *Eagle Street Pier, 1 Eagle Street, Tel. 3229-2194.* One of Brisbane's very best seafood restaurants, offering everything from fish-and-chips to lobsters. For a real treat, try the blackened barramundi. Good wine selections.

❑ **Jimmy's on the Mall:** *Queen Street Mall, Tel. 3229-9999.* A long-time favorite, this elegant brasserie with its open kitchen offers an extensive menu of local favorites.

❑ **Kim Thank Chinese and Vietnamese Restaurant:** *99 Hardgrave Road, West End, Tel. 3844-4954.* Serves excellent Chinese and Vietnamese dishes. Try the barbecued prawns wrapped in sugarcane and Mongolian lamb.

ENJOYING YOUR STAY

Brisbane is one of the best organized cities in providing information to tourists. One of your first stops in Brisbane should be to the **Queensland Government Travel Centre** at Edward and Adelaide Streets, (Tel. 3213-1801). This office has a wealth of travel information on the city as well as the State of Queensland. You can book tours and hotels through this office. It also has a small information booth at the airport near the arrival area.

Brisbane Tourism, the city tourist and convention office, is located in the City Hall Building at King George Square (Tel. 3221-8411). It also provides maps and brochures on the city. In the middle of Queen Street Mall you will find a tourist information kiosk which has maps and brochures and personnel to answer questions.

The **Brisbane Visitors and Convention Bureau**, the official tourism and convention marketing authority for Brisbane, operates information booths at the following areas: Queen Street Mall Information Centre (Tel. 3229-5918) and City Hall, King George Square (Tel. 3221-8411).

Look for several useful publications provided by these tourist information offices both in the city and at the airport: *Hello Brisbane*, *This Week in Brisbane*, and *Dining Out in Brisbane*.

If you're interested in taking a city tour or visiting the Gold Coast, Noosa Heads, and the Sunshine Coast, contact **Australian Pacific Day Tours** (Brisbane Transit Centre, Roma Street, Level 3, Tel. 3236-4165).

Brisbane has a great deal to offer visitors in addition to shopping, hotels, and restaurants. Within the city you will find several historical and cultural sites worth visiting for their architectural interest: **The City Hall, Parliament House, The Treasury Building, Albert Street Uniting Church, St. John's Cathedral, The Observatory**, and **The State Library of Queensland**.

The **Queensland Cultural Centre**, located along the bank of the Brisbane River and directly across from the Victoria Bridge on Melbourne Street, is especially worth visiting. This is one of Australia's finest cultural centers. Consisting of a

Performing Arts Complex, Queensland Art Gallery, Queensland Museum, and State Library, you can easily spend a day exploring this attractive complex. Guided tours are available and take nearly three hours to complete. Look for special art exhibits and special performing arts groups.

You may want to cruise the Brisbane River. The **Kookaburra Queen**, a paddlewheeler, cruises the river daily from Eagle Street Pier, 1 Eagle Street. Call 3221-1300 for information on current departure times and costs.

Outside the city center you will find several interesting places to visit:

❑ **Lone Pine Koala Sanctuary:** This is one of Australia's most popular attractions and its largest sanctuary for more than 80 species of Australian native animals and birds, including koalas, kangaroos, wallabies, emus, wombats, platypus, and cockatoos. Located on Jesmond Road, Fig Tree Pocket (Tel. 3378-1366), 12 kilometers west of Brisbane, it is open seven days a week from 9:30am to 5pm. You can reach this sanctuary by taking a tour coach, taxi, or the ferry from North Quay at 2pm each day (Tel. 3378-1366).

❑ **Mount Coot-tha Botanic Gardens and Planetarium:** Located five kilometers west of the city at the foot of Mt. Coot-tha, this is a good place to get a panoramic view of the city as well as the D'Aguilar Mountains. The botanic gardens also include a planetarium.

❑ **New Farm Park:** *Located on Brunswick Street in New Farm,* this park has nearly 12,000 rose bushes that bloom from September to November, jacaranda annuals that bloom in October and November, and poinciana trees that bloom in November and December.

❑ **Alma Park Zoo:** *Alma Road, Kallangur, Tel. 3204-6566, Open daily, 9am-5pm.* Located 28 kilometers north of Brisbane, this popular zoo includes koalas, kangaroos, monkeys, camels, buffalo, and lots more. Hold the koalas during feeding times, 12:30-3pm daily.

❑ **Chinatown:** Located five minutes north of the city center in the suburb of Fortitude Valley, this is a good place for sampling Oriental foods, watching cultural performances, and shopping.

❑ **The Australian Woolshed:** *148 Samford Road in Ferny Hills, Tel. 3351-5366 (reservations).* Located 11 kilometers northwest of Brisbane, this popular program includes trained rams, sheep shearing, spinning, and sheepdog demonstrations. You can purchase wool products at their award-winning craft shop.

❑ **Sunshine Coast:** Located two hours north of Brisbane and centered in the town of Noosa Heads, this is a major seaside resort with fine beaches and hotels.

❑ **Gold Coast:** Located two hours south of Brisbane and centered in and around Surfers Paradise, this is Australia's most popular and commercialized resort area. A booming area of resort communities, high-rise hotels, condominiums, restaurants, entertainment spots, seven golf courses, Dreamworld, and shopping. If you like Miami, Fort Lauderdale, Waikiki, or Costa del Sol, and prefer to relax along beautiful beaches with thousands of others, you'll like the Gold Coast.

Nightlife in Brisbane can be most rewarding. Brisbane has a very active program of cultural events, from concerts, ballet, opera and theater to jazz and gambling. For upcoming events, be sure to look at Thursday "What's On Magazine" and the Saturday edition of the *Courier-Mail.* Most of Brisbane's major cultural activities are centered at the **Performing Arts Complex** (Melbourne Street, Tel. 3840-7444). If you're interested in gambling, head for the **Conrad Treasury Casino** at William and Elizabeth Streets, Tel. 3306-8888. Open 24-hours a day, this European-style casino includes 104 tables and 1,000+ slot machines. You'll also find several delightful bars, pubs, and nightclubs in Brisbane (try **Fridays** at 123 Eagle Street, Tel. 3832-2122) and **Hogie's Pool Bar and Nightclub** at 127 Charlotte Street, Tel. 3221-5555). Both the Gold Coast and Sunshine Coast have numerous bars, pubs, and related entertainment venues.

Whatever you do, don't just pass through Brisbane and the surrounding area on your way to the beach resorts or to other cities in Australia. Brisbane offers some wonderful shopping opportunities for unique local and Australian products. Spend at least three or four days here to enjoy its shopping and related activities. If you spend some time exploring its downtown area, suburbs, and craft towns you will be richly rewarded with some of the best shopping in Australia!

6

Cairns

C AIRNS IS A PLEASANT SURPRISE FOR THOSE who spend most of their time in the major beach resorts and cities further south or in the Outback to the south and west. A booming city along the mountainous northeastern shore of Tropical North Queensland, Cairns has become a tourist mecca for those who have discovered the many treasures and pleasures of this fascinating area. Once a small tropical town, it became famous in 1965 when one of the world's largest Black Marlins, weighing in at more than 1,000 pounds, was caught off the shores of Cairns. International sportsmen have flocked to Cairns ever since to experience the thrill of catching their own 1,000+ pounders! Today Cairns' popular marlin fleet consists of more than 30 boats that regularly take anglers on thrilling deep sea adventures, especially from late August to January.

THE NEW CAIRNS

Cairns is no longer a sleepy tropical town primarily frequented by backpackers in search of cheap eats, sleeps, and beaches. It has awakened to become a major tourist center for all classes of travelers, from budget to deluxe resort. It functions as a major gateway city to Australia's pristine rainforests, the Great Barrier Reef, the vast wilderness of Cape York Peninsula, the Northern Territory, and neighboring Papua New Guinea, Indonesia, and the Pacific Islands.

In the past few years, Cairns also has become a popular center for Japanese tourists and entrepreneurs who have invested heavily in Cairns tourist infrastructure, especially in hotels and shops that primarily cater to Japanese tourists and tour groups. In fact, the influx of Japanese tourists and investment has been a mixed blessing for locals. It was initially welcomed after a prolonged airline pilot strike in the early 1990s nearly devastated the local economy. However, for some local residents, it has been somewhat unsettling since the large and steady influx of Japanese tourists has had a major impact on the character of this city, from hotels to restaurants and shops. Cairns recent fortunes also have fluctuated with the ups and downs of the Japanese economy. In many respects, Cairns has become a Japanese tourist colony complete with Japanese shops, restaurants, and hotels. Indeed, this is a very Japanese-friendly city—signs are often in Japanese, prices are frequently quoted in Yen, and many sales personnel in shops are Japanese. Best of all, you can experience legendary Japanese service when you shop!

❑ Cairns has become a major tourist center for all classes of travelers, from budget to deluxe resort.

❑ A large and steady influx of Japanese tourists has had a major impact on the character of this city, from hotels to restaurants and shops.

❑ Expect to find some good shopping here for tribal artifacts, Australian arts and crafts, and tropical weight clothing and resort wear.

❑ We recommend spending at least three days–preferably five days–in Cairns. You'll find this area offers two to three good days of shopping and several additional days of attractions.

❑ Cairns is the best place to stop in transit to Papua New Guinea.

Still a small city with a decided resort atmosphere, Cairns offers an infinite variety of both hectic and relaxing tourist attractions to keep you busy for several days, if not weeks. It's a city that appeals to jet-setters and backpackers alike. Better still for us, it offers some very good shopping opportunities that are largely unknown to outsiders who primarily treat Cairns as a jumping-off point for recreational activities elsewhere in this part of Queensland. Indeed, visit a few of our "best of the best" shops, as well as explore the area's markets and craft towns, and you may be pleasantly surprised with what you find in Cairns as you begin viewing this city as more than just another way-station.

Getting to Know You

Cairns has long been neglected as a major destination. Preoccupied with the joys of fishing and reef walking, many visitors used to by-pass Cairns altogether. This was unfortunate because they missed some truly wonderful shopping opportunities in downtown Cairns as well as in nearby craft towns. In fact, if you read much about Australia, you still get the feeling that this is the type of town you should, at best, spend two or three hours in on your way fishing or visiting the Great Barrier Reef. But there is a lot more to Cairns these days that may entice you to visit this delight city for at least a few days.

Cairns has long had a reputation as a center, gateway, or jumping-off point for other more interesting attractions and activities in this part of the country: chartering a boat for big game fishing; visiting the Great Barrier Reef; exploring the beautiful beaches and Atherton Tablelands outside the city; discovering the world's oldest rainforests or flying from here to Papua New Guinea, Indonesia, or the Pacific Islands. As such, Cairns has exhibited little character of its own that would entice visitors to come to the city to spend more than a few hours or to actually book a hotel in the downtown area.

All this has changed during the past decade as new resort hotels, restaurants, casinos, entertainment complexes, galleries, and shopping centers have sprung up to service an increasing number of visitors who now stay here for a few days rather than just pass through Cairns on their way to elsewhere. Now you can easily spend a day or two shopping in Cairns and still need more time to enjoy its fine hotels and restaurants.

Cairns has a great deal to offer visitors, more so than many other more popular tourist destinations in Australia. This is a booming city and area. Resort complexes, such as Port Douglas 40 kilometers north of the city, cater to Cairn's growing international clientele. It has a sophisticated yet easy-going temperament—one more frequently associated with international beach resorts located in tropical areas not yet overrun by tourists. Its beautiful and varied typography of mountains, rainforests, Atherton Tablelands, rivers, ocean, reefs, and miles and miles of picturesque beaches make this one of Australia's most attractive areas to visit. It's easy to quickly fall in love with this beautiful and relaxing area.

Shopping in and around Cairns is surprising to many visitors who arrive misinformed about the city. Given Cairns' tropical setting, close proximity to Papua New Guinea, and the continu-

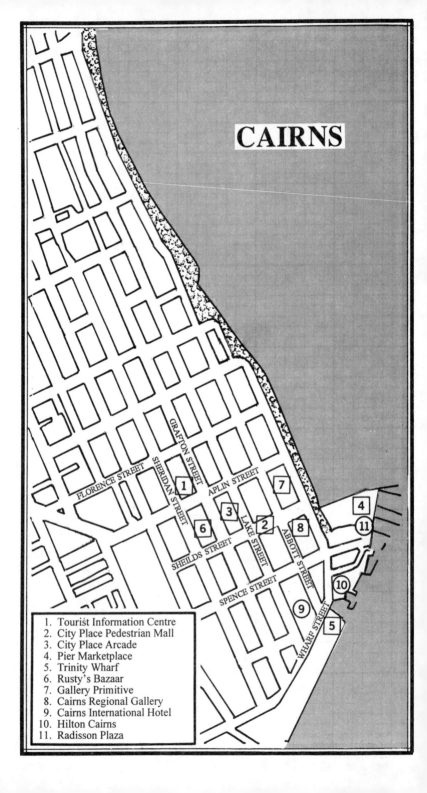

CAIRNS

1. Tourist Information Centre
2. City Place Pedestrian Mall
3. City Place Arcade
4. Pier Marketplace
5. Trinity Wharf
6. Rusty's Bazaar
7. Gallery Primitive
8. Cairns Regional Gallery
9. Cairns International Hotel
10. Hilton Cairns
11. Radisson Plaza

FLORENCE STREET
SHERIDAN STREET
GRAFTON STREET
APLIN STREET
LAKE STREET
SHEILDS STREET
ABBOTT STREET
SPENCE STREET
WHARF STREET

ing strong Australian craft tradition, expect to find some good shopping here for tribal artifacts, Australian arts and crafts, and tropical weight clothing and resort wear. And the shopping in Cairns can be exceptional. Within the downtown area, you will find one of Australia's best Papuan New Guinea tribal art (Gallery Primitive). You will also discover some very nice art galleries (Landmark Art and The Gallery Shop) and craft markets (Rusty's Bazaar and Karunda) both within and outside the city. In addition, numerous shops offer good selections of fashionable tropical weight clothing, sportswear, and swimwear. Outside Cairns, especially in the hill town of Karunda and the Tablelands as well as Port Douglas, you will find several shops offering exquisite arts and crafts unique to this area.

So plan to spend a little time here shopping and enjoying Cairns' varied recreational opportunities. We recommend spending at least three days—preferably five days—in Cairns. You will find this area offers two to three good days of shopping. You may also want to visit the many other attractions in and around Cairns. These can easily take another three days—if not a week or more!

If you plan to visit Papua New Guinea (PNG), Cairns is the best place to stop in transit to your first stop in PNG—the capital Port Moresby. In Cairns you will want to introduce yourself to what you will see in abundance in PNG—tribal artifacts. A few shops offer good selections of artifacts from PNG, many of which you may not find in PNG. You will want to see the range of artifacts as well as compare quality and prices. In general, we find the prices for PNG artifacts in Cairns to be two to three times higher than the prices in Port Moresby which, in turn, are three times higher than what you might pay along the Sepik River or 10 times more than what you might pay in remote tribal villages—if you can make such an adventure! However, the selections and quality may be better in Cairns and thus you will want to buy here rather than in Papua New Guinea.

If you plan to return to Cairns after visiting PNG, do your window shopping on your first visit to Cairns and then do your buying after you have had a chance to see your alternatives in PNG. But if you do not plan to return to Cairns, buy now since you may not find similar quality items in PNG, and certainly not from shops in most other Australian cities.

STREETS OF CAIRNS AND ENVIRONS

Shopping in and around Cairns primarily centers on three areas: downtown Cairns, the village of Kuranda, and the resort town of Port Douglas. You will find a few craft towns, such as Atherton, Mareeba, Yungburra, and Tolga, in the Tablelands west and south of Cairns.

Cairns is one of the easiest towns to get around in and shop. Similar in size to Darwin, Cairns' downtown area is laid out on a simple grid plan. The major shops, shopping centers, and hotels are concentrated in a four block area which is centered around a pedestrian mall called **City Place**. This area is bordered by The Esplanade, Florence Street, Sheridan Street, and Wharf Street, streets which front on or lead to the waterfront. The major shopping streets are Abbott, Lake, Grafton, Shields, Spence, and Wharf. Within this area you will find the Radisson Plaza Hotel, Cairns International Hotel, Hilton Hotel, Pacific International Hotel, Trinity Wharf, Orchard Plaza, Palm Court, Pier Marketplace, tourist information center, airline offices, restaurants, and banks. Most of the newer shops, as well as the whole downtown shopping area, are moving toward the Trinity Wharf. You can easily walk this whole area within 45 minutes.

The major shopping areas outside Cairns can be reached by car within 45 minutes. The tropical rainforest village of **Kuranda**, a small craft town 27 kilometers northeast of Cairns, can be reached by train, skyrail, or road. The train, which traverses a unique and mountainous 109-year old railway, leaves Cairns most days around 8:30, 9:00, and 9:30am for the scenic trip to Kuranda. The roundtrip takes approximately 3 hours. By road you can drive to the village within 45 minutes along a winding road that takes you through a tropical rainforest area. You also can reach Kuranda by the scenic 7.5 kilometer Skyrail which departs daily at 8:50am. You also can take the Skyrail one direction and the train the other direction for a thrilling day trip to Kuranda.

Within Kuranda you will find numerous shops and bazaars lining both sides of Kuranda's two main streets. Open daily— but very special when the popular Kuranda Heritage Markets are open (8am-3pm) Tuesdays, Wednesdays, Thursdays, Fridays, and Sundays—this is an attractive arts and crafts town offering many unique items for those who enjoy shopping in village bazaars and quaint crafts towns. The village also has the internationally acclaimed Tjapukai Dance Theatre (daily shows at 11am and 1:30pm) and the popular Australian Butterfly Sanctuary.

Port Douglas, an attractive resort community 65 kilometers north of Cairns, has a few shops worth visiting, especially for Queensland arts and crafts. The town can be easily reached by car within 45 minutes. However, you may want to stop along the way to enjoy the beautiful beaches that stretch for miles along this major highway to the northern end of Queensland. Within Port Douglas the major shopping is confined to the Marina Mirage Shopping Centre with its upmarket boutiques, jewelry, art, and handicraft shops as well as along Macrossan Street, the main street of the town.

Other shopping areas in the Cairns area include Paradise Shopping Village at **Palm Cove**, a small beachside resort shopping center 20 kilometers north of Cairns, and a few villages in the **Tablelands**. If you plan to drive to Kuranda or Port Douglas, you can easily stop at Palm Cove along the way. The major craft towns in the Atherton Tablelands—Mareeba, Atherton, Yungaburra, and Tolga—involve a day trip. You can stop at Kuranda along the way.

To best enjoy the Cairns area, we recommend that you rent a car as soon as you arrive in Cairns. Assuming you arrive by plane, you will find four car rental firms at the airport—Hertz, Avis, Thrifty, and Budget. If you rent a car here, you can save yourself the taxi fare into Cairns. With a car you will have the freedom to quickly cover all of the major shopping areas in and around Cairns as well as enjoy the beaches, mountains, and rainforests of this delightful area.

WHAT TO BUY

Cairn's major shopping strengths are the areas of ethnic and tribal arts, crafts, leather goods, clothes, resort wear, jewelry, and souvenirs. Unlike most other cities in Australia, the arts and crafts in Cairns come from four major groups and areas: Papua New Guinea, Indonesia, Australia, and Aborigine. You will also find many shops selling the latest in fashionwear, opals, and duty-free items.

TRIBAL AND ETHNIC ARTS

Cairns is one of the best places in Australia to shop for tribal and ethnic arts because of one shop. **Gallery Primitive** at 26 Abbott Street (Tel. 4031-1641) has one of the finest collections of primitive art from Papua New Guinea. This is a "must visit" shop for anyone interested in tribal and ethnic arts from PNG. The owner, Ed Boylan, has been in the PNG artifact collection business for more than 25 years. His eye for quality combined with his spirit of adventure takes him to some of the more remote and dangerous areas of PNG where he is able to find unique artifacts not available in other shops in Australia, or even in Papua New Guinea. You will find, for example, some very beautiful masks from the Black Water area in PNG which you seldom find elsewhere. This is the type of shop serious collectors of PNG artifacts will find interesting. Prices here are not cheap, but they are better than elsewhere in Australia as well as abroad. Best of all, you get unique and good quality items not readily available even in PNG. The shop also has a good quality Australian Aboriginal art collection which should appeal to serious collectors. This shop also does some of the best packing of any shop we encountered in Australia.

In Kuranda you will find one excellent shop—**Tropical Pulse** (1 Therwine Street, Tel. 4093-7369)—offering a unique collection of textiles, woodcarvings, and jewelry from Java and Bali in Indonesia as well as PNG. This shop has one of the best collections of Sumba ikat textiles (from Indonesia) in Australia.

FINE ART

Cairns also has its own artist colony. Several local artists produce excellent quality oils and watercolors that appear in several galleries in Cairns. One of the first places you should visit is the **Cairns Regional Gallery** (Tel. 4031-6865) at the corner of Abbott and Shields Streets in downtown Cairns. Located in a beautifully restored historical building, the gallery includes exhibitions, performances, and a shop (Gallery Shop) representing the best of northern Queensland artists. This is this best place to make contact with local artists. Indeed, some may be found sipping coffee in the gallery's café.

You'll find several other art galleries in Cairns, Kuranda, and Port Douglas. In Cairns, look for the **Landmark Gallery** (Bolands Centre, Spence Street, Tel. 4031-5735) which is Cairn's largest commercial gallery representing some of the region's top artists; **Reef Gallery** (Pier Marketplace, Tel. 4041-1292) for colorful prints, sculptures, and glass art by local artists; **Helen Wiltshire Studios** (Conservatory Arcade, 9-15 Abbott Street, Tel. 4031-7699) for colorful abstract paintings and some ceramics; and **Editions Gallery** (Village Lane, between Lake and Abbott Streets, Tel. 4031-2052) for the colorful tropical paintings of JoAnne Hook. In Port Douglas, the **Marina Gallery** (Shop 29, Marina Mirage, Tel. 4099-4310) has a good selection of paintings with nautical themes by local artists. Just outside Port Douglas, three miles off the main road (look for signs), is the small but unique **Mowbray Gallery** (Mowbray River Road, Tel. 4098-5580) which represents the works of 40 artists in the area (paintings, ceramics, glass, and jewelry). In Kuranda, look for the **Windmill Gallery** (Shop 5, Windmill Complex, 25 Coondoo Street, Tel. 4093-7223) for paintings by Ian Stephens and the **Wild North Gallery** (Shop 1/24 Coondoo Street, Tel. 4093-9310).

AUSTRALIAN ARTS AND CRAFTS

Artists and craftsmen in the Cairn's area have similar traditions as artists and craftsmen elsewhere in Australia: they tend to be a very independent group working from small houses, studios, and shops in the hills of northeast Queensland. They sell their products through several shops in downtown Cairns as well as in Kuranda, Port Douglas, and small towns in the Atherton Tablelands. You will find some exquisite work being done with ceramics, pottery, jewelry, and wood.

Some excellent arts and crafts shops to look for in **downtown Cairns** include the Cairn's branch of the excellent Sydney craft shop, **Australian Craftworks** (Shop 20 Village Lane, Lake Street, Cairns International Hotel, Tel. 4051-0725). It includes a its fine collection of quality crafts—wood, ceramics, leather, jewelry, and silk clothes. The **Gallery Shop**, which is part of the attractive Cairns Regional Gallery (Abbott and Shields Streets, Tel. 4031-6865), includes arts and crafts from the region's top artisans. **Uniquely Unique** (Shop 7 The Conservatory, 9-15 Abbott Street, Tel. 4031-3270) includes many unique Australian arts and crafts, especial ceramics, wood bowls, and casted figurines along with some paintings and prints.

Be sure to visit the major markets in Cairns for a large selection of Australian arts and crafts. For example, **Rusty's Bazaar** (Sheraton Street, between Spence and Shields Streets) on Friday night and Saturday and Sunday mornings is filled with small stalls selling a large variety of locally produced arts and crafts similar to those you will find in the markets and shops of Kuranda. **The Night Markets** on The Esplanade at Alpin Street (every night 5pm-11pm) include lots of stalls offering Australian made arts and crafts, jewelry, clothes, and souvenirs. **The Mud Markets** at the Pier Marketplace on

Saturday and Sunday include over 100 local artists and artisans offering numerous quality arts and crafts.

The rainforest village of **Kuranda** has several shops offering good quality arts and crafts. One of Kuranda's most popular attractions is the **Kuranda Heritage Markets** on Tuesday, Wednesday, Thursday, Friday, and Sunday. It's filled with many interesting arts and crafts stalls.

Port Douglas also has a few arts and crafts shops worth visiting. Most are found in the Marina Mirage shopping arcade on Wharf Street. The best shop here is the **Flying Stone Gallery** (Shop 27, Tel. 4099-5566) which represents the works of 10 artists who produce nice quality glass, ceramics, and jewelry. This shop also has a branch in Cairns (Shop 10, Village Lane, Tel. 4031-3515). Also, visit the **Candlenut Gallery** (10 Macrossan Street, Tel. 4099-4204) for locally produced woodwork, arts, craft, and furniture.

Other arts and crafts shops are scattered throughout the **Atherton Tablelands** area south of Kuranda. If you visit the towns of Mareeba, Atherton, Yungaburra, and Tolga you will find a few shops and galleries run by local craftsmen.

ABORIGINAL ART

Shops selling Aboriginal arts and crafts are by no means as numerous in Cairns as you would find in Darwin or Alice Springs. Nonetheless, you will find a few good quality shops offering some Aboriginal arts and crafts. Like so many other Aboriginal art shops in Australia, the ones in Cairns tend to carry lots of souvenir quality arts and artifacts. In **downtown Cairns**, look for The **Original Dreamtime Gallery** (Shop 22, Orchid Plaza, Abbott Street, Tel. 4051-3222). This is actually a branch shop of one of Alice Spring's leading Aboriginal galleries (63 Todd Mall). It includes a nice collection of paintings, boomerangs, didgeridoos, pottery, jewelry, boxes, books, batik and clothes. **Gallery Primitive** at 26 Abbott Street (Tel. 4031-1641) has a small but very good quality collection of Aboriginal artifacts that is more collector quality than souvenir quality. **Jabiru** (Tel. 4031-59643) at The Pier Marketplace and **Indigenous Creations** (Shop 10A, Boland Centre, Lake Street (Tel. 4031-0177) include lots of aboriginal artifacts and souvenirs. Most of the arts and crafts markets (Rusty's Bazaar, The Mud Markets, and The Night Markets) include Aboriginal arts and crafts.

In **Kuranda**, the **Tjapukai Dance Theatre** (Tel. 4093-7544) at the corner of Koondoo and Therwine Streets, which daily puts on very interesting Aborigine cultural performances, has a small shop offering Aboriginal arts and crafts. Also, visit **Doongal Aboriginal Art and Artefacts** (26 Coondoo Street, Tel. 4093-9003) for didgeridoos, boomerangs, paintings, and emu eggs. A few stalls in the **Kuranda Heritage Markets** also include Aboriginal arts and crafts.

JEWELRY AND OPALS

You will find several shops in and around Cairns offering jewelry and opals. For some of the best quality jewelry and opals, visit these two shops: **Regency Jewellers** (Orchid Plaza, 87 Abbott Street, Tel. 4031-2924), which owns an opal mine in Lightning Ridge and makes its own jewelry downstairs; and **Paragon Jewellery** (The Pier Marketplace, Tel. 4031-3848) which is branch shop of Paragon Jewellery in Brisbane (Wintergarden). Neither of these shops pay commissions to tour guides. Other popular jewelry and opal shops include **Evert Opals** (26 Abbott Street, Tel. 4051-2576); **Quilpie Opals** (The Conservatory, 9-15 Abbott Street, Tel. 4031-3688); **Gemex Opals** (57-59 Abbott Street, Tel. 4051-9833); **The Diamond Gallery** (46 Abbott, Tel. 4051-4460); and **The Sapphire and Opal Centre** (129 Abbott Street, Tel. 4051-6626). For uniquely designed jewelry and watches, stop at **Flying Stone Gallery** (Shop 10, Village Lane, Lake Street, Tel. 4031-3515).

FASHION AND RESORT WEAR

As a major resort area in Queensland, the Cairns area has numerous shops selling the latest in fashion and resort wear, from colorful swimsuits to fashionable evening wear. In downtown Cairns, most of the good quality fashion, accessory, and resort wear shops are found in The Pier Marketplace. Look for these popular shops on the ground level: **Australian Bush Trading Company, Benetton, Brian Rochford, Canterbury International, Country Road, Esprit, Hats by the Hundred, JAG, Just Jeans, Man Overboard, Mussfeldt Design, Nautica, Oroton, Shark Attack T-Shirts, The Docks, Tropic City Designs**, and **Weiss Art**.

You'll find numerous clothing shops in the many downtown shopping malls and street shops. For Australian mens wear, visit **Reef City** (29 Shields Street, Tel. 4051-1831). The popular Ken Done resortwear, swimwear, and sportswear can be found at **Done Art and Design** (4 Spence Street). For colorful knitware, visit **Coogi Connections** (Shop 5, Palm Court, 34

Lake Street). For a large selection of swimwear, stop by **Splish Splash** (78 Grafton Street, Tel. 4031-2724).

When visiting **Port Douglas**, be sure to browse through the many upmarket boutiques found in the Marina Mirage shopping center, such as the **Coogi Collection**, **Louis Vitton**, **Loewe**, **Polo Ralph Lauren**, and **Lacoste**.

AUSTRALIANA, SOUVENIRS, AND GIFTS

If you collect souvenirs or are looking for small gift items, especially T-shirts and shells, you've come to the right place. Cairn's abounds with souvenir shops selling everything from good quality arts and crafts to tourist kitsch. If you are interested in shell items, one of the largest and most unusual souvenir shops in Cairns—as well as Australia—is **The House of 10,000 Shells** at 32 Abbott Street (Tel. 4051-3638). This shop is packed with every conceivable item made from shells. **Presenting Australia** at The Pier Marketplace, The Conservatory (Abbott Street), and in Port Douglas (Marina Mirage shopping center on Wharf Street) is well stocked with all types of good quality Australiana, from clothes, stuffed koalas, sweaters, and mouse pads to boomerangs, hats, and knick knacks. In fact, you may want to do most of your Australiana, souvenir, and gift shopping in the Presenting Australia shops. Several souvenir and gift shops also can be found in The Pier Marketplace: **Jabiru**, **Glass Temptations**, **Mad's**, and **Lawrence Denham**. The Royal Flying Doctor Visitors Centre (1 Junction Street, Edge Hill, Tel. 4053-5687) also operates a T-shirt and souvenir shop called **The Outback Shop**.

For good selections of Australiana, souvenirs, and gifts, be sure to visit the **Night Markets**, **Mud Markets**, and **Rusty's Bazaar** in Cairns and the Kuranda Heritage Markets in Kuranda. We especially like the nice selections at the Saturday and Sunday indoor Mud Markets (The Pier Marketplace).

In **Kuranda** look for vendor stalls in the market as well as shops along Therwine and Coondoo Streets, especially **Things Unusual** and **Tropical Pulse**. The Marina Mirage shopping center at **Port Douglas** has a few Australiana, souvenir, and gift shops, such as **Presenting Australia** and **Crocodile Rock** (music shop).

DUTY-FREE SHOPS

Cairns major duty-free shop is **City International Duty Free** which has two locations: 77 Abbott Street (opposite the Cairns

Post Office) and the Cairns International Airport. Like duty-free shops elsewhere in Australia, this one carries a similar range of liquor, fragrances, cosmetics, watches, jewelry, fashion accessories, cameras, electronics, Australian opals, Australiana, souvenirs, and gifts.

WHERE TO SHOP

The Cairns area has three major shopping areas you can visit during your stay: downtown Cairns, Kuranda, and Port Douglas. You will also find a few shops in Paradise Shopping Village at Palm Cove and in the crafts towns of the Atherton Tablelands.

DOWNTOWN CAIRNS

Downtown Cairns is the major center for the region. Here you will find a pedestrian mall—City Place—surrounded by small shopping arcades, street shops, hotel shopping arcades, Trinity Wharf, and Rusty's Market. Somewhat worn and ticky-tacky with a decided souvenir and T-shirt look to it, it is worth spending some time browsing through the ins and outs of the arcades and shops that are found along six major shopping streets: Abbott, Lake, Grafton, Aplin, Shields, and Spence. Most of the best shopping is located near the southern end of Abbott Street toward the Cairns International Hotel and Trinity Wharf. Some of the best shops in this area are found in two shopping arcades, **The Observatory** (9-15 Abbott Street) and **Orchid Plaza** (87 Abbott Street), and along **Village Lane** (next to the Cairns International Hotel). A few shops in this area really stand out as exceptional: **Gallery Primitive** (26 Abbott Street, Tel. 4031-1641); **Australian Craftworks** (Shop 20, Village Lane, Cairns International Hotel, Tel. 4051-0725); **Gallery Shop** (Cairns Regional Gallery, corner of Abbott and Shields Streets, Tel. 4031-6865); **Regency Jewellers** (Orchid Plaza, 87 Abbott Street, Tel. 4031-2924); **Uniquely Unique** (Shop 7 The Conservatory, 9-15 Abbott Street, Tel. 4031-3270); and **Landmark Gallery** (Bolands Centre, Spence Street, Tel. 4031-5735).

Much of downtown Cairn's best shopping is found at **The Pier Marketplace** which is located adjacent to the Radisson Plaza Hotel and Marlin Marina. This expansive indoor air-conditioned shopping mall includes more than 100 specialty shops, restaurants, and tour operators. It includes numerous fashion and accessory shops, such as the popular **Brian Rochford, Canterbury International, Country Road, JAG, Oroton,** and **Weiss Art,** as well as a few excellent quality jewelry shops (**Paragon Jewellery**), Australiana stores (**Presenting Australia** and **Jabiru**), and art galleries (**Reef Gallery**). The Pier Marketplace is especially lively on the weekends when the ground floor is turned into a huge indoor market called **The Mud Markets.** Over 100 local artists and artisans set up vendor stalls from which they offer a wide selection of arts and crafts. Live entertainment adds to the festive atmosphere.

Immediately south of The Pier Marketplace is **Trinity Wharf** which includes several fashion, resortwear, and souvenir shops along with restaurants.

In addition to The Mud Markets, you may want to browse through the nightly **Night Markets** on The Esplanade (Alpin Street, 5pm-11pm). It consists of numerous stalls offering arts and crafts, jewelry, clothes, souvenirs, and produce. If you're looking for inexpensive gifts and souvenirs, this is good place to do some evening shopping. On Friday night and Saturday and Sunday morning, you may want to visit another local arts and crafts market, **Rusty's Bazaar** (Sheraton Street, between Spence and Shields Streets). The many small stalls here offer a large variety of locally produced arts, crafts, clothes, and fresh produce.

The rainforest village of **Kuranda** has several shops offering good quality arts and crafts. Be sure to visit the **Kuranda Heritage Markets** on Tuesday, Wednesday, Thursday, Friday, or Sunday.

KURANDA VILLAGE

The small tropical rainforest village of Kuranda is located 27 kilometers northwest of Cairns. As very popular tourist center, it can be reached by train, skyrail (cable car), and road. A gateway to the Atherton Tableland area, Kuranda is famous for its arts and crafts shops, the Kuranda Heritage Markets, the award-winning Tjapukai Dance Theatre (daily performances at 11am and 1:30pm), and the Australian Butterfly Sanctuary (daily 10am-3pm). You will find numerous shops lining Kuranda's two main streets—Therwine and Coondoo Streets. Most of these shops are open seven days a week and they offer some of the best selections of arts, crafts, and clothes in the Cairns area. Be sure to visit the Kuranda Heritage Markets which are open on Tuesdays, Wednesdays, Thursdays, Fridays, and Sundays.

Over 100 vendors set up tables to sell their products: arts, crafts, clothes, leather goods, T-shirts, Australiana, souvenirs, and gifts. There's a little of something for everyone here. The markets are larger versions of Rusty's Market found in downtown Cairns on the weekends.

While Kuranda is more crowded, touristy, and festive during the market days, you may want to visit Kuranda on the non-market days (Saturday and Monday) when there are fewer crowds and tour groups descending on the town. Most of the shops remain open during the week, and these other days will give you an opportunity to shop Kuranda at a much more leisurely pace. While the markets are the big drawing card to visiting Kuranda, they are by no means exceptional given their decidedly tourist orientation. The really good shopping in Kuranda is found in a few quality shops that line the two main streets of Kuranda.

Some of our favorite shops in Kuranda are the **Windmill Gallery** (Shop 6, Windmill Centre, 25 Coondoo Street, Tel. 4093-7223), **Kuranda Inn Crafts** (Tel. 4093-7142), **Wild North Gallery** (Shop 1/24 Coondoo Street, Tel. 4093-9310), **Jasmine Opals** (Windmill Centre, Tel. 4093-9087), **The Rainforest Shop** (Windmill Centre, Tel. 4093-8945), and **Tropical Pulse** (1 Therwine Street,Tel. 4093-7369).

PORT DOUGLAS

Port Douglas, located approximately 65 kilometers north of Cairns, is an attractive resort community of special appeal to upmarket travelers who enjoy the comforts and convenience of a full service resort complex, complete with a golf course and marina.

Port Douglas has three major shopping areas. The downtown area of the original town has one main street—**Macrossan Street**. You'll find a few arts and crafts shops as well as tour companies here.

Less than 1 kilometer from the main street is the relatively quiet **Sunbird Centre** of the Mirage Port Douglas Resort. This is a small shopping complex with a few clothing stores and services.

The real center for shopping is the **Marina Mirage** shopping complex on Wharf Street. It includes nearly 40 upmarket shops catering to the shopping tastes of Port Douglas' resort clientele. For fashion and accessories, look for **Coogi Collection, Louis Vuitton, Loewe, Polo Ralph Lauren**, and **Lacoste. Presenting Australia** offers good quality Australiana, gifts, and souvenirs. **Marina Gallery** includes a nice selection of paintings by local artists. **Flying Stone Gallery** is an upscale craft gallery. You'll also find several nice restaurants in this area.

PALM COVE

Palm Cove is located 20 kilometers north of Cairns. You can easily stop here on your way to either Kuranda or Port Douglas. As you travel north of Cairns, look for a small sign on your right which directs you to the Ramada Reef Resort. This is the Palm Cove area.

Palm Cove is a lovely, quiet beachside resort area where you will find the Novotel Palm Cove Resort, Ramada Great Barrier Reef Resort, Alamanda, and the Reef House hotels and a few other smaller hotels. It has a small shopping center—**Paradise Shopping Village**—with a few shops selling resort wear and arts and crafts.

ATHERTON TABLELANDS

Time permitting, you may want to drive to the Atherton Tablelands area which is located approximately 40 kilometers south of Kuranda. Four roads lead into this area. Lying at an elevation of 760 meters above sea level, the Atherton Tableland has a temperate climate, up to 10 degrees cooler than the tropical coastline. Here you will find several small towns with arts and crafts shops.

The major towns to visit for shopping purposes are Mareeba, Atherton, Tolga, Kairi, and Yungaburra—all within 100 kilometers of Kuranda. In Tolga, visit **Tolga Woodworks** (Kennedy Highway, Tel. 4095-4488) for uniquely crafted wood bowls, platters, vases, knife blocks, plates, and boxes as well as local pottery, leather hats, and prints by local artists. In Kairi look for **Kairi Pottery** (40-42 Irvine Street, Tel. 4095-8318) for dinner ware, platters, terracotta, and lamp bases.

BEST OF THE BEST

AUSTRALIAN ARTS AND CRAFTS

❑ **Australian Craftworks:** *Shop 20, Village Lane (Cairns International Hotel), Tel. 4051-0725.* Outstanding collection of fine arts and crafts from Australia's best artisans and craftspeople. Wonderful ceramics, woodcraft, glass, and clothes.

❑ **Gallery Shop:** *Cairns Regional Gallery, corner of Abbott and Shields Streets, Tel. 4031-6865.* Offers some of the best quality arts and crafts from the region.

❑ **Uniquely Unique:** *Shop 7 The Conservatory, 9-15 Abbott Street, Tel. 4031-3270.* A small shop but offers a nice selection of unique Australian works of art, wood turned bowls, paintings, and prints to ceramics and casted figurines.

TRIBAL AND ABORIGINAL ART

❑ **Gallery Primitive:** *26 Abbott Street, Tel. 4031-1641.* One of Australia's very best tribal arts shops with a terrific collection of good quality artifacts from Papua New Guinea and the Aborigines.

❑ **Original Dreamtime Gallery:** *Shop 22, Orchid Plaza, Abbott Street, Tel. 4051-3222.* Includes a good range of Aboriginal arts, crafts, and souvenirs, from paintings, didgeridoos, and boomerangs to pottery, jewelry, and clothes. Part of the Original Dreamtime Gallery in Alice Springs.

FINE ART

❑ **Landmark Gallery:** *Bolands Centre, Spence Street, Tel. 4031-5735.* Owned by painter Dean Vella, who produces very vibrant colored paintings of animals, this is the largest commercial art gallery in Cairns. Represents some of Australia's bestselling artists, including Pro Hart.

OPALS AND JEWELRY

❑ **Regency Jewellers:** *Orchid Plaza, 87 Abbott Street, Tel. 4031-2924.* Nice selection of opals directly from the shop's mines in Lightning Ridge. Makes jewelry on premises using opals and Argyle diamonds. Offers several unique designs.

❑ **Paragon Jewellery:** *The Pier Marketplace, Tel. 4031-3848.* Offers a good range or opal and gold jewelry. Also has a shop in Brisbane.

ACCOMMODATIONS

❑ **Hilton Cairns:** *Wharf Street, Cairns, Qld 4870, Australia, tel. (61 7) 4050-2000, Fax (61 7) 4050-2001. Web site: www.hiltoncairns.com.au.* The Hilton Cairns offers all the amenities expected from a five-star hotel and having recently completed a major renovation (1997) offers exceptional luxury as well. Guests enter the lobby from a raised level which affords views across the glass-enclosed lobby to Trinity Inlet and mountains beyond. A clear glass dome in the lobby serves as a huge skylight for the open atrium and accommodation tower decked with hanging tropical gardens and birds. The 265 guestrooms include in-room safe, tea and coffee making facilities as well as a mini-bar. Modem connections are provided. Bathrooms provide separate bathtub and shower facilities. Executive Floor guests enjoy extra amenities and services. Winner of several awards, Breezes Restaurant, located off the main lobby, enjoys a beautiful view of Trinity Inlet and serves a wide selection of Australian cuisine. Mondo Café Bar and Grill, winner of *Best Café Bistro* award from the Australian Hotel Association, serves light snacks, grills and beverages. Fitness Facilities; Business Center; Meeting & Banquet Facilities. Winner (1998) of excellence award for best meeting venue in North Queensland.

❑ **Radisson Plaza Hotel at the Pier:** *Pierpoint Road, Cairns, Qld 4870, Australia, tel. (61 7) 4031-1411, Fax (61 7) 4031-5340, toll-free from U.S. or Canada 800-333-3333. Web site: www.radisson.com/cairnsau.* A luxury accommodation award winner (1999), the Radisson Plaza Hotel boasts a large expanse of water frontage at the edge of Trinity Bay and a distinctive Queensland design. The rainforest lobby is accented by a Great Barrier Reef aquarium enhanced by natural timbers on the boardwalk. The spacious 219 guestrooms, including 21 suites, feature private balconies with seating. In-room safe deposit boxes, tea and coffee making facilities and mini-bar in rooms as well as other amenities expected from a 5-star international hotel. Business class rooms have individual dataports. Large bathrooms feature oversized bathtub and a separate shower. The award winning Sirocco Restaurant overlooks the water inlet. Themes Restaurant offers casual indoor or outdoor dining overlooking the poolside terrace and tropical gardens, or enjoy a candlelight dinner on your private balcony. With over 100 speciality stores adjoining the hotel and only two minutes from the city center, the location is convenient. Fitness Center; Business Center; Meeting and Banquet Facilities.

❑ **Cairns International Hotel:** *17 Abbott Street, Cairns, Qld 4870, Australia, Tel. (61 7) 4031-1300, Fax (61 7) 4031-1801, toll-free from U.S. 800-327-0200.* From the moment the guest enters the lobby, the Cairns International exudes luxury. The marble floor, warm wood of the balconies, soft white columns and walls, and brass and glass chandeliers are all suggestive of the elegance within. 321 rooms, including 5 suites, provide expected amenities which include in-room safe, tea and coffee making facilities, and mini-bar. The Kingsford Restaurant for fine dining or Café Coco for informal all-day dining. Hotel connects to Village Lane, a retail shopping village set under a canopy of verandahs and tropical trees. Fitness Facilities; Business Facilities; Conference and Banquet Facilities.

❑ **Pacific International Cairns:** *The Esplanade, Cairns, Qld 4870, Australia, Tel. (61 7) 4051-7888, Fax (61 7) 4052-1385.* With a waterfront location on the Esplanade overlooking Trinity Harbour, the Pacific International is a four-star hotel which has gained a reputation for award winning cuisine and good service. A soaring three story lobby, classic rattan furniture, Queensland timbers, gleaming brass, and island tapa create a tropical ambience. 180 guestrooms, including 16 suites, offer mini-bar and tea and coffee making facilities among the amenities. The award winning Waterfront Seafood Restaurant features fresh local seafood; the new Café Pacifico specializes in fast, efficient service. Monsoon Wood Fired Piazza Kitchen serves gourmet pizzas and freshly made pasta. Fitness Center; Business Center; Conference and Banquet Facilities.

RESTAURANTS

Like other cities in Australia, Cairns has a good selection of Australian and ethnic restaurants as well as food courts and outdoor eateries. Given Cairns many Japanese visitors, you'll find several good Japanese restaurants here. Some of Cairns best restaurants include:

AUSTRALIAN

❑ **Sirocco Restaurant:** *Radisson Plaza Hotel at the Pier, Pierpoint Road, Tel. 4031-1411. Open for lunch, Tuesday to Friday; dinner, Tuesday to Saturday. Reservations essential.* This outstanding fine dining restaurant serves both modern Australian and international cuisines. Try the many inventive Australian dishes, such as char-grilled fresh reef with sweet potato mash and smoked duck breast. Great desserts. Excellent service.

❑ **Red Ochre Grill:** *43 Shields Street, Tel. 4051-0100. No lunch on Sunday.* This modern Australian restaurant serves creative char-grilled dishes using many exotic ingredients such as lemon aspen, bunya nuts, kurrajong seed, illa-warra plums, macadamias, pepper leaf, wattle seed, quandong, and kakadu plums. It's often an adventure in dining as well as great table conversation when ordering kangaroo, emu, baked wattle seed damper, and pepper leaf foccacia. Also serves excellent seafood.

❑ **Dundees:** *Corner of Aplin and Sheridan Streets. Tel. 4031-2155. Open nightly from 6pm for dinner.* Serves exotic Australian cuisine in an informal, tropical setting—seafood, crocodile, buffalo, emu, beef, and pasta.

INTERNATIONAL

❑ **Kingsfords:** *Cairns International Hotel, 17 Abbott Street, Tel. 4031-1300.* An award-winning restaurant serving international cuisine in informal and elegant surroundings.

❑ **Themes Restaurant:** *Radisson Plaza Hotel, The Pier Marketplace, Tel. 4031-1411. Open daily for breakfast and* *dinner. Reservations essential.* This innovative restaurant constantly offers new menus, new dishes, and new dining themes from around the world.

SEAFOOD

❑ **Breezes Brasserie:** *Hilton International Cairns, Wharf Street, Tel. 4052-6786. Dinner only.* This very attractive restaurant with a nice view of Trinity Inlet, serves an excellent seafood and Asian buffet nightly.

❑ **Tawney's:** *Wharf Street, Tel. 4051-1722. Reservations essential.* This award-winning longtime favorite restaurant serves excellent seafood in a waterfront setting.

❑ **Pesci's:** *The Pier Marketplace, Tel. 4041-1133.* Open daily from 7:30am until late. This bar and bistro offers both indoor and outdoor dining. Serves local seafood with a Southern European influence.

JAPANESE

❑ **Yamagen:** *40 Abbott Street, Tel. 4031-6688.* Excellent Japanese restaurant located next to the Cairns International Hotel.

❑ **Cherry Blossom:** *Corner of Spence and Lake Streets, Tel. 4052-1050.* This popular Japanese restaurant is open for lunch Monday through Friday and dinner daily. Includes sushi bar, teppanyaki bar, and a-la-carte restaurant.

ITALIAN AND GREEK

❑ **Roma Roulette:** *48 Aplin Street, Tel. 4051-1076.* No dinner on Monday or Tuesday. Popular Italian restaurant known for its friendly atmosphere and popular dishes, such as *pasta tricolore* and *scaloppine al vino bianco*. Serves excellent seafood dishes.

❑ **Greek Taverna:** *Corner of Aplin and Grafton Streets, Tel. 4041-1500. Open nightly for dinner.* If you're hankering for Greek cuisine, here's the restaurant you've been waiting for. Serves innovative Greek and seafood cuisine.

CHINESE

❑ **Welcoming Dragon Restaurant:** *Corner of Spence and Grafton Streets, Tel. 4031-0688.* Features contemporary Chinese cuisine. Specializes in Peking/Cantonese style cooking with excellent seafood and noodle dishes.

INDIAN

❑ **Indian Restaurant:** *Corner of Spence and Sheridan Streets (61 Spence Street), Tel. 4051-2228.* This award-winning Indian restaurant offers excellent curries and vegetarian dishes. Authentic cuisine but adjusts the spices to individual palates, from mild to very hot and spicy.

ENJOYING YOUR STAY

As noted earlier, most people come to Cairns for everything other than shopping. It's only after being in the area for a few days that they begin discovering many of Cairns' shopping delights. And some visitors leave too little time to shop downtown Cairns, Kuranda, Port Douglas, Palm Cove, or the Atherton Tablelands. If you enjoy shopping, we recommend that you include two days in your schedule just for shopping. We also suggest that you rent a car to shop this area on your own. Use tours to do what most other visitors to the Cairns area do—see the Great Barrier Reef and go sportfishing.

If you don't know where to initially stay or what to do, be sure to stop at the information and booking office in the arrivals area of the international airport terminal or at the currency exchange in the domestic terminal for tourist information. These offices should be able to give you a great deal of useful information for getting oriented to Cairns and its surrounding areas. You should be able to pick up lots of free tourist literature, such as *Hello Cairns*, *Welcome to Cairns*, and *Cairn's Ultimate Shopping Guide*.

Most visitors come to Cairns to see the **Great Barrier Reef** to do reef walking, snorkeling, scuba diving, or just lying on the sandy beaches to soak up the sun. Indeed, Cairns is one of the major departure points along the East Coast for visiting the reef. Green Island is the major reef watching destination from Cairns. Several tour groups sponsor day cruises to the Great Barrier Reef.

You will find a great deal of literature in your hotel and at the tourist information center which advertises tours to the Great Barrier Reef. We do not recommend any particular tours since each one is slightly different in terms of cost, itinerary, and group and ship size. Some tours, for example, allow you time to walk on the reef, snorkel, and swim whereas others spend most of the time getting to and from the reef, with little time available for recreational activities. On the other hand, you may not want to spend four hours waiting for everyone else to enjoy the water. Therefore, it's best to look over the literature, compare tours, and decide on which tour best meets your interests and needs.

If you enjoy **sportfishing**, you've come to the right place. Cairns has a well deserved reputation as the world's center for Black Marlin fishing. Sport fishermen come from all over the world to fish in the waters outside Cairns where Black Marlins weighing more than 1000 lbs. (455 kgs.) have been caught. You can charter fully equipped boats in Cairns to take you on a fishing adventure of a lifetime. If you don't catch the big Black Marlin, there are plenty of good-sized sail fish, Spanish mackeral, tuna, dolphins, barracuda, and sharks to keep your fishing interests high.

The Cairns area is also famous for its **rainforests and Tablelands**. As we noted earlier, Kuranda is one of the gateways to the tropical Atherton Tablelands. This picturesque area includes rainforests, extinct volcanic lakes, waterfalls, gorges, rich farmlands, ancient limestone caves, and rolling plains. You can easily spend a full day or two exploring this area. While you can take a tour to Kuranda as well as into the Tablelands, you can also rent a car and easily drive to this area. We recommend starting in Kuranda and then proceed to Mareeba, the largest town in the Tablelands only 37 kilometers from Kuranda. Proceed from there to Tolga, Kairi, Lake Tinaroo, Atherton, Yungaburra, and Malanda. In addition to seeing interesting sights in the Tablelands, you will also find several small arts and crafts shops in these towns. You can return to Cairns by way of Lake Barrine or Innisfail.

Whatever you do, you will find plenty to do in Cairns. More adventuresome visitors might head further north to the **Cape York area**, the northern most point in Australia. Indeed, you will find regular air service from Cairns to Australia's remote northern areas such as Cooktown, Mt. Isa, Normanton, Karumba, Buretown, Mornington Island, and Doomadgee as well as nostalgic 'Gooney Bird' air tours of Cape York Peninsula (contact DC-3 Queensland at 4053-7819). Others might want to try a wilderness safari into the **Daintree River** and **Daintree**

National Park areas northwest of Port Douglas or go white-water rafting, hot air ballooning, or para-sailing.

If you plan to proceed on to **Papua New Guinea**, Cairns is a good place to relax before encountering a totally different culture and society. In Cairns you can prepare for your new adventure. For Papua New Guinea is different—wild, colorful, and intriguing. Get a glimpse of this fascinating country by visiting the tribal artifact shop in downtown Cairns (Gallery Primitive) as well as contacting Air Niugini Cairns (Tropical Arcade, Shields Street, Tel. 4031-1611) for information on tours to the Highlands (Ambua Lodge) and the Sepik River (Karawari Lodge). Papua New Guinea is a different world than what you have seen in Australia thus far. You will be entering a country that has quickly moved from the Stone Age into the 20th century, a country where over 700 languages are spoken amongst its hundreds of diverse ethnic and cultural groups. This is a beautiful and fascinating country of former headhunters, remote valleys and villages, raging rivers, steaming jungles, colorful tribes, proud warriors, and incredibly rich and continuously productive artistic traditions. However you travel and wherever you stay in Papua New Guinea, you will have fond memories of your Cairns experience and look forward to returning there again.

7

Darwin

DARWIN IS A SURPRISING CITY FOR MANY
first-time visitors. Very friendly and laid back, it's
Australia's only tropical capital. Situated at the
Top End of Australia's Northern Territory, an area
larger than the U.S. State of Texas, Darwin still has
the look and feel of a frontier town that is content in being left
alone to develop its own unique character.

With a population of only 80,000 and a suburban area of
nearly 20,000, over 50 percent of the Northern Territory's
population of 200,000 live within a 40 kilometer radius of
Darwin. Functioning as Australia's gateway to Southeast Asia,
Darwin is relatively isolated from the rest of the country.
Accessible primarily by air, its closest state capital is Adelaide,
a 3,620 kilometer trek south along the hot and boring Stuart
Highway. In many respects, Darwin is a case of splendid
isolation. If you're like us, you'll really enjoy this unique place.

DELIGHTFUL DISCOVERIES

While more and more tourists are discovering this delightful
city and its wonderful environs, Darwin still remains off the
beaten tourist path. It's a city tourists are likely to visit only

after stopping first in Sydney, Melbourne, Brisbane, Perth, and Adelaide. It's a particularly popular city for backpackers and budget travelers who arrive here from Thailand, Malaysia, Singapore, and Indonesia (only a 2½ flight from Bali) on their way to other parts of Australia or who use Darwin as their gateway city to Southeast Asia, especially for visiting inexpensive neighboring Indonesia.

Best of all, Darwin, its suburbs, and the Tiwi islands of Bathurst and Melville offer some of Australia's most unique shopping. Here, you will find very lovely Aborigine arts, Australian crafts, and uniquely designed jewelry largely unavailable elsewhere in Australia. Being a small and well laid out city, it's relatively easy to shop Darwin in a couple of leisurely days.

GETTING TO KNOW YOU

Darwin is an interesting **city of contrasts, commitment, and cultures**. Begun with Australia's gold rush in 1871, the city survived 60 Japanese bombings during World War II and three devastating cyclones, the most recent being Cyclone Tracy in 1974. Completely rebuilt since the 1970s, today Darwin is a pleasant mix of modern architecture in the midst of Top End residential relics from the pre-1974 cyclone period.

It's a city long ago discovered by Asian immigrants, Greeks, Italians, sailors, fishermen, investors, and budget travelers, and more recently by Asian gamblers, resort-goers, curious fans of *Crocodile Dundee*, and Australians themselves. It's a city that is discovered by more and more tourists each year who enjoy urban comforts while participating on the edge of the rugged and ever fascinating Outback of Aborigines, natural beauty, and incomparable flora and fauna. It's one of Australia's best adventure travel destinations where visitors can explore the rugged Outback by four-wheel drive vehicles, small aircraft, or seaplanes. Spend a week here and you will feel you have just begun to discover the "real Australia" so many others miss by only visiting the East Coast, Sydney, and Melbourne.

Darwin is Australia's **gateway city to Southeast Asia** and an important expression of the Australian character. More than any other Australian city, Darwin is more oriented to its Asian neighbors than to cities in the southeast. Indeed, it recently became a major supplier of live cattle to Vietnam (12,000 to 40,000 head per year), and it expects trade relations with Vietnam and other parts of Asia to expand considerably in the coming years. International flights from Singapore, Brunei, Jakarta, and Bali, for example, regularly fly in and out of

Darwin. Many local residents still find it cheaper to travel and shop in Singapore and Bangkok or lie on the beaches of Southern Thailand, Eastern Malaysia, and Bali than to head for Australia's more expensive Sydney, Melbourne, and the East Coast. Darwin's multiracial population and ethnic restaurants and markets reflect the fact that this city has become a popular home for Australia's resident Chinese, Vietnamese, Malays, Thai, and Indonesians.

Here's the city of *Crocodile Dundee*, where hard-driving, beer-drinking, Outback cowboys come in from the never-never land of the Northern Territory. Sometimes wild, but often wacky, Darwin is very much a part of the Australian character that is so often communicated abroad. This is where stereotypes of Australia, however true or false, tend to arise and take on a life of their own.

Darwin is also a center for some of Australia's most interesting **Aboriginal tribes** as well as a central marketing and distribution point for **Aboriginal art**. On the one hand, you will find Aboriginal artists from Arnhem Land (east of Darwin, near Kakadu National Park) producing bark paintings in "Dreamtime" themes. On the other hand, you encounter the Tiwi peoples of Bathurst and Melville Islands who produce bark baskets, carved poles, and textiles in colorful abstract designs completely devoid of "Dreamtime" themes. At the same time, and to the dismay of many local residents and visitors, you may meet small groups of Aborigines roaming the streets of downtown Darwin. Not all are sober nor friendly, but they do not bother visitors.

❑ Darwin still has the look and feel of a frontier town that is content in being left alone to develop its own character.

❑ More than any other Australian city, Darwin is more oriented to its Asian neighbors than to cities in the southeast. Indeed, many local residents still find it cheaper to travel and shop in Singapore and Bangkok or lie on the beaches of Southern Thailand, Eastern Malaysia, or Bali than to head for Australia's more expensive Sydney, Melbourne, and the East Coast.

❑ Since the city and suburbs are spread over a 25 kilometer area, expect to do a great deal of walking as well as traveling by car or bus between major shopping areas.

❑ Darwin is famous for its pearls because of the close proximity of pearl farms in the Darwin area and the presence of Paspaley Pearls, one of the world's pioneers of South Sea pearl farming.

This is also a **resort city** for tourists who have discovered Darwin's irresistible combination of great weather, fine hotels and restaurants, a colorful Outback, wild and wonderful Kakadu National Park, outstanding boating and sportfishing opportunities, picturesque islands, beautiful beaches and sunsets, dramatic lightning, a fine museum, a fun casino, colorful markets, and some of Australia's most interesting

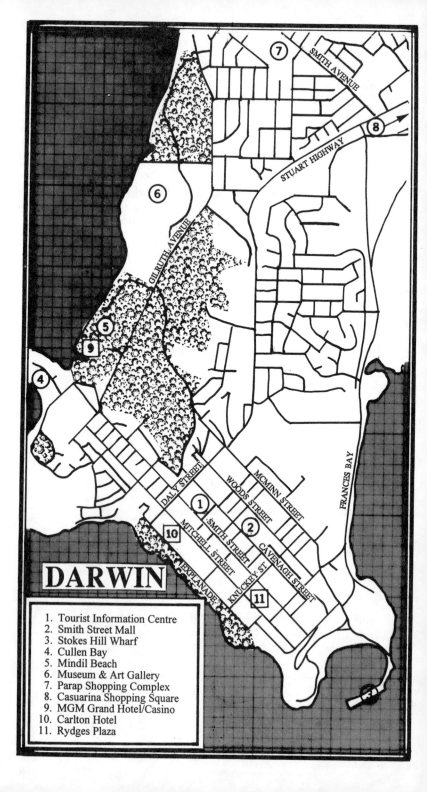

DARWIN

1. Tourist Information Centre
2. Smith Street Mall
3. Stokes Hill Wharf
4. Cullen Bay
5. Mindil Beach
6. Museum & Art Gallery
7. Parap Shopping Complex
8. Casuarina Shopping Square
9. MGM Grand Hotel/Casino
10. Carlton Hotel
11. Rydges Plaza

SMITH AVENUE
STUART HIGHWAY
GILRUTH AVENUE
FRANCES BAY
DALY STREET
MCMINN STREET
WOODS STREET
SMITH STREET
CAVENAGH STREET
MITCHELL STREET
KNUCKEY ST.
ESPLANADE

shopping. It's all set here in the bright and bustling town of Darwin where there's plenty to see and do in splendid isolation from the rest of Australia, and Asia.

Darwin also has the feel of tropical Southeast Asia. Famous for its frequent lightning and its two-season climate (hot and wet), Darwin's hot and humid weather, palm trees, beaches, and sunny and balmy days remind one of similar places in Indonesia, Singapore, and Malaysia. No need to pack your winter clothes for Darwin. The pleasant sunny, but occasionally wet, climate calls for causal summer clothes, an umbrella, hat, and suntan lotion.

THE STREETS OF DARWIN

Being a relatively small yet sprawling city, Darwin is easy to get around by bus or car. Taxi stands are plentiful, but taxis seem to be few and far between. Since the city and suburbs are spread over a 25 kilometer area, expect to do a great deal of walking as well as traveling by car or bus between major shopping areas. It's most convenient to rent a car and drive this rather expansive urban area.

Shopping is largely confined to six areas in the city and suburbs: Downtown Darwin, Cullen Bay, Mindil Beach, Parap Shopping Centre, Casuarina Shopping Square, and Palmerston Shopping Centre. Each area can be easily covered on foot, but distances between areas require some form of transportation. Downtown Darwin, Cullen Bay, and Mindil Beach are the major shopping areas for visitors; Parap, Casuarina, and Palmerston shopping centers cater primarily to local residents.

Downtown Darwin is the hub of shopping in the Northern Territory. Laid out as a grid system, it is easily accessible on foot from the major hotels on the Esplanade. The center for shopping is the Smith Street Mall, a pedestrian mall crammed with shopping arcades and bordered by Knuckey and Bennett Streets. The adjacent Knuckey, Mitchell, Smith, and Cavenagh Streets also have some shops of interest to visitors. The downtown area also extends southeast to the Wharf which includes several interesting shops, restaurants, and tourist attractions.

Cullen Bay, located four kilometers northwest of the Smith Street Mall, is Darwin's delightful waterfront community of upscale shops and restaurants. It's a great place to spend a couple of hours of el fresco dining at breezy Buzz's Café or Yots overlooking the sheltered Cullen Bay Marina with its many boat slips and browsing through adjacent specialty shops. Better still, come here to see the sunset over the marina and its many luxury craft.

Mindil Beach, located less then two kilometers north of Cullen Bay—just off the Stuart Highway and next to the MGM Grand Darwin casino—becomes a popular outdoor food and craft market (Mindil Beach Sunset Market) only open Thursdays from May to October (5-10pm) and Sundays from June to September (4-9pm). Here you will find 60 food stalls offering delicacies from 20 different countries and 200 arts and crafts vendors selling a wide range of international and locally crafted products. In the midst of all the crowds, local residents dine on the beach—complete with tables, chairs, candles, and wine—as they watch the sun produce another gorgeous Darwin sunset.

Fannie Bay is located immediately north of Mindil Beach—just off Stuart Highway or approximately 10 kilometers from Smith Street Mall. Here you will find the Museum and Art Gallery of the Northern Territory, with its fine shop and restaurant, and the **Parap Shopping Centre** which has a few small arts, crafts, and clothing stores. The shopping village really comes alive on Saturdays when the Parap Markets are held here from 8am to 2pm.

The **Casuarina Shopping Square** is located approximately 17 kilometers northeast of Parap Shopping Centre via Stuart Highway, Bagot Road, and Trower Road. This is Darwin's premier shopping mall with over 120 specialty shops as well as the popular Kmart, Big W, Woolworths, and Coles stores. It also caters to the upscale local market.

The **Palmerston Shopping Centre**, located nearly 7 kilometers from Darwin in one of Australia's fastest growing suburbs, includes over 50 specialty stores along with the large Target, Coles, and Liquorland stores and numerous eateries.

Outside the Darwin metropolitan area is the **Outback** which has little to offer shoppers. One major exception are the islands of the Aborigine Tiwi peoples—**Melville and Bathurst Islands**. Located 30 minutes by air, just off the northwest coast of Darwin, Melville Island offers some unique shopping opportunities for Tiwi art, clothes, and pottery while one also learns about the local history, culture, flora, and fauna. Here, you can buy direct from the Tiwi at savings of 50 percent over what you will pay for comparable items in the shops of Darwin.

WHAT TO BUY

Darwin's major shopping strengths are in the areas of Aboriginal arts, Australian arts and crafts, jewelry, and locally produced sportswear. Prices for Aboriginal art in Darwin appear to be lower than in other cities because Darwin is located near the production sources and thus prices reflect the involvement of fewer middlemen in the marketing process.

ABORIGINAL ARTS AND CRAFTS

The shops in Darwin offer Aboriginal arts from four different groups in the Northern Territory:

- **Central Australia:** Acrylic Papunya paintings, woodcarvings, and Utopia Batik from artists and settlements near Alice Springs—1,000+ kilometers south of Darwin.

- **Arnhem Land:** Bark paintings with "Dreamtime" themes, clap sticks, and totemic objects from tribes east of Darwin in the area of Kakadu National Park.

- **Bathurst and Melville Islands:** Bark baskets, carved Pukamani burial poles, woodcarved animals, silk screen materials, and pottery using distinctive Tiwi patterns that are both colorful and abstract. Since the Tiwi have no "Dreamtime," their designs are less mysterious and thus need little interpretation.

- **New South Wales:** Weapons and utilitarian items, such as boomerangs, clubs, and small shields.

Shopping for Aboriginal arts, artifacts, and textiles is centered in downtown Darwin and the Mindil Beach area as well as on Bathurst Island. It's best to start in and around Smith Street Mall in downtown Darwin. Here you will find several shops selling Aboriginal items. The range in quality is from tourist kitsch and souvenirs to serious collector art. Many are operated by the owners who are extremely friendly and informative about their products as well as about Darwin in general, including the best restaurants and sightseeing. Striking up a conversation in one of these shops can be a truly rewarding experience in meeting the locals and learning a great deal about the community.

Our four favorite shops in downtown Darwin are Aboriginal Fine Arts, Raintree Aboriginal Fine Arts, Karen Brown Gallery, and Wadeye Art and Craft Gallery:

❑ **Aboriginal Fine Arts:** *1ˢᵗ Floor (upstairs), corner of Mitchell and Knuckey Streets (can enter from both streets), Tel. 8981-*

1315, www.aaia.com.au. This attractive and expansive gallery includes top quality acrylic and bark paintings, baskets, carved poles, didgeridoos, boomerangs, books, videos, and music. Famous Aborigine painters, such as Emily, Clifford Possum, and his daughter Gabriella Possum, are well represented here.

❑ **Raintree Aboriginal Fine Arts:** *Shop 3, 20 Knuckey Street, Tel. 8981-2732.* This long established shop (formerly the Raintree Gallery) offers excellent quality Aboriginal arts and crafts, including Tiwi sculptures, Central desert sand paintings, bark paintings, carvings, didgeridoos, weapons, weavings, and silk screen printed fabrics as well as T-shirts, books, cards, and music. The prices here are some of the best we have found for any retail shop in Australia, and the service, including packing and shipping, is excellent.

❑ **Karen Brown Gallery:** *NT House, 1-22 Mitchell Street, Tel. 8981-9985.* Represents the acrylic paintings of six top Aborigine artists, including the Josiah sisters, from the Northern Territory.

❑ **Wadeye Art and Craft Gallery:** *31 Knuckey Street, Tel. 8981-9362, www.topend.com/au/~wadeye/.* This relatively new gallery represents the works of 16 Aborigine artists, including the noted Timothy Dumoo, who work on canvas (acrylic and ochre) and Arches paper. Includes some bark paintings, didgeridoos, mats, and dilly bags.

You'll also find a few souvenir quality shops in downtown Darwin that offer numerous popular Aboriginal arts and crafts along with Australiana, especially didgeridoos, boomerangs, paintings, cards, and T-shirts. Three such shops are operated by Indigenous Creations (Tel. 8941-2515; also found at the Boland Centre on Lake Street in Cairns). Look for **Indigenous Creations** at two locations on The Mall (corner of Knuckey and Smith Streets on The Mall and at the center of the Mall) and **Cultural Images** at Mitchell and Daly Streets.

It's well worth making a special trip to two great places for Aboriginal arts and crafts which are located about 15 minutes north of downtown Darwin:

❑ **Framed: The Darwin Gallery:** *55 Stuart Highway, Stuart Park, Tel. 8981-2994, www.framed.com.au.* Located just a few minutes from the Museum and Art Gallery of the

Northern Territory (between Fannie Bay and Parap), this is North Australia's largest fine art gallery. It includes two rooms, at the back of the gallery, that make up an "Aboriginal Gallery" with a nice eclectic collection of acrylic and bark paintings, bark baskets, carved poles, hand-printed fabrics (Tiwi and Injalak silks and cottons), didjeridoos, and books.

❑ **The Museum Shop:** *Museum and Art Gallery of the Northern Territory, Conacher Street, Fannie Bay, Tel. 8999-8201.* Offers a small collection of books, posters, videos, music, jewelry, cards, and T-shirts with Aboriginal themes. But the real draws here are the Aboriginal Art Gallery and the Cornucopia Museum Café!

The other major shopping area for Aboriginal arts is on the Tiwi island of Bathurst. This is one of the most interesting Aboriginal shopping adventures in Australia. If you take the wonderful full-day tour (also has two-day camping tours) of this island organized by Tiwi Tours (reservations through your hotel reception desk, travel agent, or call Tiwi Tours directly at Nguiu, Bathurst Island, Tel. 1-800-183630), you will have an opportunity to visit the arts and crafts centers and shop for Tiwi arts and crafts and screen printed fabrics in the main settlement town of **Nguiu** (check the Tiwi Prima Arts Centre (varously called "The Keeping Place" and "The Sistine Chapel" for colorful bark baskets and carved Pukamani (burial) poles and animal figures. You can purchase the items here at half the price you would pay in Darwin and one-fourth the price you might pay in Sydney. The center takes credit cards, and Tiwi Tours will transport your purchases back to Darwin free of charge. This is the same place dealers from Darwin and other cities come to make their purchases, and they pay the same prices you will pay. In fact, you may pay for your tour to this island from the savings on your island purchases!

You will also find three workshops in Nguiu producing uniquely designed womenswear (Bima Wear), menswear (Tiwi Design), and pottery (Tiwi Pottery). The colors, designs, and overall quality of these products may or may not appeal to you, but they are unique.

AUSTRALIAN AND IMPORTED ARTS AND CRAFTS

Darwin has its own local artists and craftsmen who produce unique arts and crafts. The single best center for fine art in all of the Northern Territory is **Framed: The Darwin Gallery** (55

Stuart Highway, Stuart Park, Tel. 8981-2994, *www.framed.com. au*). It includes changing exhibitions as well as permanent collections of contemporary art. It's an eclectic gallery which offers the area's best quality paintings, prints, sculptures, jewelry, glass work, and ceramics. If you're interested in paintings, be sure to ask to see the photo book which includes the works of several artists in the Northern Territory.

The **Parap Shopping Centre** in Parap Village (suburb of Fannie Bay) includes a few good arts and crafts shops. Look for **Aussie Potz** (Shop 4, Tel. 8981-7071) for colorful and fun pottery from around the Darwin area. The nearby **24 HR Art** gallery which is operated by the Northern Territory Centre for Contemporary Art has changing exhibitions. Craft lovers will also enjoy the **The Parap Markets** which are held in this shopping area every Saturday from 8am to 2pm. The market offers everything from Asian foods and fresh produce to jewelry and secondhand books.

The Thursday and Sunday evening food and craft market at **Mindil Beach** also is a popular area for purchasing local arts and crafts from vendor stalls. Amongst all the Asian food vendors, hot dog stands, and ice cream trucks, you will find several local craftspeople selling pottery, leather goods, jewelry, and candle holders as well as clothes, stuffed animals, and books. Several stalls also offer international arts and crafts.

JEWELRY

Darwin is famous for its pearls because of the close proximity of pearl farms in the Darwin area and the presence of Paspaley Pearls, one of the world's pioneers of South Sea pearl farming. If you are unfamiliar with South Sea pearls, you can get a quick education by visiting the **Australian Pearling Exhibition** at the Darwin Wharf Precinct (Tel. 8999-6573, open daily 10am-5pm) which is located just south of the city center. Two of Darwin's top pearl shops include:

❑ **Paspaley Pearls:** *19 The Mall, at the end of The Mall on Bennett Street, Tel. 8981-9332, www.paspaleypearls.com.* Now here is a shopping surprise in Darwin! If you like pearls—both big and top quality—you'll love Paspaley Pearls. Indeed, in Australia pearls and Paspaley are nearly synonymous. Darwin is the headquarters for this world-renowned pearler and jeweler that produces 80 percent of the world market in South Sea pearls from its extensive high-tech farms in both Darwin and Broome. But Paspaley is more than just a pearler. Paspaley also is a top jeweler with designs that can hold their own in Paris, London, and New York. After all, Paspaley uses some of the world's top jewelry designers. It simply doesn't get better than the exquisite jewelry designs and classy offerings at this shop. The retail operation is in the small shop at the ground floor. Dealers go upstairs where the bulk of the inventory is found and the big deals are made. Everything here is very expensive and very special. If you've visited Paspaley's other shops in Sydney and Broome, you know what to expect here. Be sure to ask for a copy of their magazine as well as visit their Web site.

❑ **Bynoe Harbour Pearl Company:** *Shop 11, Darwin Wharf Precinct, Tel. 8981-2744, www.octa4.net.au/bynoe.* This is the only retail outlet for this company which operates one pearl farm in Darwin. Includes a wide range of jewelry. Does some of its own designs. Has its own gemologist and goldsmith on the premise.

You'll find several jewelry shops offering opals and pearls in and around the Smith Street Mall. For pearls, check out **Pearl Island Jewellers** (Paspalis Centrepoint, Smith Street Mall). For opals, one of the best shops is **The World of Opal** (44 Smith Street Mall, Tel. 8981-8981) which includes black, boulder, and solid white opals direct from their own mine in Cooper Peedy. Also look for **Sterns Jewellers** (The Galleria, Smith Street Mall, Tel. 8941-1818 and at Casuarina Square, 247 Trower Road, Tel. 8927-2883) for pearl, opal, and diamond jewelry. You'll find lots of other small jewelry shops in the various arcades that lead to and from the Smith Street Mall.

For handcrafted jewelry from various artisans and crafts-people in the Northern Territory, be sure to examine the nice selections at **Framed: The Darwin Gallery** (55 Stuart Highway, Stuart Park, Tel. 8981-2994, *www.framed.com.au*).

For nice quality 9 to 18 karat theme jewelry, including attractive X-ray art jewelry, stop at **JA Manufacturing Jewellers** in Cullen Bay (4/52 Marina Boulevard, Tel. 8981-7070). This shop also does jewelry repairs and offers a wide range of jewelry using gold, diamonds, rubies, and sapphires.

CLOTHES, FASHIONWEAR, AND ACCESSORIES

While Darwin is not a noted fashion center, given its warm and humid climate, you can expect to find a great deal of light weight cotton clothing in numerous shops throughout the city and suburbs. Smith Street Mall has several shops offering the latest in fashion design. The Paspalis Centrepoint shopping center on the mall has several fashion and sportswear shops. **Shady Lady** (Shop 8, Westlane Carkpark Arcade or through the Vic Arcade off of Smith Street Mall) has a unique collection of hats, from Akubras to holiday, wedding, and fashion hats.

AUSTRALIANA, GIFTS, AND SOUVENIRS

You will find several gift and souvenir shops throughout Darwin offering a wide variety of Australiana, T-shirts, Aboriginal artifacts, stuffed animals, leather goods, and memorabilia. Most of these shops, however, tend to concentrate in the downtown area around Smith Street Mall. Look for three Australiana and souvenir shops operated by **Indigenous Creations** (two on the mall and one called **Cultural Images** at Mitchell and Daly Streets). Many of the Aboriginal art and craft shops, fine art shops, and markets identified earlier offer nice gift items.

WHERE TO SHOP

The most interesting shopping is centered in and around the Smith Street Mall in downtown Darwin, the Wharf Precinct, Cullen Bay, the suburban shopping centers of Parap Village and Casuarina Shopping Square, the markets at Mindil Beach and Parap Village, and the settlement town of Nguiu on the Tiwi island of Bathurst. Hotel shopping for the most part involves small gift and souvenir shops that primarily service their own hotel guests.

While you can easily cover each of these shopping areas on foot, it is best to take a bus or car between the shopping areas because of the long distances involved in going from one area to another. If you don't rent your own car, you may find the bus more convenient since taxis tend to be very irregular. In the case of Bathurst Island, you must take an authorized tour (Tiwi Tours, Tel. 1-800-183639) since this island is not open to the general public. You will travel to Bathurst Island by plane, by mini bus on both Bathurst and Melville Islands, and by a short boat trip between the two islands. This is a well-organized and thoroughly enjoyable tour for anyone interested in the Tiwi culture or artifacts.

DOWNTOWN DARWIN

The center of shopping in Darwin is the Smith Street Mall, a pedestrian mall similar to Adelaide's and Brisbane's pedestrian malls but smaller in scale. Bordered by Knuckey and Bennett Streets, the mall consists of 12 small shopping arcades crammed with over 250 specialty shops. You can easily spend half a day exploring the arcade and sampling the international foods offered by several restaurants and take-away eateries. If you want stock up on groceries, head for the big **Woolworth** store.

Some of our favorite shops in and around the Smith Street Mall include **Aboriginal Fine Arts**, **Raintree Fine Art Gallery**, **Wadeye Art and Craft Darwin**, **Karen Brown Gallery**, **Paspaley Pearls**, **The World of Opal**, and **Shady Lady** (see contact information in the previous sections on Aboriginal art, jewelry, and clothes).

Be sure to visit the **Stokes Hill Wharf** (also known as the Wharf Precinct) which is located south of the city center. Here you'll find one of Darwin's major attractions (Australian Pearling Exhibition), one of its best restaurants (Christo's), and a good pearl and jewelry shop, the **Bynoe Harbour Pearl Company**.

CULLEN BAY

Located about five minutes northwest of the city center, this upscale community with its yacht-jammed marina is a pleasant place to stop for lunch or dinner. You'll also find a few boutiques, art, and jewelry shops here just as **JA Manufacturing Jewellers** and **Framed at the Bay**. Our recommendation: come here for the fabulous summer berry dessert at the Buzz Cafe!

SUBURBS

Numerous suburban shops are located throughout the greater Darwin area: Hibiscus Shopping Town, Malak Shopping Square, Nightcliff Shopping Complex, Northlakes Shopping Centre, Palmerston Shopping Centre, Rapid Creek Shopping Centre, and Winnellie Shopping Centre. However, two suburban shopping areas are of some interest to visitors: Parap Shopping Centre and Casuarina Shopping Square.

Parap Shopping Centre in Parap Village of the suburb of Fannie Bay includes a few interesting shops such as **Aussie Potz** and **Flame Tree Crafts**. However, these shops as well as others in this small shopping center do not warrant a special trip except for the Parap Markets on Saturday (8am-2pm).

Casuarina Shopping Square (247 Trower Road, Casuarina, Tel. 8927-8209) is the largest shopping center in the Northern Territory. From Darwin, bus numbers 4 and 10 stop here. Located 20 minutes from downtown Darwin and 5 minutes from the airport, it includes 170 specialty stores selling everything from health food to opals. Considered upscale by local standards, Casuarina Shopping Square has four major department stores—Coles, Kmart, Woolworths, and Big W—as well as numerous restaurants (huge food court on the lower level) and specialty shops. Primarily catering to local residents, there's very little here of interest to visitors interested in acquiring unique Australian products. Includes late night shopping on Friday.

The really interesting suburban shopping for visitors is found at **Framed: The Darwin Gallery** in Stuart Park (55 Stuart Highway, near the intersection with Geranium Street, Tel. 8981-2994), a five minute drive north of the city or two minutes from the Museum and Art Gallery of the Northern Territory. Open seven days a week (Monday-Saturday, 8:30am-5:30pm and Sunday, 11am-5pm), this is the largest gallery in Northern Australia which includes top quality art, sculpture, crafts, and jewelry.

MARKETS

Darwin has five markets you may find interesting for shopping purposes. Like popular markets elsewhere in Australia, most are held on weekends and offer the usual mix of arts, crafts, and food. They are good places to sample ethnic foods and meet local artists and artisans. Darwin's major markets include:

❑ **Mindil Beach Night Market:** *Located along Mindil Beach about 10 kilometers northeast of the Smith Street Mall. Tel. 0419-837-646 (mobile).* This is a fun ethnic food and crafts market held every Thursday from May to October (5-10pm) and every Sunday from June to September (4-9pm). It's a social event for many local residents who come here to browse through nearly 200 arts and crafts stalls, snack at the 60 ethnic food stalls, picnic on the beach, and watch the beautiful sunset slip behind Fannie Bay. Many people sit on the beach or take their own tables, chairs, and lighting as they eat and drink the night away in the tropical ambience of a beautiful sunset, cool breeze, and a festive atmosphere. Be sure to get here early (by 6pm in the winter) if you want to watch the sunset. The market itself is an interesting mix of ethnic food stalls and arts and crafts vendors selling pottery, clothes, leather goods, jewelry, candle holders, books, and souvenirs. The quality of food and beachside ambience tends to out-dis-tance shopping for quality arts and crafts.

❑ **Nightcliff Markets:** *Nightcliff Shopping Centre, Pavonia Way, Nightcliff. Tel. 0414-368773.* This leisurely Sunday market (8am-2pm) is dubbed "a shady continental street-café lifestyle experience." It includes local entertainment, food, arts and crafts stalls, and recycled goods.

❑ **Parap Markets:** *Parap Shopping Centre, Fannie Bay, Tel. 8948-2373.* This festive arts, crafts, and food market is open every Saturday from 8am to 2pm.

❑ **Rapid Creek Markets:** *Rapid Creek Shopping Village, Trower Road (1.5 kilometers past the Nightcliff traffic lights), Tel. 8948-2204.* Open every Sunday from 8am to 2pm.

❑ **Palmerston Markets:** *Tel. 8932-1322.* Held every Friday 5:30-9:30pm in Frances Mall (April-October) and inside Palmerston Shopping Center (November-March).

BATHURST AND MELVILLE ISLANDS

Bathurst and Melville Islands offer an interesting opportunity to learn about the Aborigine Tiwi as well as shop for Tiwi arts, crafts, and clothing. Located 80 kilometers off the northeast coast of Darwin, these two islands are home to the unique and artistic Tiwi peoples who are noted for their colorful abstract designs.

You cannot visit the Tiwi islands on your own since this area is restricted by invitation only. The best approach is to take a half-day or full-day tour of the island operated by Tiwi Tours, Nguiu, Bathurst Island (Tel. 1-800-183630). This is one of the best tours we encountered in all of Australia. After a scenic half-hour flight, the plane lands on Bathurst Island, the smaller but more developed and more heavily populated of the two islands. The tour includes both islands, with visits to the major towns and through the countryside by minibus.

The central focus of the tour is the town of Nguiu on Bathurst Island, a community of 1,200. Begun in 1911 as a Catholic Church Mission, today it is a center for Tiwi development. This is where you will find the Tiwi Design screen printing workshop, Tiwi Pottery, Bima Wear clothing and screen printing workshop, and the Tiwi Pima Art Centre. You can shop at each of these places. If you are interested in purchasing a Pukamani ceremonial burial pole, carved figures, or bark baskets, be sure to stop at the **Tiwi Pima Art Centre**. This warehouse-shop is the central distribution point for locally produced art. You can purchase items at half the price you will pay for comparable items in Darwin.

The **Bima Wear** clothing and screen printing workshop is operated by Tiwi women who produce Bima Wear label clothes, including dresses, blouses, T-shirts, and bags with unique Tiwi designs. You can tour the workshop to observe the screen printing, cutting, and sewing rooms. Next to the work rooms is a boutique which sells the finished garments and a few books on the Tiwi people and islands. You will find changing rooms here so you can try on the garments. The same garments are also found in a few gift and clothing stores in Darwin. The quality of the prints and garments may be improving.

Near the Bima Wear shop are two additional workshops worth visiting. The **Tiwi Design** screen printing workshop is operated by Tiwi men who produce shirts, tablecloths, tea towels, T-shirts, and bolts of fabric. The designs are different from those of Bima Wear. You will not find high-quality prints, fabrics, and products here. Some of the items may make souvenir or gift items.

Next door to Tiwi Design is **Tiwi Pottery** which produces a glazed pottery with Tiwi designs. Again, don't expect top quality. Most of the pottery looks like seconds.

BEST OF THE BEST

We found the following shops, all of which we identified earlier, offer some of Darwin's best quality products. Most focus on the unique aspects of shopping in Darwin—Australia arts and crafts, Aboriginal arts and crafts, pearls, and jewelry:

ARTS AND CRAFTS

❑ **Framed: The Darwin Gallery:** *55 Stuart Highway, Stuart Park, GPO Box 585, Darwin, Northern Territory 0801. Tel. (08) 881-2994; Fax (08) 8941-0883; e-mail: framed@top end.com.au. Web site: www.framed.com.au.* Located near the Museum and Art Gallery of the Northern Territory, this is the Northern Territory's premier arts and crafts gallery. Representing numerous artists and craftspeople through-out Australia, the gallery is literally a one-stop-shop for acquiring some of the best arts and crafts found anywhere in Australia. Two rooms at the rear of this shop serve as an "Aboriginal Gallery."

❑ **Aboriginal Fine Arts:** *1st Floor (upstairs), corner of Mitchell and Knuckey Streets (can enter from both streets), Tel. 8981-*

1315, www.aaia.com.au. One of the best Aboriginal art galleries in the Northern Territory. Look for paintings of top Aboriginal artists—Clifford Possum Japaltjari, Emily Kame Kngwarreye, David Malangi, Michael Nelson Tjagamarra, Paddy Fordham, Eunice Napangadi, Pansy Napangadi, Old Mick Namarri, Jimmy Robinson, and Turkey Tolson. Also offers a good selection of baskets, carved poles, didgeridoos, boomerangs, books, videos, and music.

❑ **Raintree Aboriginal Fine Arts:** *Shop 3, 20 Knuckey Street, Tel. 8981-2732.* This long established shop (formerly the Raintree Gallery) offers excellent quality Aboriginal arts and crafts, including Tiwi sculptures, Central desert sand paintings, bark paintings, carvings, didgeridoos, weapons, weavings, and silk screen printed fabrics as well as T-shirts, books, cards, and music. The prices here are some of the best we have found for any retail shop in Australia, and the service, including packing and shipping, is excellent.

❑ **Karen Brown Gallery:** *Northern Territory House (across from the new Parliament House complex, just around the corner from Smith Street Mall and Bennett Street and next door to Paspaley Pearls), 1/22 Mitchell Street, Tel. 8981-9985.* Offers a small but fine quality collection of Aboriginal paintings produced by six major artists: the five Joshua Sisters, especially the colorful work of Gertie Huddleston and her daughter-in-law, Sheena Wilfred Huddleston, and Mitbul, also known as Prince of Wales, the last of the Larrakia.

❑ **Wadeye Art and Craft Gallery:** *31 Knuckey Street, Tel. 8981-9362, www.topend.com/au/~wadeye/.* This attractive new gallery represents the works of 16 Aborigine artists. Includes lots of interesting acrylic paintings, didgeridoos, mats, dilly bags, and bark paintings. Offers certificates of authenticity with art purchases.

JEWELRY

❑ **Paspaley Pearls:** *Paspaley Pearls Building, 19 The Mall, Tel. 8981-9332, www.paspaleypearls.com.* This is both a retail and wholesale center for the world famous pearl producer. Indeed, Paspaley Pearls produces over 80 percent of the world's South Seas pearls from its extensive farms in

Broome and Darwin. While it has retail outlets in Broome and Sydney as well as wholesale operations in New York and Hong Kong, this Darwin location is the headquarters for Paspaley Pearls worldwide operations. The downstairs showroom has a small but stunning collection of jewelry. The upstarts office is reserved for wholesales.

❏ **Bynoe Harbour Pearl Company:** *Shop 11-13 Wharf Precinct, Stokes Hill Wharf, Darwin, Tel. (08) 8981-2744; Fax (08) 8981-2704; e-mail: hynoe@octa4.net.au. Web site: www.octa4.net.au.* If you decide to dine at one of Darwin's top eateries—Christo's at the Stokes Hill Wharf—you can miss this large shop that is located in the shopping arcade next to the restaurant. You may also want to visit the Australian Pearling Exhibition, which is located near the entrance (left of the gate) to the Wharf, for a good overview of the Australian pearling industry.

ACCOMMODATIONS

❏ **MGM Grand Hotel & Casino:** *Gilruth Ave., GPO Box 3846, Darwin, NT 0801, Australia, Tel. (61 8) 8943-8888, Fax (61 8) 8943-8999.* Australia's only beachside hotel and casino is set on 18 acres of tropical gardens on the edge of Mindil Beach and is only minutes by car from the city center. On Thursday and Sunday evenings stroll to the Mindil Beach Markets set up next door. Recipient of the 1997 and 1998 Australian Hotel Association National Award for Best Hotel Accommodation, the 5-star MGM Grand Darwin offers 96 guestrooms and suites with all the necessary luxuries from private balconies to concierge. Rooms are decorated to exude a tropical feel. Suites offer spa baths, in-room safes, personal fax machines and upgraded amenities. Guests may choose from five dining outlets in the hotel and casino. The multi award winning signature restaurant , The Boardroom, offers fine dining; the Dragon Court was voted best Asian restaurant in the Northern Territory; or choose casual dining in the Sunset Café. Complimentary city shuttle service at set times during the day. Complimentary on-site security parking. Fitness Facilities; Business Facilities; Conference and Banquet Facilities.

❏ **The Carlton Hotel:** *The Esplanade, GPO Box 207, Darwin, NT 0800, Australia, Tel. (61 8) 8980-0800, Fax (61 8)*

8980-0888. Located on the Esplanade across from Darwin Harbor, the Carlton is the winner of 13 Northern Territory awards including excellence in service in 1997. Conveniently located to the central business district. Considered to be 5-star in the Northern Territory, the 163 comfortable rooms and 33 spacious suites offer the expected amenities. Most of the bathrooms provide separate bathtub and shower facilities. Ask about an upgrade to a suite—the hotel runs specials, and you may find that for just a few extra dollars you can enjoy the additional space provided by a suite. The Carlton Brasserie offers a range of international cuisine and offers great views of Darwin Tropical Harbour Parkland. Hotel received award for outstanding pastry chef of Northern Territories. Complimentary enclosed parking. Fitness Facilities; Business Services; Conference and Banquet Facilities.

❑ **Rydges Plaza:** *32 Mitchell Street, GPO Box 1750, Darwin, NT 0801, Australia, Tel. (61 8) 8982-0000, Fax (61 8) 8981-1765.* Rydges Plaza Darwin is located in the heart of the central business district. The largest hotel in Darwin has 233 rooms including 12 suites, non-smoking accommodation, executive floors and specially equipped rooms for disabled guests. Separate bathtub and shower facilities in guest baths. Two restaurants: Signatures restaurant awarded the Gold Plate award as Darwin's premier fine dining restaurant for 1998. Fitness Facilities; Business Center; Conference and Banquet Facilities.

❑ **Novotel Atrium:** *100 The Esplanade, Darwin, NT 0800, Australia, Tel. (61 8) 8941-0755, Fax (61 8) 8941-3513. Web site: www.noveldarwin.com.au.* Conveniently located on the Esplanade in downtown Darwin, just a short walk from the city center, Novotel Atrium Darwin overlooks Darwin Harbour and Bicentennial Park. The 138 guestrooms reflect the essence of the 'Top End' with use of striking color and local woodwork. Corellas restaurant offers a range of unique and exotic local dishes such as kangaroo or crocodile along with fresh seafood and tropical fruits. Or try award winning Castaways alfresco restaurant. Fitness Facilities; Business Services; Conference Facilities.

RESTAURANTS

Darwin has some surprisingly good restaurants and food stalls. Reflecting Darwin's close proximity to Southeast Asia and its ethnic mix of more than 40 different nationalities, many of the restaurants and food stalls serve Thai, Vietnamese, Chinese, Indonesian, Italian, Greek, French, and Swiss dishes. Look for exotic Aussie dishes with kangaroo, buffalo, crocodile, and camel. But be sure to sample Darwin's fresh seafood, especially the wonderful barramundi. Some of Darwin's best restaurants include:

❑ **Christo's on the Wharf**: *Stokes Hill Wharf, Tel. 8981-8658. Open Monday to Saturday, 6:30pm until late. Gilligans bar upstairs is open from 4pm until late.* This delightful seafood restaurant, with a confiscated Indonesian ship in the warehouse section of the restaurant, offers excellent dishes in a wonderful waterfront setting. Get here early to enjoy Darwin's spectacular sunsets while dining al fresco. The signature seafood dinner for two is enormous with huge and meaty mud crabs.

❑ **Cornucopia Museum Café**: *Museum and Art Gallery of the Northern Territory, Conacher Street, Fannie Bay, Tel. 8999-8201.* One of our favorite restaurants which is part of the museum. Everything is excellent here but try the local fish, barramundi, if it's on the menu. Includes both indoor and outdoor dining areas but the outside is the nicest given the garden and ocean front setting. Try the special on the chalk board. Excellent service with waitresses who really do recommend the best dishes!

❑ **Buzz Café**: *Marina Boulevard, On the Boardwalk on the Marina at Cullen Bay.* This three-level restaurant, with many triangular tables outside and facing the marina, is one of the most pleasant restaurants in Darwin for either lunch or dinner. Try the fabulous summer berry cobbler for dessert.

❑ **The Boardroom**: *MGM Grand Casino, Gilruth Avenue, Mindil Breach, Tel. 8943-8888.* Serves excellent modern Australian cuisine. Try the barramundi.

❑ **Twilight on Lindsey**: *2 Lindsey Street. Tel. 8981-8631. Open for lunch (Wednesday-Friday, 11:30am) and dinner*

(Monday-Saturday, 6:30pm to late). Operated by one of Darwin's best chefs. Offers excellent seafood dishes. Recommend dining al fresco.

❑ **Pente:** *28 Mitchell Street, Tel. 8941-1444. Open daily for breakfast, lunch, and dinner (6pm until late).* Owned by the owner of Christo's on the Wharf. Serves inventive modern Australian cuisine.

❑ **Hanuman Thai and Nonya Restaurant:** *28 Mitchell Street, next door to Pente, Tel. 8941-3500.* This is considered by many locals to be Darwin's very best Thai and Malaysian restaurant. Includes many traditional Thai dishes as well as innovative local dishes, such as barramundi baked with ginger flower.

❑ **Tim's Surf and Turf:** *Smith and Pachard Streets, Tel. 8981-9979.* Serves terrific steaks and huge seafood portions at reasonable prices. Good value.

❑ **Yot's Cafe:** *54 Marina Boulevard, Cullen Bay, Tel. 8981-4433.* Famous for its wood-fired pizzas as well as its baked barramundi.

ENJOYING YOUR STAY

Darwin and the Northern Territory is a fascinating area to visit. While there is much to do in Darwin, from enjoying the beaches, casino, ethnic restaurants, and shops to visiting the Territory's finest museum, the city is an ideal jumping-off point for exploring the Outback and for sportfishing.

TOUR INFORMATION AND SERVICES

Because there is so much to do in and around Darwin, you may want to initially stop at the **Tourist Information Centre** (38 Mitchell Street, Tel. 8981-4300, and at the Darwin International Airport) to pick up brochures and ask questions about things to do in the area. *The Top End and Darwin Regions Holiday Guide* and *This Week in Darwin* are especially useful. The personnel here are very helpful and can assist you in booking tours. You'll find a wealth of information at this office to assist you during your stay in Darwin.

A good way to see Darwin, take a walking tour of the city or purchase an all-day pass to tour the city by open-air bus. Get a copy of the free booklet *Darwin and the Top End Today* and follow its map which includes 17 historical sites, including Government House, Old Court House and Police Station, Christ Church Cathedral, Brown's Mart, Old Admiralty House, Chinese Temple, The Tunnels, and Darwin Wharf Precinct. Alternatively, pick up a series of nine informative brochures called *Discovering Darwin*; they cover the Wharf, the Esplanade, the City, the Gardens, the Northern Suburbs, East Pint, Darwin, Outer Darwin, and Fannie Bay. A tour bus service called **Tour Tub** offers a full-day pass ($16) which stops on the hour at 23 locations in the Darwin area, including hotels on the Esplanade, Museum and Art Gallery of the Northern Territory, and the Botanical Gardens. You can get on and off this bus at your own leisure. Look for the Tour Tub along Knuckey Street next to the Smith Street Mall as well as at most of the major hotels. For more information, call 8981-5233 or 8981-4300.

If you are interested in renting a car or campervan (Hertz and Budget), which we highly recommend, you can do so at the airport. The major car rental companies include the following:

Avis NT	8981-9922
Budget Rent a Car	8981-9800
Cheapa Car Cental	8981-8400
Delta Car Rentals	8941-0300
Hertz NT	8941-0944
Nifty Rent a Car	8981-2999
Prt Rent A Car	8981-8441
Territory Thrifty Car Rental	8924-0000
Value Rent A Car	8924-0000

If you're interesting in joining a **tour of the area**, you'll find numerous tour companies that offer a variety of interesting itineraries. Some of the major tour companies include:

AAT Kings	8941-3844
Aussie Adventure Holidays	8948-0091
Coo-ee Tours	8981-6116
Darwin Day Tours	8981-8696
Holiday AKT	8947-3500
Kakadu Dreams	8981-3266
Kakadu Gorge & Waterfall Tours	8979-2025
NT Adventure Tours	8981-4255
Tiwi Tours	8978-3630
Wilderness 4WD Adventures	8941-2161
Wildman Tours	8981-4255

Numerous **cruises** depart from the Darwin area. Contact
these companies for further information:

Adventure Cruises NT	8988-4547
City of Darwin Cruises	8984-4529
Darwin Pearl Lugger Cruises	8983-2892
Spirit of Darwin	8981-3711
Tropical Cruises	8984-3974
Yellow Water Cruises	8979-0149

If you're interested in fishing the waters around Darwin,
contact these companies for details on **fishing charters**:

Arafura Boat Charter	8941-8988
Cape Don Experience	8979-0263
Darwin Barra Fishing Tours	8931-0031
Fishing's Fun	8981-1444
Gove Diving and Fishing Charters	8987-3445
Kakadu Fishing Tours	8979-2025
Mark's Territory Barra Safaris	8981-1444
NT Barra Fishing Trips	8945-1841
NT Sportsfishing and Barra Safaris	8945-4637
Obsession Fishing Safaris	8948-0091
Top End Barra Fishing	8983-2280
Tropical Fishing Tours	8927-6989

MUSEUMS

Darwin boasts several excellent museums that are well worth
visiting. Each is an educational experience for greater appreciat-
ing the history and character of Darwin and the Northern
Territory. The major museums include:

❏ **Northern Territory Museum of Arts and Sciences:**
*Conacher Street, Bullocky Point, Fannie Bay, Tel. 8999-8201,
open Monday-Friday, 9am-5pm and Saturday and Sunday,
10am-5pm.* One of Australia's finest museums. The
displays on Aborigines, Papua New Guinea, Oceania, and
Southeast Asia are outstanding, some of the most informative we have found anywhere, especially on the Tiwi
Pukamani ceremonies and the Indonesia ikat textiles. You
will also find a good collection of contemporary art in this
museum. A small museum shop sells books on Australia,
Indonesian textiles, and prints. One of the additional
benefits of visiting the museum is to discover one of
Darwin's best restaurants on the premises—the Cornuco-

pia Museum Café. It's a great place for lunch or dinner, with excellent food and a nice outdoor tropical ambience.

❑ **Australian Pearling Exhibition:** *Stokes Hill Wharf, Tel. 8999-6573. Open daily 10am-5pm.* Pearling has played a critical role in the development of Darwin's economy and its ethnic make-up. This exhibition puts it all in perspective by explaining the mysterious, dangerous, and romantic history of pearling in the Northern Territories. Reveals an exciting history of luggers, hard hat divers, and modern farming and pearl culturing techniques.

❑ **Aviation Heritage Centre:** *557 Stuart Highway, Winnellie (8 kilometers north of Darwin), Tel. 8947-2145. Open April through September 8:30am-5pm and October through March 10am-4pm.* Very interesting displays emphasizing the role of aviation in the Northern Territory, including a massive B-52 bomber on loan from the U.S. and a Japanese Zero downed during the first air raid on Darwin in 1942, a B-25 Mitchell Bomber, Spitfire Replica, Mirage and Sabre jets.

❑ **Fannie Bay Gaol:** *E. Point Road, Fannie Bay, Tel. 8999-8290. Open daily 10am-5pm.* Serving as Darwin's prison between 1883 and 1979, this museum shows how prisoners lived as well as those who died at the gallows. Highlights the history of the early Northern Territory penal system.

BUILDINGS

Not many original buildings were left standing after the devastating Cyclone Tracy in 1974. Many have been reconstructed to approximate their original construction. Most are included on walking tours of the city:

- Government House
- Old Town Hall
- Brown's Mart
- Old Court House and Police Station
- Hotel Darwin
- Old Admiralty House
- Lyons College
- Victoria Hotel
- Chinese Temple
- NT Parliament House

GARDENS AND AQUARIUMS

❑ **Darwin's Botanic Gardens:** *Gardens Road, Tel. 8981-1958.* Includes a large and interesting collection of flora indigenous to the region.

❑ **Indo Pacific Marine:** *Stokes Hill Wharf, Tel. 8981-1294, Open daily 10am-5pm.* This large aquarium includes a unique self-contained coral-reef ecosystem. Very interesting displays of reef fish and other marine life.

BEYOND DARWIN

Outside Darwin we highly recommend a tour of **Bathurst and Melville Island** to meet and learn about the Tiwi people. As outlined earlier, Tiwi Tours (Tel. 1-800-183630) offers excellent tours to these two islands.

One of the most popular destinations outside Darwin is the **Kakadu National Park**, located in Aboriginal Arnhem Land approximately 150 kilometers east of Darwin. Kakadu National Park offers an excellent opportunity to view unique Northern Australian flora, fauna, wetlands, Aboriginal rock art, and picturesque countryside. Several tour companies operate day tours from Darwin to Kakadu National Park by coach or a combination of air and coach. The tours are mainly designed to view the wildlife in Kakadu National Park, but they also include a few other interesting stops along the way. You will see wildlife and termite mounds, take a boat ride on the wetlands (Yellow Waters) to observe crocodiles and birds, observe Aboriginal rock art, view the Arnhem Land escarpment, and view from a distance the world's largest uranium mine (Ranger Uranium Mine at Jabiru). You can also rent a car or camper to visit this area on your own. Keep in mind that this is a long drive which you may want to break by staying overnight in Kakadu National Park.

Several other areas outside Darwin, such as **Katherine Gorge National Park**, 350 kilometers south of Darwin, offer sightseeing, adventure touring, and sportfishing opportunities. A sportsman's country, you can golf, go horseback riding, parachute, sail, swim, or water ski. The Northern Territory has several parks you can visit to observe flora and fauna, swim, camp, and hike. Several tour operators offer trips to these areas as well as specialty fishing tours. You can charter boats, take cruises, or join a river safari to enjoy the northern inland waterways as well as the surrounding Timor Sea, Van Diemen Gulf, and Gulf of Carpentaria.

The best approach to identifying activities and tours is to contact the **Tourist Information Centre** at 38 Mitchell Street (Tel. 8981-4300 or e-mail: *drtrainfo@ozemail.com.au*) in downtown Darwin. If you visit Katherine, be sure to stop at the **Katherine Region Tourist Association** at the corner of Stuart Highway and Lindsay Street (Tel. 8972-2650 or e-mail: *krta@ nt-tech.com.au*). You also can visit the Northern Territory on the Web: *www.nttc.com.au*.

8

Broome

B ROOME IS ONE OF AUSTRALIA'S MOST IMPOR-
tant eco tourism and adventure destinations. Indeed,
it's the southern gateway to the world's last great
wilderness area, the diverse, rugged, and pristine
Kimberley region of northwest Australia—an area of
423,000 square kilometers which is home to only 25,000
people. But Broome is much more than eco tourism and
wilderness adventures. Above all, it's a surprising adventure in
shopping!

A dusty, sweltering, and isolated tropical beachfront community of only 11,000 inhabitants, friendly Broome remains
one of the country's most important towns. It's literally the
world's most important center for magnificent South Sea
Pearls, the "source" from where you can acquire beautiful, top
quality pearls and jewelry. It's where Australian entrepreneur-
ism and Japanese technical know-how meet to manage one of
the world's most fascinating underwater industries that produces more than $200 million in pearls each year. In fact,
Broome remains one of Australia's best kept travel and shopping secrets. If you've already visited the fabulous Paspaley
Pearls shops in either Sydney or Darwin, or Linneys in Perth,
you already have a glimpse of what might lie ahead in Broome.

You've come to Australia's pearl center where shopping may never be the same. Whatever you do, make sure you include Broome in your travel, and shopping, plans.

IT'S ALL ABOUT PEARLS

Spend a few days in Broome and you'll quickly discover a whole new world of traveling and shopping in Australia. No question about it—this is a unique place that may well capture your imagination and your wallet! Like many others who have come before you, Broome's intriguing, colorful, and flamboyant multicultural history—centered on the farming, wholesaling, and retailing of pearls, from risks to robbers and the gallows—reads like a Joseph Conrad novel set somewhere else in the South Pacific or Southeast Asia. Obsessed with farming the riches of the ocean, this is the place where countless people risked their lives and died in the process so only a few could make their fortunes.

In many respects, the story of Broome is more interesting and compelling than that of a gold rush town, an oil cartel, or the wine making industry. Broome is all about a small town engaged in one of the world's most risky and deadly businesses and the many fascinating characters who managed to develop an ostensibly romantic industry of farming, diving, and harvesting pearls. It's about a little-known but powerful cartel that controls the production, supply, and pricing of pearls on the world market. Best of all, it's a living history whose major growth has taken place only within the past twenty years. This business continues to thrive in the more than fifteen licensed pearling farms and five major pearl shops that define Broome's contemporary pearling industry. It's a very subtle story and industry, largely conducted at the bottom of the ocean, in wholesale pearl rooms in Broome and Darwin, and

❑ Broome is literally the world's most important center for magnificant South Sea Pearls. It remains one of Australia's best kept travel and shopping secrets.

❑ The story of Broome is more interesting and compelling than that of a gold rush town, an oil cartel, or the wine making industry. Broome is all about a small town engaged in one of the world's most risky and deadly businesses.

❑ Bill Reed of Linneys is important to Broome's living history. Without him, the whole retail end of the pearling industry, including the pearl and diamond jewelry business, may have by-passed Broome, as well as Australia, altogether. He still works behind the counter at Linneys.

❑ "Broome Time" often defines activities for this area's many hot and sunny days followed by balmy nights.

❑ Most of the popular tours tend to fill up quickly, especially during high season, mid-May to mid-September.

at the annual (September) pearl auction in Hong Kong.

Don't expect to see the streets lined with pearls in Broome. In fact, the dusty streets tend to be primarily lined with souvenir shops, restaurants, and tour companies with a small section devoted to pearls and jewelry. What you get to see in Broome is only the tip of a fascinating iceberg—a trip on a old pearl lugger, a visit to a pearl farm, a video of pearling operations, and the retail jewelry outlets.

If you want a quick introduction to this history and industry, just step into Linneys jewelry store on Dampier Terrace and meet the famed Bill Reed selling pearl and Argyle diamond jewelry behind the counter, or a strand of exquisite black pearls from a recent trip to Tahiti. You'll be dealing with a microbiologist who in 1979, with a broken leg and a can of pearls, serendipitously transformed Broome's wholesale pearl industry into retail history. Without Bill Reed, the whole retail end of the pearling industry, including the pearl and diamond jewelry business, may have by-passed Broome, as well as Australia, altogether. Or go next door to Broome Pearls to view the current collection of jewelry offered by Australia's second largest pearler, Kailis Pearls. Better still, visit the nearby showroom of Paspaley Pearls, at the corner of Carnarvon and Short Streets , and you will be viewing the fabulous work of the world's largest producer of South Seas Pearls whose exquisite European designs grace the pages of leading fashion and lifestyle magazines, the showcases of the world's major jewelers, and the bodies of the rich, famous, and beautiful.

Broome may be a very small town but its presence is felt in major cities throughout the world because it is one of the most important production sources for the world's jewelry business. From the annual pearl auction in Hong Kong to jewelry workshops and showrooms in Tokyo, Milan, Madrid, Paris, London, and New York, Broome is synonymous with the world's largest and best quality pearls. Look in most any major jewelry store that specializes in top quality pearls and you will find Broome pearls prominently on display. Visit three of the world's leading jewelry designers and houses—Frederico Buccellati, Carrera Y Carrera, and de Vroomen—and you will see some of the most fabulous pearl jewelry using top quality cultured pearls from the Paspaley farms in Broome and Darwin.

IN SPLENDID ISOLATION

Situated in splendid isolation along the Indian Ocean in the northwest part of Western Australia, Broome was established in the 1880s as a pearling port. Today, Broome is a small town of only 11,000 inhabitants which boasts one of the world's best white sand beaches as well as one of Australia's most interesting, entrepreneurial, colorful, and romantic histories—pearling. Indeed, Australia's lucrative pearling industry began and continues in the pristine waters of Broome. Today, nearly 70 percent of all South Sea Pearls come from Australia's pearl farms which are primarily found in and around Broome's tidal coves. Pearls, along with unique art produced around Broome as well as in the Kimberley region, also make Broome one of Western Australia's most interesting shopping destinations.

If you're planning a trip to Western Australia, consider including a few days in Broome. You won't be disappointed. In fact, small town Broome with its multicultural and adventuresome history, coupled with a big, diverse, and beautiful hinterland, may well become a major highlight of your Australian travel and shopping adventure.

WELCOME TO A DIFFERENT WORLD

As soon as you arrive in Broome, you feel you're in a small tropical frontier town unlike any other encountered in Australia. Palm trees and red, white, and purple bougainvillea decorate this sleepy town and resort community. Even the unusual colonial and Asian style architecture speaks volumes about a place that has developed its own unique style: low bungalows with wide verandahs often painted in green and red, the colors of the old wooden luggers that once plied the pearling waters of Broome. Visit the town's Japanese cemetery which interns many pearl divers who lost their lives diving for pearls or stroll through Chinatown and the old pearling sheds that now function as air-conditioned pearl showrooms and jewelry shops, and you'll quickly discover the uniqueness of this place. It's a different world where "Broome Time" often defines activities for this area's many hot and sunny days followed by balmy nights.

Even adventuresome local tourists add another layer of uniqueness to this place. Australian outback travelers arrive here with their rugged, supply-heavy four-wheel vehicles to cruise the wide sandy stretches of world famous Cable Beach and face the lovely sunsets with their white plastic lounge chairs, eating and drinking from their tailgates. Camel caravans —laden with tourists who often come here just for the unique sunset camel riding experience which is Broome's number one tourist attraction—pass in front of these beach lovers, casting long shadows along the beach. No, this is not the Middle East nor the camel races of Alice Spring. It's another unusual aspect of Broome that attracts thousands of visitors to its shores each year where they experience a little of "Broome Time" that makes up some of this area's many surprising treasures and pleasures.

Quiet, friendly, laid-back, and sparsely populated with lots of tropical vegetation, red earth, white sandy beaches, lightning shows, and gorgeous sunsets, this also is a town whose commercial life is centered in Chinatown. Since the first pearl was discovered in Roebuck Bay in 1861, Broome attracted thousands of Malay, Japanese, Filipino, Koepanger, and Aboriginal pearl divers who kept the industry alive and well for nearly a century. Ill equipped to dive in Broome's waters, many died here while working from the old pearl luggers. Numerous Chinese also came to Broome but they became the town merchants who gave Broome its distinctive Chinatown character.

Today, Broome remains a multicultural community with an interesting blend of influences, many of which can be observed in Chinatown. Here you'll find most of Broome's shops and restaurants along the two main streets—Dampier Terrace and Carnarvon Street—that make up the town's major commercial section.

But there is a lot more to Broome than just the small pearling town and its shops, restaurants, and local historical sites. In fact, many people fail to plan enough time in Broome because they mistakenly believe there may not be much to do in such a small town. But Broome also is the gateway to the awesome Kimberley region. Those who are familiar with Broome's many treasures and pleasures come here for several days to explore the region by plane, four-wheel drive vehicle, or boat. Broome is a popular destination for those who love to go deep sea fishing or explore the ecology of a relatively unexplored area. Here you can ride camels on the beach; visit pearl farms and learn about Broome's colorful pearling industry; take a lugger cruise; drive off-road to explore flora and fauna, rock formations, and waterfalls; gaze at the stars or experience the unique stairway to the moon; join a fishing expedition; take a float plane to visit a spectacular waterfall; or participate in an eco beach day trip or gorgeous gorges tour. To do it all, you'll need to spend several days in Broome trying to fit your traveling time into Broome time.

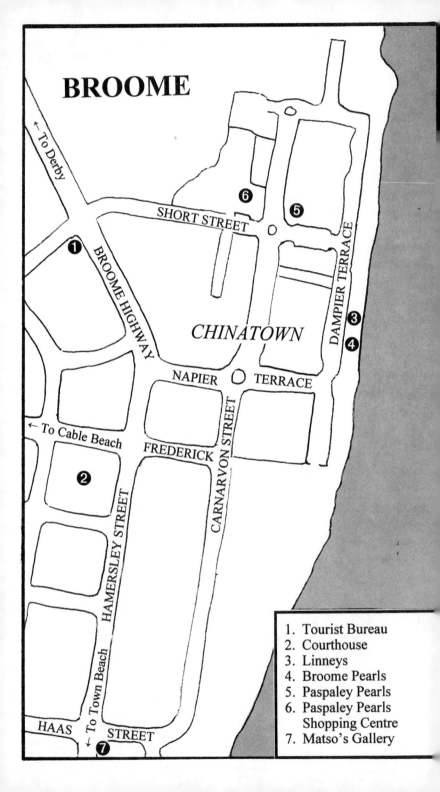

BROOME

← To Derby

❶

BROOME HIGHWAY

SHORT STREET

❻

❺

CHINATOWN

DAMPIER TERRACE

❸

❹

NAPIER TERRACE

← To Cable Beach

FREDERICK

CARNARVON STREET

❷

HAMERSLEY STREET

← To Town Beach

HAAS STREET

❼

1. Tourist Bureau
2. Courthouse
3. Linneys
4. Broome Pearls
5. Paspaley Pearls
6. Paspaley Pearls
   Shopping Centre
7. Matso's Gallery

GETTING TO KNOW YOU

Travel should be so simple! It takes less than five minutes to orient yourself to Broome. With even a mediocre map, you quickly discover that all roads lead from the airport to either Chinatown or Cable Beach. Turn left as you leave the airport and you'll be in Chinatown within three minutes. Turn right and follow the signs to Cable Beach, a six kilometer trip involving four turns, and you'll be there within ten minutes. Chances are 90 percent of your traveling in Broome will involve the airport, Chinatown, and Cable Beach.

While Broome has a public bus and several taxis, and hotels and resorts offer shuttle services, you may want to rent a car for the convenience of exploring the area. Three car rental firms have desks at the airport: Budget, Avis, and Hertz. Others are found in town. Daily rental fees tend to be higher in Broome than in many other places. Expect to pay from A$70 to A$90 a day which would include 50 to 100 free kilometers.

TOURS AND TRAVEL AGENCIES

Prior to visiting Broome, you should visit the town's Web site through which you can request tourist information, ask questions, or book tours:

www.ebroome.com/tourism

You also can call, write, fax, e-mail, or visit them through the following address and numbers:

Broome Tourist Bureau
Corner Broome Highway and Bagot Street
Broome, WA   Australia
Tel. (61 8) 9192 2222
Fax (61 8) 9192 2063
E-mail: *tourism@broome.wt.com.au*

This office also functions as a one-stop booking and information service. In addition to sending you information on Broome, they will assist you in booking hotels and arranging tours.

Broome abounds with travel agencies that basically offer the same types of tours, often with the same companies, within and beyond Broome. While your hotel or resort may have a tour desk (the Cable Beach Inter-Continental Resort has a very large and well organized operation), several agencies such as Terri's

Travel (Tel. 9192-2992 or Fax 9193-7979) are found along **Carnarvon** Street and adjacent Johnny Chi Lane in Chinatown. Some of the major tour operators include:

Broome Town Tours:

Broome Day Tours	9192-1068

Day Coach/4-Wheel Drive Tours:

Aussie Off Road Tours	9192-3617
Broome Day Tours	9192-1068
Discover the Kimberley Tours	9193-7267
Eco Beach Day Trip	9192-4844
Over the Top Adventure Tours	9193-7700
Willie Creek Pearl Farm Tour	9193-6000

Cable Beach Camel Treks:

Broome Camel Safaris (morning)	0419-916-101
Red Sun Camel Safaris (sunset)	9193-7423
Ships of the Desert	1-800-677-830
Cable Stables (sunset)	9193-5713

Nature Based Tours:

Astro Tours of the Kimberley	9193-5362
Kimberley Birdwatching, Wildlife, and Natural History Tours	9192-1246

Scenic Air Tours:

Broome Aviation	9192-1369
King Leopold Air	9193-7155
Seair Broome	9192-6208
Thousand Island Air Tours	1-800-067-939

Extended Boat Cruises:

Broome Fishing & Dive Charters	9193-6339
North Star Charters	9192-1829
Pearl Sea Coastal Cruises	9193-6131
Tropic Rover Cruises	9193-7115

Day Ocean Charters:

Willie Pearl Lugger Cruises	0418-919-781

Day Fishing Charters:

Broom Billfish Charters	9192-2127
Eco Beach	9192-4844
Broome Time Charters	9192-2458
Broome Sailfishing Charters	9192-1558
Lucky Strike Charters Broome	9193-7375
Pearl Sea Coastal Cruises	9193-6131

Diving:

North Star Charters	9192-1829
Workline Dive & Tackle	9192-2233

Extended 4-Wheel Drive Tours:

Desert Inn 4WD Adventure	9199-1257
Discover the Kimberley Tours	9193-7267
Flak Trak Tours	9192-1487
Kimberley Wilderness Adventures	1-800-804-005
Over the Top Adventure Tours	9193-7700
S-Cape Adventure Tours	9191-1271
West Coast Explorer	9198-8835
West Coast Safaris	1-800-621-625

Most of these tours can be booked directly through the Broome Tourist Bureau.

One word of caution when preparing for your Broome adventure. Most of the popular tours tend to fill up quickly. If you arrive during the high season, which usually runs from mid-May to mid-September, you may be disappointed in learning that several of the tours are fully booked, especially the air tours. You are well advised to make reservations for these tours prior to your arrival. The ten most popular tours, which fill up quickly, are:

- Camel Safari
- Pearl Farm
- Lugger Cruise
- Eco Beach
- Off Road Tour
- Astro Tour
- Fishing Charter
- Float Plane
- Gorgeous Gorges
- Bird Watching

WHAT TO BUY, WHERE TO SHOP

Shopping in Broome primarily focuses on four major items: jewelry, art, crafts, and souvenirs. Most of the jewelry is set in gold with pearls and Argyle diamonds. The art is primarily from the Kimberley region and encompasses paintings, prints, and sculpture from some of Western Australia's leading artists. While some quality Aboriginal art finds its way into Broome, most of what passes for Aboriginal art tends to be souvenir arts and crafts. Also look for some unique pottery and ceramics created by Western Australian craftspeople living in and around Broome. Souvenirs, from the truly tacky to the cool and clever, are in abundance throughout the town's many souvenir and gift shops.

Broome basically has two shopping areas. The first one is concentrated along two main streets in Chinatown and includes everything from tacky souvenirs to high quality pearls and jewelry. The second one is dispersed throughout the town in several art galleries that are attached to home studios and restaurants.

CHINATOWN

Known as Old Broome Town and located at the northern end of the town, Chinatown is where all the shopping and dining action is concentrated. Indeed, all roads in Broome tend to lead to Chinatown, Broome's central commercial area. Here you'll find two main streets where all the shopping, restaurants, and travel agencies are concentrated. The main street is **Carnarvon** which is primarily lined with souvenir shops, small cafes and restaurants, and one of Broome's most unique tourist attractions—the open air Sun Pictures movie garden. It also includes an indoor and outdoor shopping mall, Paspaley Pearls Chinatown Shopping Centre, and the famous Paspaley Pearls shop. If you're looking for assistance with tours, this street, as well as adjacent Johnny Chi Lane, are the places to go. Indeed, most tourists tend to congregate along this heavily trafficked street where they do their souvenir shopping, stop for a cup of coffee or an ice cream cone, and escape into the air-conditioned comfort of small shops.

The second, and by far Broome's most upscale shopping area, is **Dampier Terrace**, a street located one block from and parallel to Carnarvon Street. You can easily miss this street if you first visit Carnarvon Street and conclude that Broome primarily welcomes budget travelers and souvenir hunters.

However, staying too long on Carnarvon Street may mean missing out on Broome's best quality shopping. Get over to Dampier Terrace as soon as possible. Here, you'll find several of Broome's top shops: Linneys Pearls, Broome Pearls, Pearl Fishers Jewellery Gallery, Pearlers Row Gallery, David Rees Designer and Goldsmith, Catanach's Antique and Art Gallery, and Moonlight Pearls. Except for Paspaley Pearls at the corner of Carnarvon Street and Short Street, and the faux pearls offered at Moonlight Pearls, the shops along Dampier Terrace represent the best of the best shopping in Broome for top quality pearls, jewelry, art, and antiques. You may need a couple of hours to shop this small but highly concentrated street of shops.

ART AND CRAFT GALLERIES

Broome offers a delightful mix of good quality art produced by local Broome artists and others from the Kimberley region. While you can find a few tourist shops offering souvenir quality Australiana and Aboriginal arts and crafts, the galleries we identify are not touristy arts and crafts shops. They represent the works of leading painters, sculptors, and potters who use colors, designs, and mediums that reflect the local area. The following galleries are well worth visiting: Durack Gallery, Matso's Gallery, Monsoon Gallery, Cockatoo Gallery, Pearlers Row Gallery, Krim Benterrak, Art Thingz, and Chimaera Pottery. We profile each of the places, along with contact information, in our "best of the best" section.

SHOPPING CENTERS

Broome boasts a few small shopping centers that primarily cater to the shopping needs of local residents. These shopping centers also are good places to shop for groceries or get a bite to eat. You may even find a few shops of interest for your own needs. The major such centers include:

❑ **Paspaley Pearls Shopping Centre:** Located at the intersection of Carnarwon and Short Streets, across the street from Paspaley Pearls, this indoor and outdoor shopping mall includes a Coles supermarket along with a few arts and crafts shops offering souvenirs and T-shirts, a couple of restaurants, a pharmacy, sports shop, travel agent, photo processing shop, and bookstore. Open from 8:30am to 5pm, Monday through Friday; 8:30am to 1pm on Saturday; and 10am to 4pm on Sunday.

❑ **Boulevard Shopping Centre:** Located on Frederick Street near the road to the airport, this pleasant indoor air-conditioned shopping mall includes 22 shops: supermarket, liquor store, pharmacy, news agency, cafe, optometrist, hairdresser, travel agent, florist, shoe shop, and photo processing shop. Open from 8:30am to 6pm, Monday through Friday; 8:30am to 1pm on Saturday; and 10am to 4pm on Sunday.

❑ **Seaview Shopping Centre:** Located on Robinson Street. A small shopping center which includes a supermarket, pharmacy, news agency, and fast food outlet. Open from 8:30am to 5pm, Monday through Friday; 9am to 1pm on Saturday; and 10am to 4pm on Sunday.

BEST OF THE BEST

The following shops are well worth visiting during your stay in Broome. While most of the pearl and jewelry stores are found in Chinatown, within easy walking distance of each other, most of the arts and crafts shops are dispersed throughout the town and surrounding area. Consequently, you'll need transportation to visit these places.

PEARLS AND JEWELRY

❑ **Linneys:** *Dampier Terrace, Tel. 9192-2430.* Also includes an affiliated shop, independently operated by their original partner Alan Linney, in Sabiaco, a suburb of Perth. Owned and operated by Bill Reed, who literally developed the retail pearl industry in Australia, this is one of Australia's best quality jewelry shops. This spacious and inviting shop includes beautiful designs produced by its two local Swiss designers as well as by Alan Linney and his designers in Sabiaco. Look for pearl and Argyle diamond jewelry set in gold. Includes a good range of medium priced jewelry along with high-end pieces. This is not a direct-from-our-pearling-farm shop. Focusing on designing jewelry, Linneys acquires pearls from many different sources, including many beautiful black pearls from farms in Tahiti.

❑ **Paspaley Pearls:** *Chinatown Shopping Centre, 2 Short Street (corner of Short and Carnarvon Streets), Tel. 9192-2203, www.paspaleypearls.com.* This is one of three retail outlets of Australia's major pearler and pearl jewelry. Its other more upscale retail shops are located in Darwin and Sydney. The showcases here are jam-packed with excellent quality pearl jewelry which reflects Paspaley's premier name in the pearl industry. Not only does Paspaley own nearly 60% of the Australian pearl business, with its 20 pearl farms off the coasts of Broome and Darwin, it also uses some of the world's top designers for crafting exquisite jewelry.

❏ **Broome Pearls:** *38 Dampier Terrace, Tel. 9192-2061.* Owned and operated by the M.G. Kailis Group which has also pioneered Australia's pearling industry. Includes a wide range of jewelry. Includes a very informative 15-minute video on the pearling industry in Australia. If you know little about this industry, it's well worth sitting through this video before making any jewelry purchases.

❏ **Willie Creek Pearls:** *Lot 34, Challenor Drive, Cable Beach, Tel. 9193-6000, www.williecreekpearls.com.au.* This small gallery includes pearl jewelry, gifts, and souvenirs. Operates one of the most popular pearl farm tours (Willie Creek Pearl Farm Tours, A$17.50 if you drive on your own or $45.00 for the coach tour, although the coach tour is recommended because high tides can flood the road) which starts 38 kilometers north of Broome. You can see the cultured pearling process, including live oyster seeding, view a video, enjoy tea, and shop in the showroom for locally handcrafted jewelry and loose pearls. Also operates the nearby Monsoon Gallery.

❏ **Pearl Fishers Jewellery Gallery:** *Shops 5 and 6 Pearlers Row, Dampier Terrace, Tel. 9193-7244.* This small jewelry shop offers pearls from its local farm.

❏ **David Rees Designer Goldsmith:** *44 Dampier Terrace, Tel. 9192-2414.* Located near Broome Pearls, this shop offers some interesting jewelry designs.

❏ **Catanach's Antique Jewellers:** *Shop 1-2, 26-28 Dampier Terrace, Tel. 9192-7311.* In addition to jewelry, this nice shop includes furniture from Indonesia.

❏ **Moonlight Pearls:** *Corner of Dampier Terrace and Johnny Chi Lane, Tel. 9193-7300.* Somewhat surprising shop given Broome's reputation for real pearls. Operated by noted designer Susan Pender, who supplies the Myer department stores with costume jewelry, here's the shop for beautifully designed faux pearl jewelry made of glass or plastic. Looks like the real thing for a fraction of the real price. So if you like pearls but not the prices, check out the attractive costume jewelry at this interesting shop.

ARTS AND CRAFTS

❑ **Durack Gallery:** *31 Robinson Street, Tel. 9193-6114 or Fax 9192-3133. E-mail: perpetua@tpgi.com.au. Web site: www.oz pages.com/eddieburrup. Open 10am to 5pm on weekdays and by appointment.* Good idea to call before visiting, just in case the gallery would be temporarily closed. Considered by many professionals to be Broome's most important art gallery because of its key role in promoting and support-ing the small but vibrant art movement in Broome and the Kimberley region. Operated by Perpetua Durack, the daughter of one of Western Australia's most famous artists, Elizabeth Durack. Includes a wonderful collection of top quality Australian and Aboriginal paintings and prints (both historic and contemporary) housed in an old pearl dealer's house. Sponsors regular solo and group exhibitions. For a look at Elizabeth Durack's paintings, visit a separate Website devoted to her work: *www.cygnus. uwa.edu.au/~edburrup*. Eddie Burrup's paintings can be viewed at *www.ozpages.com/eddieburrup*.

❑ **Matso's Gallery:** *60 Hamersley Street, Tel. 9193-5811 or Fax 9192-1995. Open daily, 10am to 5pm.* Housed in the historic Captain Gregory House and adjacent to Matso's Store and Brewery which includes an exhibition hall operated by the gallery. The exhibits change monthly. The gallery includes a diverse mix of paintings, prints, pottery, sculpture, and crafts from some of the top local and Kimberley artists. Also displays a small collection of Aboriginal artworks, including rugs. A top quality opera-tion.

❑ **Monsoon Gallery:** *Challenor Drive, Cable Beach, Tel. 9193-5379. Also at the Broadwalk Gallery, Cable Beach Inter-Continental Resort.* This attractive gallery includes nicely displayed paintings, arts and crafts, ceramics, textiles (ikat), and Indonesian furniture. Represents several artists (see photo album with extensive inventory). The Cable Beach Inter-Continental Resort shop is an extension of the café (Sketches) and includes similar items but on a much smaller scale.

❏ **Pearlers Row Gallery:** *Shops 3 and 4 Pearlers Row, Dampier Terrace, Tel. 9192-6330.* A small but very nice gallery located across from Linneys. Includes some Aboriginal art as well as up and coming Kimberley and Australian artists. Look for the attractive works of Peter Coad.

❏ **Cockatoo Gallery:** *19 McDaniel Road, Tel. 9192-1647. Open daily 9am to 5pm.* Newly reopened after being closed for two years, this is the home gallery of one of Western Australia's most successful and colorful artists, Helen Norton.

❏ **Chimaera Pottery:** *McDaniel Road off Archer and Port Drive. Tel. 9192-1056. Open daily 9am to 12 noon and weekends by appointment.* The pottery studio of Angela Bakker.

❏ **Krim Benterrak:** *P.O. Box 332, Broome, WA 6725. Tel. 9192-1490 (for private viewing).* Born in Morocco, educated in Paris, and moved to Western Australia in 1977. Paints colorful expressionist landscapes, still lives, and nudes. One of Western Australia's most distinctive artists whose works have been exhibited throughout Australia as well as in Japan.

❏ **Art Thingz:** *Kanagae Drive '12 Mile' (18 kilometers from town) off Broome-Derby Highway. Tel/Fax 9192-1454.* Open daily from Easter to September. The home studio and gallery of Mary Kirby who does original paintings and prints of Broome and the surrounding area.

❏ **Courthouse Markets:** *Hamersley Street.* Every Saturday morning this popular market is held on the grounds of the historic Courthouse. Includes lots of arts and crafts as well as foods.

ACCOMMODATIONS

Top quality accommodations tend to be limited in Broome. The two best places to stay are the Cable Beach Inter-Continental Resort at Cable Beach and the Mangrove Hotel in Broome. We prefer the Cable Beach location because of its nice range of facilities.

❑ **Cable Beach Inter-Continental Resort:** *Cable Beach Road, GPO Box 1544, Broome, Western Australia 6725, Australia, Tel. (61 6) 9192-0400, Fax (61 6) 9192-2249.* A short drive from town, located across from Cable Beach, this resort offers the most upscale accommodations in Broome. Set on 26 acres of tropical gardens, the resort reflects the style of Broome's original pearling masters' quarters with wide wooden verandahs and lattice screens and shutters. The green and red colors of the pearling luggers are used for the exterior of the resort. 263 rooms are divided into three categories—studio rooms, bungalows and suites—and are designed with Oriental, Dutch and European influences. Studio rooms have a private balcony and sitting area. The bungalows are self-contained and ideal for families or friends traveling together. Bungalows feature separate dining, bathrooms and cooking facilities. A renovation was completed in early 2000. Six restaurants offer a range of choices. Kimberly Grill features local products such as barramundi, kangaroo and emu, and an Asian style noodle bar. Lord Mac's features a variety of foods for all-day dining; Sketches serves fresh pastas. The award winning Pandanus restaurant blends Asian and Mediterranean cooking styles and features Western Australian wines. Fitness Facilities; Tour Desk; Kids Club; Conference Facilities.

❑ **Mangrove Hotel:** *120 Carnarvon Street, Broome, Western Australia 6725, Australia, Tel. (61 8) 9192 1303, Fax (61 8) 9193 5169.* The Mangrove Hotel overlooks Roebuck Bay and is only a 5-minute walk to Chinatown—the commercial center of Broome. The location is perfect for viewing the 'stairway to the moon' on full moon evenings. Rooms have private balconies. Charters Restaurant serves an a la carte menu; Tides Gardens Restaurant and Palms Café Bar provide additional choices. Fitness Facilities; Conference Facilities.

RESTAURANTS

Given Broome's long multiethnic history, it has a surprisingly good range of restaurants as well as its own brewery-restaurant which also functions as an art gallery. Many of the best restaurants are small cafes or bistros that offer very good blackboard specials. The largest number of restaurants are found at the Cable Beach Club Resort.

❑ **Pandanus:** *Cable Beach Inter-Continental Resort, Cable Beach Road, Tel. 9192-0400. Open 6:30-10:30pm.* An award-winning restaurant, this is Broome's best fine dining restaurant which combines Australian, Asian, and Mediterranean cooking styles and features Western Australian wines. Reservations are essential.

❑ **Old Zoo Café:** *Challenor Drive, Cable Beach, Tel. 9193-6200.* Located next to the Monsoon Gallery and Willie Creek Pearls, this popular restaurant is open daily from 7am until late (closed Monday night). Dine outside in the beautiful tropical gardens.

❑ **Blooms:** *Shop 2, 31 Carnarvon Street, Tel. 9193-6366.* Deli and café. Dine indoors or al fresco along the sidewalk. Check the specials on the blackboard. The chef's specialty here is risotta. Offers many tempting desserts, especially the Mississippi Mud Pud.

❑ **Matso's Coffee House:** *Matso's Store, 60 Hamersley Street, Tel. 9193-5811. Open Monday-Thursday 8am-5pm and Friday-Sunday 8am-9pm.* This combination café, art gallery, and brewery serves good sandwiches and main courses for breakfast, lunch, and dinner. Pleasant dining on the veranda. Be sure to try the fresh juices and a Broome Brewery ale.

❑ **Nippon Garden Restaurant:** *Nippon Inn, Dampier Terrace.* This combination restaurant and nightclub offers excellent Thai and Chinese dishes.

❑ **Conti Bar and Bistro:** *Mercure Inn Continental Hotel, Weld Street, Tel. 9192-1002.* Serves good Continental and seafood dishes in a pleasant setting. Check out the blackboard specials.

❑ **Kimberley Grill:** *Cable Beach Inter-Continental Resort, Cable Beach Road, Tel. 9192-0400.* This seasonal restaurant features many local dishes such as barramundi, kangaroo, and emu.

❏ **Sketches:** *Cable Beach Inter-Continental Resort, Cable Beach Road. Tel. 9192-0400. Open for lunch and dinner.* Offers a variety of fresh pastas.

❏ **Palm's Café Bar:** *The Mangrove Hotel, Carnarvon Street,* Tel. 9192-1303.

Enjoying Your Stay

There's lots to do in Broome both inside and outside the town. The major highlights include:

❏ **Camel Rides on Beach:** This is Broome's most popular tourist activity, a signature tour of Broome. Whatever you do in Broome, be sure to join a camel safari on the beach, especially the late afternoon sunset safari. Several companies offer morning (½ hour) and late afternoon (1 hour) camel treks along beautiful Cable Beach. The oldest and most experienced firm is Ships of the Desert (Tel. 1-800-677-830).

❏ **Willie Creek Pearl Farm:** *Lot 34 Challenor Drive, Tel. 9193-6000 (for information and bookings).* Located 28 kilometers north of Broome, this is the only pearl farm in the Kimberley region open to the public. Includes daily tours.

❏ **Chinatown:** *Carnarvon Street.* As noted in our examination of shopping in Broome, this is Broome's central business district where most of Broome's pearl history flourished—pearl sheds, billiard saloons, and Chinese eateries. Today, it's where all the commercial action is found. The streets here are now lined with pearl showrooms, art galleries, souvenir shops, cafes, ice cream parlors, grocery stores, and tour companies.

❏ **Broome Historical Society Museum:** *Located in the Old Customs house, behind the Seaview Shopping Centre, Tel. 9192-2075. Open Monday-Friday 10am-4pm and Saturday-Sunday 10am-1pm (April to November).* This museum chronicles the town's fascinating history. Includes a display on pearling and many old photos.

❏ **Pearl Luggers:** *44 Dampier Terrace, Tel. 9192-2059.* Chronicles Broome's pearling history and includes two of

Broome's original pearl luggers, the *Same Male* and the restored *DmcD*.

❑ **Cable Beach:** The beautiful long beach is ideal for swimming, parasailing, jet-skiing, camel riding, or just enjoying the spectacular sunsets.

❑ **Staircase to the Moon:** This natural phenomenon occurs from March to October when the full moon reflects off the exposed mudflats of Roebuck Bay. The resulting illusion looks like a staircase reaching to the moon. Many local artists depict this phenomenon in their art work.

❑ **Sun Pictures:** *Carnarvon Street*. This is one of Broome's more interesting downtown attractions. Built in 1916, Sun Pictures is considered the world's oldest operating outdoor picture garden. Here you can really enjoy "Broome Time" by watching a movie under the stars while laying back in a deck chair!

❑ **Japanese Cemetery:** Lots of local history is buried here with this testimony to the perils of the early pearling industry. Includes the graves of over 900 pearl divers.

❑ **The Courthouse** and **Courthouse Markets:** *Hamersley Street*. This is one of the best examples of the original distinctive "Broome style" architecture. The popular Courthouse Markets are held on the grounds of the historic Courthouse.

❑ **Broome Crocodile Park:** Home to over 1,000 reptiles: salt water crocodiles, alligators, New Guinea caimans, and freshwater species. Houses some of Australia's largest crocodiles.

❑ **Specialty tours:** As noted earlier, several companies (see previous listing of tours and companies) in the Broome area offer a variety of exciting land, sea, and air tours, from pearl lugger cruises, diving, and fishing charters to four-wheel drive adventure tours into the Kimberley region. Contact any tour company in Broome or Cable Beach for information and reservations. The tour desk at the Cable Beach Inter-Continental Resort is especially good. Be sure to make reservations well in advance during the high season since many of the most popular tours, such as Eco Beach, Astro Tour, Fishing Charter, Float

Plane, and Gorgeous Gorges, are fully booked several days in advance.

Whatever you do, enjoy the many treasures and pleasures associated with "Broome Time." This is a very pleasant and surprisingly interesting place to visit for both shopping and traveling. Our warning is well worth repeating: Plan to stay an extra day or two here since you are bound to find many things to do that you may have failed to plan for initially.

9

Perth and Fremantle

V ISITING PERTH AND NEIGHBORING FREMAN-
tle takes special effort. Located along the southwest
coast of Australia, Perth is nearly 2,000 miles from
any other large metropolis. While extremely isolated
from the rest of cosmopolitan Australia, nonetheless,
Perth has developed its own unique character that makes this
delightful city of 1.3 million residents a major highlight of any
Australian adventure. A sophisticated metropolis of business,
government, culture, arts, and sports, this clean and well laid
out city lacks the traffic congestion found in other major cities.

   If you have the time, plan to spend at least three days in the
Perth and Fremantle area—a week would be much better.
There's lots to see and do here, from exploring gorgeous
beaches, sailing, and snorkeling to visiting museums, quaint
towns, and wineries. This very sunny and friendly city also
offers great shopping, dining, and entertainment. For many
first-time visitors, this is a pleasantly surprising city.

GETTING TO KNOW YOU

There is a saying in Perth that perhaps best characterizes one
of this city's major attractions: *"Perth has the climate California*

thinks it has!" Indeed, bright sunny skies and delightful temperatures make this one of Australia's most pleasant places to visit.
Its idyllic Mediterranean climate and near total absence of
pollution (no heavy industry) make this an great place to live
and visit. The pleasant climate partly explains this area's
decided beach and water culture—locals and visitors alike flock
to the gorgeous beaches both day and night. Sailing enthusiasts
know this area very well, especially for hosting the Americas
Cup yacht race at Fremantle in 1988.

But Perth is a lot more than just beaches and sailing. This is
a thriving business and government center that dominates
Western Australia, a state of only 1.8
million people. A huge state, it literally dwarfs Britain and Europe together or even most Southeast Asian
countries. From the tropical north to
the temperate forests in the south,
and from the sun drenched beaches
of the west and south to the arid
goldfields of the center, this is one
very big, varied, and sparsely populated state. Here you can enjoy the
cosmopolitan treasures and pleasures
of Perth, Fremantle, surrounding
suburbs, and nearby rural villages to
more rugged adventure destinations
elsewhere in the state. Sample the
unique wildlife of cuddly koalas to
huge ferocious salt water crocodiles,
dine on famous crayfish (rock lobsters) and prawns, or enjoy Perth's
vibrant nightlife of great restaurants,
theatrical performances, concerts, a
casino, and world class entertainment in the southern hemisphere's

❏ Located nearly 2,000 miles
from any other large metropolis, Perth is extremely isolated from the rest of cosmopolitan Australia.

❏ Perth's idyllic Mediterranean
climate and near total absence of pollution make this
a great place to visit.

❏ Perth is one of the easiest and
most pleasant cities in which
to drive a car.

❏ For a panoramic view of the
city, be sure to visit King's
Park.

❏ Subiaco is an upscale community with several nice
boutiques, art, and jewelry
stores as well as cafes and
restaurants.

❏ Western Australia is well
known for its production of
fine Argyle diamonds, South
Sea pearls, opals, and gold.

largest Entertainment Centre, and you'll wonder what is so
isolated about this place and why more don't know about the
attractions of this unique area. Indeed, Perth is a world class
city that both looks and feels good.

THE STREETS OF PERTH

Perth is relatively easy to get around in given its well laid out
streets and convenient transportation system. While taxis and
buses are plentiful, you may want to rent a car to get around

this sprawling city as well as visit its suburbs and the many interesting areas outside the metropolitan area. This is one of the easiest and most pleasant cities in which to drive a car.

The best way to get oriented to Perth is to first stop at the **Western Australian Tourist Centre** (Albert Facey House on Forest Place, next to the main post office near the train station and Wellington Street, Tel. 9483-1111) to pick up free maps and tourist literature. Open daily from 8:30am-6pm (but opens at 10am on Sunday and closes at 7pm on Friday and 5pm on Saturday and Sunday), this office is jam-packed with tourist literature on the city and state. The counter personnel are very helpful in answering questions, giving advice, and making travel arrangements. You also may want to visit the nearby **Perth Tourist Lounge** (Level 2, Carillion Arcade, 680 Hay Street Mall, Tel. 9481-8303) for information on tours and travel in Perth and Western Australia; they also provide Internet access to travelers. In both places you'll find lots of useful tourist information on everything from tours and accommodations to shopping, restaurants, and sightseeing. Be sure to pick up these useful booklets: *Hello Perth and Fremantle*, *Your Guide to Perth and Fremantle*, *What's On in Perth and Fremantle*, and *West Coast Visitors Guide*. You also should visit the Western Australian Website and a few others prior to arriving in Perth:

www.westernaustralia.net
www.countrywide.com.au
www.whatson.com.au

For a panoramic view of the city, be sure to visit **King's Park** which remains the city's number one tourist attraction. Located southeast of the city center, just off Thomas Street, Kings Park Road, and Fraser Avenue, this 1000 acre park overlooks the city. Viewed from Fraser Avenue, Perth is especially romantic at night when the bright city lights reflect into the Swan River.

Stretching along the banks of the delightful Swan River, Perth is both a relatively compact and sprawling city. It's compact in terms of its city center where you will find its major hotels, restaurants, shops, and historical sites. It's sprawling in terms of its suburbs which stretch to the north, south, east, and west of the city. The port city of Fremantle lies 19 kilometers southwest of Perth.

Shoppers focus much of their attention and energy on the city central which is bordered by **Wellington Street** on the north and **St. George's Terrace** on the south and **King Street** on the west and **Barrack Street** on the east. Within this

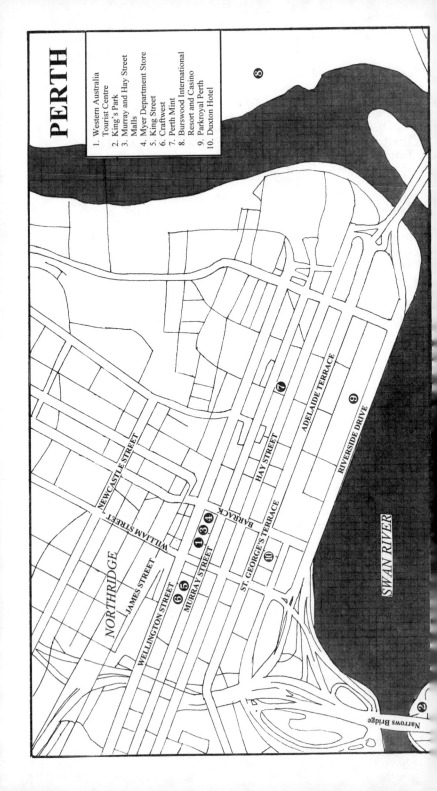

expansive six block area lie most of Perth's major shopping arcades, two major department stores (Myer and Aherns), and the city's two connected east-west pedestrian malls (Murray Street Mall and Hay Street Mall). If you choose to stay at one of the centrally located hotels, such as the Park Royal, Duxton, or Hyatt Regency, you can easily walk the central business district and its shopping centers.

Immediately east of the central business district, across the Swan River, is the imposing 10-story **Burswood International Resort & Casino** with its huge hotel, restaurant, shopping, gambling, convention, and entertainment complex.

While Perth has several surrounding suburbs, only two are of particular interest to visitors. Immediately north of the city's central shopping district and train station (Wellington and William Streets) is **Northbridge** with its many restaurants, pubs, bars, and sex shops. A somewhat seedy and highly overrated area, it's especially popular at night with young people in search of cheap beer, entertainment, and pleasures of the flesh. The centrally located Brass Monkey Pub and Brasserie at 209 William Street (corner of William and James Streets) is one of the more popular watering holes in this area.

For shoppers and dinners, the western suburb of **Subiaco** is well worth visiting. Located only 10 minutes from downtown Perth (via Hay Street), Subiaco is an upscale community with several nice boutiques, art, and jewelry stores as well as cafes and restaurants located near the intersections of Hay and Rokeby Streets. The famous pearl jeweler **Linneys** (affiliated with the pioneering Linneys in Broome), for example, is located here along with one of Perth's best Aboriginal art galleries, **Indigenart**.

Further west is the oceanfront suburb of **Cottesloe** which is popular for surfing, swimming, and kayaking. It's also where you will find one of the best theme restaurants in the area, the award-winning oceanfront **Indiana Tea House** celebrated for its east-meets-west architecture, ambience, and cuisine as well as for its wonderful view which includes gorgeous sunsets.

Southwest of Perth is the popular port city of **Fremantle** made famous worldwide for hosting the World Cub. While it may have a glamorous image beyond southwest Australia, in reality Fremantle is a somewhat disappointing city with a decided working class orientation. The shops and restaurants here leave much to be desired. While you may want to spend a few hours visiting this city, it's not worth staying overnight when you can have a much better time in Perth, Subiaco, and Cottesloe.

A good way to get quickly oriented to Perth and the

surrounding area is to take a city tour. The **City Tram Company** (Kings Park and University, Tel. 9367-9404), for example, conducts daily 1½ tours of the city which includes visiting Kings Park, Burswood International Resort Casino, Barrack Street Jetty, Perth Mint, the city shopping areas, and Perth's major tourist attractions. You don't need to book ahead. Just look for the red City Tram and get on board where you can purchase a ticket ($12 for regular adults). You also can take a free walking tour of the city by picking up a copy of the free tourist guide *What's On* (pick up a copy from the Western Australian Tourist Centre) and following the map and suggested itinerary found in the booklet under the section entitled "Perth City Tour." The recommended walk will take you to 24 major sites in the downtown area.

SHOPPING HOURS

Most shops in Perth and nearby suburbs are open 8:30am-5:30pm, Monday to Friday, and 8:30am-5pm on Saturday. Late night shopping in downtown Perth is until 9pm on Friday. Late night shopping in the suburbs is until 9pm on Thursday. Most shops are open 12noon-5pm on Sunday. Weekend markets tend to have varying hours, with some opening at 8am and closing at 4pm and others opening at 9am and closing at 5pm.

WHAT TO BUY

Like many other large cities in Australia, Perth is noted for its jewelry, arts, crafts, antiques, and fashion clothing. Many shops offer items that are particularly unique to Western Australia and Perth.

GEMS AND JEWELRY

Western Australia is well known for its production of fine Argyle diamonds, South Sea pearls, opals, and gold. Look for both the usual and unusual in gems and jewelry. Most jewelry shops offer some combination of Australian opals, Argyle diamonds, Kalgoorlie gold, and South Sea pearls. Some of the best pearls, with unique jewelry designs, are found at **Linneys** in Subiaco (37 Rokby Road, Tel. 9382-4077). Owned and operated by one of Western Australia's most important pioneering jewelers (Alan Linney), this shop also offers Argyle diamond and Kalgoorlie gold jewelry; it literally pioneered the

Australian jewelry industry in diamonds and pearls in the mid-1980s! **Lyndale Galwey** (Shop 7A, Bayview Terrace, Claremont, Tel. 9385-3937) also offers a wide selection of pearls from Australia as well as from Tahiti, Japan, China, and the United States. For opals, look for several jewelry shops in the various shopping arcades in downtown Perth. One of the best such shops is **Quilpie Opals** (Shop 6, Piccadilly Arcade, off Hay Street Mall, Tel. 9321-8687). Also try the **Opal Gallery** (1st Floor, 81 Barrack Street, Tell 9221-2992); **Opal Exploration Co.** (616 Hay Street, Tel. 9325-2907); **Opal Strike** (Shop 22, Carillon Arcade, Murray Street Level, Tel. 9324-2882). **Costello's** (Shop 5-6 London Court, Tel. 9325-8588, *www.costellos.com.au*) is famous for it fine collection of Argyle diamonds, including pink and champagne diamonds, South Sea pearls, and opals. For excellent quality pink Argyle diamonds, stop at **Charles Edward Jewellers** (45 King Street, Tel. 9321-5111). For a wide range and selection of jewelry, crystal, and animal collectibles, shop at **City Gems** (Shop H16, City Arcade, Hay Street Level, Tel. 9321-5853). **Koro Fine Australian Jewellery** (Shop H27, City Arcade, 207 Murray Street, Hay Street Level, Tel. 9485-0880), with its five designers and goldsmiths, offers a good collection of diamonds, opals, sapphires, Broome pearls, and Kalgoorlie gold. For one of the most interesting tours of the gold minting process, be sure to visit the **Perth Mint** (310 Hay Street, corner of Hill Street, Tel. 9421-7277); its shop also includes gold jewelry. **Exclusive Gold** (Plaza Arcade, off Hay Street Mall, Tel. 9325-8296) also has a wide range of gold jewelry. For nice quality antique jewelry, visit **Trinity Antiques** (Trinity Arcade, 205 Hay Street Level, Tel. 932-8321).

Australiana

Like other Australian cities, Perth offers the usual range of Australiana which is popular with tourists. Several of the shops are branches of shops found in other cities. **Purely Australian** (London Court, Hay Street Mall, and City Arcade, Tel. 9325-4328) offers a wide range of Australiana. **R. M. Williams** (Carillon Arcade, Hay Street Mall, Tel. 9321-7786) offers the usual range of Australian leather goods, including moleskin trousers, boots, and Akubra hats.

Aboriginal Arts and Crafts

Several shops in the Perth area offer a wide range of both Aboriginal arts and crafts from Western Australia. Some of the best quality Aboriginal arts and crafts found in the Perth areas are at **Indigenart** (The Mossenson Gallery, 115 Hay Street, Subiaco, Tel. 9388-2899). **Desert Designs** (28 King Street) has an excellent art gallery on the lower level (clothes upstairs) which represents several Aborigine artists. Many of the other shops tend to offer more souvenir quality arts and crafts, such as the popular **Creative Native** (32 King Street, Tel. 9322-3398); it also has a similar shop in Fremantle (65 High Street, Tel. 9335-6993). However, you'll find some serious Aborigine paintings in the upstairs gallery.

AUSTRALIAN ARTS, CRAFTS, AND GIFTS

The arts and crafts are well and alive in Western Australia. They are particularly well represented in Perth's many museums and shops. If you're interested in fine art, be sure to visit the **Art Gallery of Western Australia** at the Perth Cultural Centre (51 James Street, Tel. 9492-6655). At the information desk, ask for literature on arts and crafts galleries in the Perth area. They have a free directory entitled "Gallery Circuit" which outlines the major galleries in and around Perth. Some of the most important galleries include **Artplace** (Upstairs Old Theatre Lane, off 52 Bayview Terrace, Claremont, Tel. 9384-6964); **Perth Galleries** (61 Forrest Street, Subiaco, Tel. 9380-9595); **Stafford Studios** (102 Forest Street, Cottesloe, Tel. 9385-1399); **Goddard/de Fiddes** (31 Malcolm Street, West Perth, Tel. 9324-2460); and **Greenhill Galleries** (37 King Street, Tel. 9321-2369).

Several shops offer good quality crafts from Western Australia. One of the best shops is the **Craftwest Shops** (Centre for Contemporary Craft, King Street Arts Centre, 357 Murray Street, Tel. 9226-2799). One of our favorite places is a very tiny shop in London Court—**Fine Presence** (Shop 43, Tel. 9325-3050). **Mineral Kingdom** (City Arcade, Murray Street Level, Tel. 9321-9730) has a nice selection of wood turned bowls, minerals, and jewelry. If you're looking for small gift items and souvenirs at good prices, try the reliable **Chanelle** (Shop 6, City Arcade, Murray Street Level, Tel. 9321-6885). Also in the City Arcade, look for **Olsson's** for nice quality Australian glassware and gift items.

FASHION AND ACCESSORIES

Perth's downtown shopping arcades and department stores are jam-packed with the latest apparel, both Australian and imported. If you're interested in the latest in European designer fashion, head for **King Street** which recently has become Perth's "Bond Street." Here you'll find upscale shops offering such popular brand labels as Gucci, Valentino, Armani, Versace, Moshini, Louis Vuitton, and Kookai. Across the street is the combination clothing and art gallery called **Desert Designs** (28 King Street) which offers fashionable clothes with Aboriginal designs for children to adults. For Australian clothes, check out several branches of the popular **Purely Australian Clothing Co.** (Shop M1 City Arcade, 731 Hay Street Mall, and Shop 38-39 London Court). For factory outlet shopping for brand name Australian made fashions, visit **Factory Outlets Direct** (52 Lord Street, East Perth, Tel. 9221-8881).

WHERE TO SHOP

There is much more to shopping in Perth than just the shops concentrated in and around the downtown pedestrian mall. Perth's major shopping is concentrated in small pedestrian malls, shopping arcades, department stores, street shops, markets, museums, and factory outlets. Each has its own character and offers a special shopping adventure.

SHOPPING ARCADES

Perth's major shopping area is located in the central business district, immediately south of the Perth Cultural Centre, train station, and bus station. It consists of a six block high density shopping area bordered by Wellington Street, King Street, Georges Terrace, and Barrack Street. At the center of this area are two east-west pedestrian mall streets, Murray Street Mall and Hay Street Mall, which are linked to a series of seven small shopping arcades and two department stores that run north and south: Piccadilly Arcade, Carillion Arcade, City Arcade, Plaza Arcade, St. Martins Arcade, London Court, Trinity Arcade, Gledden Arcade, Myer Department Store and Ahrends Department Store. Within this area you will also find Perth's two major tourist information offices, the Western Australian Tourist Centre (Albert Facey House on Forrest Place) and the Perth Tourist Lounge (Carillon Arcade, Level 2).

   The whole shopping area is very mixed in terms of both people and products. Unfortunately, Forrest Place and the pedestrian malls tend to be popular destinations for derelicts and heroin addicts. Street musicians occasionally entertain shoppers. The shops range from the cheap, junky, and transient $2 shops to upscale jewelry, gift, and fashion shops.

You can easily wile away several hours of browsing through the various shops in each of these arcades as well as in shops found along nearby streets. Like shopping arcades elsewhere in Australia, you'll find lots of food courts, cafes, take-away shops, and restaurants in this area. In City Arcade, look for **Oroton** for quality leather goods; **Olssons** for nice contemporary Australian glassware and gift items; **Koro Jewellers** for pearls and gold nuggets; and **Mineral Kingdom** and **Chanelle** for arts, crafts, and souvenirs. Piccadilly Arcade includes one of Perth's best opal and jewelry shops, **Quilpie Opals**. The charming English Tudor-style lane known as London Court has **Costello's** for excellent jewelry and **Fine Presence** for good quality crafts.

DEPARTMENT STORES

Perth's two major department stores are found across from each other in the downtown pedestrian mall area: **Myer Department Store** at Forest Place and Murray Street Mall and **Aherns Department Store** at Murray Street Mall and Hay Street Mall.

DOWNTOWN STREETS

A few streets adjacent to the pedestrian malls and shopping arcades offer some of Perth's best shopping. Be sure to head one block west to King and Murray Streets. King Street, between Hay and Murray Streets, has become Perth's upscale shopping street ("Bond Street") with fine boutiques and art galleries. Here you'll find **Desert Designs** and **Creative Native** for Aboriginal paintings, clothing designs, and arts and crafts; **Greenhill Galleries** for paintings of top Australian artists; and **Louis Vuitton**, **Cartier**, **Kookai**, and **King Street Couture** for brand name (Gucci, Valentino, Armani, Versace, Moshini) fashion clothes, accessories, and jewelry. You'll also find a few nice cafes and restaurants along this street. Just around the corner, along Murray Street, is one of Western Australia's best craft centers, **Craftwest Shop** of the Centre for Contemporary Crafts (357 Murray Street).

MUSEUMS AND GALLERIES

Just north of the train station and downtown shopping center is the large Perth Cultural Centre complex with its four buildings: Perth Institute of Contemporary Art, Western Australian

Museum, Art Gallery of Western Australia, and Library. The Museum Shop in the Art Gallery has a good selection of art books. From the Art Gallery you can take the walkover, which crosses the railway station and Wellington Street, and connects with Myer Department Store.

One of the highlights of visiting Perth is making a trip to the Government of Western Australia's **Perth Mint** (310 Hay Street, corner of Hill Street) in downtown Perth to see the gold minting process, view the large collection of gold nuggets and memorabilia, and perhaps have your own souvenir medallion minted while you wait. The Perth Mint also has a shop which includes gold nuggets, coins, jewelry, and souvenirs.

SUBURBAN SHOPPING

While the northern suburb of Morley has the largest shopping center (Galerie), it's mostly of interest to local residents. The best suburban shopping for visitors tends to be found in nearby Claremont and Subiaco. In Claremont look for shops, especially boutiques and home decorative, at Bayview Terrace (look for **Plantation Trading Company** with its furniture and accessories from India). But Subiaco, especially along Hay Street and Rokeby Road, is really the place to go. Here you'll find nice jewelry shops, art galleries, boutiques, and gift shops along with several appealing cafes and restaurants. Be sure to visit the famous **Linneys** (37 Rokeby Road) for top quality South Sea pearls and jewelry designs. For some of the best quality Aboriginal art, especially paintings and sculptures, in Western Australia, visit **Indigenart** (115 Hay Street). The large home decorative shop next door, **Empire Homewares**, with its extensive collection of distinctive international furniture, pillows, and tableware, is well worth visiting. If you're in this area around lunch time, be sure to stop at the popular bistro Oriel (483 Hay Street); on a nice day, get an outdoor table facing the main street.

MARKETS

Like other communities in Australia, Perth and its nearby communities host several markets. Some are weekend markets, others are Sunday markets, and a few are evening markets. Most offer some combination of handicrafts, fresh produce, second hand clothing, and food outlets. Located within 50 kilometers of Perth, some of the most popular markets include:

❑ **Canning Vale Markets:** *Canning Vale, Market City markets (corner of Ranford and Bannister Roads). Open Sunday 7am-2pm.* This is Western Australia's largest undercover market. It's one big flea market with over 1,000 stalls offering new and secondhand goods.

❑ **The E Shed Markets:** *Fremantle, Victoria Quay. Open on weekends.* This waterfront market includes about 100 stalls offering arts and crafts, souvenirs, and gift items.

❑ **Fremantle Markets:** *Corner of South Terrace and Henderson Streets, Fremantle, Tel. 9335-2515. Open Friday 9am-9pm, Saturday 9am-5pm, and Sunday and Monday 10am-5pm.* Housed in the old Victorian Market Hall which was built in 1897, this popular and award-winning market includes more than 150 stalls offering everything from prints, pottery, jewelry, clothing and accessories to antiques, sheepskin and leather goods, jarrah and cane products, dried wildflowers, opals, and fresh produce.

❑ **Galleria Art and Craft Market:** *Located in downtown Perth adjacent to the Art Gallery of Western Australia. Open weekends 9am-5pm.* Offers a good range of locally produced arts and crafts.

❑ **Gosnells Railway Markets:** *Gosnells, Albany Highway. Open Thursday, Saturday, and Sunday 10am-5:30pm and Friday 10am-8:30pm.* A replica of an old Australian railway station, this market includes over 100 arts and crafts stalls as well as a growers market and international food hall.

❑ **Mardi Gras Markets:** *Malaga, corner of Alexander Drive and Beach Road. Open Friday 12noon-5:30pm and weekends 9am-5:30pm.* Includes over 100 stalls offering a wide range of handmade Western Australian products and produce.

❑ **Midland Military Markets:** *Bellevue, corner of Clayton Street and Military Road. Open Friday through Monday 9am-5pm (Tel. 9250-2998).* Offers jewelry, antiques, souvenirs, knick knacks, fruits, vegetables, flowers, and entertainment.

❑ **Midland Sunday Markets:** *Midland, Crescent Car Park. Sunday 8am-4pm.* This open air market has numerous stalls offering jewelry, crafts, and food items.

❑ **Scarborough Fair Markets:** *Scarborough, corner of Scarborough Beach Road and West Coast Highway. Open weekends 9am-5:30pm.* The area's only seaside markets which are located next to the Rendezvous Observation City hotel.

❑ **Stock Road Markets:** *Bibra Lake, corner of Stock Road and Spearwood Avenue. Open weekends 9am-5pm.* Has numerous stalls offering a wide range of clothes, jewelry, used furniture, gift items, produce, and baked goods.

❑ **Subiaco Station Street Markets:** *Subiaco, just north of the Subiaco Railway Station. Open Saturday, Sunday, and Monday 9am-5:30pm.* One of Perth's largest undercover markets with numerous stalls offering arts, crafts, souvenirs, jewelry, rugs, pottery, gems, wildflowers, and gift items. Includes international food stalls.

❑ **Subiaco Pavilion:** *Subiaco, opposite the train station, corner of Roberts and Rokeby Roads. Open Thursday and Friday, 10am-9pm, and Saturday and Sunday 10am-5pm.* Includes 15 international food stalls as well as 60 specialty stalls located in an air-conditioned converted warehouse. Within a couple of minutes walk to the Subiaco Station Street Markets.

❑ **Wanneroo Weekend Mega Market:** *Wangara (just south of Wanneroo), Prindiville Drive. Open weekends and Monday 9am-5pm.* One of the largest markets in Perth with nearly 180 stalls offering everything from gift items and novelties to fresh produce, gardening items, and food stalls.

FACTORY OUTLET SHOPPING

Perth's factory outlets are found at **Factory Outlets Direct** (52 Lord Street, East Perth, Tel. 9221-8881). Open daily 10am-5pm (Sunday 12noon-5pm), here you'll find several name brand clothing and accessory clearance centers with savings of up to 70% over the normal retail prices. Look for **Intangible**, **Just Jeans**, **Table Eight**, **Brown Sugar**, **Surf Lords**, **Corfu**, **Menswear Direct**, and **Martins Shoes**. Includes a food court.

BEST OF THE BEST

We've found the following shops in Perth and Subiaco (we examine Fremantle separately in the next section) to be well worth visiting. They offer quality products and appear to be especially reliable.

GEMS AND JEWELRY

❑ **Linneys:** *37 Rokeby Road, Subiaco, Tel. 9382-4077.* The Australian jewelry industry using diamonds and pearls is a relatively new industry—started in the mid-1980s. Alan Linney, a talented jeweler who owns this shop, along with Bill Reed, a geologist and pearler who operates Linneys in Broome, are largely responsible for starting this industry. If you're looking for excellent quality diamonds, opals, and pearls as well as unique designs, be sure to visit this shop. Nearly 50% of the jewelry stock at Linneys in Broome comes from this shop. You'll often find Alan Linney at this shop working with his own designs or with his design team.

❑ **Quilpie Opals and Gems:** *Shop 6 Piccadilly Arcade, off Hay Street Mall, Tel. 9321-8687.* Known as Australia's first producer of the Queensland Boulder Opal, this long esta-blished (since 1969) family company is a leading specialist on opal and opal jewelry and a key pioneer of the Boulder Opal. As you may quickly discover when visiting this shop, like the pearl trade in Australia, there is a interesting history related to this company and the revival of the Boulder Opal trade in Australia due to the key role of one individual. Discovered in Western Queensland in the 1880's, the Boulder Opal enjoyed a brief period of prosper-ity during the 1880's and 1890's. It wasn't until 1969 that a local pharmacist, Desmond Burton, in the small Western Queensland town of Quilpie (population 747) literally revived the opal mining industry by introducing modern machinery. Reintroducing the Boulder Opal into the market after an absence of 50 years, Quilpie Opals became the leaders in mining several fields in Western Queensland. Today the mining area of Quilpie Opals and other compa-nies now encompasses nearly 250,000 square kilometers. Many of today's opal miners, wholesalers, jewelers, and retail buyers are heavily indebted to the pioneering work of Desmond Burton, the proprietor of Quilpie Opals. This shop offers a wide range of stones and jewelry, from budget souvenir pieces to investment quality pieces. Be sure to visit the new museum upstairs. Quilpie Opals also has shops in Brisbane, Cairns, Surfers Paradise (Gold Coast), Quilpie, and Tokyo.

❑ **Costello's:** *Shop 5-6, London Court, Tel. 9325-8588, www. costellos.com.au.* Offers a good selection of Argyle diamonds, South Sea pearls, and opals. Specializes in pink and champagne diamonds. Also includes black pearls.

ABORIGINAL ARTS AND CRAFTS

❑ **Desert Designs:** *28 King Street.* The new art gallery in the downstairs area displays the works of many top Western Australian Aborigine artists. The upstairs area is primarily devoted to unique clothes in Aboriginal designs. Ask about their shop in Fremantle which is called Japingka Gallery (114 High Street). That gallery may have additional prints and paintings not found in this gallery.

❑ **Indigenart:** *The Mossenson Gallery, 115 Hay Street, Subiaco, Tel. 9388-2899.* Offers nice quality art work of Aborigines in Western Australia, including Wandjinas produced by Lily Karadada. Changes exhibits every three weeks. Includes paintings, didgeridoos, wood sculptures (Tiwi poles), baskets, prints, scarves, ceramics, boomerangs, and books.

❑ **Creative Native:** *32 King Street, Tel. 9322-3398.* This large Aboriginal art and souvenir shop has a huge inventory of tourist quality arts and crafts, including didgeridoos, boomerangs, T-shirts, placemats, jewelry, and hats on the ground floor. The upstairs gallery area includes rugs and paintings. The better quality stuff is found upstairs.

AUSTRALIAN ARTS AND CRAFTS

❑ **Craftwest Shops:** *Centre for Contemporary Craft, King Street Arts Centre, 357 Murray Street, Tel. 9226-2799.* This is the state center for craft professionals in Western Australia. The small shop includes wood crafts, jewelry, pots, ceramics, and scarves by its members. You may find similar items by the same craftspeople in other commercial galleries in the city. The adjacent gallery changes exhibits every four weeks.

❑ **Olsson's:** *City Arcade.* Very nice contemporary Australian glassware and gift shop. Excellent quality and selections.

❑ **Fine Presence:** *Shop 43, London Court, Tel. 9325-3050.* This tiny shop has an excellent selection of quality arts and crafts from some of Western Australia's top craftspeople.

ACCOMMODATIONS

Perth has a good range of accommodations, from five-star to budget. Some of the best hotels and resorts in the city include:

❑ **Parkroyal Perth:** *54 Terrace Road, Perth, WA 6004, Australia, Tel. (61 8) 9325-3811, Fax (61 8) 9270-4299. Web site: www.parkroyal.com.au.* The Parkroyal Perth should technically be listed as a four star international hotel, but we were so impressed with this gem and consider it such good value, that it appears first. If you are determined that your hotel should have several restaurants, three telephones in your room and a hairdresser on premises, then look elsewhere. But if you are looking for a well furnished room, guestroom and bath with expected amenities, friendly staff who will try to accommodate your needs, and good value, take a good look at the Parkroyal Perth. The Parkroyal overlooks the Swan River and parkland, and is near the city center. With a new wing added to the hotel in 1999, and the existing guestrooms renovated, each of the 191 rooms have been well-appointed both for comfort and working ease. With the feel of a boutique hotel, the rooms are spacious and undoubtably the best lighted of any we have encountered—which is wonderful whether you have tasks to complete for business, need to write some postcards home, or just want to read in bed. The crisp white down filled coverlets and many pillows propped on the bed are inviting. The closets are quite spacious and the bath has all the expected amenities and a shower enclosure that is separate from the bathtub. There are 2 Presidential suites, king rooms, queen rooms and double-double rooms available. Three queen rooms are equipped for disabled guests. Data points in every room for plug-in access to the internet or email. Gusti's serves contemporary Mediterranean cuisine and offers an option of alfresco dining under rustling palm trees. Free valet parking and courtesy vehicle service to key business destinations. Fitness Center; Business Center; Conference and Banquet Facilities.

❑ **Burswood International Resort & Casino:** *Great Eastern Highway, P.O. Box 500, Victoria Park, WA 6100, Australia, Tel. (61 8) 9362-7777, Fax (61 8) 9470-2553. Web site: www.burswood.com.au.* The Burswood Resort is very nearly a self-contained city offering myriad recreational choices for the leisure traveler, full business facilities and a casino.

Overlooking the Swan River, the 414 rooms are accessed from a 47 meter atrium which surrounds many of the public areas with more than a half an acre of glass. Rooms feature the expected amenities. Both guestrooms and bathrooms are spacious. In-room TV even has a casino gaming instruction channel! 17 River suites provide a spacious lounge, dining-bar area, and large exterior balcony. International Floor rooms offer extra services and amenities. The Presidential Suite provides two bedrooms and two full bathrooms along with sauna, spa, bar, boardroom, dining areas, living area and a large balcony. Guests have the choice of dining in several restaurants in the hotel, including The Garden Terrace Restaurant, Atrium Buffet, Edo Kerin Japanese Restaurant or Windows—the Burswood's award winning signature restaurant. Within the casino are several additional restaurants including Paddy Hannan's, Carvery Corner. Genting Palace Chinese Restaurant, Victoria Station Steak and Seafood, La Rotisserie, and Spinners Café and Bar. Four Hundred and fifty employees service the Burswood's 414 rooms for an impressive employee-guest ratio which translates into service for the guest. Fitness Facilities; Business Center; Convention and Banquet Facilities including the Burswood Dome—the biggest indoor venue in the Southern Hemisphere. It is column-free and reputed to have superb acoustics.

❑ **Duxton Hotel:** *No. 1 St. George's Terrace, Perth, WA 6000, Australia, Tel. (61 8) 9261-8000, Fax (61 8) 9261-8020. Web site: www.duxton.com.au.* Situated next to the Perth Concert Hall in the city center, the Duxton is bordered to the south by the Swan River. Opened in 1996, this newest luxury hotel's 306 rooms and suites offer true luxury and all the amenities a guest expects and more. Many hotels claim to offer luxury; the Duxton Perth delivers. Club rooms situated on the top two floors offer additional services and amenities including Continental breakfast, canapes and cocktails every evening and security accessed express elevators. The Brasserie offers informal dining in a stylish atmosphere specializing in contemporary Australian cuisine. Fitness Facilities (claim to be Perth's largest hotel fitness center); Business Center; Conference Facilities.

❑ **Hyatt Regency:** *99 Adelaide Terrace, Perth, WA 6000, Australia, Tel. (61 8) 9225-1234, Fax (61 8) 9325-8899.* Situated within easy walking distance of the central business district, on the banks of the Swan River, the Hyatt's 367 rooms are spacious and tastefully decorated. Regency Club rooms offer extra amenities including complimentary Continental breakfast and cocktails and canapes in the evening. Gershwin's, the signature restaurant, periodically features special theme evenings such as Flamenco Night or Winemakers' and Musical evenings. Joe's Oriental Diner serves a wide range of Eastern-style cuisine or enjoy a meal in the Café. Fitness Facilities; Business Center; Conference and Banquet Facilities.

❏ **The Melbourne:** *Corner of Hay and Milligan Streets, Perth, WA 6000, Australia, Tel. (61 8) 9320-3333, Fax (61 8) 9320-3344.* Situated in the West End of Perth near shopping boutiques, restaurants and many businesses, The Melbourne is a luxury boutique hotel. Decorated in a New Orleans style, the 35 deluxe rooms and suites offer casual, but elegant furnishings. Some guestrooms have balconies; others open onto a private garden atrium for hotel guests. Executive suites provide additional seating area space. Non-smoking rooms are available and Fax machines are available upon request. Louisiana's Restaurant offers Australian, Cajun style, Italian and Asian influenced dishes. Fitness center nearby; Business Services; Conference and Banquet Facilities.

❏ **The Sebel of Perth:** *37 Pier Street, Perth, WA 6000, Australia, Tel. (61 8) 9325-7655, Fax (61 8) 9325-7383.* Situated in the city center, the Sebel is a short walk to the Swan River. The 119 spacious luxury guestrooms and suites feature large desks for working travelers. The Pyrenees Restaurant and the Office Bar and Café provide dining options. Fitness Facilities; Business Services; Conference and Banquet Facilities.

❏ **Rendezvous Observation City Hotel:** *The Esplanade, Scarborough Beach, WA 6019, Australia, Tel. (61 8) 9245-1000, Fax* (61 8) 9245-1345. Located 15 minutes from downtown Perth, directly on the beach, Hotel Rendezvous offers 333 guestrooms and suites appointed in luxury. Bathrooms clad in marble and mirrors add to the effect. Plaza Club floors receive additional amenities and services which include Continental breakfast and evening cocktails. Four restaurants include Dragon Palace for Chinese cuisine, Pines Grand Buffet and Carvery for international buffet selections, Café Estrada for wood fired pizzas and tapas grill, and Savannahs Restaurant. Shopping Arcade; Complimentary Shuttle to Perth and Fremantle; Fitness Facilities; Business Services; Convention and Banquet Facilities.

If you decide to stay over in Fremantle, the best hotel is the Esplanade Hotel Fremantle:

❑ **Esplanade Hotel Fremantle:** Corner Marine Terrace & Essex Streets, Fremantle, WA 6160, Australia, Tel. (61 8) 9432 4000, Fax (61 8) 9430 4539. Web site: *www.espla nade-freo.net.au*. The Esplanade Hotel Fremantle is located within the city center, within easy walking distance to many restaurants, shops and sights, yet offers seafront accommodation and great ocean views. Its 259 guestrooms and suites are nicely appointed in contemporary decor and offer the most upscale accommodations in Fremantle. Rooms have views overlooking the boat harbor, the Indian Ocean or the tropical garden and swimming pool. The Atrium Garden Restaurant offers an international smorgasbord; Café Panache serves local foods prepared with a cosmopolitan flair. Fitness Center; Conference and Banquet Facilities.

RESTAURANTS

The Perth area has many excellent restaurants. Since most of these places are very popular, and dining out seems to be a very popular form of evening entertainment, most of our restaurants require reservations. The dress style for even fine dining restaurants tends to be smart casual. Some of Perth's best restaurants include:

MODERN AUSTRALIAN

❑ **Fraser's Restaurant:** *Fraser Avenue, King's Park, Tel. 9481-7100.* It's difficult to top the view from this fine restaurant. Overlooks the Swan River and the Central Business District. Includes both indoor and outdoor dining. The well appointed restaurant serves numerous inventive dishes with a daily changing menu. Try the mixed seafood with couscous—if available.

❑ **Coco's:** *Southshore Centre, 85 The Esplanade, South Perth, Tel. 9474-3030. Open daily (starts at 9am Monday-Saturday and 8:30am on Sunday) for breakfast, lunch, and dinner.* Extremely popular Northern Italian restaurant serving great fresh seafood and char-grilled steaks. Menu changes daily. Great views of the city skyline and river. Excellent service.

❑ **Chez Uchino:** *120 Wellington Street, Mosman Park, Tel. 9385-2202.* This elegant restaurant offers excellent fusion cuisine which combines Japanese and French cuisine. Operated by one of Perth's top chefs, Osamu Uchino.

❑ **Indiana Tea House:** *99 Marine Parade, Cottesloe, Tel. 9385-5005.* This is one of Western Australia's most interesting restaurants for its architecture and cuisine. Located on the beach, it's grand colonial ambience transports you to South or Southeast Asia. Serves an interesting combination of Indian, Thai, Chinese, Malaysian, and Japanese dishes. Go early for the beautiful sunsets but wait until you can order from the full menu at 6:30pm (the early abbreviated menu offers limited choices).

ITALIAN

❑ **Perugino:** *77 Outram Street, West Perth, Tel. 9321-5420. Closed Sunday. No lunch on Saturday.* Great for lunch or dinner. Try the many seasonal specials, especially the risotto and pasta dishes. Good service.

❑ **Romany:** *188 William Street, Northbridge, Tel. 8328-8042. Closed Sunday. No lunch on Saturday.* This is Perth's oldest and most authentic Italian restaurant. The linoleum tables and chairs add to the aging quality of this old fashioned restaurant. Watch what you order since the kitchen here serves enormous portions. Good wine list. Reasonably priced.

FRENCH

❑ **Chanterelle:** *210 Rokeby Road, Subiaco, Tel. 9381-4637. Closed Sunday and Monday. No lunch on Saturday.* This elegant restaurant serves excellent traditional French dishes. Try the salmon, emu, or souffles.

❑ **Loose Box:** *6825 Great Eastern Highway, Mundaring, Tel. 9295-1787.* Located 30 minutes from the city, this fine dining restaurant turns out classic French cuisine with a contemporary touch. Nice ambience.

JAPANESE

❑ **Matsuri Sushi Bar:** *903 Hay Street, Tel. 9324-2420. Lunch (12noon-2:30pm) and dinner (6-10pm) Monday through Saturday.* Outstanding sushi and always consistent. Excellent service and good value.

❑ **Cheers Japanese Restaurant:** *375 Hay Street, Subiaco, Tel. 9388-2044. Lunch (12noon-2pm) Monday through Friday and dinner (6-9:30pm) Monday through Saturday.*

ASIAN

❑ **Genting Palace:** *Burswood International Resort Casino, Great Eastern Hwy., Burswood, Tel. 9362-7777.* Primarily serving excellent Cantonese cuisine, this is Perth's best Chinese restaurant. Excels with seafood dishes. Try the exceptional Peking Duck, shark's fin soup, and lobster. Serves dim sum for lunch (until 3pm) on weekends.

❑ **Joe's Oriental Diner:** *Hyatt Regency, 99 Adelaide Terrace, Tel. 9225-1268. Closed Sunday. No lunch on Saturday.* Serves excellent Thai, Indonesia, Malaysian, and Singapore dishes. The Thai dishes are exceptionally good.

ENJOYING YOUR STAY

There's lots to see and do in Perth in addition to shopping and dining. The city's many highlights include the following:

❑ **City Walking or Tram Tour:** For a quick overview of the city, including visiting its major attractions, take the City Tram to several sites around the city or take a self-directed walking tour of the city (see earlier discussion under "The Streets of Perth" section). The major sites include:

- Perth Rail Station
- Forrest Place
- London Court
- Perth Town Hall
- St. George's Cathedral
- The Deanery
- St. George's Hall
- Young Australia League
- Perth Fire Station League

- Royal Perth Hospital Museum
- St. Mary's Cathedral
- Perth Mint
- Concert Hall
- Government House
- Supreme Court Gardens
- Francis Burt Law Museum
- Old Perth Port
- The Weld Club
- Allan Green Conservatory
- Old Perth Boys School
- The Cloisters
- Barracks Arch
- His Majesty's Theatre
- King Street

❏ **King's Park:** *Located on a hill southeast of the city, off Thomas Street, Kings Park Road, and Fraser Avenue.* This is Perth's top tourist attraction. A 1,000 acre park with beautiful views of the Swan River and central business district (from the Forrest Drive end of the Broadwalk Vista and the top of the DNA tower), King's Park also has a botanical garden with a collection of over 2,500 native plants. In the evening, try Fraser's Restaurant on Fraser Avenue for excellent dining overlooking the city lights.

❏ **Burswood International Resort & Casino:** *Great Eastern Highway, Burswood, Tel. 9362-7777.* You can't miss this huge 10-story glass atrium hotel which also functions as Western Australia's largest casino and entertainment complex. Includes numerous restaurants, shops, and a casino offering 24-hour slots, roulette, blackjack, baccarat, keno, craps, and two-up games. Check out what's playing at the adjacent auditorium. Many international stars pack the house here with popular concerts.

❏ **Western Australian Museum:** *Perth Cultural Centre, James and Francis Streets, Tel. 9427-2700. www.museum.wa.gov.au. Open Sunday to Friday 10:30am-5pm and Saturday 1pm-5pm.* This is Western Australia's natural and cultural museum. Traces 3.5 billion years of fossil history. Includes exhibits on Aboriginal culture and Western Australia's birds, butterflies, mammals, and meteorites. The Marine Gallery includes an 80 foot long Blue Whale skeleton and exhibits of creatures found in the oceans and waterways of Western Australia. Includes some changing exhibitions.

❑ **Art Gallery of Western Australia:** *Perth Cultural Centre, James Street Mall, Tel. 9492-6600. www.artgallery.wa.gov.au. Open daily 10am-5pm.* This is one of Australia's most attractive museums. Offers an excellent permanent collection (2nd level) of Aboriginal art (paintings, sculptures, artefacts) from all over Australia (Arnhem Land, Central Desert, The Kimberley, Great Sandy Desert, and Cape York Peninsula). Also includes excellent paintings and sculptures produced by noted Western Australian artists. Be sure to stop at the **Art Gallery Shop** for art publications, art reproductions, cards, and gift items. The popular **Art Gallery Café** is good place for coffee, tea, or lunch. The **Information Desk** on the ground floor has lots of useful literature on art and galleries in Perth as well as Western Australia. The personnel here are very helpful and will answer most of your questions concerning the Western Australian art scene as well as the city of Perth!

❑ **Perth Mint:** *310 Hay Street, corner of Hill Street, Tel. 9421-7222. www.perthmint.com.au. Open weekdays 9am-4pm and Saturday and Sunday 9am-1pm (gold pouring demonstrations take place on the hour weekdays 10am-3pm and Saturday and Sunday 10am-12noon.* If you've not visited already as part of your Perth shopping adventure, be sure to stop here to see the gold minting process. This is Australia's oldest operating mint that has been refining gold since 1899. Mints the Australian Nugget coin. Highlights of a visit here include viewing the huge collection of gold nuggets and memorabilia, watching the pouring of gold, handling a $200,000 gold bar, and having your own souvenir medallion minted.

❑ **Perth Zoo:** *20 Labouchere Road, South Perth, Tel. 9474-3551. www.perthzoo.wa.gov.au. Open daily 9am-5pm.* This award-winning tourist attraction is located across the Narrows Bridge in South Perth. One of Australia's best zoos. Includes a wide range of Australian and international wildlife. Be sure to visit the Great Ape complex with its Orangutans, the Nocturnal House, the walk through aviary, the Great Cat enclosure, and the wild bird lake.

❑ **Swan River Cruises:** *Captain Cook Cruises, Pier 3, Barrack Street Jetty, Perth and East Street Jetty, Fremantle. Tel. 9325-3341. www.brimstone.com.au/cook.* Offers a variety of day (9:45am and 2pm departures) and evening cruises along the Swan River. Day time cruises ($24) take 2 hours and

45 minutes and pass by the restored Swan Brewery, Royal Perth Yacht Club, and Millionaire's Row. Saturday evening dinner cruise ($60) departs at 8pm and returns around 11:30pm. Also can take one-way cruises during the day (from either Perth, 9:45am and 2pm, or Fremantle, 11am and 3:15pm; cruise to Perth includes wine tasting). Also check out the less expensive ($12-14) competition—the MV Classique operated by **Oceanic Cruises** (Tel. 9325-1191 in Perth or Tel. 9430-5127 in Fremantle).

❑ **Underwater World:** *Located 20 minutes north of Perth at Hillary's Boat Harbour. Open daily 9am-5pm. Tel. 9447-7500. www.coralworld.com.* A fun place to meet dolphins, sharks, and other water animals. Popular shark feeding time is 11am and 2pm; dolphins get fed at 10:30am, 1:30pm, and 4pm. Includes a Touch Pool at noon and 3pm.

If time permits, you may want to make excursions to two of the area's major wine regions which also include shopping opportunities for arts and crafts. The two major areas, Swan Valley and Margaret River, are within an hour or two drive from Perth:

❑ **Swan Valley:** Located 30-45 minutes northeast of Perth, this is Western Australia's oldest wine region and one of its most popular holiday destinations. Enjoy touring wineries and breweries, cruising the Swan River, horseback riding, playing golf, and enjoying the area's many restaurants and shops. For good quality arts and crafts, be sure to stop at **Guildford Village Potters** (22 Meadow Street, Guildford, Tel. 9279-9859—also functions as the Swan Valley Visitor Information Centre) and **Maali Gallery** (8991 West Swan Road, Henley Brook, Tel. 9296-0704).

❑ **Margaret River:** Located 180 kilometers south of Perth, this town of 8,000 lies at the center of one of Western Australia's most popular wine regions. Includes several interesting arts and crafts shops in Margaret River as well as the surrounding area. The area also is famous for its excellent surfing. Stop at the **Augusta/Margaret River Tourist Bureau** (Bussell Highway, Tel. 9757-2911) for brochures and maps of the wineries in this region (they also are available through the Western Australian Tourist Centre in downtown Perth). Since there are over 40 wineries and numerous shops in this area, you may want to stay overnight in Margaret River in order to fully enjoy this area. You'll find several nice hotels and bed and breakfast places in and around the town.

Perth's **nightlife** tends to be centered around restaurants, bars, pubs, and the casino. Perth's major entertainment complex is found at the **Burswood International Resort & Casino** (Great Eastern Highway, Burswood, Tel. 9362-7777). The bar and pub scene is alive and well in Northbridge, which is immediately north of the downtown shopping center. It tends to be centered around William and James Streets. A somewhat honky-tonk area, with nightclubs and sex shops, one of the most popular and attractive pubs in this area is the **Brass Monkey Pub and Brasserie** (209 William Street, at the corner of James Street, Northbridge, Tel. 9227-9596). Get a table on the 2nd level balcony with a view of the city and street below. This is a pleasant location from which to spend the evening dining, drinking, and people watching.

For information on what's going on in the evenings, be sure to get a copy of the Saturday edition of the *Western Australian* which includes a weekly guide to cultural events and entertainment in the Perth area. Also, pick up a free copy of *X-Press Magazine* which includes lots of useful information on what's going on in the music, concert, and movie scene as well as covers pubs and clubs.

FREMANTLE

Located 19 kilometers southwest of Perth, Fremantle is the principal seaport for the State of Western Australia. Facing the ocean (but with few good ocean views) as well as located at the entrance to the Swan River, the city has developed into a combination historical city, arts and crafts center, water sports center, and restaurant and entertainment center. Many visitors come here for the day to shop, see a few sites, and enjoy the cafes and restaurants. It's most lively on the weekends when its two main markets—Fremantle Markets and E Shed Markets— are fully functioning.

Fremantle received major international recognition in 1988 when it hosted the Americas Cup yacht race. It also received a major facelift at that time in anticipation of a huge influx of tourists, which indeed descended on this relatively tranquil community. Since then, the city has continued to attract tourists but not of the same class as those who attended the Americas Cup event. Indeed, the city now serves many day-trippers who visit for only a few hours or budget travelers who decide to stay for a few days and hang out in the city's many cafes.

While you will find several things to see and do in this area, you also may find Fremantle to be somewhat overrated. It has a decided working class and budget travel character to it which at times gives it a seedy, frontier character. While it has a few interesting shops and markets, for the most part this is not a quality destination; its most popular shops tend to be the ubiquitous $2 shops which further add to the city's unexciting character. Indeed, Fremantle's shopping and attractions don't warrant staying overnight in this city. You can easily take the train or drive to Fremantle within a half hour. This city does have enough going on to justify spending a few hours there. Make sure you visit Fremantle, but don't have excessive expectations of having a great time here. It's an interesting old port town with a decided colonial atmosphere.

At the same time, Fremantle is a "work in progress." Many of the old warehouses are being restored and converted into studios, apartments, and townhouses. The downtown historic area, when fully restored, may some day attract better quality shops, restaurants, cafes, and visitors.

GETTING TO KNOW YOU

Fremantle is a small city which is relatively easy to get around in. For a quick orientation to the city, visit the city's Web site: *www.fremantle.wa.gov.au*. Once in Fremantle, be sure to stop at the **Fremantle Tourist Bureau** (Town Hall, Kings Square, corner of Adelaide and William Streets, Tel. 9431-7878) for maps and brochures. The helpful personnel here can answer most of your questions and will do tour and accommodation bookings for you. Also stop at the **Notre Dame Shop** (47 Henry Street which is part of the Department of Land Management and Conservation, Tel. 9430-8600, open 10am-5:30pm). This shop has lots of useful brochures on the area as well as promotes its own Aboriginal cultural tours.

The major town area is centered along High Street, William Street, South Terrace, Marine Terrace, Henry Street, Bannister Street, Nairn Street, Essex Street, and Norfolk Street. Within this area you'll find many shops, restaurants, cafes, and hotels. **South Terrace** is known as the city's cappuccino strip because it's lined with many outdoor cafes. Here you'll also find several souvenir shops, bookstores, and the ubiquitous $2 stores. The colorful **Numbats Gifts and Souvenirs** (60 Market Street) is a one-stop shop for Australian arts, crafts, gifts, and souvenirs. **Elysian Glass** (255 South Terrace) offers handcrafted glassware by local artist Elizabeth Mavrick.

High Street is the central shopping street. Starting at Little High Street in the east and ending at William Street (Kings Square) in the west, this street is lined with antique, art, and craft shops (look for **Desert Designs**, **Staircase Gallery**, **Quay West Gallery**, **Japingka Gallery**, and **Creative Native**) as well as two of the city's shopping arcades which fan off from the High Street pedestrian mall—Atwell Arcade and Manning Arcade. These arcades also lead into eight other small to medium-sized shopping arcades and malls—Woodsons Arcade, Wesley Way Arcade, Westgate Mall, Woolstores Shopping Centre, High Street Arcade, Paddy Troy Mall, South Terrace Plaza, and Henderson Mall. With the exception of Atwell Arcade (look for **Desert Designs** for colorful clothes, **The Nugget Shop** for gold jewelry and opals in small glass blown figures, and the **Porcelain Art Shop** for hand painted porcelain by local artists and gold jewelry), most of these places are filled with nondescript clothing, souvenir, and $2 shops.

Along **Marine Terrace**, look for **Artisans of the Sea** (The Bank, corner of Marine Terrace and Collie Street, Tel. 9336-3633) which is the world headquarters for Kailis Broome Pearls. In addition to offering excellent quality pearl jewelry (smaller and more practical that than larger and more expensive Paspaley Pearls), this shop shows a 10-minute video upstairs explaining the pearling trade in Australia.

Some of the streets leading into the central downtown area yield a few excellent shops, including antique and craft centers. Look for **J Shed** along Fleet Street for arts and crafts studios (**Greg James Sculpture Studio** and **Beaufort Pottery**) as well as shops along Bannister Street (**Craft Works** and **Klopper Pottery**). Henry Street is the **Moores Building Art Gallery** (46 Henry Street) which houses the contemporary art gallery of the Artists Foundation of Western Australia.

Outside the city center you'll find a small but nice craft shop at the **Fremantle Arts Centre** (1 Finnerty Street, Tel. 9335-8244, *www.fac.org.au*), Fremantle's former lunatic asylum. Across the street from the Centre is a nice craft shop specializing in leaded glass, **The Artists Window** (1A Tuckfield Street). Also look for a few antique shops which are found together in North Fremantle along Queen Victoria Street and Tydeman Road (**Matilda's Antique Centre, Antichita Antiques, Waratah Antiques, The Church Antique Centre,** and **Antiques and Meubles**).

Fremantle is especially famous for the **Fremantle Markets** (corner of South Terrace and Henderson Street, Tel. 9335-2515) which are held Friday (9am-9pm), Saturday (9am-5pm), and Sunday and Monday (10am-5pm). Housed in an old Victorian building, the markets include over 150 stalls offering a wide range of arts, crafts, and food. The weekend **E Shed Markets** at Victoria Quay include over 100 stalls offering local arts, crafts, gifts, souvenirs, and fresh fruits and vegetables.

Best Shopping

If you have limited time in Fremantle, you may want to focus your shopping efforts on a few of Fremantle's best quality shops. Since Fremantle tends to attract many artists and craftspeople, you'll find many shops offering arts and crafts. We found these shops in Fremantle to warrant special attention:

❑ **Artisans of the Sea:** *The Bank, corner of Marine Terrace and Collie Street, Tel. 9336-3633.* This attractive jewelry shop also functions as the headquarters for Kailis Pearls in Broome. Excellent quality pearl jewelry. Ask to see the 10-minute video (upstairs) if you don't know much about the Australian pearling industry. Excellent and friendly service.

❑ **Japingka Gallery:** *47 High Street, Tel. 9335-8265.* Operated by Desert Designs (also has a gallery in its King Street shop in Perth), this is one of the area's best Aboriginal art galleries. Showcases some of Australia's top Aborigine artists from Warman (East Kimberley), Balgo (Western Desert), Oenpelli (Arnhem Land), and Utopia and Yuendemu (Central Desert). In addition to paintings and prints, the gallery includes didgeridoos, books, and pure wool rugs (produced in India and Belguim) with designs by Jimmy Pike and Doris Gingingara. The upstairs gallery includes exhibits that change every six weeks. The gallery appeals to both the causal arts and crafts shopper and serious collectors of top quality Aboriginal art. Represents such well known artists as Kathleen Petyarre, Helicopter Tjungerai, Rover Thomas, George Milpurrurru, Peter Nabarlambarl, Daisy Napaltjarri, Lily Karadada, Doris Gingingara, and Jimmy Pike.

❑ **Staircase Gallery:** *57 High Street, Tel. 9430-6447, http:// interway.ois.net.au/fremart.* Walk in the front door and this small shop makes an immediate statement with its massive and fascinating wood sculptured staircase to the upper level. Offers lots of interesting wood crafted items, from Jarrah wood bowls and boxes to wine racks and furniture.

❑ **Creative Native:** *65 High Street, Tel. 9335-6993.* This is the branch shop of the same shop on King Street in Perth. Offers lots of Aboriginal art and artefacts, from paintings, jewelry, and pottery to didgeridoos and boomerangs.

❑ **The Nugget Shop:** *Shop 6 Atwell Arcade, Tel. 9430-8994, www.nettrek.com/au/~aurum.* Offers an interesting collection of natural good nuggets, iron ore, gemstones, jewelry, watches, and clocks.

❑ **Desert Designs:** *114 High Street Mall, Tel. 9430-4101.* Offers colorful fashion clothes for both children and adults using traditional Aboriginal designs. Includes everything from ladies' and men's fashion in silk and linen, scarves, bags, T-shirts, to children's wear, rugs, and art. Includes the same wool rugs as found in Japingka Gallery.

❑ **Beaufort Pottery:** *3/J Shed, Fleet Street, Tel. 9430-7887.* Also known as **J Shed Studios.** Produces attractive fountains. This is a working ceramic studio which also sells its items to wandering shoppers. Look for Ian Macrae's unique tiered ceramic fountains (also ask to see his photo album of different styles) and Jenney Dawson Ceramics.

❑ **Greg James Sculpture Studio:** *J Shed, next door to Beaufort Pottery.* This working studio produces large sculptured figures for outdoor display. You'll see his works in several public places in Perth.

❑ **Elysian Glass:** *255 South Terrace, Tel. 9336-3922. Open Wednesday to Sunday, 11am-6pm or by appointment.* The glassware gallery of local artist Elizabeth Mavrick. Includes many beautiful and unique glassware pieces.

❑ **Bannister Street Craftworks:** *8-12 Banister Street, Tel. 9336-2035. Open Tuesday-Sunday 11am-5:30.* This craft cooperative includes the studios of several artists who produce a large variety of craft items, from woodcrafts, leather goods, and ceramics to hand-blown glass, metal-work, and souvenirs.

❑ **Porcelain Art Shop:** *Shop 10, Atwell Arcade, Tel. 9430-8902.* Operated by Heather Tailor, this unique craft shop includes hand painted porcelain (plates, cups, saucers) by local artists as well as gold jewelry and China painting supplies.

❏ **Numbats Gifts and Souvenirs:** *60 Market Street, Tel. 9430-8838.* In any other setting, this might be considered a shop full of tourist kitsch. However, given its close proximity to the South Terrace area, it stands out as one of the best souvenir shops. Its two floors are crammed with Australian made crafts, from hand painted furniture (upstairs) and pottery to pewterware, clothes, woodcrafts, stuffed animals, and Aboriginal artefacts.

❏ **Craft Shop:** *Fremantle Museum and Arts Center, James and Finnerty Street.* Includes a small but very nice collection of wood bowls and boxes, ceramics, glassware, textiles, and silver jewelry. The tiny adjacent bookshop has many interesting art books, novels, and travel books.

❏ **Matilda's Antique Centre:** *222 Queen Victoria Street, North Fremantle, Tel. 9335-6881.* Includes lots of good quality furniture and collectibles, especially silver, glass, boxes, jewelry, ceramics, and clocks.

ENJOYING YOUR STAY

If you decide to stay over in Fremantle, the best hotels are the **Esplanade Hotel Fremantle** (corner of Marine Terrace and Essex Street, Tel. 9432-4000 or Fax 9430-4539), **Fremantle Biscuit Factory Apartments** (330 South Terrace, South Fremantle, Tel. 9430-5255 or Fax 9430-5266), and **Fothergills** (bed and breakfast, 20-22 Ord Street, Tel. 9335-6784 or Fax 9430-7789).

Restaurants abound in Fremantle. Some of the best restaurants include **Granita's** (330 South Terrace at Jenkins Street, Tel. 9336-4660) for Italian seafood and pasta; **Chunagon** (46 Mews Road, Tel. 9336-1000) for excellent Japanese cuisine); **Roma** (9 High Street, Tel. 9335-3664, no credit cards) for top Italian cuisine.

You can easily cover Fremantle's major attractions in a couple of hours. Pick up a copy of the free *Your Guide to Perth and Fremantle* or the *Fremantle Specialist Tourist Map and Information Guide* and follow the self-guided city walking tours outlined in these publications. Following these guides, you'll encounter most of the city's major landmarks. We've highlighted the most interesting attractions:

- A Shed
- Cy O'Connor Statue
- Duyfken Replica

- E Shed Markets
- Fremantle Boy's School
- **Fremantle Markets**
- **Fremantle Prison Museum**
- Fremantle Railway Station
- Fremantle Town Hall
- **Historic Boats Museum**
- **King's Square**
- Proclamation Plaque and Tree
- Samson House
- St. John's Anglican Church
- St. Patrick's Catholic Church
- The Moores Building
- **The Round House**
- University of Notre Dame
- **Western Australian Maritime Museum**
- Wesley Church
- Western Power Energy Museum

Other major attractions that go beyond the walking tours include:

- Artillery Barracks or Army Museum (corner of Tucker and James Streets)
- **Fremantle Museum and Arts Centre** (1 Finnerty Street)
- Fremantle War Memorial and Park (corner of High and Bateman Streets)

10

Alice Springs

ALICE SPRINGS IS A RELATIVELY ISOLATED FRON-
tier town of nearly 25,000 residents. Noted for hosting
nearly 200,000 visitors a year, as well as serving as
home for a large community of U.S. citizens who
operate a highly secured communication facility, Alice Springs
also is an important center for Aborigine art and culture and
adventure travel. Located in the heart of Australia's famous
Outback, this is the second largest town in the Northern
Territory. The largest city, Darwin, is situated 1,305 kilometers
directly north via the Stuart Highway at the coastal Top End of
Australia. Adelaide lies 1,316 kilometers directly south by way
of the Stuart Highway; it also can be reached by rail (Adelaide
to Alice Springs in 20 hours) via Australia's great train adventure, the Ghan. Most visitors, however, arrive in Alice Springs
by air. Located in the center of the country, Alice Springs can
be reached from most major cities within 2 to 2¾ hours by air
(2 hours from Darwin and Adelaide; 2½ hours from Sydney
and Melbourne; and 2¾ hours from Perth and Cairns).

Thought by some as a hot, flat, dusty, fly-ridden, and
uninteresting place, there's much more to Alice Springs than
what initially meets the eye. Local residents, including its many
American expats, love this friendly, quirky, and irreverent little
community (even has its own yacht club and surf shop in the

middle of the desert!). Also known as The Red Centre, for its deep orange and red colored soil, this is the area of Ayers Rock and The Olgas—two of the world's most unique and impressive rock formations. It's also an area of Aborigines, festivals, camels, a casino, pedestrian shopping mall, shopping arcades, boutiques, and unusual festivals. While many cities in Australia are surprising to visitors, Alice Springs is more surprising than most other Australian communities. It's not what you would expect for such a remote Outback community.

GETTING TO KNOW YOU

Once a shabby town of rugged individualists, Alice Springs still retains its Outback frontier character while it also functions as a major tourist destination for those who want to sample the sights of the unique Outback. While by no means a shopper's paradise, it can claim to be a shopper's oasis. For it offers some surprising opportunities for those who are particularly interested in Outback art and the local Aboriginal cultures.

❑ This isolated frontier town is located in the center of the country. It can be reached from most major cities within 2 to 2¾ hours.

If you arrive in Alice Springs from any of Australia's major cities, you will experience a very sudden and striking transformation in Australia's physical, social, and cultural landscapes. First of all, Alice Springs is a small town with some big-city ideas about attracting tourists with unique festivals, a casino, hotels, tour companies, recreational opportunities, and a shopping mall. Arrive at the impressive new (1991) airport and you'll feel you've come to a special place. But take a drive to Anzac Hill overlooking the town or a hot air balloon ride, and you'll quickly discover that this indeed is a

❑ Alice Springs is a shopper's oasis. It offers some surprising opportunities for those who are particularly interested in Aboriginal art and culture. Here you'll find a large concentration of Aboriginal art galleries offering excellent quality arts and crafts at reasonable prices.

❑ On a hot day, the mixture of pesky flies, wind, dust, and sand confirms the fact that Alice Springs is a harsh area for rugged individualists.

❑ The town is very easy to get around on foot or by taxi. Most shops, hotels, restaurants, and sights are within walking distance.

small and remote town. Attend Alice Spring's famous Camel Cup races or Henley-On-Todd Regatta bottomless boat races on the dry bed of the Todd River, and you sense that some things are very different here in the Outback! This is a small town that likes to have fun in the hot, dusty, fly-ridden desert.

Second, Alice Springs is surrounded by an arid, harsh, and barren landscape exhibiting dramatic contrasts—temperature extremes, beautiful floral, unique fauna, unusual rock formations, and spectacular hues and colors. The landscape itself generates a sense of timelessness, an ethereal quality captured in many Aboriginal paintings. At night you can look up at the sky and see fabulous constellations, especially the Milky Way and Southern Cross.

Third, this area impresses you with its flies, wind, dust, and sand. The Outback flies are everywhere. You can't escape them except for fleeing into a fly-free air-conditioned vehicle or building. Depending on the time of year you visit, the flies can be either a mild annoyance—the winter months—or a major irritation—the rest of the year. The wind is often strong, blowing tons of dust and sand in all directions—but not removing the flies from your body! On a hot day, the mixture of pesky flies, wind, dust, and sand confirms the fact that Alice Springs and its surrounding countryside is indeed a harsh area for rugged individualists.

Fourth, Alice Springs quickly introduces you to the Aborigines and their unique culture as well as their socio-economic problems. Walk along the Todd Street Mall and you will see several groups of seemingly poor, dusty, and unkept Aborigines sitting around socializing with each other or drinking. Socially and economically dislocated, many of these Aborigines live on the outskirts of town or sleep in the dry bed of the Todd River next to trees and logs. And still others are visiting town from settlements to sell their paintings and carvings to local shops, galleries, and middlemen as well as to purchase additional art supplies, food, drink, clothing, and household provisions. The sight of these Aborigines in Alice Springs' major shopping areas may at first startle you with their primitive looks, charcoal skins, deep features, unkept appearance, and loud and aggressive manners amongst themselves. Nonetheless, they are a very shy people with outsiders and tend to keep to themselves; they will not bother you. Remember, you should not take photographs of them since they may take offense at such an invasion of their privacy.

THE STREETS OF ALICE SPRINGS

Thanks for small towns after shopping in Australia's big cities! Alice Springs is very easy to get around on foot and by taxi. The city is somewhat spread out over a 12 kilometer area, running north to south adjacent to the west bank of the Todd River (usually a dry river bed), but most places of interest are concentrated within a four block area in the center of the town.

Before arriving in Alice Springs, you may want to visit these Web sites for an introduction to the area:

> *www.ozemail.com/au/~asnews/* (local newspaper)
> *www.alicesprings.nt.gov.au*
> *www.nttc.com.au*
> *www.northernterritory.com/3-1.html*

Upon arriving in Alice Springs, you should pick up a map and tourist literature which are available at the airport and hotels as well as through the CATIA (Central Australian Tourism Industry Association) office's Visitor Centre (Tel. 8952-5800 and *www.cati.asn.au*). This Centre is located at the river end of Gregory Terrace next to the Town Library and opposite Todd Mall and is open Monday-Friday 9am-6pm and Saturday and Sunday 9am- 4pm. It also maintains an Information Centre at the airport. It's very helpful in providing literature, answering questions, and booking hotels and tours. Look for the following publications:

> *Welcome to Central Australia*
> *Four Wheel Drive Tracks and Unsealed Roads of C.A.*
> *Alice Springs Attractions*
> *Scenic Drive Guide to Central Australia*
> *The Guide to Central Australia*

Alice Springs has one main shopping street, Todd Mall–Todd Street–Gap Road. Just one block west of South Terrace–Leichhardt Terrace, which is adjacent to the river, the main shopping sections of Todd Street and Todd Mall intersect with the east-west streets called Stott Terrace, Gregory Terrace, and Parsons Street. Like many other streets in Australia, Todd Street changes its name three different times. The street stretches for more than 7 kilometers and is where most major shops and shopping centers are located. Being a very long street and not conveniently located within easy walking distance from such major hotels as Lasseters Hotel Casino and the Rydges Plaza Hotel (Barrett Drive), you may need to take a hotel bus or taxi into the center of town at the Todd Mall to begin your shopping adventure. After shopping along the Todd Mall and a few adjacent streets (Terrace and Hatley), you may wish to take a taxi (3 kilometers) until Todd Street becomes Gap Road and resume shopping (between Strehlow and Kempe Streets).

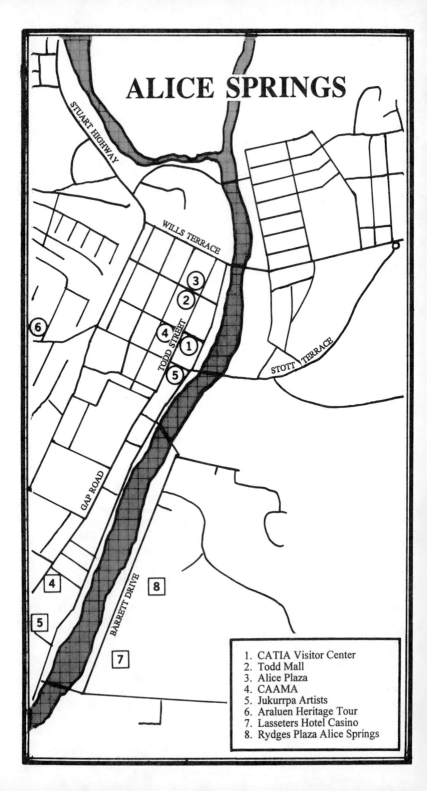

ALICE SPRINGS

STUART HIGHWAY

WILLS TERRACE

TODD STREET

STOTT TERRACE

GAP ROAD

BARRETT DRIVE

③
②
⑥
④
①
⑤

4

5

8

7

1. CATIA Visitor Center
2. Todd Mall
3. Alice Plaza
4. CAAMA
5. Jukurrpa Artists
6. Araluen Heritage Tour
7. Lasseters Hotel Casino
8. Rydges Plaza Alice Springs

SHOPPING ALICE SPRINGS

Shopping hours in Alice Springs are Monday through Friday 9am-5:30pm. Many shops are open on Saturday and Sunday. Every second Sunday morning of the month arts, crafts, food, and entertainment markets are held along the Todd Mall. Between September and Christmas, Thursday Night Markets (6-9pm) also are held at Todd Mall.

Alice Springs offers one of the easiest and most rewarding shopping experiences in all of Australia. It's easy because most shops are located within easy walking distance of each other in and around the Todd Mall area. It's rewarding because you'll find a large concentration of Aboriginal art galleries offering excellent quality arts and crafts at reasonable prices. Indeed, you can buy Aboriginal paintings in Alice Springs for a third of the price you'll pay for comparable art in Sydney and Melbourne. However, be forewarned that you may have to do some probing in order to find the top quality Aboriginal art. A few shops, such as the Australian Aboriginal Dreamtime Gallery and the Original Dreamtime Gallery, keep their top quality paintings in a special room, usually designed "Private", in the back of the shop or upstairs. A shop that may essentially look like a touristy arts and crafts shop may also be a serious art dealer. The front part of the shop brings in daily cash flow while the private section is more unpredictable. Always ask if a shop has a private gallery. You may be surprised at what you discover!

Shopping in Alice Springs is all about Aboriginal arts and crafts. In fact, Alice Springs has played a major role in the recent evolution of acrylic "sand" paintings with the emergence of the Papunya school of art. In the early 1970s Aboriginal artists in the Alice Springs area began painting in oils on canvas. Since then, this art form has flourished both domestically and internationally. The story of the evolution of this relatively recent art movement, from Alice Springs to major museums and art galleries around the world, is fascinating. It's well documented in Alice Springs' many galleries and museums.

WHAT TO BUY

Alice Springs has full service shopping centers and shops selling the latest in fashionwear, accessories, gift items, and Australiana. However, Alice Springs' major shopping strength is **Aboriginal arts**. Next to Darwin in the north, this town functions as the most important center for marketing arts and crafts produced by numerous Aboriginal groups in the Northern Territories.

Compared to similar quality items found in Sydney and Melbourne, Aboriginal art prices in Alice Springs are very good. A similar acrylic or bark painting to one selling for $1,000 in Sydney or Melbourne may sell for $350 in Alice Springs. The prices are less here, because you buy with only one or two middlemen between you and the artists; in Sydney and Melbourne you may be buying items that have already passed through the hands and mark-ups of three or four middlemen and rents are higher for shops in Sydney and Melbourne. However, a Tiwi bark basket that sells for $50 on Melville Island off the coast of Darwin, may cost $80 in Darwin, $100 in Alice Springs, and $200 in Sydney, because it first passes through middlemen who collect such items on Melville Island before marketing them in Darwin, Alice Springs, and Sydney. Bark paintings that primarily originate in the Darwin area will be cheaper there than in Alice Springs, but cheaper in Alice Springs than in Adelaide, Melbourne, Sydney, or Brisbane.

Several shops in downtown Alice Springs sell a good variety of Aboriginal arts and crafts from the western desert. The best buys in this area are the unique **acrylic dot paintings** which used to be done only in sand and then destroyed. Lacking trees for wood and bark—found more abundantly further north near Darwin—the local Aboriginal art traditions were committed to sand and rocks, until the twentieth century. First developed by Geoff Bardon, an art and craft teacher at the nearby Papunya School, today there are over 100 Aboriginal artists using the acrylic and canvas mediums to paint colorful dreamtime themes and stories. Associated with the Papunya Tula art school, this is one of Australia's most important contemporary art movements, and it's centered here in Alice Springs. Consequently, you will find the best prices on these paintings in the shops of Alice Springs; prices are higher in Darwin, Adelaide, Melbourne, and Sydney. If you appreciate this art style, you can spend a great deal of time going from one shop to another to learn more about this school of art as well as discover just the right painting with the right colors, designs, and dream time story.

Another good buy in Alice Springs are the beautiful handmade **batik cloth designs** which we have not seen outside Alice Springs. Marketed under the name Utopia Batik, this textile work is being done on Aboriginal settlements near Alice Springs and marketed through the **CAAMA Shop** (Central Australian Aboriginal Media Associate at 101 Todd Street). **Gondwana II** (2/11 Todd Mall) also offers some lovely batik silk textiles which make ideal wall hangings.

Several shops also sell **woodcarvings** of small animals using a traditional Aboriginal wood burning process; **bark paintings** from the Darwin area; **carved poles** and **bark baskets** from the Tiwi tribe of Melville Island; didgeridoos, clap sticks, boomerangs, and music.

WHERE TO SHOP

Knowing where to shop in Alice Springs is very simple: go to the shops and shopping centers in and around the tree-lined Todd Mall, the town's only pedestrian mall, as well as Todd Street, Hartley Street, and Gregory Terrace. All the shops and shopping centers are conveniently located within easy walking distance of each other.

Alice Springs has two major shopping centers: Alice Plaza on Todd Mall and Yeperenye Centre on Hartley Street, which is located one block north of Todd Mall. **Alice Plaza** (formerly the Ford Plaza) will probably be your first shopping stop in Alice Springs, because it lies at the city center. This small but nice air-conditioned shopping mall includes several souvenir, clothing, shoe, camera, book, and music stores as well as a food court, supermarket, and liquor store. The upper level houses the Museum of Central Australia which focuses on prehistory and geology and includes a nice book shop.

Outside these shopping centers you'll find several shops concentrated in a four block area along Todd Mall, Todd Street, Gregory Terrace, and Stott Terrace. Some of the most interesting shops here include:

❑ **Australian Aboriginal Dreamtime Gallery:** *71 Todd Mall, Tel. 8953-0222.* Formerly known as the Central Australian Artifacts shop, which was housed in the former Ford Plaza, this is one of Alice Springs best galleries. It offers a wide range of arts and crafts, from souvenirs to museum quality art. The front part of this shop primarily offers paintings, boomerangs, didgeridoos, and large carvings priced appropriately for the average tourist interested in Aborigine art and artefacts. The adjacent gift shop is really into tourist souvenirs—T-shirts, stuffed toys, key rings, and coffee mugs. But the really "good stuff" of museum quality is found in the "private" back room of the first shop. If you are a serious collector, ask to see this special art gallery. This shop is a supplier to major museums. It does excellent packing and shipping.

❏ **The Original Dreamtime Gallery:** *63 Todd Mall, Tel. 8952-8861.* This rather large Aboriginal arts, crafts, and gift shop includes lots of didgeridoos, paintings, boomerangs, carvings, jewelry, pottery, T-shirts, and clothes. Serious art collectors should ask to see the "private" gallery on the upper level which includes many high quality and expensive ($2000+) paintings and carvings. This company also has branch shops in Cairns and Sydney.

❏ **Aboriginal Art and Culture Centre:** *86-88 Todd Street, Tel. 8952-3408. http://aboriginalart.com.au.* Also refers to itself as the Australian Aboriginal Art Gallery. This Aboriginal owned (Pwerte Marnte Marnte Aboriginal Corporation, a Southern Arrernte Tribal group) and operated shop offers a nice selection of arts, crafts, and souvenirs: paintings, rugs, didgeridoos, boomerangs, pottery, screens, carvings, baskets, shields, spears, and jewelry along with T-shirts, books, and post cards. But this is more than just a shop. It includes a Living History Museum profiling Arrernte culture, art gallery (upstairs and on Internet), cultural performances, and a "Didgeridoo University" where you can learn to play this unique musical instrument. The Centre also sponsors half- and full-day Aboriginal cultural tours to Arrernte Country (Mparntwe).

❏ **Papunya Tula Artists:** *78 Todd Street, Tel. 8952-4731.* Founded in 1972, this cooperative is one of the most important art galleries promoting Aboriginal art of the central and western deserts—the Papunya Tula school of artists. Represents the works of nearly 100 artists. Known for their high quality paintings which are found in major museums, galleries, and collections worldwide. Also includes some craft items such as necklaces, carvings, and traditional weapons.

❏ **Gallery Gondwana:** *54 Todd Mall, Tel. 8953-1577.* Specializes in Aboriginal and tribal art. Serves as the local agent for paintings from the East Kimberley and Balgo Hills regions of Western Australia. Includes paintings and craft work from Western, Central and Eastern Desert regions of Central Australia, Arhemland, Bathurst and Melville Islands, Papua New Guinea, Timor, and other areas of Southeast Asia. Also offers wood carvings, fabrics, and pottery as well as handcrafted contemporary jewelry by Australian jeweler Richard Ivey.

❑ **Gondwana II:** *2/11 Todd Mall, Tel. 8953-5511.* Essentially a home decorative shop with many interesting furniture (wood and metal) and accessory pieces, such as lamps, textiles, paintings, and sculptures. Many items are imported from Indonesia. A very nice craft and design center that represents a good range of contemporary Australian arts and crafts.

❑ **CAAMA:** *101 Todd Street, Tel. 8952-9207.* Known as the Central Australian Aboriginal Media Association or CAAMA, this shop offers a good range of Aboriginal arts and crafts, including paintings, carvings, prints, fabrics, didgeridoos, music, and books. Includes attractive hand-painted scarves Much of the art work comes from Utopian artists. The shop is run by an Aboriginal organization that operates a major radio station beamed to Aboriginal communities.

❑ **Aboriginal Desert Art Gallery:** *87 Todd Mall, Tel. 8953-1005.* Includes one of the largest collections of Aboriginal art in Australia, although most of it is found in its shops in Melbourne and Sydney. The front part of this shop includes lots of the usual tourist quality arts, crafts, and souvenirs, such as didgeridoos, paintings, boomerangs, carvings, jewelry, T-shirts, and leather hats. Quality paintings are found in the rear of this shop in the section called "Collectors Gallery." If you plan to visit Melbourne and Sydney, be sure to visit their other shops (Melbourne, 31 Flinders Lane; Sydney, 203 Clarence Street).

❑ **Jukurrpa Artists:** *Stott Terrace, Tel. 8953-1052.* One of four Aboriginal-owned galleries in Alice Springs. This 23-member coop represents nearly 800 different artists who are mainly Aboriginal women. Includes some carved animals. Paintings tend to be piled on the floor and must be pulled out like rugs for viewing. Sponsors cultural tours to Aboriginal settlements.

❑ **Mbantua Gallery:** *71 Gregory Terrace, Tel. 8952-5571. www.mbantua.com.au.* Includes a wide range of arts, crafts, and souvenirs, especially paintings, didgeridoos, boomerangs, carvings, and T-shirts. Recently expanded gallery has a permanent display of Aboriginal artefacts and weapons. Includes paintings of noted artists such as Albert Namatjira, Gabriella Wallace, Emily Kngwarreye, Ada Bird, and artists of the Hermannsburg school.

❑ **Arunta Art Gallery and Book Shop:** *Todd Street (near Papunya Tula Artists at 78 Todd Street),* Tel. *8952-1544.* Mainly stocks books and art supplies. Includes a few interesting paintings.

❑ **Lightning Ridge Opal Mines:** *75 Todd Mall (next to Scotty's Tavern),* Tel. *8952-4444.* Includes a good selection of opal stones and jewelry.

❑ **The Gem Cave:** *85 Todd Mall (opposite the French Café),* Tel. *8952-1079.* Offers one of the largest selections of opal stones and jewelry in the Northern Territory. Includes daily opal cutting demonstrations and a video of opal mining at Cooper Pedy.

❑ **Outbush:** *95 Todd Mall,* Tel. *8952-1922.* Includes a large selection of outback clothes: Akubra hats, Drizabone oilskins, Thomas Cook adventure clothing, R. M. Williams moleskins and boots, and Coogi knitwear. Also has travel accessories, crafts, souvenirs, jewelry, and T-shirts.

❑ **Todd Street Markets:** *Todd Mall. Operates every second Sunday from 9am to 1pm.* A lively art, craft, clothing, food, and entertainment market lining the pedestrian mall.

❑ **Airport shopping:** Don't forget to stop at the shops in the Alice Springs airport. It include a few shops offering attractive Aboriginal arts and crafts, Australiana, souvenirs, opals, and jewelry.

That's it for shopping in this town, except for a few other small arts, crafts, souvenir, and clothing shops in and around the four block Todd Mall, Todd Street, Gregory Terrace, and Hartley Street area. You can do it all in half a day. And there's no need to hunt for a great variety of product lines nor look for hotel shopping arcades, department stores, suburban shopping centers, and towns outside Alice Springs. Most of your time may be taken in comparing products and asking questions to learn more about the unique Aboriginal arts found in the town's many shops. For shopping in Alice Springs is primarily shopping for Aboriginal arts, crafts, and souvenirs. It's the simplest shopping adventure you will encounter in Australia, but it also yields some of the nicest products at relatively reasonable prices for all of Australia. The only thing left is to enjoy the rest of Alice Springs and the Outback, which is, after all, what most people come here to do anyway.

ACCOMMODATIONS

Two of Alice Springs' best properties include the following hotels and resorts:

❑ **Rydges Plaza Alice Springs:** *Barrett Drive, Alice Springs, NT 0870, Australia, Tel. (61 8) 8950-8000, Fax (61 8) 8952-1373. Web site: www.rydges.com.* This resort is located 1.5km from the town center, adjacent to the Todd River, an 18-hole International Desert Golf Course, and the local casino! Upscale for Alice Springs, (advertised as 4.5 star luxury) and the most luxurious hotel in town, its 235 rooms include 2 premier suites and 5 junior suites. All expected amenities in guestrooms and all rooms have balconies. Award winning Bradshaws restaurant and Balloons Brasserie, 2 lounge bars and a poolside bar provide choices for meals and relaxing with friends. High Powered Telescope for stargazing; Onsite Helipad; Fitness Facilities; Business Center; Conference and Banquet Facilities.

❑ **Alice Springs Resort:** *34 Stott Terrace, Alice Springs, NT 0870, Australia, Tel. (61 80 8951 4545, Fax (61 8) 8953 0995. Web site: www.alicespringsresort.com.au.* Located in the downtown area on the bank of the Todd River, the Alice Springs Resort enjoys a quiet garden setting. The 108 guestrooms include a selection of first class and deluxe rooms as well as rooms configured for disabled guests. Low rise buildings with wide corridors and ramps allow easy access. New Rivergum Court deluxe rooms have private balconies and baths feature separate shower and bathtub. Palms restaurant offers a wide ranging menu with an emphasis on Northern Territory cuisine. Pool and Games room; Conference and Banquet Facilities.

If you plan to take a side-trip from Alice Springs to visit Ayers Rock, you will need to stay overnight. The best property at Ayers Rock is the Ayers Rock Resort:

❑ **Ayers Rock Resort:** *Yulara Drive, NT 0872, Australia, Tel. (61 8) 8957-7888, Fax (61 8) 8956-2018. Web site: www. ayersrockresort.com.au.* Ayers Rock Resort lies entirely below the level of the highest sand dune. Everything about the resort reflects sensitivity to the environment and respect for the area's traditional owners. The resort consists of five hotels, nine restaurants, four bars, four swimming pools plus tennis courts, art galleries, designer shops, bakery, supermarket, ice creamery, conference center and many other facilities to make guests comfortable. *Sails in the Desert* is the resort's premier hotel with 220 deluxe rooms, 6 deluxe spa rooms, and two suites—each with a choice of one king size or 2 double beds. All have a private balcony or verandah. *Desert Gardens Hotel* offers 100 standard rooms with one double and one single bed, and 60 deluxe rooms with balconies overlooking Uluru. *Outback Pioneer Hotel & Lodge* offers 125 standard hotel rooms with ensuite bathrooms and 12 budget cabins as well as 4 or 20 bed air-conditioned dormitories. *Emu Walk Apartments* provide a choice of fully self-contained one and two bedroom apartments with sofa beds. *Spiniflex Lodge* offers twin or quad bunks with kitchenette; bathroom facilities are shared. *Ayers Rock Campground* provides 220 tent sites plus 198 powered sites, 6 coach sites and 14 air conditioned cabins. In addition to nine restaurants in the resort complex, the resort offers very special dining options. For *Sounds of Silence*, guests are driven to a special site in the desert shortly before sundown. As a didgeridoo player weaves his magic spell, diners enjoy canapes and witness a spectacular sunset. After a feast of Northern Territory specialities including barramundi, kangaroo, emu, crocodile, bush salads and Australian desserts, guests are treated to some of the world's best stargazing with the assistance of a resident astronomer. Or consider the *Desert Dinner for a Duo* which includes private transfer from the resort to a secluded place amongst the sand dunes for champagne at sunset, a four-course dinner at a formally-laid candlelit table, plus the exclusive services of a chef and a waiter for the evening. This romantic dinner must be booked a minimum of four days in advance. Inquiries should be directed to *rockpr@ayersrock. aust.com.*

RESTAURANTS

Don't expect to find a wide selection of international restaurants in Alice Springs. This is Outback country, so expect lots of Outback food and pub fare. Some of Alice Spring's best restaurants include:

❑ **Overlanders Steakhouse:** *72 Hartley Street, Tel. 8952-2159.* While somewhat touristy, nonetheless, this fun restaurant dispenses good food and atmosphere. This is a rustic meat and potatoes Outback restaurant for hearty diners. Try the famous A$35 buffet-style "Drovers Blowout" of buffalo, crocodile, kangaroo, camel, emu, barramundi, beef, lamb, and specials plus salads, potato, soup, and dessert—if you can handle it!

❏ **Ristorante Puccini:** *Todd Mall and Parsons Street, Tel. 8953-0935. Open for dinner (lunches by appointment only). Closed Sunday.* A surprisingly good Italian restaurant in the heart of town. Try the fettuccine Calabrese, Barramundi baked in lemon, and tournedos funghi.

❏ **Oriental Gourmet:** *80 Hartley Street, Tel. 8953-0888. Dinner only.* This is Central Australia's best Chinese restaurant. Everything is good, but especially try the honey prawns and duck with lemon sauce.

❏ **Balloons:** *Rydges Plaza Hotel, Barrett Drive, Tel. 8952-8000. Open daily 6:30am until late.* This delightful casual restaurant with a view of the nicely landscaped hotel grounds, offers a good menu. Includes a popular lunch buffet and a Sunday champagne brunch.

❏ **Bradshaw's Restaurant:** *Rydges Plaza Hotel, Barrett Drive, Tel. 8952-8000. Open Tuesday-Saturday 6-10pm* This elegant dining restaurant offers an extensive menu of local and international dishes. Try the "Discovers" menu.

❏ **Golden Inn Chinese Restaurant:** *9 Undoolya Road, Tel. 8952-6910. Open 12noon-2pm and 5-10:30pm Monday through Friday and 5-10:30pm on Saturday and Sunday.* Offers a good selection of Szechuan, Cantonese, and Malaysian cuisines.

❏ **Kings Restaurant:** *Lasseters Casino, 93 Barrett Drive. Open 6:30am-3am.* Offers the area's famous "Centralian Buffet." Also includes a la carte and snack menus.

ENJOYING YOUR STAY

Alice Springs is a popular destination for those interested in visiting the popular **Ayers Rock**, one of the world's largest monoliths located 462 kilometers southwest of Alice Springs, and enjoying adventure tours to the Outback. Many visitors stay in Alice Springs and visit Ayers Rock on a two-day tour; others proceed directly to the village of **Yulara** where they will spend a night or two at one of the resort hotels. You'll also find a couple of good Aboriginal art and craft shops here. And others sign up for several four-wheel drive tours. In any case, you will pass through Alice Springs. The question is what to do while in Alice Springs.

If you decide to stay in Alice Springs for a few days, you will find several things to do in addition to shopping. Be sure to pick up maps and tourist literature at the CATIA (Central Australian Tourism Industry Association) office on the corner of Gregory Terrace and Hartley Streets (Tel. 8952-5199). They have several tourist booklets and brochures that outline festivals, walking tours, historical sites, and adventure holidays, in and around Alice Springs.

One of the first things you may want to do in Alice Springs is to take a walking tour of the town. This will not take you long since the town's highlights are within a five block area—Hartley Street, Todd Mall, Willis Terrace, Railway Terrace, Parsons Street, Stott Terrace, Todd Street, and Stuart Terrace. You'll basically discover twelve major sites along the way. We've highlighted the ones that are especially worth visiting:

- Flynn Memorial Church
- Adelaide House
- **Museum of Central Australia**
- The Old Court House/National Pioneer Women's Hall of Fame
- The Residency
- Old Stuart Gaol
- **Old Hartley Street School**
- **Panorama Guth**
- Old Government Homes
- **Royal Flying Doctor Service**
- Billy Goat Hill
- **Anzac Hill**

Outside this downtown walking tour area are few other places you may want to visit. Many visitors take **The Araluen Heritage Tour** which consists of visiting seven adjacent attractions on the outskirts of town. You may want to take a cab to this area (corner of Memorial and Larapinta Drives) since it's a hot 30 minute walk from Todd Mall. The focus here is on history, culture, arts, and crafts. The self guided tour consists of visiting these several buildings and areas:

- Araluen Centre
- Araluen Homestead
- Pioneer Cemetery
- Transport Museum
- Aviation Museum
- Crafts Council
- Strehlow Centre

While you may find a few interesting things here, especially the transportation and aviation museums, some attractions tend to be over-hyped, especially the Shrehlow Centre (very controversial museum and a tribute to someone on a real ego trip). The Araluen Centre houses two art galleries and is the site for an annual Australian-wide craft exhibition.

Outside Alice Springs you'll find several additional attractions worth visiting:

❑ **The Transport Heritage Center:** *Norris Bell Avenue (8 kilometers south of Alice Springs—look for the old diesel locomotive and truck on the Stuart Highway), Tel. 8955-5047, Open daily 9am-5pm.* Interesting displays of rail and road transportation, include the Old Ghan Train.

❑ **Decca Date Gardens:** *Located 5 kilometers south of the town (take Stuart Highway through Heavitree Gap and then turn left into Palm Circuit). Open Monday-Saturday 9am-5pm and Sunday 10am-4pm (closed on Sundays from November to April). Tel. 8952-2425.* Australia's oldest date plantation and now one of the Northern Territory's major tourist attractions. Walk amongst the palms, try the date ice cream and chocolate dates; enjoy tea under the palms; and shop for souvenirs, Aboriginal artefacts, and paintings.

❑ **Royal Flying Doctor Service:** *Stuart Terrace. Open Monday-Saturday 9am-4pm and Sunday 1-4pm, Tel. 8952-1129.* Tour the RFDS base and learn about the unique aeromedical-communication-emergency services of the famous Royal Flying Doctor Service. Includes a video, museum, and souvenir shop.

❑ **Frontier Camel Farm:** *Located 4 kilometers south of Alice Springs on the Ross Highway.* Learn about camels in Australia, enjoy a short camel ride, and discover how a camel farm operates. Includes tours of the farm which cover a reptile house, kangaroo enclosure, and camel museum.

❑ **Chateau Hornsby Winery:** *Petrick Road. Open daily 9am-5pm.* Located 10 kilometers southeast of Alice Springs and overlooking the MacDonnell Ranges, this is the first and only winery in the Northern Territory. Take the tour and then enjoy the restaurant. Offers popular Sunday afternoon jazz concerts from 1-4pm.

❑ **Alice Springs School of the Air:** *80 Head Street. Open 8:30am-4:30pm and Sunday 1-4pm.* Learn about Australia's first radio school which currently broadcasts to an area of 1.3 million square kilometers as it serves the educational needs of children living in the Outback. Explore its history, technology, and projects. If the schedule permits, you can listen to a live radio broadcast.

❑ **The Gem Tree:** *Located 140 kilometers (Bitumen Road) northeast of Alice Springs along Plenty Highway. Tel. 8956-9855.* Have a great time looking for your own gems in the nearby gem fields. Includes equipment, a tour, and gem cutting.

While you can visit may of these places on your own, you may want to contact a local tour group for information on these and other tours of the area. The best known groups include:

AAT King's Tours	Tel. 8952-1700
Alice Springs VIP	Tel. 1-800-806-6411
Anangu Tours	Tel. 8956-2548
Central Sightseeing Tours	Tel. 8952-2111
DesertTracks	Tel. 8956-2144
Down Under Tours	Tel. 8953-4455
Frontier Camel Tours	Tel. 8953-0444
Rest Australia Tours	Tel. 8953-5030
Rod Steinert Tours	Tel. 8957-7377
Sahara Outback Tours	Tel. 1-800-806-240
The Outback Experience	Tel. 8953-2666
V.I.P. Travel Australia	Tel. 1-800-806-412
Winjeel Tours	Tel. 53-0870

Alice Springs is well known for its unique, entertaining, and irreverent festivals. If you're in Alice Springs during the following months, you may get caught up in all the fun and festivities. The most famous festivals are the **Lions Camel Cup** (camel races) and the **Henley-on-Todd Regatta** (bottomless boat races along the dry river bed!). Shoppers will enjoy the **Corkwood Festival** of arts and crafts:

April-May

- Alice Springs Cup Racing Carnival
- Heritage Week
- Country Music Festival
- Bangtail Muster
- King of the Mountain

June - July

- Shell Finke Desert Race
- Alice Springs Show
- Lions Camel Cup

August

- Alice Springs Rodeo
- Harts Range Races
- Alice Springs Marathon

September - October

- Henley-on-Todd Regatta
- Honda Masters Games
- International Multicultural Festival

November

- Corkwood Festival (arts and crafts)

Alice Springs, the MacDonnell Ranges, gorges, historical landmarks, and local flora and fauna are interesting to see from the air. If you can get up early in the morning, consider taking a **hot air balloon ride** over the area. The following firms offer half-hour and one-hour balloon flights over Alice Springs and the MacDonnell Range:

Ballooning Down Under	Tel. 8952-8816
(Alice Springs Tour Professionals)	
Outback Ballooning	Tel. 8952-8723
Spinifex Ballooning	Tel. 1-800-677-893

You will be picked up at your hotel early in the morning, assist with inflating the balloon, take a peaceful ride, watch the sun rise over the MacDonnell Ranges, and finish with a traditional chicken and champagne brunch.

You will most likely want to visit **Ayers Rock** and **The Olgas**, the two most popular tourist attractions outside Alice Springs. Ayers Rock is located 462 kilometers southeast of Alice Springs. The Olgas are only 25 kilometers from Ayers Rock. We recommend that you take a scheduled tour to this area rather than drive yourself. It's a long boring drive with little help along the way should you have car trouble. One of the best tour companies is **AAT King's Tours** which is located at 74 Todd Street (Tel. 8952-5266). You also can fly to the area from Alice Springs. We took the AAT King's Tour by bus and were favorably impressed with the trip. The bus was comfortable and passengers were able to enjoy the outback scenery during the morning drive to Ayers Rock. Two films relating to Australia were shown on the bus during the return trip. A stop was made for dinner—included in the price of the tour—and a later short coffee stop along the highway gave us a view of the southern skies we will never forget. Out on the desert, away from city lights, the Milky Way was a thrilling attraction for those of us who had never seen it before.

Many visitors to Ayers Rock plan to stay overnight at the resort village, Yulara. You will find several nice hotels here: **Sails in the Desert** (Tel. 8956-2200), **Desert Gardens** (Tel. 8956-2100), and **Outback Pioneer Hotel and Lodge** (Tel. 8956-2170). The **Spinifex Lodge** (Tel. 8956-2131) provides budget accommodations, and **Ayers Rock Campground** (Tel. 8956-2055) is for campers.

Ayers Rock itself is a fascinating monolith, 9 kilometers in circumference and 348 meters high. Many visitors choose to climb the Rock, a rather ambitious endeavor considering its steep and exhausting incline. It looks easier than it is and will take you at least two hours to complete. The Rock is a great photo opportunity, especially for its changing colors during the day. The nearby Olgas consist of several smaller but picturesque rocks with huge cliffs and gorges. Both Ayers Rock and The Olgas are sacred areas of the Aborigines who still live in this area.

If time permits, you may want to take some other tours to various Outback locations. Most of these are adventure tours. Again, we recommend AAT King's Tours, a very reputable firm which offers a wide variety of tours: Heritage Tour (Old Ghan), Aboriginal Culture, Alice Springs Town, Palm Valley by 4WD, Stanley Cham-Glen Helen-Ormiston George-Simpsons Gap, Ross River, and Outback Bushmans Dinner.

RIDING THE SOUTHERN RAIL

Whether you are coming to Alice Springs from the south or leaving Alice Springs heading south to Adelaide (a 1,316 kilometer journey), consider taking the famous **Ghan** (*www.gsr. com/au/theghan*). One of the world's great train journeys, this railroad adventure between Alice Springs and Adelaide is named after the Afghan Cameleers who provided the early transportation link between the Red Center and the rest of the country. First Class sleeping cars convert from a lounge by day to cosy beds for two by night. With reading lamps, wardrobes, en-suite shower and toilet, the traveler has the choice of enjoying privacy or mingling with other guests in the Oasis Bar or Dreamtime Lounge. You enjoy the scenery of the Outback as the Ghan passes through the spiritual lands of The Dreaming. Southbound trains—Alice Springs to Adelaide—depart Alice Springs at 2pm two days a week (presently Fridays and Tuesdays) and arrive in Adelaide between 11am and 11:30am the following day. Northbound trains depart Adelaide at 2pm—presently on Fridays and Tuesdays–and arrive in Alice Springs at about 10:30am the following day. The chefs on board the Ghan serve local specialities such as Baked Barramundi Almondine with Australian wines as you sightsee through the desert. Travel between Alice Springs and Adelaide on The Ghan offers a unique opportunity to see some of the least populated areas of the Outback from the comfort of your moving lounge car.

Residents of the U.S. and Canada who want more information on The Ghan should contact the following tour groups: **ATS Tours** (100 N. First Street, Burbank, CA 91502, Tel. 310-643-0044 or 1-800-423-2880); **Goway** (2400 Yong Street, Suite 2001, Box 2331, Toronto, Ontario M4P 1E4, Tel. 416-322-1034; and Suite 409, 402 West Pender Street, Vancouver B68 1T9, Tel. 604-687-4004, 1-800-663-9418, or 1-800-663-9107). Residents of other countries should contact their travel agent or visit the booking section of the Great Southern Railway Web site: *www.gsr.com.au/booking2.htm*. For more information on The Ghan, as well as other rail trips in Australia, visit this section of the Web site: *www.gsr.com.au/index.htm*.

Adelaide

ADELAIDE, AUSTRALIA'S FOURTH LARGEST CITY
with a population of over one million, is a charming
community of beautiful architecture, bountiful parklands, enticing museums, attractive churches, vibrant
downtown and suburban areas, terrific restaurants
and outdoor cafés, and a festive atmosphere accented with
numerous festivals year-round. It's a surprising city for visitors
who primarily think of Australia as being made up of Sydney,
Melbourne, and the beaches of Queensland.

We're still unabashed fans of Adelaide. We like its leisurely
pace, openness, and convenience. It's a big city, but with a
small town feel to it best captured by walking its many downtown and suburban streets. It's a surprising city for shopping,
touring, and enjoying the ambience of a friendly and inviting
South Australia. It has the look of a frontier city but with all
the amenities of a modern metropolis. It's Denver without
Denver's elevation, snow-capped mountains, and lingering
pollution. Australia's best planned city, it boasts wide streets
and squares laid out on an inviting one square mile grid scheme
with green buffer zones that make this an extremely easy city
to navigate.

Come to Adelaide and you will discover one of Australia's
best kept travel and shopping secrets, all available on the edge

of the Outback and in the midst of Australia's major wine producing country, the Barossa Valley, Clare Valley, and McLaren Vale. Come here before you venture further north into the interior Outback, the Northern Territory of Alice Springs and Darwin. For Adelaide makes a wonderful transition from the more cosmopolitan metropolises of Melbourne and Sydney.

GETTING TO KNOW YOU

Once considered to be Australia's most conservative city, today Adelaide is a city of great diversity, energy, and a delightful Mediterranean climate. Host to the annual Australian Formula One Grand Prix and the biennial Adelaide Festival of the Arts, world famous for its opals and wines, renowned for its arts and crafts, noted for its gambling casino and vibrant central business district, and considered the gateway to the vast Outback and the center for Australia's movie industry, Adelaide has placed itself in league with Australia's other cosmopolitan cities. It's a city with a great deal of character. Best of all, it offers some excellent shopping opportunities.

Stroll down Rundle Mall in downtown Adelaide or head for the upmarket suburbs of Hyde Park (King William and Unley Roads), Glenside (Burnside Village at Greenhill and Portrush Roads), Norwood Parade, and North Adelaide (Melbourne Street), and you will quickly discover a unique city which has much to offer shoppers. While many shops have gone out of business during the past decade, due to South Australia's severe recession, you will still find some excellent arts and crafts shops, chic boutiques, department stores, opal and jewelry stores, and numerous fine restaurants and charming cafés dotting this city's major shopping areas. While not on the same scale as Sydney and Melbourne, shopping in Adelaide does hold its own in comparison to Brisbane and Perth and other cities in Australia. Better yet, shopping in Adelaide is easily managed because of its smaller population size and convenient street system. You can easily shop this city in two days and then head for even more

❏ Adelaide is a big city with a small town feel to it. It's a surprising city for shopping, touring, and enjoying the ambience of a friendly and inviting South Australia.

❏ This is Australia's best planned city with wide streets and squares laid out on an inviting one square mile grid scheme with green buffer zones.

❏ Outside Adelaide are several small towns with shops selling some of South Australia's best arts and crafts.

❏ Adelaide's major shopping strengths are handcrafted items and opals. Outside Adelaide, crafts and wine predominate as major shopping attractions.

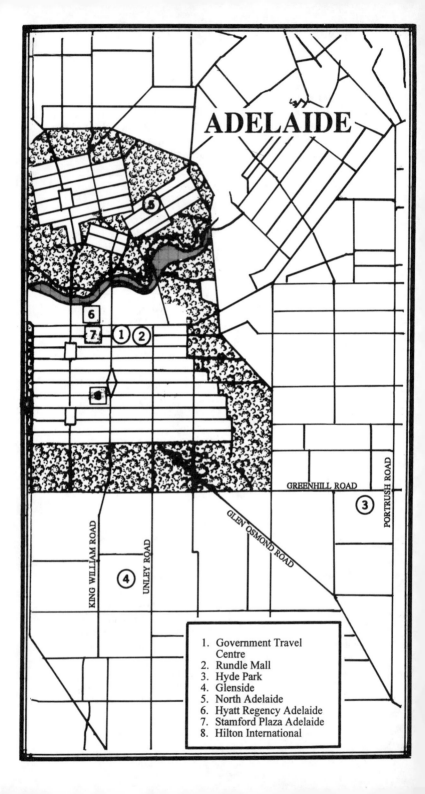

ADELAIDE

1. Government Travel
   Centre
2. Rundle Mall
3. Hyde Park
4. Glenside
5. North Adelaide
6. Hyatt Regency Adelaide
7. Stamford Plaza Adelaide
8. Hilton International

GREENHILL ROAD

PORTRUSH ROAD

GLEN OSMOND ROAD

KING WILLIAM ROAD

UNLEY ROAD

shopping in the many charming arts and crafts towns in the surrounding hills (Hahndorf) and valleys (Barossa and Clare). Indeed, these out of town trips yield some very interesting shopping for unique South Australian products not found elsewhere in Australia.

THE STREETS OF ADELAIDE

No question about it—Adelaide is Australia's best planned city, thanks to Colonel William Light who laid out the city in 1836 with great foresight. The plan was simple: create a city center as a grid of broad streets running north, south, east, and west, surround it with a buffer of parks, and put a large square at the center and smaller squares in each of the city's four corners. The plan worked amazing well and to the envy of more congested cities in Australia and elsewhere in the world. Today, **downtown Adelaide** consists of a one mile square grid of wide streets, surrounded by green parklands, and situated along the charming Torrens River. This whole area is bounded by North, South, East, and West Terrace Roads, each one mile in length.

Downtown Adelaide is best approached on foot. As you will quickly discover, this is a walking city for shoppers, diners, and night owls. The main shopping, dining, and entertainment area is the east-west **Hindley Street** which flows at the east end into **Rundle Mall**, a pedestrian mall between King William and Pultney Streets, similar in appearance to the central pedestrian malls in Brisbane and Darwin. Indeed, Hindley Street has become Adelaide's non-stop 24-hour center for entertainment (40 restaurants, 6 cinemas, 9 hotels, 15 amusement venues, 20 nightclubs) and shopping (Millers and Station Arcades). You'll find within the highly congested three block Rundle Mall commercial area hundreds of shops and three department stores crammed into 16 different shopping arcades, centers, and plazas that feed into Rundle Mall. Here you can spend hours—day and night—walking from one shopping arcade to another as you untangle Adelaide's many clothing, arts and crafts, jewelry, and sporting goods shops as well as dine at its many restaurants, cafés, and fast-food establishments within the Rundle Mall area as well as along adjacent Hindley Street. At the eastern end of Rundle Mall which also becomes Rundle Street, beginning at East Terrace, the road is used annually by the Australian Formula One Grand Prix as part of its downtown trackway.

Just one block off Rundle Mall to the north along North Terrace are major hotels, the Lion Art Centre Complex, and

Adelaide's famous gambling casino. Other surrounding streets define the central business district of commercial and government offices. King William Street, for example, is where you will find a tourist information center, the post office, and the city's major banks and insurance offices.

Outside the downtown area are a few suburban areas worth including in your shopping plans. You can easily get to these areas within 10 minutes by bus or taxi. **North Adelaide** used to be Adelaide's major upmarket shopping area during the 1980s until many of the area's best shops moved to the southern and eastern suburbs. Centered along **Melbourne Street**, just a five minute taxi ride from the downtown area, the shops here offer a nice mix of clothes, accessories, arts, and crafts. You can easily spend two to three hours browsing through the many boutiques and curio shops that line both sides of this pleasant street and leisurely enjoy its many delightful restaurants and cafés.

Other popular suburban areas for shopping include **Burnside Village** (Greenhill Road), a small upmarket shopping center in Glenside to the southeast of the city center; **Norwood**, with its boulevard (The Parade) of restaurants and shops; and **Hyde Park** (King William and Unley roads), a major upmarket shopping area filled with boutiques. The Hyde Park area requires a major walking effort especially given the length of King William Road.

Outside Adelaide you will find several small towns with shops selling some of South Australia's best arts and crafts. While you can join bus tours of these areas, it may be more convenient to rent a car and drive yourself. You will pass through some lovely countryside of rolling hills and colorful vineyards. **Hahndorf**, 40 kilometers southeast of Adelaide, is a popular craft town with tourists. Shops here offer everything from the latest tourist kitsch to good quality arts and crafts. Nearby is the quaint and less touristed town of **Aldgate** with a few nice arts and crafts shops. To the north of Adelaide is the popular **Barossa Valley**, best known for its vineyards, but an excellent center for quality arts and crafts. Here you can visit galleries and shops throughout the valley but especially in the small towns of Bethany, Tanunda, Nuriootpa, and Angaston. Time permitting, you also may want to venture further north to the quaint towns in the Clare Valley wine area or south to the craft towns of the McLaren Vale wineries or even to the nearby historical port city of Port Adelaide located 20 minutes northwest of the city. Whatever you decide to do, you'll have many surprising places to shop, dine, and tour.

GETTING ORIENTED

Like other cities in Australia, Adelaide's shopping hours vary depending on whether you're shopping in the city or suburbs. Late night shopping (until 9pm) takes place on Thursday in the suburbs and on Friday in the city. Most shops and shopping arcade in the city are open as follows:

Monday - Thursday	9am - 5:30pm
Friday	9am - 9pm
Saturday	9am - 5pm
Sunday	11am - 5pm

In the suburbs, most shops and shopping centers are open the following hours:

Monday, Tuesday, Wednesday, Friday	9am - 5:30pm
Thursday	9am - 9pm
Saturday	9am - 5pm
Sunday	Limited hours

Given the size and planned nature of Adelaide, it is very easy to get oriented to this city. It's best to start your Adelaide shopping adventure at Rundle Mall in the downtown area. From here you can visit the major shopping centers and gather information on the city and surrounding area. One of your first stops should be the **South Australian Travel Centre** at the corner of King William Street and North Terrace (Tel. 8212-1505), near Rundle Mall; it's open Monday through Friday 8:45am-5pm and Saturday and Sunday 9am-2pm. This office has maps and tourist literature and can answer your questions and help you book tours. Be sure to pick up maps as well as current copies of *Today in Adelaide* and *Visitor's Guide to Adelaide and Environs*. Your hotel also should have copies of these and other helpful publications.

A good way to get oriented to the city is to purchase an unlimited day travel pass on the **Adelaide Explorer** (Tel. 8364-1933). This bus-tram stops at Adelaide's major attractions, such as the HMS Buffalo restaurant and Museum, Adelaide Casino, Old Parliament House, Marineland, Festival Centre, Botanic Gardens, and Adelaide Zoo. You also can purchase special Daytrip or Multitrip tickets for travel on the city buses, trams, and trains.

You should be able to shop Adelaide and the surrounding

areas on your own. We recommend renting a car and driving to the suburban areas as well as Hahndorf, Aldgate, and the Barossa Valley. Several rental car firms are located in downtown Adelaide. It's best to reserve a car the day before since many of the firms have few cars available, and those that are seem to be gone by 9am. Alternatively, you can book day and overnight tours through several tour companies or through the South Australian Travel Centre.

Should you wish assistance with your shopping, contact **Day Shopping Tours** (Tel. 8326-6848). This group focuses on factory and warehouse shopping. Tours are Monday through Saturday from 9am to 4:30pm.

WHAT TO BUY

Adelaide's major shopping strengths are handcrafted items and opals. Outside Adelaide, crafts and wine predominate as major shopping attractions. Indeed, since South Australia is the country's largest producer of wine and opals, expect to see such production well represented in the shops of Adelaide. At the same time, you will find many clothing, art, antique, leather, Australiana, gift, souvenir, and duty-free shops in and around Adelaide to round out your shopping adventure.

ARTS AND CRAFTS

The city, towns, and hills are alive with some of Australia's finest arts and crafts as well as some of the best shopping for handcrafted items in all of Australia. In fact, many of the arts and crafts found in the shops of Brisbane, Sydney, and Melbourne come from artists and craftspeople who live and work in South Australia. Adelaide is the city that hosts the popular biennial Adelaide Festival of the Arts which attracts hundreds of craftspeople from all over Australia.

You will find numerous shops in the shopping arcades along Rundle Mall offering good quality arts and crafts. One of the best shops in South Australia is found here: **L'Unique** (City Cross Arcade, Tel. 8231-0030). It includes nice quality handcrafted items such as wood bowls, hand-blown glass, ceramics, and jewelry. It also has a shop in Hahndorf (33 Main Street). Also look for **Australian Quality Crafts** (The Myer Centre, Promenade Level, Tel. 8212-3340) for a good range of handcrafted gifts and quality souvenirs, including pottery, metal, woodwork, glassware, paintings, clothing, and jewelry as well as some Aboriginal arts and crafts.

Adelaide also has its own state promotional craft and design center which is operated by the South Australian Craft Authority. Known as **The Jam Factory** (Lion Art Centre Complex at 19 Morphett Street, Tel. 8410-0727), it is similar in concept to The Meat Market Craft Centre in Melbourne. The Jam Factory has a gallery as well as offers training workshops in four major craft areas: knitted textiles, ceramics, glass, and leather. It also has a retail craft shop on the ground floor which sells top quality handcrafted items from South Australia: ceramics, glass, metal, leather, and jewelry. It also operates a small shop called **City Style** at 74 Gawler Place (Tel. 8223-6809).

Along Grenfell Street, look for **East End Pottery** (242 Grenfell Street, Tel. 8232-6284) which has a good selection of South Australian pottery, ceramics, paintings, silk scarves, and woodcrafts. It's located across the street from one of Adelaide's best Aboriginal art, craft, and cultural centers—**Tandanya** (253 Grenfell Street, Tel. 8224-3200), the National Aboriginal Cultural Institute.

Some of the most interesting shopping for arts and crafts is found outside Adelaide in Hahndorf and the Barossa Valley. If you rent a car, you can cover the two areas in a single day. However, it will be a long and rushed day, especially once you become captive of the Barossa Valley where you'll probably be tempted to go wine tasting while doing arts and crafts shopping. The town of **Hahndorf**, located 33 kilometers southeast of Adelaide, is Australia's oldest German town. In recent years it has become an arts and crafts mecca for tourists. Disdained by many locals for its commercial atmosphere and heavy emphasis on tourist kitsch, it does have a few quality shops worth visiting. It's true, on a busy weekend as many as 30 tourist buses will descend on this small town and disgorge its camera-toting tourists as they proceed to overwhelm many of the small shops. Try to visit this town during a weekday so you may miss much of this activity.

Hahndorf's one main street is lined for 1 kilometer with restaurants, arts and crafts shops, trash and treasure stores, and antique bric-a-brac shops offering a wide range of handcrafted items. You can buy arts, crafts, antiques, opals, Australiana, skins and hides, and clothing in Hahndorf's many shops. You will find, for example, a branch shop of **L'Unique** (33 Main Street, Tel. 8388-7934) here which offers good quality arts and crafts. Our favorite place here is a small shop called **Bamfulong Fine Crafts** (34 Main Street, Tel. 8388-1199); it has a wonderful collection of quality crafts, especially ceramics and woodcrafts, produced by some of South Australia's top craftspeople. **Tineriba Tribal Gallery** (89 Main Street, Tel. 8388-7218) includes an interesting collection of tribal arts and crafts from Papua New Guinea as well as Australian Aboriginal paintings, carvings, books, and music. You will find a few unique items in other shops but most of them seem to offer the same types of souvenir items.

The **Barossa Valley** is another excellent source for arts and crafts. A one hour drive north of Adelaide, the Barossa Valley is most famous for its vineyards, wineries, and small craft towns. One of the best places to shop for quality arts and crafts is a small shop in the town of **Angaston**, the **Bethany Art Gallery** (corner of Washington and Fife Streets, Tel. 8564-3344). This shop offers an excellent collection of handcrafted ceramics, and glassware. Two other towns in the Barossa Valley also have a few interesting arts and crafts shops: **Tanunda** and **Nuriootpa**. On your return trip to Adelaide, you may want to take the road directly south of Angaston which goes through **Eden Valley** and **Springton** which have a couple of interesting arts and crafts shops.

CLOTHES AND FASHIONWEAR

Similar to other cities in Australia, Adelaide has its own budding group of fashion designers who produce some very attractive and trendy garments. Local designers, such as Walter Kristensen, Bowie's, Harry Who, George Gross, Naffines, and Skins and Things, create some of Australia's most attractive and fashionable clothes for women. While by no means as large and well known a group as the designers in Melbourne and Sydney, nonetheless, they do offer unique designs which attract the eyes of many visitors to Adelaide.

You will find numerous clothing stores and boutiques in the various arcades of Rundle Mall. However, the best concentration of good quality boutiques and clothing stores is found in the suburbs of Hyde Park, Burnside, Norwood, and North Adelaide.

Indeed, King William and Unley roads in Hyde Park are the fashion centers for all of South Australia. This is to Adelaide what Toorak Road is to Melbourne and Double Bay is to Sydney. Here you can easily spend a full day walking these two long streets to visit the numerous boutiques and shops along the way.

Along **King William Road**, for example, you will find **Toffs Fashion House** (169-171 King William Street) for a good selection of designer label clothes from several of Australia's major designers. The street is lined with many small boutiques, gift shops, bakeries, and flower shops. Some of the best boutiques here include **Penny Mitchell** (#124), **Anastasia Michos** (#141), **Kenzo** (#165), **Rogues** (#165), **Biba** (#165), **Lorenzini** (#165).

Unley Road is a 10 minute walk from the intersection of King William Road and Mitchel Street/Park Street. The intersection of Park Street and Unley Road is a major shopping area for fashion clothes and accessories. Here you'll find the **Metro**, with numerous designer shops. Across the street are such shops as **Carla Zampatti**, **Country Road**, and **Esprit**.

Burnside Village and **Village Shopping Centre** in Glenside (corner of Greenhill and Portrush roads) also have a few nice clothing stores and boutiques. The **Demasius Department Store** stocks several designer labels, and locals like to shop here because of prices and selections. The nearby enclosed shopping complex includes nearly 70 specialty shops, including a Liz Davenport shop.

Norwood, which is located directly east of the city center, is a center for fashion boutiques. Both sides of the main street, The Parade, are lined with interesting shops.

North Adelaide, especially along Melbourne Street, used to be Adelaide's most upmarket fashion center. However, this changed with the continuing development of the Rundle Mall area as well as the growth of King William Road and Unley Road as the fashion center for Adelaide. As a result, several boutiques along Melbourne Street relocated to these other areas, and Melbourne Street has fewer boutiques than it did more than a decade ago. But you'll still find some nice clothing stores here amongst the art galleries, restaurants, and cafes.

In downtown Adelaide, the **Gallerie Shopping Centre** (North Terrace and Gawler Place, just off of Rundle Mall) has a large collection of upmarket boutiques and clothing stores. Also check out the various fashion, accessory, and footwear shops in **City Cross Shopping Centre** on Rundle Mall. If you interested in Outback clothing, be sure to visit **Bonnetts** (242 Hutt Street, Tel. 8232-0324).

OPALS AND JEWELRY

Adelaide and South Australia are also the centers for Australia's opal industry. One of Australia's largest opal mining areas, for example, is found in Coober Pedy (960 kilometers northwest of Adelaide) as well as in Andamooka. Opals mined in these areas find their way into numerous shops in Adelaide.

One of our favorite opal and jewelry shops is **Southern Cross Opal** (114 King William Road, Hyde Park, Tel. 8357-9797). Operated by Michael and Robyn Evans, this small shop produces very nice opal jewelry. It also includes some estate pieces and Aboriginal art. Another favorite is **The Opal Factory** (36 King William Street, Tel. 8212-2652); it does opal cutting in the upstairs shop as well as includes a good selection of Aboriginal art (ask to see albums). Some of the better known opal and jewelry stores in Adelaide include: **Adelaide Gem Center** (12 Hindley Street, Tel. 8212-3600); **Opal Field Gems** (33 King William Street, Tel. 8212-5300); **Olympic Opal Gem Mine** (5 Rundle Mall, Tel. 8211-7440, and 142 Melbourne Street, North Adelaide, Tel. 8267-5100—an underground opal cutting factory and showroom); **The Opal Mine** (30 Gawler Place, Tel. 8223-4023); **Harlequin Opal** (5 Hindley Street, Tel. 8212-7577); **Opal Australia** (Forecourt Hyatt Hotel, North Terrace, Tel. 8231-0700); **Precious Gems of Australia** (9 Hindley Street, Tel. 8212-3493). Duty-free shops as well as some souvenir shops also carry opals and jewelry.

One of the nicest jewelry shops in downtown Adelaide is **Gerard McCabe** (Shop 12, Adelaide Arcade, Tel. 8232-1000). This is not the typical opal and jewelry store catering to tourists. A jewelry manufacturer, it includes some very nice designs along with a good collection of quality estate jewelry.

AUSTRALIANA, GIFTS, AND SOUVENIRS

You will find the usual assortment of Australiana, gifts, and souvenirs—stuffed fur animals, leather goods, mugs, spoons, pottery, kangaroo and lambskin rugs, jumpers, tea towels, boomerangs, postcards, and T-shirts and sweatshirts—in many of Adelaide's downtown and suburban shops. They range from the truly tacky to excellent quality arts and crafts. The Rundle Mall area has the largest concentration of such shops.

One of the best Australiana shops in the Adelaide area is found in Burnside Village—**Australiana Design** (Shop 5, Burnside Boulevarde, Tel. 8338-2476). Also look for **Outback Australiana** (36 Regent Arcade, Tel. 8232-3405), **Adella Gallery** (12-14 Hindley Street, Tel. 8212-3600) for Aboriginal souvenirs; **Hats and Caps** (56 Pulteney Street, Tel. 8232-6627) and **Adelaide Hatters** (Shop 36, Adelaide Arcade, Tel. 8224-0131) for lots of leather bush hats, traditional Outback fur felt hats, and other uniquely designed headwear; **Talk to the Animals** (Myer Centre, Promenade Level; also Shop 3, 42 Main Street, Hahndorf) for stuffed animals; and **Central Market Souvenirs** (17-18 Central Market, Gouger Street entrance, Tel. 8268-5744) for a wide assortment of sheep and kangaroo products and souvenirs; **Adelaide Arcade Souvenirs and Gifts** (Shop 39 Adelaide Arcade, Tel. 8223-3467),

Outback Experiences (Myer Centre, Rundle Mall Level, Tel. 8231-5900), and **Aussie Gifts** (173 Rundle Street, Tel. 8223-7353) for numerous tourist gifts and souvenirs.

ARTS AND ANTIQUES

Several shops in and around Adelaide offer arts and antiques from Australia and abroad. For excellent Aboriginal art which goes beyond the typical souvenirs found in many Australiana shops, try these places: **Dacou Gallery** (110 Melbourne Street, North Adelaide, Tel. 8239-1353); **Tandanya Retail Shop** (Tandanya, National Aboriginal Cultural Institute, 253 Grenfell Street, Tel. 8224-3200); **Gallerie Australis** (Forecourt Plaza, Hyatt Regency, North Terrace, Tel. 8231-4111); and **Adella Gallery** (12-14 Hindley Street, Tel. 8212-3600).

Fine arts, from paintings to sculptures, can be found in several galleries along Melbourne Street in North Adelaide. For contemporary art, visit **BMG Art** (100 Melbourne Street) and **Aerodrome Gallery** (102 Melbourne Street). You'll also find several home decorative shops in this same area, such as **Blue Heeler Interiors and Tribal Art** (80 Melbourne Street), **Raffi's Gallery** (97 Melbourne Street), and **Kismet's Decorating Treasures** (105 Melbourne Street). Also nearby in North Adelaide is **Greenhill Galleries** (140 Barton Terrace, Tel. 8267-2933).

In the Ruddle Mall area, one of the best art shops in Adelaide is **Gallery 27A** (Apt. 37, The Mansions, 3rd Floor, 21 Pulteney Street, Tel. 8223-3365). This gallery includes the works of some of Australia's top artists such as Pro Hart, Alan Tregenze, Peter Coad, and Stephen Gunner. Also look for the **Anima Gallery** (2nd Floor, 187 Rundle Street, Tel. 8232-3936); **Hill-Smith Fine Art** (113 Pirie Street, Tel. 8223-6558) **Antique Print Room** (132 King William Road, Hyde Park, Tel. 8272-3399); **Art Images Gallery** (32 The Parade, Norwood, Tel. 8363-0806); and **Kensington Gallery** (39 Kensington Road, Norwood, Tel. 8332-5752).

Many of Adelaide's antique shops are found in the city center as well as south of the city along Unley Road and east of the city along Magill Road. In the downtown area, look for these antiques centers which include numerous antique shops and stalls offering a wide range of antique furniture and collectibles: The **Antique Centre** (26 Leigh Street, Tel. 8231-3071); **Antique Market** (32 Grote Street City, opposite the Hilton International Hotel and Central Market, Tel. 8212-6421); and **Culpeper Antique Centre** (115 Pirie Street, Tel. 8232-0189).

Several years ago we discovered a very interesting shop offering Asian arts and antiques which used to be located along Unley Road in Glenside: **Zen Oriental Design**. It has now moved into the owners' home gallery in Flagstaff Hill and is only open by appointment (Tel./Fax 8298-5927). This shop offers some of the best selections of Asian arts and antiques in all of Australia, especially Japanese chests, Chinese panels, Thai Buddhas and lacquerware, and textiles.

WHERE TO SHOP

If you want to fully shop Adelaide, your shopping adventure should take you to several shopping areas: downtown (Rundle Mall, Hindley Street, and adjacent streets), suburbs (Hyde Park, Malvern, Glenside, Norwood, North Adelaide), and small craft towns (Aldgate, Hahndorf, Barossa Valley) each within one hour of Adelaide. You will also find some shops in other suburbs (Glenelg and Port Adelaide), and in several small craft towns (McLaren Vale, Strathalbyn, Clarendon, Milang, Auburn, Goolwa, Bridgewater, Kapunda, Blyth, Mitcham, Birdwood, Clare, Springton, Victor Harbor, Watervale, and Mt. Torrens).

DOWNTOWN SHOPPING ARCADES

Downtown Adelaide is the city shopping center. **Rundle Mall**, stretching from Pulteney Street to King William Street, is one of Australia's largest and most compact pedestrian malls, similar to the ones found in Brisbane and Darwin. This is where you will find Adelaide's major shopping arcades, department stores, and shops. It's where most visitors to Adelaide begin their shopping, where Adelaide's young people congregate, and where the annual Grand Prix races draw crowds at the Rundle Street section of the race track. The nearby streets house Adelaide's major banks, hotels, restaurants, and the Adelaide Casino.

The **Rundle Mall** area consists of a web of 16 separate shopping arcades that feed into adjacent streets and each other:

- Adelaide Arcade
- Citi Centre Arcade
- City Cross Arcade
- De Costa Arcade
- Gays Arcade
- John Martins Plaza
- Myer Centre

- Regent Arcade
- Renaissance Arcade
- Renaissance Centre
- Rundle Arcade
- Southern Cross Arcade
- The Gallerie Shopping Centre
- Twin Plaza Arcade

Walking one block west of Rundle Mall into Hindley Street you'll find two more small shopping arcades on the north side of the street: Millers Arcade and Station Arcade.

Most of these arcades are small to medium size, housing 10 to 50 shops. The most upscale shopping arcade is **The Gallerie Shopping Centre** which houses several of Adelaide's best boutiques, clothing stores, and jewelers. The **Renaissance Arcade, John Martin Plaza,** and **City Cross Arcade** are also relatively upscale. You will also find three major department stores in this area: **Myer, David Jones,** and **John Martin's.**

Some of our favorite shops in the Rundle Mall area include **L'Unique** (City Cross Arcade, Tel. 8231-0030) for outstanding quality South Australian arts and crafts; **The Opal Factory** (36 King William Street, Tel. 8212-2652) for opals and Aboriginal art; **Outback Australiana** (36 Regent Arcade, Tel. 8232-3405) for good quality souvenirs; and **Gerard McCabe** (Shop 12, Adelaide Arcade, Tel. 8232-1000) for quality jewelry.

DOWNTOWN SHOPS

While most shopping in the downtown area is concentrated in and around Rundle Mall, you'll also find several interesting shops along other streets in the downtown area. Three of our favorites are **The Jam Factory** (Lion Art Centre Complex at 19 Morphett Street, Tel. 8410-0727) for top quality South Australian arts and crafts; **East End Pottery** (242 Grenfell Street, Tel. 8232-6284) for good quality pottery, ceramics, paintings, silk scarves, and woodcrafts; **Tandanya Retail Shop** (National Aboriginal Cultural Institute, 253 Grenfell Street, Tel. 8224-3200) for quality Aboriginal arts and crafts; **Antique Centre** (26 Leigh Street, Tel. 8231-3071), **Antique Market** (32 Grote Street City, opposite the Hilton International Hotel and Central Market, Tel. 8212-6421), and **Culpeper Antique Centre** (115 Pirie Street, Tel. 8232-0189) for antiques and collectibles; **Gallerie Australis** (Forecourt Plaza, Hyatt Regency, North Terrace, Tel. 8231-4111) for Aboriginal arts and crafts; and **The City Market** (Gouger Street) for fresh produce as well as some arts, crafts, and souvenirs.

HYDE PARK

Adelaide's four major shopping suburbs are within 10 minutes driving distance from the downtown area. **Hyde Park**, located 3 kilometers directly south of Rundle Mall, is Adelaide's second major shopping area. Here you can easily spend the day walking up and down two major parallel streets—King William Road and Unley Road—that are lined with some of Adelaide's best boutiques, jewelry, and gift shops. This is definitely one of the most upscale shopping areas in Adelaide, similar in concept and style to Double Bay in Sydney as well as Toorak Road in Melbourne. It's best to start shopping this area at the northern end of King William Road and continue walking south until you reach the intersection with Park and Mitchel streets. Turn left onto Park Street and walk approximately 1 kilometer until you reach Unley Road. Take another left and walk north along Unley Road for approximately two kilometers. You will initially see the **Metro**, Adelaide's fashion center with its numerous designer label boutiques, on the corner of Park Street and Unley Road. Similar to King William Road, you will find shops along both sides of Unley Road.

Some of our favorite shops along **King William Road** include **Southern Cross Opal** (#114) with its nice jewelry and art and Toffs Fashion House (#169-171) for major designer label clothing and accessories. While the shops along King William Road primarily sell upmarket clothing, many shops along **Unley Road** offer arts and antiques along with top name brand clothes. Most of the major clothing and accessory shops are found at the intersection of Park Street and Unley Road.

GLENSIDE

Glenside is another upscale shopping area you may wish to visit if time permits. Located 3 kilometers southeast of Rundle Mall, Glenside's major shopping area is the **Burnside Village** shopping complex. Located at the corner of Greenhill and Portrush roads, across the street from the Glenside municipal office, this is a small shopping area of nearly 70 specialty shops frequented by many of Adelaide's upmarket shoppers.

NORWOOD

Located directly east of the downtown area, Norwood is a popular shopping and dining area. Its major boulevard, **The Parade**, is lined with specialty shops, fashion boutiques, and cafes. One block north of The Parade is **Magill Road** which is home to many interesting antique and bric-a-brac shops.

NORTH ADELAIDE

North Adelaide used to be the major upmarket suburban shopping area. Centered on **Melbourne Street**, just a five minute drive from Rundle Mall, this area still has some very nice shops and restaurants although it has the appearance of an area in decline. It's best to start shopping this area just west of the intersection of Jerningham and Melbourne streets, which is directly across the street from **The Old Lion Hotel**. Some of the most interesting shops along this street include the **Dacou Gallery** (#110) for Aboriginal art; **BMG Art** (#100) for contemporary art; **Blue Heeler Interiors and Tribal Art** (#80) for tribal art from Indonesia, Papua New Guinea, and Africa; **Melbourne Street Fine Wine Cellars** (#95) for a good selection of local wines; **Raffi's Gallery** (#97) for Persian, Oriental, and tribal carpets; **Aerodrome Gallery** (#102) for paintings; **4B2 Design** (#119) for unusual art and sculpture; and **The Banana Room** (#125) for vintage fashions, accessories, and jewelry.

MARKETS

Like other Australian cities, Adelaide has its share of markets, both daily and weekend. The major markets include:

❑ **Adelaide Central Market:** *Gouger Street, Tel. 8203-7494. Open Tuesday 7am-5:30pm, Thursday 11am-5:30pm, Friday 7am-9pm, and Saturday 7am-1pm.* Also known as The Central Market, this is reputed to be the largest fresh produce market in the Southern Hemisphere, and the oldest continuously operating market in Australia (since 1870). Also includes several stalls offering souvenirs. For an interesting behind-the-scenes guided tour of this market, including meeting vendors and sampling foods, contact **Market Adventures** (Tel. 018-842-242).

❑ **East End Markets:** *Rundle Street, Tel. 8232-5606.* Open every Friday, Saturday, and Sunday from 9am to 6pm. This popular weekend market includes a Market Bazaar offering arts and crafts, a Produce Market with fresh fruits, vegetables, meats, breads, cheeses, and nuts, and a food court.

❑ **Orange Lane Market:** *Corner of Edward Street and Orange Lane, off The Parade, Norwood. Tel. 8414-1346. Open Saturday, Sunday, and Monday 10am-5pm.* Includes everything from antiques, artwork, furniture, used clothes, and nurseries to cafes and food stalls offering many international dishes.

❑ **The Fishermen's Wharf at Port Adelaide:** *Wharfshed on Queens Wharf next to the Lighthouse at the end of Commercial Road, Port Adelaide, Tel. 8341-2040. Open Sunday and public holidays 9am-5pm.* This popular weekend market has everything—arts, crafts, bric-a-brac, curios, collectibles, CDs, records, books, fresh fish and vegetables, and prepared food.

CRAFT TOWNS

You will find numerous small towns with craft shops in South Australia. Many of these towns service large numbers of tourists who come to shop and dine while visiting nearby wineries. Indeed, South Australia is wine county with the Clare Valley, Barossa Valley, and McLaren Vale being three very popular wine centers located to the north, northeast, and south of Adelaide. Most of these places can be reached within 30 to 90 minutes from the city. Other places, such as Hahndorf, are famous rural ethnic communities noted for their arts and crafts.

You may want to concentrate your shopping on two major areas within a day's drive of Adelaide. The first area, **Hahndorf**, is located approximately 40 kilometers southeast of Adelaide just off Route 1. An excellent four-lane highway will get you there by car within 30 minutes. Hahndorf, is the oldest German town in Australia. In recent years it has become a major tourist attraction because of its many arts and crafts shops. Both sides of the street are lined with arts and crafts shops and German restaurants. While the town is somewhat overrun by tourists and disliked by many South Australians for its touristy atmosphere and trinket quality shopping, you can still find some good quality shopping in this town. The best shop here is **Bamfurlong Fine Crafts** (34 Main Street, Tel. 8388-1199) with its excellent collection of top quality hand-crafted items, especially ceramics and some woodcrafts, produced by Australian craftspeople. Across the street is **L'Unique** (33 Main Street, Tel. 8388-7934), a branch shop of L'Unique at City Cross Arcade in Adelaide, which also offers an excellent section of South Australian fine arts and crafts. The **Tineriba Tribal Gallery** (79 Main Street, Tel. 8388-7218) seems somewhat out of place here, but it offers an interesting collection of tribal art from Aboriginal groups as well as Papua New Guinea. Next door is **Australian Minerals** (79 Main Street) with a nice collection of minerals, stones, and jewelry. If you're in Hahndorf for lunch or dinner, try **Karl's** (17 Main Street, Tel. 8388-7171), a German coffee house restaurant that serves excellent German dishes.

On the way to or from Hahndorf, you may want to stop at the nearby town of **Aldgate** which has a few interesting arts and crafts shops. It's located just 5 kilometers west of Hahndorf. **Aldgate Crafts** (4 Strathalbyn Road, Tel. 8339-2639), with its excellent collection of pottery, jewelry, woodcraft, glass, leather, and paintings, alone is worth a stop in Aldgate.

The **Barossa Valley** is another good place to go shopping for South Australian arts and crafts. Located a little more than one hour from Adelaide by way of Route 1 and Main North Road, the Barossa Valley is dotted with numerous wineries and small craft towns. While you may wish to spend two or three days relaxing, tasting wine, and shopping in this lovely valley, you can easily drive to and from the Valley in one day. Once you arrive in the main town of Tanunda, be sure to stop at the **Barossa Wine and Visitor Centre** at 66 Murray Street (Tel. 63-0600) for maps, brochures, and advice. Tanunda has a few interesting arts, crafts, and antique shops along the main street. Two of best here are **Eve's Apple** (38 Murray Street, Tel. 8563-0557), for its innovative arts and crafts and **Tanunda Pottery Shop** (101-103 Murray Street, Tel. 8563-3494). The town is especially good place for lunch or dinner. Try the **Zinfandel Restaurant** (58 Murray Street, Tel. 8563-2822), a small, homey, and extremely popular restaurant; it serves some of best German food, including excellent desserts, in Australia. The **1918 Bistro and Grill** (94 Murray Street, Tel. 8563-0405) is also a good choice.

Further north of Tanunda is the Valley's commercial center, **Nuriootpa.** You may decide to skip this town altogether as you head directly east along Angaston Road for the town of **Angaston.** This town has a few interesting arts, crafts, and antique shops. The best one here is **Bethany Art Gallery** (12 Washington Street, corner of Washington and Fife Streets, Tel. 8564-3344). If offers top quality ceramics and glasswork.

If time permits, you may want to visit these three towns which offer some interesting shopping opportunities:

❑ **Port Adelaide:** Located only 20 minutes northwest of Adelaide, this charming historical town is noted for its arts and crafts galleries, cafes, and popular Sunday Fisherman's Wharf markets. Be sure to visit the **New Land Gallery** (1 McLaren Parade), the **South Australian Maritime Museum** (126 Lipson Street), and the **Jane Lane Gallery** (24 Divett Street).

❑ **Clare:** Located 136 kilometers north of Adelaide, this is the commercial center for the Clare Valley, one of Australia's premium wine growing regions. Stop at the Clare Valley Tourist Association Information Office at the Clare Town Hall for information on visiting the local wineries, shops, and restaurants. This area includes a few nice art and craft shops such as **Russell Pick Warenda Creek Studio Gallery** (Warenda Road) and **Springfarm Galleries** (Guarry Road/Springfarm Road).

❑ **McLaren Vale:** Located 39 kilometers south of Adelaide, this is another popular wine region with over 50 wineries. Includes several nice art and craft shops such as **Chapel Hill Winery and Gallery** (Chapel Hill Road), **Dridan Fine Arts** and **Fleurieu Showcase Craft Gallery** (Sand Road), and **The Barn Gallery** (Main Road).

BEST OF THE BEST

Adelaide's best shops tend to offer quality Australian and Aboriginal arts, crafts, souvenirs, and jewelry. While most of the best shops are found in Adelaide, a few also are found in the suburbs and in Hahndorf. While wine is one of the major products and attractions of South Australia, we have not included it as a "best of the best" category. You'll need to do you own wine tasting on a journey through the area's major wine country—Barossa Valley, Clare Valley, and McLaren Vale. Let us know what you discover!

AUSTRALIAN ARTS AND CRAFTS

❑ **L'Unique:** *City Cross Arcade (Rundle Mall Entrance), Tel. 8231-0030. Also has a branch shop in Hahndorf at 33 Main Street, Tel. 8388-7934.* Represents some of South Australia's best artists and craftspeople. The selections here are beautiful, from pottery, hand-blown glass, and wood craft to jewelry and paintings. If you're looking for something very special for your own collection or a gift, be sure to visit this attractive shop.

❑ **The Jam Factory:** *Lion Art Centre Complex, 19 Morphett Street, Tel. 8410-0727. Open Monday-Friday, 9am-5:30pm and Saturday and Sunday 10am-5pm. Also has a branch shop called City Style at 74 Gawler Place, Tel. 8223-6809.* This is the city's craft and design center. It includes three floors of shops, galleries, and workshops. The retail is located on the ground floor and includes some of the best quality handmade ceramics, glass, metal, leather, and jewelry available in Adelaide.

❑ **Bamfurlong:** *34 Main Street, Hahndorf, Tel. 8388-1199. Open daily 11am-5pm.* Offers top quality crafts from some of Australia's leading craftspeople. Includes an excellent selection of beautiful ceramics and woodcrafted items.

❑ **Bethany Art and Craft Gallery:** *12 Washington Street, Angaston, Tel. 8564-3344.* Occupying the towns Old Police Station and Courthouse, this small gallery in the sleepy town of Angaston offers an excellent range of craft items from some of the areas finest craftspeople. Includes beautiful ceramics and glassware.

ABORIGINAL ARTS AND CRAFTS

❑ **Tandanya Retail Shop:** *Tandanya, National Aboriginal Cultural Institute, 253 Grenfell Street, Tel. 8224-3200. Open daily 10am-5pm.* This is a cultural center for Aboriginals that includes exhibitions of Aboriginal art, theatrical performances, seminars, a café, and a retail shop. The shop includes a large and diverse range of Aboriginal paintings, artefacts, souvenirs, books, music, jewelry, and clothing. The quality ranges from serious art to tourist souvenirs. Includes the works of many well known artists.

❑ **Dacou Gallery:** *110 Melbourne Street, North Adelaide, Tel. 8239-1353. Open Tuesday-Friday 9am-5pm and Saturday and Sunday 1-5pm.* Housed in an old church building, this Aboriginal art gallery functions as the Dreaming Art Centre of Utopia. Includes many interesting paintings of the Utopia artists.

❑ **Gallerie Australia:** *Forecourt Plaza, Hyatt Regency, North Terrace. Tel. 8231-4111.* A leading aboriginal art and craft gallery offering everything from crafts and jewelry to books, videos, and T-shirts.

❏ **Adella Gallery:** *12-14 Hindley, Tel. 8212-3600.* Offers Western Desert and bark paintings, bird carvings, boomerangs, didgeridoos, fashion accessories, scarves, sheepskins, fur products, gifts, souvenirs, and T-shirts.

ASIAN ARTS AND ANTIQUES

❏ **Zen Oriental Design:** *5 Katherine Court, Flagstaff Hill, Tel./Fax 8298-5927. Open by appointment only.* This is one of those "rare finds" for connoisseurs of Asian arts and antiques, a place you would not expect to find in South Australia or even Australia in general. Collectors and experts Alan Myron and Lee Grafton, who used to have a shop on Unley Road in Glenside many years ago, now operate this shop from their residence in the southern suburb of Flagstaff Hill (20 kilometers south of Adelaide). The shop includes top quality furniture from Japan and China, Buddhas and lacquerware from Thailand and Myanmar, antiques and collectibles from India, textiles, and a few art pieces from Papua New Guinea. Everything here is first-rate and the owners are extremely knowledgeable. If you collect quality Asian arts and antiques, be sure to visit this place. Their outdoor aviary filled with gorgeous black cockatoos is wonderful!

OPALS AND JEWELRY

❏ **Gerard McCabe:** *Shop 12, Adelaide Arcade, Tel. 8232-1000.* Produces nice quality jewelry. Unique designs. Includes estate pieces.

❏ **Southern Cross Opal:** *114 King William Road, Hyde Park, Tel. 8357-9797.* This combination jewelry and art (Aboriginal) produces very nice Opal jewelry. Cuts own opals. Includes some estate jewelry.

❏ **The Opal Factory:** *36 King William Street, Tel. 8212-2652.* Includes two upstairs shops—one specializes in opals, including cutting, and the other displays Aboriginal art. Includes a large selection of opal jewelry.

AUSTRALIANA AND SOUVENIRS

❏ **Outback Australiana:** *36 Regent Arcade, Rundle Mall, Tel. 8232-3405.* Offers good quality souvenirs, especially woodcrafted items. Includes many unique items made in South Australia.

❏ **Australiana Design:** *Shop 5, Burnside Boulevarde (adjacent to Burnside Village), Tel. 8338-2476.* Offers top quality Australian clothing and gift items.

ACCOMMODATIONS

Adelaide has many excellent hotels conveniently located within the central business district. The best hotels include:

❏ **Hyatt Regency Adelaide:** *North Terrace, Adelaide, SA 5000, Australia, Tel. (61 8) 8231-1234, Fax (61 8) 8231-1120.* Hyatt Regency Adelaide is located in the city center adjacent to the casino, convention center and festival theater. A towering granite lobby features the first of four soaring atriums in the hotel and is a fitting welcome to Adelaide's premier hotel. 369 spacious guestrooms and suites are beautifully appointed. The octagonal towers create interesting room shapes—a refreshing change from standard rooms. Marble bathrooms offer a shower cubicle that is separate from the bathtub and bathrooms have all expected amenities. The Regency Club floors offer extra services including Continental breakfast, evening cocktails and hors d'oeuvres. Blakes serves a variety of Continental cuisines and a tandoor oven allows an eclectic variety. Shiki, the award winning Japanese restaurant, offers choices from teppanyaki, to tempura, to sashimi in a modern setting. Fitness Facilities; Business Center; Conference and Banquet Facilities.

❏ **Hilton International Adelaide:** *233 Victoria Square, Adelaide, SA 5001, Australia, Tel. (61 8) 8217-0711, Fax (61 8) 8231-0158.* Overlooking Victoria Square and in the heart of the city, the Hilton's 380 spacious guestrooms and 15 suites offer the extensive facilities and professional well trained staff expected from the Hilton. Grange Restaurant serves outstanding fusion dishes drawing from Mediterranean and Asian cuisines and combined with Australian specialities for some unique dishes. Fitness Facilities; Business Center; Conference and Banquet Facilities.

❑ **Stamford Plaza Adelaide:** *150 North Terrace, Adelaide, SA 5000, Australia, Tel. (61 8) 8461-1111, Fax (61 8) 8231-7572. Web site: www.stamford.com.au.* Located in the heart of the city across from Parliament House, the casino, convention and exhibition centers, shopping, entertainment and businesses are all a short walk. Winner of South Australia tourism awards in 1997 and 1998. All 334 guestrooms and suites are nicely furnished and come with all the expected amenities. All guestrooms have executive sized desks. Some bathrooms have a spa. Café de L'Orient serves Asian cuisine, Pasta Hound presents homestyle Italian food and the Terrace Garden Restaurant offers lavish buffets. Fitness Facilities; Business Facilities; Conference and Banquet Facilities.

❑ **Stamford Grand Adelaide:** *Mosley Square, Glenelg, Adelaide, SA 5045, Australia, Tel. (61 8) 8376 1222, Fax (61 8) 8376-1111. Web site: www.stamford.com.au.* Also part of the Stamford Hotels and Resorts, you may choose the city center hotel listed above, or Adelaide's only resort-style corporate hotel situated on the beach—about 20 minutes from the city center. The architecture and decor exude 'old world' charm while the comforts and amenities are definitely up-to-date. 241 guestrooms including suites and apartments reflect the character of grand Victorian-era European hotels. Bathrooms have separate bathtub and shower enclosure. Chose among the terrace-style Promenade Restaurant or try Café de L'Orient for market-style Asian cuisine, Café Tesoro for Italian cuisine or Charlotte's Coffee Shop. Fitness Facilities; Business Services; Conference and Banquet Facilities.

RESTAURANTS

Adelaide has many excellent restaurants offering a wide range of cuisines, from Australian Outback to French and Italian. If you visit Hahndorf, you'll have a choice of several excellent German restaurants. Some of Adelaide's best restaurants include:

AUSTRALIAN

❑ **Red Ochre Grill:** *129 Gouger Street, Tel. 8212-7266. Closed Sunday. No lunch on Saturday.* Inventive chef Andrew Fielke continues to create a new Australian cuisine with his unique use of Aboriginal foods and knowledge. Every meal here is an adventure in dining. Includes a gourmet retail section with native products such as bush tomato salsa, wattle seed pasta, lemon aspen macadamia dressing, and pepper leaf mustard.

❑ **Red Lobster Café:** *108 Gouger Street, Tel. 8212-5885, Lunch Monday-Friday 11:30am-2:30pm and dinner daily from 5pm. Also has the Rock Lobster Revolving Restaurant in Glenelg, 760 Anzac Highway, Tel. 8376-0050. Lunch Wednesday-Sunday 11:30am-2:30pm (closed Saturday) and dinner Wednesday-Sunday 5:30pm-late.* Specializes in Australian seafood, shellfish, and steaks. House specialty is live lobster and lobster dishes. Includes many Thai dishes such as garlic prawns, chick and prawn tom yum, and garlic prawn. Casual dining. The revolving Glenelg restaurant provides a panoramic view of Adelaide and St. Vincent's Gulf.

MODERN AUSTRALIAN

❑ **Grange Restaurant:** *Hilton Adelaide International, 233 Victoria Square, Tel. 8217-2000. Open lunch on Friday and dinner Tuesday-Saturday from 7pm until late.* This fine Asian influenced restaurant, under the direction of one of Australia's most influential chefs, Cheong Liew, consistently turns out some of Adelaide's best dishes. Try the inventive Kangaroo Island chicken braised with abalone shitaki and oyster mushrooms, pigeon mughlai style, and ragout of possum with root vegetables and basil noodles.

❑ **The Brasserie:** *Hilton Adelaide International, 233 Victoria Square, Tel. 8217-2000. www.bestrestaurants.com.au/brasserie. Open for breakfast, lunch, and dinner.* This award-winning restaurant, commanded under the care of Chef Bethany Finn, is one of Adelaide's leading a la carte restaurants. Try the linguini with roast butternut, Sri Lankan prawn curry with jackfruit and lemon sambal, and the Barossa roast chicken with rosemary and garlic potatoes.

❑ **Sweet Water:** *187 Rundle Street, Tel. 8223-6855. Open daily for lunch 12noon-3pm and dinner 5pm-late.* Specializes in contemporary Thai cuisine using fresh Australian meats and seafood. Try the wok or red curry dishes with lamb, prawn, kangaroo, or crocodile; char-grilled barramundi; and pad Thai. Good wine list.

❑ **Nediz tu:** *170 Hutt Street, Tel. 8223-2618. Closed Sunday and Monday. Dinner only.* This award-winning restaurant, which manages to nicely synthesize Chinese, Vietnamese, and French cuisines is commanded by chefs Le Tu Thai and Kate Sparrow. Try the roast squab with parsley ravioli with truffle sauce and the lobster dishes. Excellent desserts.

ITALIAN

❑ **La Casalinga:** *77 Unley Road, Parkside, Tel. 8271-7991. Open for lunch Tuesday-Friday 12noon-3pm and dinner Tuesday-Saturday 6-10pm.* This award-winning restaurant, housed in a charming villa, offers a provincial Italian menu of home made pasta and other delicacies. Try the risotto with porcini mushrooms, *bauletti* (crepe filled with veal mince), *gamberoni alla sambuca* (king prawns), and *fritto misto all'ascolana* (lamb loin cuts, prawns, and stuffed olives).

❑ **Amalfi Pizzeria Ristorante:** *29 Frome Street, Tel. 8223-1948. Closed Sunday. No lunch on Saturday and Monday.* This popular bistro consistently turns out excellent pizza and pasta dishes which also are very large. Check out the specials board which is usually very reliable.

CONTINENTAL AND FRENCH

❑ **La Guillotine:** *125 Gouger Street, Tel. 8212-2536. Open for lunch Wednesday-Friday from 12noon and dinner Monday-Saturday from 5:45pm.* This popular French restaurant offers excellent balcony views overlooking busy Gouger Street. Serves French provincial cuisine in a rustic, cosy atmosphere. Try the French onion soup, frogs legs, pork fillet with prunes and pine-nuts, rabbit with Dijon mustard, and chicken breast filled with smoked-salmon mousse. For dessert, go for the Profiteroles au Chocolat.

❑ **Magic Flute Restaurant and Cafe:** *109 Melbourne Street, North Adelaide, Tel. 8267-3172. Open for lunch Monday-Friday from 12noon and for dinner Monday-Saturday 6pm-midnight.* This is Adelaide's oldest restaurant noted for its casual dining and fine cuisine. Try the beef fillet rossini, blackened Moroccan fish fillets, kangaroo filled with red pepper corn, and lamb shanks braised with garlic, green peppers, olives, and beans. Good blackboard specials.

❏ **The Manse Restaurant:** *142 Tynte Street, North Adelaide, Tel. 8267-4736. Open for lunch Thursday and Friday from 12noon and dinner Monday-Saturday from 6:30pm.* One of the city's oldest restaurants housed in a historic and elegant Victorian mansion. Serves modern French cuisine with Asian influences. Try the grilled tiger prawns, seared fillet of tuna, and loin of venison with red currant sauce and black peppered noodles. Excellent desserts.

ECLECTIC

❏ **Blake's:** *Hyatt Regency Adelaide, North Terrace, Tel. 8238-2381. Closed Sunday. No lunch.* This cozy restaurant is the Hyatt Regency's best. Try the blackened fish with vegetable couscous sauce as well as its tandoor oven dishes. Excellent wine list.

❏ **Mona Lisa's Mediterranean Bistro and Café:** *160 Hutt Street, Tel. 8223-3733. Open for lunch Monday-Friday 12noon-3pm and for dinner Monday-Saturday 6-10pm.* Housed in a historic former general store, and complete with the ambience of 130 year old blue stone walls, tribal rugs, ethnographica, paintings, and open fires in the winter, this place is especially noted for its wine list and inventive dishes. Try the tagine of corn fed Kangaroo Island chicken, char-grilled chilli lamb kebab, Arabian fish curry, and seared sugar cured kangaroo fillet with gilled figs, radicchio and crisp prosciutto.

JAPANESE

❏ **Shiki:** *Hyatt Regency Adelaide, North Terrace, Tel. 8238-2381. Closed Sunday and Monday. No lunch.* This elegant restaurant offers four set menus in addition to its a la carte selections. Includes five *teppanyaki* tables which come complete with flamboyant chefs who produce a breathtaking spectacle. Local favorites include kangaroo fillet and tempura of barramundi.

❏ **Matsuri Japanese Restaurant:** *167 Gouger Street, Tel. 8231-3494. Open Friday for lunch, 12noon-2pm, and Wednesday-Monday for dinner, 6pm-late.* Offers a wide range of authentic Japanese food, such as Sushi, Tempura, Ishiyaki, Nabe dishes.

ASIAN

❑ **Spices Restaurant:** *150 North Terrace, Tel. 8217-7552. Open for lunch Tuesday-Saturday 12-noon and dinner Tuesday-Saturday 6pm.* Offers many interesting dishes from North India, Indonesia, Malaysia, and Thailand. Try the *murgh makhani* (North India), *rendang ayam* (Malaysia,), *mie goreng istimewa* (Indonesia), and *kaeng phed nuer* (Thailand).

❑ **Lemon Grass Bistro:** *289 Rundle Street, Tel. 8223-6627. Open daily for lunch 12noon-3pm and dinner 5pm-late.* Centrally located in the heart of Adelaide, this popular restaurant offers modern Thai and Japanese *teppanyaki* cuisine. Try the set menus.

❑ **Jasmin:** *31 Hindmarch Square, Tel. 8223-7837. Closed Sunday and Monday. No lunch on Sunday.* This well-appointed Indian restaurant specializes in Punjabi cuisine. Try the tandoor fish and chicken. Excellent wine list.

ENJOYING YOUR STAY

Adelaide and South Australia have a great deal to offer visitors who have a few days to enjoy the many and varied pleasures of this city and state. In addition to shopping, the area offers a number of attractions to make any holiday a memorable experience. In addition to taking the Adelaide Explorer (see discussion at the beginning of this chapter), one of the first things you may want to do is take a 2-hour walking tour of the city. Some of the tourist books and brochures available through the South Australian Travel Centre (1 King William Street) outline 20 places to visit on this self-directed walking tour:

- The Beehive Corner
- Renaissance Tower
- Ruthven Mansions
- Scots Church
- Tandanya
- East End Markets
- Ayers House
- Botanic Gardens
- University of South Australia
- Adelaide University
- Art Gallery of South Australia
- South Australia Museum

- State Library of South Australia
- Migration Museum
- National Ware Memorial
- Government House
- Festival Centre
- Parliament House
- Old Parliament House
- Adelaide Casino

Adelaide's major attractions for visitors include the following:

❏ **Adelaide Casino:** *North Terrace, Tel. 8212-2811. Open Monday-Friday 10am-4am and weekends 24 hours a day.* Located next to the luxury Hyatt Regency Hotel and the Adelaide Convention Centre, this is Adelaide's premier gaming center. The casino is part of the restored heritage Adelaide Railway Station which was built in the 1920s. Includes over 100 gaming tables, more than 600 gaming machines, 3 bars, live entertainment, and a restaurant.

❏ **Adelaide Festival Centre:** *King William Road, Tel. 8216-8600.* Located on the banks of the Torrens River, this is the city's performing arts complex. It houses the State Opera, the South Australian Theatre Company, and the Adelaide Symphony Orchestra. Tours are available, but you may want to attend one of the many regularly scheduled theatrical or musical performances. Offers champagne brunches on Sunday mornings at its bistro (Tel. 8216-8744).

❏ **Art Gallery of South Australia:** *North Terrace, Tel. 8223-7200. Open daily 10am-5pm.* Houses a substantial collection of Australian, English, and European paintings.

❏ **Ayers House:** *288 North Terrace, Tel. 8223-1234. Open Tuesday-Friday 10am-4pm and Saturday and Sunday 1-4pm.* This old restored 41-room mansion serves as the headquarters for the National Trust of South Australia. Offers a one-hour tour. Includes two restaurants.

❏ **Botanic Garden:** *North Terrace, Tel. 8228-2311. Open Monday-Friday from 7am to sunset and Saturday and Sunday from 9am to sunset.* This 40-acre (16 hectares) of beautiful gardens displays a fine collection of Australian and exotic plants. The garden features the oldest glasshouse in an Australian botanic garden. Guided tours on Tuesday and Friday at 10:30am. Includes an excellent restaurant, the Botanic Gardens Restaurant, with a nice view of the city.

❑ **HMS Buffalo:** *Patawalonga Boat Haven, Adelphi Terrace, Glenelg. Tel. 8294-7000. Open daily 10am-5pm.* Located in the ocean front suburb of Glenelg, this is a full scale model of the Buffalo, the ship that brought the first colonist to Glenelg in 1836 (but wrecked in New Zealand in 1840). Contains a good maritime museum and a popular seafood restaurant for lunch and dinner.

❑ **Light's Vision:** *Corner of Pennington Terrace and Montefiore Road, North Adelaide.* Montefiore Hill provides a panoramic view of the city, Adelaide Hills, Torrens River, and parklands. A great place for taking photos of the city.

❑ **Parliament House:** *Corner of North Terrace and King William Road, Tel. 8237-9100.* Located adjacent to Old Parliament House, the impressive Greco-Roman facade on this building, with its 10 Corinthian columns, is best noted for its architecture. The building, of course, is the seat of South Australia's government.

❑ **St. Peter's Cathedral:** *Corner of King William Road and Pennington Terrace, North Adelaide, Tel. 8267-4551. Open Monday-Friday 9am-5pm. Free guided tours every Wednesday at 11am and Sunday at 3pm.* Completed in 1904, this is one of Adelaide's most famous historic and architectural landmarks. Noted for its beautiful towers and spires, pealing bells, and 20 stained glass windows by Adelaide artist Cedar Prest.

❑ **South Australian Museum:** *North Terrace, Tel. 8223-8911. Open daily 10am-5pm.* This museum houses the world's best collection of Aboriginal artifacts (only a few on display) as well as excellent displays on Melanesia and the Pacific Islands.

❑ **Zoological Gardens:** *Frome Road, Tel. 8267-3255. Open daily 9:30am-5pm and until 8pm on Wednesday and Sunday in January. Daily feeding times are 11:45am and 3:45pm.* One of Australia's most interesting zoos. It's particularly noted for its fine collection of Australian birds as well as its ability to breed rare animals such as the red panda and Persian leopard. Includes a special Children's Zoo. Beautifully landscaped with walk-through aviaries and a reptile house.

In addition to visiting the Barossa Valley, Hahndorf, and Aldgate **outside Adelaide**, you will find several other interesting towns and hill areas worth visiting for their historical sites, museums, wineries, and recreational opportunities: Belair, Birdwood, Blackwood, Bridgewater, Clarendon, Cudlee Creek, Glen Osmond, Gumerache, Hersbrook, Lobethal, Mount Baker, Mount Lofty, Norton Summit, One Tree Hill, Springfield, and Windy Point. Further outside the metropolitan area—requiring more than one day to visit—are such popular destinations as **Coober Pedy** for opal mining; the **Eyre Peninsula** for its coastal resorts; **Flinders Ranges** for its spectacular mountain scenery and bushwalking; **Kangaroo Island** for its wildlife and beaches; the **Murray River** for its cruises; and **Mt. Gambier** for its lakes.

Adelaide also offers over 32 kilometers of lovely **beaches** and seaside resorts within a 30-minute drive from the city. The beaches have excellent facilities for swimming and boating. If you enjoy fishing from jetties, go to the popular fishing beaches at Brighton, Glenelg, Henley Beach, Grange, Semaphore, and Largs Bay.

The **Barossa Valley**, as noted earlier in our discussion of shopping and craft towns, is a popular destination for both its wineries and craft shops. Located less than two hours drive north of Adelaide, the Barossa Valley begins around the town of Grawler. Many visitors to Adelaide plan to stay two or three days in this area enjoying the wineries, quaint towns, interesting historical sites, excellent restaurants and bakeries, friendly accommodations, and varied recreational opportunities. Indeed, you will find 50 wineries open to the public for tours, wine tasting, and retail sales. Settled by German Lutherans in the early 1800s, the Valley has retained much of its old world charm and hospitality. There's plenty to see and do, from touring the many wineries to taking hot air balloon rides to sampling the many marvelous old bakeries and restaurants in the towns. You will find many small country hotels, motels, traditional farms houses, and camping sites for accommodations. The **South Australia Travel Centre** at 1 King William Street (Tel. 8212-1505) in Adelaide as well as the **Barossa Wine and Visitor Centre** at 66 Murray Street in Nuriootpa can assist you with your plans to visit the Valley.

Another popular area for famous South Australian vineyards and wineries is the **Clare Valley**, located in the hills of the northern Mt. Lofty Ranges. The historic town of Clare is the center for visiting this area.

Known as the "Festival City", Adelaide is a great place to visit during the biennial crafts festival that draws hundreds of craftspeople from all over Australia. This festival is held during the month of March in even-numbered years. The Australian Grand Prix is held every October. Small towns, such as Hahndorf, Tanunda, Willunga, and McLaren Vale, also have festivals.

There is a lot to do at night in Adelaide. For performing arts, check what's on (opera, theater, concerts) at the **Adelaide Festival Centre** (box office is open Monday-Saturday 9:30am-8:30pm). The **Adelaide Casino** (North Terrace, Tel. 8212-2811, open 10am-4am) offers the usual gaming alternatives for gamblers.

Adelaide's trendy spot for young people is in the heart of the city along **Hindley and Rundle Streets**. Here you'll find numerous nightclubs, bars, restaurants, and cafes that stay open until early morning. Some are 24-hour establishments. One of the city's top nightclubs is found at the Hilton International Adelaide Hotel (Victoria Square)—**Margaux's on the Square** (Tel. 8217-0711, open Thursday-Saturday 9pm-3am).

Melbourne

MELBOURNE IS AUSTRALIA'S BEST ATTEMPT to capture the old world elegance, charm, and culture of Europe. Frequently compared to Boston, Philadelphia, and Edinburgh, but regularly contrasted with more energetic and exuberant Sydney, Melbourne is a city of tree-lined boulevards, beautiful parks and gardens, Victorian architecture, towering glass and steel commercial buildings, fashionable shops, charming street cars, fine ethnic restaurants, and distinct neighborhoods and villages. Touted by locals as *"the world's most livable city"* for its climate, lifestyle, and ambience, Melbourne is one of Australia's truly unique cities. A city of casual elegance, it's a melting pot of European ethnic and cultural groups as well as a center of political and financial influence in direct competition with the bolder and brasher Sydney. It's a very boastful and trendy city that loves to lay claim to many so-called "firsts": Australia's art, culture, fashion, shopping, sports, commercial, banking, and financial capital. It leaves little of distinction to other cities that are expected to live in the shadow of Melbourne's excessive pride.

But many claims to fame are really true about this city. Above all, Melbourne is a shopper's paradise for fashion, arts, antiques, and crafts. You've come to the right city if you want antiques, and crafts. You've come to the right city if you want to do some serious, yet fun, shopping in some of Australia's best shopping streets, arcades, department stores, neighborhoods, markets, and craft centers. You should leave this city with a very different view of the "real Australia," a view partially shaped by Melbourne's many shopping discoveries.

GETTING TO KNOW YOU

Melbourne has a certain character, class, and charm largely absent in other Australian cities. Indeed, if Sydney is Australia's Los Angeles, then Melbourne is its London. Compared to its fast-paced arch rival, Sydney, Melbourne is more laid-back and sedate. Whereas Sydney appears bold, brash, and innovative, Melbourne seems more reserved, traditional, and conservative.

❑ Melbourne is a very boastful and trendy city that loves to lay claim to many "firsts". It leaves little of distinction to other cities that are expected to live in the shadow of Melbourne's excessive pride.

❑ Melbourne is a shopper's paradise for fashion, arts, antiques, and crafts.

❑ If Sydney is Australia's Los Angeles, then Melbourne is its London.

❑ This is Australia's fashion capital, where leading designers and factories turn out the latest in fashion clothes and accessories.

❑ The emphasis in the suburbs tends to be on opening more and more trendy youth-oriented clothing stores as well as small cafes and restaurants that cater to the weekend shopping crowds.

It projects a refined and cultured image that challenges the popular stereotype of a male dominated Australia disproportionately populated by crude, vulgar, uncultured, beer-drinking, beach-bumming, party-going, Crocodile Dundee cowboys.

Many people fall in love with this city of over 3 million people. It may not have Sydney's fabulous weather nor the symbolism of the uniquely designed Opera House perched on a visually appealing harbor, but it has a compelling style that puts this city in a class of its own. If you take a tram, stroll its wide tree-lined boulevards and parks, attend a play or opera, visit its many museums and buildings, dine its ethnic restaurants, and shop in its fashionable department stores, shops, galleries, and weekend markets, you will quickly learn why so many Australians love to call Melbourne their home.

If you liked shopping in Sydney, you may enjoy it even more in Melbourne. This is Australia's fashion capital, where the country's leading designers and factories turn out the latest in fashion clothes and accessories. It's the city that boasts the country's largest (Myer) and most elegant (David Jones and Georges) department stores and shopping complex (Melbourne

Central) and the finest collection of designer boutiques (Toorak Road). It's where you can spend thousands of dollars on haute couture (Toorak Village) or save up to 70 percent on brand names by shopping in Australia's largest concentration of factory outlets (metro area but especially near Sydney Road in Brunswick). It's where you will find Australia's best collection of serious Aboriginal art (Bourke Street and Flinders Lane) and Asian art and antique shops (Chapel and High Streets), its finest arts and craft shop (Craft Shop in the Meat Market Craft Centre), and its largest and most fascinating open-air market (Queen Victoria Market).

Like many other cities in Australia, Melbourne also is a city that recently has gone through some tough economic times, especially with the recession of the 1990s that resulted in closing many shops, including the venerable upscale Georges department store (now reopened). The result was less conspicuous consumption and the increased popularity of second-hand stores. While a few new trendy shopping complexes have opened in recent years, such as Melbourne Central and South-gate, the overall quality of shopping in Melbourne has not changed much in the past decade; in some respects it has actually declined. The arts and crafts remain well and alive in many of the city's shops and markets, and more and more Aboriginal art galleries have opened or expanded their operations in recent years. Much of the suburban shopping remains somewhat disappointing, except for the many art and antique shops that seem to hold their own. The emphasis in the suburbs tends to be on opening more and more trendy youth-oriented clothing stores as well as small cafes and restaurants that cater to the weekend shopping and entertainment crowds.

Spend four days shopping in Melbourne and you'll be thoroughly exhausted with your shopping experience. Spend two weeks shopping in Melbourne and you will learn a great deal about Australia's many highly talented designers, artists, and craftspeople and its leading Aboriginal artists. You will have a unique and fascinating travel adventure known to few people who visit Australia.

This is not a city of large shopping arcades or trendy centers such as Sydney's Queen Victoria Building, Strand Arcade, Centrepoint, or Marketplace. In Melbourne the best shopping is found in the small shops that line the main streets (Toorak, Chapel, High) of suburban Toorak, Armadale, South Yarra, Prahran, and Malvern; in the central commercial district along Collins and Bourke Streets; and in the numerous shops and small arcades that feed into or face the Bourke Street Pedestrian Mall. Stroll along these streets and arcades and you will

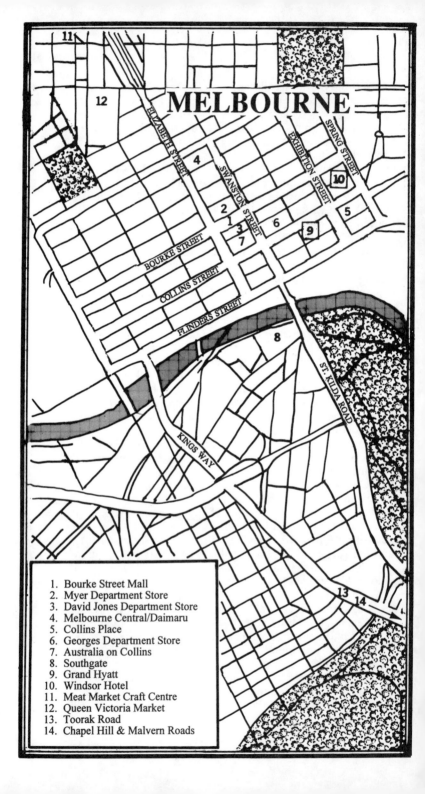

MELBOURNE

1. Bourke Street Mall
2. Myer Department Store
3. David Jones Department Store
4. Melbourne Central/Daimaru
5. Collins Place
6. Georges Department Store
7. Australia on Collins
8. Southgate
9. Grand Hyatt
10. Windsor Hotel
11. Meat Market Craft Centre
12. Queen Victoria Market
13. Toorak Road
14. Chapel Hill & Malvern Roads

quickly discover Melbourne's—and Australia's—many shopping delights. Shoppers who love to explore factory outlets and warehouses head east to Bridge Road in Richmond as well as north to the Sydney Road area of Brunswick. At the same time, Melbourne is beginning to move in the direction of the large shopping center with the recent additions of Highpoint (300 shops) in Maribyrnong (8 kilometers from the city) and Melbourne Central (160 shops) in the city center.

Walk through the elegant department stores and shopping arcades on Collins, Bourke, and Elizabeth Streets, take a tram to the upmarket suburbs of Toorak and Armadale, and visit the numerous shops that front on the main streets (Toorak, Chapel, High) and in shopping centers (Toorak Village) and you will experience some of the best quality shopping found anywhere in Australia.

THE STREETS OF MELBOURNE

Melbourne is a large sprawling metropolis with a high-rise central business district situated next to the charming Yarra River and with suburbs stretching in all directions. In addition to the central business district, you will find major shopping opportunities south and east of the central business district in the upmarket suburbs of Toorak, Armadale, South Yarra, Prahran, Maribyrnong, Richmond, Brighton, and St. Kilda.

Melbourne is a relatively easy and pleasant city to get around in. The central business district is laid out in a grid plan—1½ kilometers long by ½ kilometer wide—with major shops and shopping arcades located along Bourke, Elizabeth, Collins, and Flinders Streets and within easy walking distance of each other. You'll want to put on a good pair of walking shoes to spend a day just walking up and down these streets to explore the many department stores, shopping arcades, and shops that define this area as one of Australia's major shopping areas.

Several of Melbourne's suburbs, especially Toorak, Armadale, Richmond, and Prahran are "must" stops for serious shoppers. Located a few kilometers east and southeast of the central business district, they are best reached by tram, bus, or taxi. The most pleasant and inexpensive way to get to these suburbs is to take the tram (Nos. 6 or 9) from Swanston Street, between Bourke and Collins Streets, in the central business district. The tram ride takes only 10 minutes and puts you in the heart of these up-market suburbs. Once there, you can easily spend another day walking the streets to discover numerous shops and shopping arcades along Toorak Road and Chapel and High Streets. Since these are long streets, be sure to wear a good pair of walking shoes for a full day of walking. The Bridge Street area of Richmond, which is only 3 minutes east of the central business district, includes numerous factory outlets, boutiques, and cafes.

One other major shopping area is located just to the north of the central business district at the corner of Queen and Victoria Streets (Queen Victoria Market) and the corner of Blackwood and Courtney Streets (Meat Market Craft Centre). While within 30-minute walking distance from the central business district, we recommend taking a tram from Elizabeth Street or a taxi to reach these areas.

Melbourne's wide streets, tree-lined boulevards, green parks, Yarra River, Victorian architecture, and trams make it an inviting city for most visitors. Melbourne boasts some attractive architecture—more than any other Australian city. It's a quaint, but by no means beautiful, city with character. However, its emerging new skyline of architecturally adventuresome highrise commercial buildings, hotels, and shopping centers is transforming the character of this city.

GETTING ORIENTED

You will find plenty of resources to help orient you to Melbourne. Indeed, Melbourne provides a great amount of tourist literature on the city and surrounding area, from detailed maps to specialty tours. Most free tourist guides, such as *The Official Visitors' Guide*, *This Week in Melbourne*, and *Melbourne Events*, include a general map of the central business district—the area with the most shops. But this is not necessarily the best area for quality shopping. Be sure you get a good map of Melbourne's suburbs, most of which lie southwest of the downtown area.

Prior to arriving in Melbourne, you may want to visit the city online through these three sites:

www.melbourne.org
www.tourism.vic.gov.au
www.melbourne.citysearch.com.au

One of the first stops you should make in downtown Melbourne is the **Victoria Visitor Information Centre** which is located at the Melbourne Town Hall (corner of Little Collins and Swanston Streets, Tel. 9658-9955, open Monday-Friday 8:30am-5:30pm and weekends 9am-5pm). This center includes information on Melbourne and Victoria. You also can book accommodations and tours through AUSRES which operates from this office. The **City Experience Centre**, also located at Melbourne Town Hall (Tel. 9658-9955, open Monday-Friday 9am-7pm and weekends 10am-5pm), provides information on attractions, tours, events, activities, and Internet access. It provides volunteer "Greeters" (30 different languages) who will take you on a free one-on-one orientation of the city (need to book at least three days in advance). You also will find **Information Booths** at the Flinders Street Station (corner of Flinders and Swanston Streets, open Monday-Thursday 9am-5pm; Friday 9am-6pm; Saturday 10am-4pm; and Sunday 11am-4pm) as well as a useful new visitor information service for comprehensive information, maps and brochures on Melbourne and Victoria: **Victorian Tourism Information Service** (Tel. 132-842).

You will find plenty of bookstores in and around Bourke Street which stock maps of the city. Similar to the maps found in the tourist literature, most of these maps cover the central business district and a few outlying suburbs. Unfortunately, most of these maps cut off the eastern section of Melbourne's two most important shopping suburbs—Toorak Road (Toorak Village area) and High Street (Armadale). One of the better maps, which includes separate sections on the major shopping precincts of Toorak, Prahran, Armadale, and Malvern, is the pull-out map that is included in the free weekly guide entitled *This Week in Melbourne*. For detailed coverage of these areas, you'll need to purchase a copy of a thick street atlas used by taxi drivers and local residents—an expensive and cumbersome publication.

You will find a few guidebooks to Melbourne in the local bookstore. However, few are useful for shopping purposes. Most guides cover the usual history, sightseeing attractions, hotels, restaurants, and entertainment you will find in much of the free literature provided by local businesses and available through the Victoria Visitor Information Centre, City Experience Centre, and Information Booths. There are two exceptions, useful shopping directories not found in most bookstores. If you are interested in shopping in Melbourne's factory outlets, be sure to get a copy of Pamela Durkin's latest edition of *Pamm's Guide to Discount Melbourne* (Magpie Books, P.O. Box 2038, Brighton North, Victoria 3186, $15.95). This book identifies more than 400 of Melbourne's factory outlets by name, address, telephone number, hours of operation and products as well as includes summaries of the best buys in each outlet and money saving coupons. Also look for *Shopping*

Secrets Melbourne which identifies over 100 interesting shops by area. For more information on this book, visit the publisher's Web site (*www.shoppingsecrets.com*) or order it directly from the publisher ($14 + $5 shipping, P.O. Box 12830, Melbourne 8006, Tel. 613-9329-9663 or Fax 613-9329-9664). The publisher produces a similar book on Sydney.

Another useful, but less focused, publication outlines discount buying in Melbourne: *Bargain Shoppers' Guide to Melbourne*. Widely available in major bookstores, this publication is most appropriate for local residents who want to know where to get the best bargains on local household goods, furniture, second hand items, beauty care, pets, gardening supplies, office furniture, as well as items of interest to tourists, such as clothes, Australiana, and crafts.

Be sure to pick up free tourist literature at the airport, your hotel, and the Victoria Visitor Information Centre (corner of Little Collins and Swanston Streets, Tel. 9658-9955). Look for *Hello Melbourne*, *Discover Melbourne*, *Melbourne Events*, *Melbourne Guest Guide*, *The Official Visitors' Guide*, *Walking Melbourne*, and *This Week in Melbourne* which include maps, ads, and information on what to do and where to go in Melbourne.

SHOPPING SERVICES

Equipped with a good map, this book, walking shoes, and dogged persistence, you can easily do most shopping in and around Melbourne on your own. Hop on a tram and you're on your way to a new shopping area which may be even more rewarding than the last one. But you also may want to consider joining a shopping tour that will take you to Melbourne's many factory outlets and warehouses where you can buy everything from fashion and accessories to costume jewelry, cookware, watches, glass, crystal, chocolates, and toys. One of the well established and award-winning such tours is:

> Shopping Spree Tours
> P.O. Box 119, Gardenvale 3185
> Tel. (6 13) 9596-6600
> Fax (6 13) 9596-6388

This fully escorted tour goes to 8-10 of Melbourne's best factory outlets and warehouses, includes lunch, and stops at the Rialto Observation Deck for a panoramic view of the city. You'll also find other shopping groups offering similar services. Check the Yellow Pages of the local telephone directory as well as the information kiosks at the Victoria Visitor Information Centre for brochures on these and other shopping tours.

WHAT TO BUY

Melbourne is a shopper's paradise for all types of products. Shops, shopping arcades, and factory outlets bulge with the latest Australian-produced and imported goods. Your choices range from high fashion and trendy clothes to fine Aboriginal arts and crafts to great selections of handcrafted items from all over Australia and the world. This is a cosmopolitan city which clearly displays its worldliness in its many city and suburban shops.

FASHION CLOTHES AND ACCESSORIES

Melbourne is Australia's fashion center. Here, you find Australia's leading men's and women's clothing designers as well as struggling young designers intent on breaking into the highly competitive and glamorous world of Australian fashion. The exciting world of fashion in Melbourne is very much a cottage industry of creative artists-designers. Such noted designers and companies as Collette Dinnigan, Teena Varigos, John Cavill, Perri Cutten, Lou Wiseman, Adele Palmer, Angela Padula, Anthea Crawford, Shelley A. Neill, David Medwin, Squire Sport, Feitel, Stunning, and Bell, Book, and Candle have all been based in Melbourne. Many of their seasonal designs and collections set the pace for high fashion and trendy clothes in hundreds of boutiques and department stores throughout Australia. You can visit their boutiques in downtown and suburban Melbourne. While many of the fabrics are imported from Europe, the finished garments are designed, cut, and assembled in the many workshops of South Yarra where several top designers also have their own boutiques.

Toorak Road in suburban South Yarra and Toorak is Melbourne's fashion street. Here you will find numerous upmarket boutiques lining both sides of the road from Punt Road to Toorak Village. Starting at Punt Road and walking east, you'll come to such lovely shops as **Style of South Yarra** (#17) for wedding gowns, **Ido** (#29) for bridal and evening wear, and **Peaches and Creme** (#35) for upscale children's clothing, including christening dresses. The multi-level **Country Road** shop, at the corner or Toorak Road and Chapel Street, is the main shop of this popular Australian retail giant (great window displays). Also, look for **Digbys** (#57), **Teena Varigos** (#67), and **Trevor West** (#79) for good quality women's and men's clothes. **Morrissey and Edmiston** offers stylish men's shirts; **Scanlan and Theodore** has unique women's wear; **Bisonte** has exclusive leather and suede jacks; **Succhi** is good for fashionable shoes; and **Saba** is into classic fashion for men and women. At the classy Como Gaslight Gardens shopping center (corner of Chapel and Toorak), look for **Trent Nathan**, **Robert Burton**, **Keith Matheson**, **La Donna**, **Collette Dinnigan**, and **Night Affair**. A good portion of Toorak Road serves as a major center for bridal shops. The Toorak Village area, which is a 15 minute walk from Chapel Street, includes several nice boutiques such as **Liz Davenport** (#412), **di Parigi**, **Fells**, and **della Spiga** (#428).

While the shops on **Chapel Street** and **High Street** in the suburbs of Prahran and Armadale primarily offer arts, antiques, and ethnic foods, you will find a few nice fashion stores and trendy clothing stores in this area. Further north, where Chapel Street becomes Church Street, you will come to the suburb of **Richmond**. This area, especially along Bridge Street, has stores and factory outlets housing many of Australia's young designers. Other suburban areas with shops offering fashion clothes are located along **Lygon Street** (Carlton), **Burke Road** (Camberwell), and **Puckle Street** (Moonee Ponds).

Other fashion and clothing shops are found in the two major department stores on Bourke Street Pedestrian Mall—**David Jones** and **Myer**. **David Jones** actually has two stores, one across the street from the other. The **David Jones** store next to **Myer** only carries womenswear whereas the other branch across the street specializes in menswear. The **Myer** department store, Bourke Street Building, has women's clothes and accessories on Levels B, G, 1, 2, and 3 and menswear and accessories on Level 4. You will also find children's clothes and accessories on Level 5. Both the **David Jones** and **Myer** department stores carry fashion clothes created by Australia's leading designers. For high fashion clothes, be sure to visit the exclusive Australian designer boutique on Level 2 of Myer Department Store, Bourke Street Building.

Melbourne Central shopping center includes numerous women's, men's, and children's clothing and accessory shops as well as the adjacent Daimaru Department Store. Here you'll find such noted shops as **Brian Rochford**, **Country Road**, **Laura Ashley**, **Portmans**, **R. M. Williams**, **Shepherds**, **Jag**, and **Shortsgirl**.

You will also discover other menswear and womenswear shops in and around the shopping arcades along Bourke, Collins, and Swanston Streets as well as in the exclusive

Georges Department Store (Collins Street) and shopping arcades at the **Grand Hyatt Hotel** (Collins Street) and **Southgate** (along river). The **Galleria Shopping Plaza, The Block, Collins 234, Australia on Collins, The Welk, Centrepoint, Royal Arcade**, and **Collins Place** have numerous shops offering the latest in fashionwear and accessories for both men and women as well as children.

Collins Street is one of Australia's most upscale fashion and accessory centers, comparable to Sydney's Castlereagh Street. Here you'll find several international brand name fashion and accessory shops such as **Hermes, Ferragamo, Bally, Harrold's, Raphael, Versace**, and **Louis Vuitton.** Also look for **Cose Ipanema** (Grand Hyatt) and **Le Louvre** (74 Collins) for exclusive labels as well as one of Australia's top designers, **Teena Varigos** (182 Collins).

Further east on Collins Street is the **Grand Hyatt Hotel**. In the adjacent shopping arcade you'll find several men's and women's apparel shops selling excellent quality clothes and accessories.

For strong Australian and Aboriginal themes in clothing and accessories, be sure to visit **Aboriginal Creations** at 50 Bourke Street (Shop 3, Tel. 9662-9400). It specializes in Australian indigenous design in clothing, textiles, accessories, and artifacts. Look for everything from T-shirts, blouses, and knitwear to swimwear, childrenswear, and neckties. **Australian Way** at Melbourne Center (Shop 305), Australia on Collins (Shop 213), and Royal Arcade (Shop 18) carries the distinctive and colorful Coogi collection of knitwear.

Factory outlets and **clearance centers** offering designer label clothes and accessories are scattered throughout the Melbourne metropolitan area. For example, you can buy samples and seconds of well-known Australian designer labels for nearly half price at several outlet shops along **Bridge Road** in Richmond: **Satch** (#49 and #162), **JeansWest** (#52), **Eastbound Clothing** (#137), **Portmans Warehouse** (corner of Bridge Road and Lennox Street), **Nif Naf** (#184), **Paddington Coat Factory** (#194), **Thomas Cook Clothing** (#223), **Sportsgirl-Sportscraft Aywon Clearance Centre** (#236), **Unlimited Factory Outlet** (#243), **Country Road Wearhouse** (#261), and **Richmond Plaza Shopping Centre** (corner of Bridge Road and Church Street).

FURS AND LEATHER

Melbourne also is Australia's center for elegant furs. Run by several famous Jewish-Greek furrier families who have been in the trade for decades, Melbourne's fur shops offer selections of nicely tailored mink, fox, and opossum coats and jackets. While most of the pelts are imported from Russia, China, Canada, and the United States and then cut and tailored in Melbourne, a few of the furs, such as fox and opossum, come from Australia and New Zealand.

You may find Melbourne's fur selections limited in comparison to what you may find back home. Nonetheless, you may get lucky and find some unique furs and styles not available elsewhere. Indeed, some of the styling here is better than what we find in Hong Kong and Korea. Prices, however, vary; they may or may not be to your advantage.

Most furriers are located in downtown shopping arcades, such as **Planinsek** at Collins Place (Shop 19, 45 Collins Street). Several of these also carry leather coats, jackets, and accessories. Several outlet shops offer leather goods along Bridge Road in Richmond: **Larosa Leathergoods** (#72), **Joloni Leather** (#121), **SaRAY Leather** (#139), **Stitching Horse Bootery** (#191).

JEWELRY

Melbourne has several jewelry stores offering the usual selection of jewelry with special emphasis on set and unset Australian opals. You will find a few jewelers offering fine craft, contemporary, and antique jewelry. **Makers Mark Gallery**, for example, at 101 Collins Street (Tel. 9654-8388, *www.makersmark.com.au*), offers some of Australia's most unique silver and gold jewelry with elegant arts and crafts themes. Look for their special displays at the front of their store. Other noted jewelry designers which produce unique and award-winning designs include **MDT Design** (166 Swanston Walk, Tel. 9654-7235, *www.mdt design.com*); **Genesis** (Beehive Building, 94 Elizabeth Street, Tel. 9650-9839); **Arna Setters** (125 Swanston Street, Tel. 9654-6708); **John Schultz Manufacturing Jeweller** (Room 204, 125 Swanston Street, Tel. 9654-6478); and **Sawatzky Designs** (220 Collins Street, Tel. 9650-3861). Fine craft jewelry is found at the award-winning **Craft Shop** at the Meat Market Craft Centre on the corner of Courtney and Blackwood Streets in North Melbourne.

For top quality jewelry, **Costello's** at the Melbourne Centre (Shop 205, 300 Lonsdale Street, Tel. 9639-2233) has an excellent selection of Argyle diamonds, South Sea pearls, and Australian opals. You'll find several other jewelry shops in this shopping center, including **Franco Jewellers** (Shop 276, Tel. 9663-5751). For good quality Broome pearls and Argyle diamonds, stop at **Rutherford Pearls** at 174 Collins Street.

A nice shop selling antique jewelry, porcelain, silverware, and related items, such as uniquely handcrafted candlesticks, is **Schlager Antique Jewellery** at 308 Little Collins Street (corner of Royal Arcade, Tel. 9650-4391). You should find some very nice new and antique pieces at the beautiful shop of this well-established Melbourne jeweler.

OPALS

Many people claim the opal shops in Melbourne are the best in all of Australia for both quality and price. You'll have to judge these claims for yourself. But one thing is true—you'll find numerous shops throughout Melbourne selling opals. Most of the stores specializing in opals are found along Bourke, Exhibition, and Collins Streets. Some of Melbourne's most popular opal shops are: **Melbourne Opal Centre** (169 Bourke Street, Tel. 9654-6302); **Altmann and Cherny** (120 Exhibition Street, Tel. 9650-9685); **J. H. Mules Opals** (110 Exhibition Street); **Andrew Cody Opals** (119 Swanston Street Walk, Tel. 9654-5533); **Ashley Opals Jewellers** (85 Collins Street, Tel. 9654-4866); **Rochi's Opals** (210 Little Collins Street, Tel. 9654-4258); **Abbess Opal Mine** (218-220 Swanston Street, Tel. 9639-2188); **Johnston Opals** (124 Exhibition Street, Tel. 9650-7434; 65 Queens Road, Tel. 9510-6393; 111 Little Collins Street, Tel. 9650-7744; *www.sofcom.com.au/johnstonopals*); and **Opal World** (137 Bourke Street).

AUSTRALIANA, GIFTS, AND SOUVENIRS

Australiana shops abound in the downtown department stores and shopping arcades as well as in the suburban shopping districts. Most of these shops, such as **Australianway** at Australia on Collins (270 Collins Street) and the **Australiana General Store** at 1227 High Street in Armadale, have good selections of quality souvenirs and curios.

ABORIGINAL AND TRIBAL ARTIFACTS

Melbourne has several good shops specializing in Aboriginal and tribal arts and crafts. Serious collectors will find a few top quality Aboriginal art galleries here that are some of the best in all of Australia. One of the best shops is the **Aboriginal Gallery of Dreamings** at 73-77 Bourke (Tel. 9650-3277, open Monday-Saturday 10am-5:30pm and Sunday 12noon-5pm).

Indeed, if you only visit one Aboriginal art gallery in Australia, make sure it's this one. This is the largest Aboriginal art gallery in Australia. Under the direction of Hank Ebes, a tireless promoter of Aboriginal art worldwide, this gallery has become a rich depository of art and artefacts. It has played an important role in the promotion of Aboriginal art throughout Australia as well as abroad. The gallery is jam-packed with over 5,000 Aboriginal paintings either displayed or stored on three floors. The gallery represents many top Aboriginal artists such as Clifford Possum, Billy Stockman, Eunice Napangardi, Malcolm Jagamarra, and Emily Kngwarreye (now deceased). The ground floor includes numerous acrylic dot paintings from various areas of the central desert region as well as a wide range of handcrafted artifacts, such as boomerangs, didgeridoos, batik from Utopia, pottery, and jewelry, as well as prints, music, books, bark paintings, and Tiwi totem poles. The upper floors include galleries and demonstration and lecture areas.

Other nice Aboriginal galleries in Melbourne include the **Aboriginal Desert Art Gallery** at 31 Flinders Lane (Tel. 9654-2516) with its nice collection of paintings, didgeridoos, carvings, books, and music (see their ongoing video on Aboriginal art); **Kimberley Australian Aboriginal Art** at 76 Flinders Lane (Tel. 9654-5890) with it's intriguing paintings from the Kimberley region (check out their extensive inventory which is stored in the back room); **Gallery Gabrielle Pizzi** (141 Flinders Lane, Tel. 9654-2944) for quality Aboriginal paintings and sculptures; and **Alcaston Gallery** at 2 Collins Street (Tel. 9654-7279) with works from major Aboriginal artists.

Melbourne also as two very nice tribal arts shops that include quality arts and artefacts from Papua New Guinea and Australian Aboriginals. **Tribal Art Gallery** at 103 Flinders Lane (Tel. 9650-4186) includes some very unusual traditional and contemporary Melanesian sculptures as well as musical instruments, weapons, tools, masks, and ancestral figures. It also includes some Aboriginal art. **Aboriginal and Pacific Art Gallery** (42 Hardy Terrace, Ivanhoe, Tel. 9499-4699, by appointment), operated from the home of Rene and Mal Davidson, has a wonderful collection of art and artifacts from Papua New Guinea as well as some old Aboriginal bark paintings, Aranta watercolors, and contemporary paintings by Rene Davidson. In fact, this is one of the best sources for quality art from Papua New Guinea. Serious collectors will definitely want to visit this place which is one of the best in all of Australia.

Only 20 minutes from downtown Melbourne is the award-winning **Mia Mia Gallery** (Westerfolds Park, Fitzsimons Lane, Templetowe, Tel. 9846-4636, closed Monday and Tuesday) which is operated by local and central desert artists and includes dance and musical performances.

AUSTRALIAN AND IMPORTED ARTS AND CRAFTS

Melbourne has a well deserved reputation for producing excellent quality arts and crafts. These arts and crafts range from trendy jewelry to fine ceramics. You will find them in numerous arts and crafts shops in the downtown and suburban areas as well as in several craft towns outside Melbourne.

For one of the best selections of arts and crafts produced in the state of Victoria, be sure to visit the **Meat Market Craft Centre** (42 Courtney Street, corner of Blackwood Street, North Melbourne, Tel. 9329-9966, open Tuesday-Sunday 10am-5pm). This is one of Australia's most unique and innovative centers for promoting the development and appreciation of quality arts and crafts. While it went through some tough times in the early 1990s when it lost many of its state subsidies and subsequently went bankrupt, the center is now more entrepreneurial than ever. In addition to offering a series of workshops and exhibits representing over 650 craftspeople throughout Australia (2/3 from the State of Victoria), the Centre houses what is considered by many Australians to be one of the best arts and crafts stores in Australia—the award-winning **Craft Shop**. The Craft Shop sells only the best of Australian pottery, ceramics, glass, leather, basket work, knitwear, wood work, and hand-crafted opal and Broome pearl, gold, and silver jewelry. Items are nicely displayed, personnel are extremely informative and helpful, and the prices are excellent—the same items selling for 20-30 percent less than in other shops we visited. Also look for the **Gallery of Handweavers and Spinners Guild of Victoria** (Tel. 9329-6191) which offers some very nice hand-woven and handspun sweaters, hats, shawls, and scarves produced by its members and sold here on consignment.

You will also find a few arts and crafts shops around the **Queen Victoria Market** at Queen and Victoria Streets. While the majority of this vast market is devoted to food, house wares, clothes, and souvenirs, several shops along Victoria Street offer good selections of Australian arts and crafts, including Aboriginal artefacts and handcrafted jewelry. You'll also find leather and sheepskin shops in this area.

Several arts and crafts shops in and around Melbourne also offer good quality Australian arts and crafts. **Australian Creations** (50 Bourke Street, Tel. 9662-9400), for example, has a very nice selection of clothes, textiles, accessories, artefacts and gift items which all reflect Australian indigenous designs. At Southgate along with river, look for **Potoroo Fine Craft Gallery** (Shop U10, St. Kilda Road Level, Southgate Arts and Leisure Precinct, Tel. 9690-9859) which offers an excellent collection of top quality Australian ceramics, studio glass, textiles, and woodcraft produced by local artists. The National Gallery of Victoria (also has a nice shop, **Arts Centre Shop**, offering a nice selection of handcrafted jewelry, porcelain, glassware, and woodcraft, along with the usual public gallery assortment of books, postcards, videos, and music.

If you shop Toorak Road in South Yarra, be sure to stop at **Sheil Abbey and Gallery** (53 Toorak Road, Tel. 9866-6886; also at 21 Carpenter Street in Brighton, Tel. 9592-8192). Don Sheil produces limited editions of some of the loveliest trays, bowls, and dinnerware we have seen anywhere. Using a special aluminum-based alloy metal he terms "Sheil Silver," his designs are outstanding contributions to the Australian craft industry. He also will do special commissioned pieces. You may see some of his work in other shops in Melbourne and elsewhere in Australia. In nearby East Prahran is **Hurnall's Antiques and Decorative Arts** (691 High Street, Tel. 9510-3754) with a very nice collection of Australian ceramics.

If you are in the market for some unique designs and excellent quality gold and silver handcrafted jewelry, don't miss **Makers Mark** at 101 Collins Street (Tel. 9654-8488). This is the main shop of Makers Mark which is also found at Chifley Plaza in Sydney. This remains one of Australia's very best arts and crafts shops. They offer some of the nicest handcrafted gold and silver jewelry we have seen anywhere in Australia. Once a decidedly mid-range arts and crafts shop, Makers Mark has definitely gone upscale in recent years as it represents the best of the best of Australia's craftspeople and artisans.

A few shops along Chapel and High Streets offer good selections of Australian and imported arts and crafts. If you're interested in international arts and crafts, especially inexpensive clothes, rugs, handicrafts, shoes, jewelry, and carvings imported from China, Thailand, and Indonesia, visit **Ishka Handcrafts** at 409A Chapel Street (Prahran). This shop imports items, many of which have a decided "hippie" look, from over 50 countries. They are particularly strong on Asian arts and crafts. Ishka Handcrafts also has seven other shops plus a warehouse in the Melbourne metropolitan area: 146 High Street (Kew), 541 Riversdale Road (Camberwell), 82 Church Street (Brighton), 257 Coventry Street (South Melbourne), 362 Lygon Street, Carlton, Chadstone Shopping Centre (Shop B98), Malvern Central Shopping Centre (Shop 9), and 300 Nicholson Street, Fitzroy (warehouse). **The Camels** (458 High Street), an alternative lifestyle shop, offers rugs and artifacts relating to camel themes; one room actually has a sand floor to approximate the desert!

And don't forget the weekend craft markets in and around Melbourne. The **St. Kilda Sunday Art Bank**, at Upper Esplanade, St. Kilda, on Sunday from 9am to 6pm, consists of 190 craft stalls selling handcrafted leather, jewelry, pottery, glass, toys, cottage crafts, and woodcrafts. It's also popular for its ethnic foods and pleasant seaside ambience. The St. Kilda weekend market is located only 5 kilometers south of Melbourne and can be reached by a No. 15 or 16 tram. **Camberwell Market**, Union Street, Camberwell, is open Sunday mornings from 6am to 1:30pm. The **Dingley Village Craft Market** (Marcus Road, Dingley) is located 25 kilometers from Melbourne. It is open the first Sunday of every month from 9am to 2pm.

Several small towns outside Melbourne have craft shops worth visiting. Most are within one or two hours driving distance from the city and make wonderful day trips to discover many unique Victorian arts and crafts. **Mornington Peninsula**, located 50 kilometers south of the city via Nepean Highway, for example, is a center for craft galleries and workshops. Here you will find several shops selling paintings, pottery, ceramics, textiles, leather work, wood work, gold and silver jewelry, and glass.

Two of the best craft galleries near Melbourne (10 to 30 minutes southeast of the city) are found in Hawthorn and Camberwell: **Distelfink Gallery** (432 Burwood Road, Hawthorn, Tel. 9818-2555—contemporary ceramics, glass, sculpture, jewelry, furniture) and **Designs Australia** (536 Riversdale Road, Camberwell, Tel. 9882-8635—represents over 100 furniture designers, from traditional to contemporary, from conservative to whimsical). See additional recommendations in the section entitled "Craft Towns of Greater Melbourne."

FINE ARTS, ANTIQUES, AND DECORATIVE ITEMS

Melbourne has a good reputation for offering excellent quality Australian, European, and Asian arts, antiques, and home decorative items to complement its reputation as Australia's center for high fashion and culture. In fact, you may be overwhelmed with the number of such shops available in and around Melbourne. Serious art and antique shoppers should pick up free copies of several useful guides to Melbourne's art and antique scene: *Antiques of High Street and Malvern Road Area, Antiques & Arts in Victoria, Art Almanac, A Cultural Guide to*

Melbourne: Arts, Museums, and Heritage, and *The Australian Antique Dealers Association (List of Members)*. Most of these publications are available free from shops along High Street and Malvern Road or through the Victoria Visitor Information Centre (corner of Little Collins and Swanston Streets). The first publication provides a detailed map and summaries of over 100 art and antique shops in Prahran, Armadale, and Malvern. The other publications include informative articles, advertisements, and descriptions of major art and antique dealers in Victoria, arranged by community.

Fortunately for shoppers, Melbourne's art, antique, and home decorative shops are primarily concentrated along Toorak Road, Chapel Street, High Street, and Malvern Road in the suburbs of Toorak, South Yarra, Prahran, Armadale, and Malvern as well as in a few downtown shopping centers and hotel shopping arcades and in small communities outside the metropolitan area.

Numerous shops carry a full line of investment quality traditional and contemporary Australian oils, watercolors, etchings, lithographs, and screen prints. Some of the top galleries in downtown Melbourne include **Melbourne Fine Art Gallery** (422 Bourke Street, Tel. 9670-1707), **Flinders Lane Gallery** (137 Flinders Lane, Tel. 9654-3332), and **Adam Galleries** (105 Queen Street, Tel. 9642-8677).

Several art galleries outside the central business district offer excellent selections. The suburbs of Fitzroy, South Yarra, and Toorak are centers for such galleries.

The **Arts Centre Shop** (National Gallery of Victoria, 180 St. Kilda Road) offers a full range of art books, exhibition catalogues, hand-painted silk scarves, and replica jewelry from some of the world's leading collections. You'll want to stop at this shop when visiting the National Gallery of Victoria.

Shops selling European and Australian antiques and collectibles are found throughout the Melbourne metropolitan area and in nearby small towns. However, the major antique shops are concentrated five kilometers southeast of the central business district along High Street in the suburbs of Prahran and Armadale and along Malvern Street in the suburb of Malvern. Several additional antique shops are found on Chapel Street near the intersection of Toorak Road in the suburb of South Yarra and along Burwood, Auburn, and Burke Roads in the nearby suburbs of Hawthorn and South Camberwell.

The best approach to shopping for antiques in East Prahran and Armadale is to pick up a free copy of *Antiques of High Street and Malvern Road Area*. This booklet is an indispensable guide to over 300 antique dealers who operate from nearly 100 individual antique shops and six antique markets over a 2.5 square kilometer area—reputed to be the largest concentration of antique shops in the southern hemisphere. It is the center for Australia's antique trade. We suggest that you start at the corner of Williams Road and High Street in Prahran and walk east for three blocks until you come to Glenferrie Road. Nearly 60 art and antique shops line both sides of this section of High Street. Turn left at Glenferrie Road, go one block, and turn right at Malvern Road. Another 25 art and antique shops line this section of Malvern Road. And if you proceed west on Malvern Road, between Orrong and Williams Roads, you will come to another five art and antique shops lining both sides of this section of Malvern Road.

The High Street collection of art and antique shops has something for everyone. A shop such as **Edward Clark Antiques** (69 Sutherland Road, Armadale, Tel. 9509-1777, by appointment) has a nice collection of French and Australian antique furniture, paintings, and collectibles. **Graham Cornall Antiques** at 731-735 High Street, Armadale (Tel. 9576-1151) offers a good collection of 17th and 18th century period and provincial furniture and decorative art from Europe (French, English, Spanish, Italian).

If you are in the market for fine and rare books, **Peter Arnold** (606 High Street, Tel. 9529-2933) and **Kenneth Hince** (604 High Street, Tel. 9525-1649), noted antiquarians, should be on your shopping list. For rare prints and antique maps, be sure to stop at **Sandilands Antique Prints** (546 High Street, Tel. 9529-8011).

The **Antiques and Decorative Arts Centre of Melbourne** at 941 High Street (Tel. 9822-3700) is High Street's largest and oldest antiques center with over 50 antique shops and stalls under one roof selling a wide range of antique and decorator items. The **Armadale Antique Centre** at 1147 High Street (Tel. 9822-7788) has 30 independent dealers, and **Park Lane Antiques Centre** at 1170 High Street, Armadale (Tel. 9500-9723) also has 30 antique dealers.

Other European and Australian antique shops can be found in the city, nearby suburbs, and small towns in Victoria. In the city, for example, you may want to visit **Kozminsky** at 421 Bourke Street (Tel. 9670-1277) for fine antique and estate jewelry, silver, and objects d'art.

You will also find a few antique shops along Chapel Street, Queens Avenue, and Auburn, Burwood, and Burke roads in South Yarra, Hawthorne, and Camberwell South—suburbs just to the east and south of High and Malvern Streets in Prahran, Armadale, and Malvern. Along Chapel Road near the intersection with Toorak Road in South Yarra you will find a few good antique shops. The **Chapel Street Bazaar** (217 Chapel Street, Tel. 9529-1727) has an assortment of varying quality antiques, collectibles, old wares, and vintage clothing. In the nearby suburbs of Hawthorne and Camberwell South, you'll find several antique shops offering everything from antique furniture and accessories to antique clocks, paintings, silver, porcelain, and jewelry.

We are especially impressed with the small number of high quality shops offering Asian arts and antiques. Most are found in the suburb of Prahran, along High and Commercial Streets and Malvern Road. Japanese arts and antiques have been very popular in Melbourne during the past decade. One of the best shops for lovely Japanese interior items—antiques, chests, ceramics, and furniture—is **Kazari** at 290 Malvern Road, Prahran (Tel. 9521-1107). **Soo Tze Oriental Antiques** at 46 Commercial Road, Prahran (Tel. 9521-2892) has a nice collection of Burmese, Thai, Tibetan, and Nepalese arts, antiques, and home decorative items, with special emphasis on furniture and textiles. **Kenneth Lay** at 608 High Street, Prahran East (Tel. 9510-5978) has a good collection of colonial furniture from India, Sri Lanka, and Indonesia.

DUTY-FREE SHOPS

Like Sydney, Brisbane, and Adelaide, Melbourne has similar duty free shops offering the same types of duty-free goods— liquor, electronics, perfumes, clothes, opals, jewelry, leather goods, and sporting equipment. Since we are not duty-free shoppers and we have yet to find any real bargains in these stores, we have nothing in particular to recommend. Again, if you are from New Zealand, Japan, India, or any other country that puts high import duties on such items, these stores offer good bargains in comparison to prices back home.

Most of the duty-free shops, such as **City International Duty Free** (Swanston Street) are located in the central business district along Swanston, Collins, and Queen Streets.

WHERE TO SHOP

The shopping scene in Melbourne can be best divided into city, suburban, and small town areas as well as into distinct styles of shopping—hotel shopping arcades, department stores, factory outlets, and markets. Each area and style of shopping tends to specialize in particular types of products.

THE CITY

The city shopping area is located in the central business district. Here you will find Melbourne's only pedestrian mall (Bourke Street), numerous shopping arcades and malls, major department stores, small shops, art galleries, restaurants, and Chinatown all seemingly tied together from Collins Street in the south to Latrobe Street in the north and between Elizabeth Street to the west and Swanston Street to the east. This whole downtown area is bordered by Spring, Flinders, King, and Latrobe Streets and bisected by two major shopping streets—Bourke and Collins. Despite continuing efforts to transform this into Melbourne's central shopping area, it remains a mixed area. You will find the city's three major department stores here—Myer, David Jones, and Daimaru—as well as a few upscale shopping centers and arcades, such as Melbourne Central, Australia on Collins, Block Arcade, Collins 234, and Collins Place, and the small but exclusive Georges Department Store at 162 Collins Street. But this area also has some relatively nondescript stores in and around the Bourke Street Pedestrian Mall in such shopping arcades as The Walk, Centrepoint Mall, and the Royal Arcade.

One of the best ways to shop the city area is to start at the top of **Bourke Street**, beginning at the intersection with Spring Street, directly opposite the Parliament House. To the north of Bourke Street is Little Bourke Street which houses Melbourne's colorful Chinatown, between Exhibition and Swanston Streets. To the south of Bourke Street is Little Collins, which has few shops, and Collins Street, which is one of Melbourne's major upmarket shopping areas.

As you proceed west along Bourke Street from Spring Street, you will come to **Australian Creations** (Shop 3, 50 Bourke Street, Tel. 9662-9400) which has a very nice selection of quality Australian arts, crafts, textiles, clothing, and gift items; it specializes in Australian indigenous designs. Across the street is Australia's premier Aboriginal art gallery, **Aboriginal Gallery of Dreamings** (73-77 Bourke Street). If you turn left at the corner of Exhibition Street, you will come to three of Melbourne's major opal dealers: **Johnston Opals** (124 Exhibition Street), **Altman & Cherny** (120 Exhibition Street), and **J. H. Mules Opals** (110 Exhibition Street).

The major shopping section along Bourke Street is found along the **Bourke Street Pedestrian Mall**, a crowded pedestrian mall between Swanston and Elizabeth Streets. A tram traverses the center of the mall. **Myer** and **David Jones** department stores and three shopping arcades—**Centrepoint**

Mall, **The Walk**, and **The Royal Arcade**—feed into the mall. You will encounter several representatives of jewelry shops in the mall handing out literature on their shops as well as sidewalk vendors from Myer Department Store selling discounted items.

Both Myer and David Jones department stores dominate the mall. **David Jones Department Store** occupies two buildings across from one another on the mall. The first building is on the south side of the mall, next to Centrepoint Mall. This branch specializes in menswear. The second branch is directly across the mall next to Myer; it specializes in women's wear and accessories. Another small David Jones store is behind this store off of Little Bourke Street. The **Myer Department Store** on the Mall is the largest in all of Australia. It's the most popular department store for local residents. A monsterous complex, it extends to two blocks, stretching from the Bourke Street Mall to Little Bourke and Lonsdale Streets and connected by overhead walkways.

We have little to recommend in the **three shopping arcades** that feed into the Bourke Street Mall. You may be able to shop all three arcades within 25 minutes. **Centrepoint Mall** has several nondescript shops selling clothing, shoes, and jewelry—none of particular note. **The Walk** has an assortment of jewelry, shoes, clothes, leather, gift, and boutique shops of varying quality. The **Royal Arcade** extends from Bourke Street Pedestrian Mall to both Elizabeth and Little Collins Streets. This arcade has the usual assortment of small clothing, jewelry, leather, and souvenir stores. At the end of the Royal Arcade on Little Collins Street is one of Melbourne's nicest antique jewelry stores—**Schlager**. A well established and reputable firm, this store carries a fine selection of old and new jewelry, porcelain, and paintings. You will find several unique pieces here.

If you exit the Royal Arcade on Elizabeth Street, directly across the street on the corner of Bourke and Elizabeth Streets you will see the **Galleria Shopping Plaza**. This shopping plaza includes menswear, shoe stores, jewelers, boutiques, and restaurants as well as the interesting **Australian Geographic Shop**.

The remainder of Elizabeth and Bourke Streets have several book shops, restaurants, and gift shops. If you continue south on Elizabeth Street, between Collins Street and Flinders Lane, you will come to the state travel service offices for South Australia and Western Australia. These are good offices to visits for information and reservations should your travel plans include stops in Adelaide and Perth. At this point we recommend turning east on Collins Street to explore the shops along Collins Street between Elizabeth and Swanston Streets.

The 200 block of **Collins Street**, between Elizabeth and Swanston Streets, is a mixture of office buildings, shopping arcades, shops, and state travel offices. You will find the state travel service offices for Victoria, Tasmania, Canberra, and Queensland clustered along this block. Two relatively upscale and attractive shopping arcades on the north side of the street include numerous clothing, accessory, and gift shops, and eateries—the food and fashion centers: Australia on Collins and Collins 234. **Australia on Collins** includes more than 60 stores on five levels as well as a food court. **Collins 234**, which used to be known as the Sportsgirl Centre, includes several Australian and imported fashion shops.

Once you reach Swanston Street, you can either turn left on Swanston Street or proceed further east on Collins Street. **Swanston Street** is a major transportation artery for taking trams to the southern suburbs of South Yarra, Toorak, Prahran, Armadale, and St. Kilda. You will also find several gift, jewelry, shoes, and clothing shops along both sides of this street but primarily on the west side. We particularly recommend **Aboriginal Handcrafts** at 125-133 Swanston Street. A small shop located on the 9th floor of the Century Building, it offers good prices on its limited selections of Aboriginal bark paintings, didgeridoos, clap sticks, music, and books.

Returning to **Collins Street**, turn left and go east into the 100 block. This area, from the 100 block of Collins Street to Spring Street, is one of Melbourne's classiest and most upmarket shopping areas. Both sides of the street, but especially the north side, are lined with exclusive designer boutiques and jewelry stores such as **Hermes, Ferragamo, Bally, Harrold's, Monards, Anthony Squires, Makers Mark, Janil, Raphael, Versace, Louis Vuitton**, and **Ashley Opals**. One of the really unique shops here for top quality Australian crafted jewelry is **Makers Mark** (101 Collins Street). For interesting designer fashions, stop at **Cose Ipanema** (123 Collins Street), **Ipanema**, and **Teena Varigos** (182 Collins Street). Be sure to visit Melbourne's classiest department store, **Georges** (162 Collins Street).

Two blocks east on Collins, between Exhibition and Spring Streets, is **Collins Place**, a shopping arcade attached to the twin-Hotel Sofitel. Here you will find over 40 fashion, jewelry, gift, and food shops. Every Sunday between 8am and 4pm, this area becomes a popular all-Australian-made Art and Craft Market.

Melbourne's largest shopping complex is located three blocks north of the Bourke Street Pedestrian Mall area, in the block encircled by Latrobe, Elizabeth, Lonsdale, and Swanston

Streets and connected to Myer Department Store—**Melbourne Central** (300 Lonsdale Street). This attractive six-level shopping complex is anchored by the **Daimaru Department Store** and includes over 150 specialty shops, restaurants, and cafes. You can't miss this complex with its distinctive 20-story glass cone encapsulating the old restored shot tower (National Trust) building. The huge clock at the center of this mall draws crowds on the hour with its entertaining program. This shopping complex is filled with many well recognized name shops, such as R. M. Williams, Country Road, Done Art & Design, Just Jeans, The Irish Shop, Carla Zampati, Esprit, Laura Ashley, Sportsgirl, and Brian Rochford. The **Focal Point Gallery** (#208), located near the clock on the second level, is a very nice gallery offering attractive glass and ceramics.

Be sure to visit **Southgate** on the southern bank of the Yarra River and adjacent to the Victorian Arts Center (take Swanston Street south across the bridge). This delightful shopping and dining area includes 41 shops and 19 restaurants and cafes. You'll find several local designers, galleries, and jewelry shops here. One of Melbourne's best craft shops is located here, **Potoroo Fine Australian Craft**. **JoAnne Hook Gallery**, **Billich Gallery**, **Outback Opal Mine**, and **Made in Japan** add to the quality shopping found in this shopping center which has a very nice indoor/outdoor ambience.

You will find a few other shops scattered throughout the downtown section. However, Melbourne Centre, Daimaru Department Store, Myer and David Jones department stores on Bourke Street Pedestrian Mall, and the shops and shopping arcades from the 100 block of Collins Street to Spring Street offer the best of the city shopping. The rest of the city area is mixed for shopping. You will discover an occasional shop or two in the downtown area that offers special items for international travelers interested in unique quality products. But most such shops will be found in exclusive suburban shopping areas which have a reputation for upmarket shopping.

SUBURBAN VILLAGES

Suburban Melbourne has the look and feel of small villages. Most of these areas have their own shopping and dining areas, from upscale to ethnic and Bohemian. Suburban shopping areas tend to specialize by products with similar shops congregating in the same areas. Therefore, your suburban shopping strategy should focus on particular products of interest to you. If, for example, you are interested in **arts and antiques**, then you will want to go to High and Malvern Streets in Prahran, Armadale, and Malvern. If you are interested in **fashion clothes**, then head for Toorak Road and Bridge Road in South Yarra, Toorak, and Richmond. If you are just out for the day exploring suburban shopping opportunities, we suggest concentrating on **Toorak Road** in South Yarra and Toorak, **Chapel Street** in Prahran, and **High Street** in Armadale. All three of these streets are connected to one another within a two to three kilometer radius. While we identify the various suburban communities, you should focus your shopping on the specific streets that flow from one suburb into another. As you will quickly discover, these suburbs, or so-called villages, do not have readily identifiable boundaries. You literally need to go with the street flow.

SOUTH YARRA AND TOORAK (TOORAK ROAD)

One of the best ways to shop these suburban areas is to take a No. 8 tram on Swanston Street in downtown Melbourne to Toorak Road. This four kilometer ride is a pleasant way to see part of the city. It's best to get off near Punt Street, within one minute after the tram enters onto Toorak Road. You shouldn't have difficulty finding this stop—you will see several restaurants and shops on this corner, including **Style of South Yarra**.

Begin your shopping adventure at this corner and proceed east along Toorak Road until you come to Toorak Village at the corner of Canterbury Road. It's a long, long walk from Punt Street to Canterbury Road. You may want to take a tram part of the way, skipping sections of Toorak Road, that offer few good shopping opportunities. We will point out those sections as we take you down Toorak Road.

Beginning at the intersection of Punt Road and Toorak Road, walk east along Toorak Road until you come to Darling Street. This section of Toorak Road has several of Melbourne's leading boutiques, Australiana stores, and menswear shops. Look for **Polly Courtir Gallery** (#21) for very bold and colorful paintings; **Sheil Abbey and Gallery** (#53) for unique Don Sheil silver pieces; **Trés Belle** (#55) for nice handbags and scarves; **Digbys** (#57) for locally designed and produced clothes; **Teena Varigos** (#67) for Australian designer fashion; and **Trevor West**.

In the 100 block of Toorak Road you will come to the **South Yarra Arcade** (101-105 Toorak Road) which has a few nice shops: **El Dorado Gallery** for pre-Columbian reproduction gold jewelry; **Bottoni** for exclusive buttons; **Antique Selections** for quality antiques; and **La Modiste** for exclusive fabrics and clothing designs.

At this point you will be near Darling Street. You will find very few shops from here until you reach the 200 block of Toorak Road. Look for **Masons** (#111), **Kimberley Smith** (#135), and **Trossart** (#141) for clothes and jewelry. Rather than walk the long distance, you may want to take a No. 8 tram to the next shopping section along Toorak Road.

In the 200 block of Toorak Road, you will come to one of suburban Melbourne's classiest indoor shopping centers, **Como Gaslight Gardens** (corner of Chapel and Toorak Roads). Here you'll find several local designer boutiques and home decorative shops. Look for **Digbys**, **Midas**, **La Donna**, **Keith Matheson**, **Robert Burton**, and **Trent Nathan**. Across the street are a couple of interesting art galleries: **Andrew Ivanyi Gallery** (#262) and **Gould Galleries** (#270). **Country Road**, on the corner of Chapel Street and Toorak Road, is the headquarters shop and office for this large chain of popular Australian clothing and accessory shops.

If you walk 15 minutes west of Chapel Street, you'll come to the 400 block of Toorak Road which is known as the Toorak Village area. While there is not a lot here to justify the long walk, you will find a few nice shops, such as **Liz Davenport** (#412), **di Parigi**, **Fells**, and **dellas Spiga** (#428) for women's clothes. **The Little Gallery** (3 Village Walk, 493 Toorak Road) is a small but very nice shop offering glassware, paintings, and gift items.

You complete your Toorak Road shopping adventure once you reach the intersection of Toorak and Canterbury Roads. At this point you can take another No. 8 tram going west toward the city, but get off near the intersection of Toorak Road and Chapel Street, a 10-minute ride that may have taken you 40 minutes to walk. Alternatively, you can return to the tram stop on Swanston Street in The City and take a No. 6 tram which will put you directly on Chapel Street.

SOUTH YARRA AND PRAHRAN (CHAPEL STREET)

As soon as you get to Chapel Street, walk south until you come to the intersection of Chapel and High Streets. This is another major suburban shopping area—**South Yarra and Prahran**—which is filled with a large variety of varying quality shops offering antiques, clothes, trendy jewelry, and home decorative items, along with several inexpensive ethnic restaurants. This area is especially noted for its trendy clothing shops and small restaurants and cafes, and the **Jam Factory** with its theater, restaurants, and shops. It may be more of a cultural experience than a worthwhile shopping area. Indeed, despite a lot of local hype about this area, we find it rough and somewhat dumpy—a real mixed area of little interest to serious shoppers. Melbourne City shopping and dining is much more interesting than this so-called trendy area. Nonetheless, you'll find a few interesting shops and markets here. We especially like **Made in Japan** (533 Chapel Street) for its beautiful collection of Japanese chests and furniture (go to rear of gallery); **Ishka** (409A Chapel Street) for its international collection of arts and crafts; and **Prahran Market** for its large number of food stalls, bakeries, deli, and shops.

PRAHRAN, ARMADALE, MALVERN (HIGH/MALVERN STREETS)

High and Malvern Streets are an antique lover's delight with their numerous antique, art, designer, and home decorative shops. The best way to shop this area is to pick up a free copy of the local antique shop directory, *Antiques of High Street and Malvern Road Area*. Summarizing over 300 antique dealers in a 2.5 square kilometer area, this directory is literally a road map to Australia's largest concentration of antique shops. You can easily spend a full day exploring the many shops on both sides of these two long streets.

If you are going south and turn left at the intersection of Chapel Street and High Street, you will enter into a major shopping area—**High Street**, in the upmarket suburbs of East Prahran and Armadale, and **Malvern Road**, in the suburb of Malvern. Alternatively, you can take a No. 6 tram to High Street or a No. 72 tram from Malvern Road along Swanston Street and St. Kilda Road.

It's a very long walk from Chapel Street to Glenferrie Road via High Street. You may wish to skip the first section of High Street altogether since few shops in the Chapel Street and William Road area offer quality goods; most shops in this rather run-down area sell household items, office furniture, and auto parts. It's best to start shopping this street near Williams Road. Take a tram or taxi to the first major quality antique shop along High Street, **Peter Bidwell** (457 High Street). Starting here, keep walking east along High Street until you reach Glenferrie Road. You'll find over 50 shops offering a large variety of antiques and collectibles as well as a few clothing, arts, and crafts shops.

Some of our favorite High Street shops include **Westbury Antiques** (#463), **The Cellars** (#467), **The Camels** (#458), **Behruz Studio** (#471), and **Gallery 21** (#485).

One of the most concentrated shopping areas along High Street is between Kooyong and Glenferrie Roads. This is a more diverse section of antique, home decorative, rug, clothing, and jewelry shops. One of our favorite shops is **The Australiana General Store** (1227 High Street) with its excellent collection of Australiana. At this point, the intersection of Glenferrie Road and High Street, you have reached the end of the High Street shopping area.

If you walk one block to the north on Glenferrie Road, you will reach the Malvern Road shopping area. This area primarily has art and antique shops similar to the High Street shops. One of our favorite shops along this road is **Kazari** (290 Malvern Road) with its nice collection of Japanese furniture, screens, paintings, and decorative pieces. You will also find a few shops three blocks directly west on Malvern Road, between Orrong Road and Williams Road. **Soo Tze Orientique** (46 Commercial Road, Prahran) has a good collection of Southeast Asian and Tibetan, artifacts, and textiles.

RICHMOND

Nearby these major suburban shopping areas are several other suburbs offering unique shopping opportunities. Bridge Road, Swan Street, and Victoria Street (Little Saigon) in **Richmond**, one kilometer north of the Chapel Street and Toorak Road intersection, are the centers for Melbourne's Greek and Vietnamese communities. But **Bridge Street** is where the dining and shopping action is found. Here's where you will find numerous ethnic restaurants, shops, and factory outlets, especially retail outlets of Australia's top designers as well as factory outlet shops of Melbourne's garment manufacturers which sell seconds and discontinued stock. From downtown Melbourne, you can easily reach this area by taking No. 70 tram for Swan Street, Nos. 75/76 for Bridge Road, and Nos. 44/45 for Victoria Street.

FITZROY

Fitzroy, which is located about 15 minutes north of downtown Melbourne, is one of Melbourne's "Bohemian" centers. **Brunswick Street** is the central focus with its numerous ethnic restaurants and many exotic shops, from clothing and gift to used furniture and crafts. You can easily get here from the central business district by taking Nos. 9/10/11 trams for Brunswick Street and 88/89 for Smith Street.

CARLTON

Immediately to the west of Fitzroy is **Carlton**. Home to one of the largest Italian communities outside Italy, as well as noted for its Victorian architecture, Carlton's main center for restaurants, cafes, and shops is found along **Lygon Street**. While you can easily walk here from the city center, tram Nos. 1/15/21/22 go to Lygon Street.

ST. KILDA

St. Kilda is located south along the seashore, about 20 minutes from downtown Melbourne by tram. Long known as the center for Melbourne's Jewish community and Melbourne's playground, St. Kilda is still a lively center for dining and shopping, especially along Fitzroy and Acland Streets. There's nothing really upscale about this place. **Fitzroy Street** is noted for its many take-away food shops, restaurants, and all-night bars. **Acland Street** is famous for its delicatessens and cake shops. St. Kilda really comes alive on weekends when day-trippers come here to dine, drink, shop, and stroll along the breachfront, marina, and St. Kilda Pier. People-watching seems to be everyone's favorite pastime. The sidewalks along Fitzroy Street are crowded with tables and chairs of restaurants and cafes, baby strollers, and dogs and their owners. Sunday is especially lively when the Upper Esplanade is transformed into the open air **St. Kilda Esplanade Sunday Market** which offers an interesting array of arts and crafts, from handcrafted jewelry and ceramics to clothes and leather goods. The quality here varies from excellent to mediocre. Retail shopping in St. Kilda is so-so with lots of knick knacks and souvenirs to complement the often honky-tonk character of St. Kilda. Most people come here for the seaside ambience and the Sunday market. Getting here is very easy from downtown Melbourne: take the St. Kilda Light Rail along Bourke Street, trams Nos. 15/16 along Swanston Street, or Nos. 10/11 along Collins Street. The tram stops right in the heart of Fitzroy Street, in the midst of all the shops and restaurants.

DEPARTMENT STORES

Melbourne has four major department stores each found in the central business district within a few minutes walking distance of each other.

❏ **Georges:** *162 Collins Street, Tel. 9650-4864.* This is Melbourne's most upscale department store located on Melbourne's most upscale street. Small and exclusive, attention to detail here is important. The entry way is lined with lovely flowers and your receipt is presented in a classy gray envelope. After three years of troubled history—closed, reopened, closed, and reopened again in 1998—Georges is once again all about style, class, and taste. Includes such designer labels as Clements Ribeiro, Lawrence Steele, and Slowik. Especially famous for its gorgeous accessories (hats, hair clips, chokers, scarves, pendants, and rafia disco bags). Includes the Southern Hemisphere's first branch of a Conran housewares shop.

❏ **Myer Department Store** is located on the Bourke Street Pedestrian Mall next to and directly across the street from the two David Jones Department Stores. This is the favorite department store of many local residents because of its size, service, and prices. It's Australia's largest department store consisting of eight levels and two huge buildings (Bourke Street Building and Lonsdale Street Building) spanning two blocks which are joined by bridges and a subway. You can easily spend a day shopping the numerous departments of this mammoth place as well as get lost several times as you become overwhelmed attempting to find different departments and products! As soon as you enter the store from Bourke Street, look for the Information Desk which will give you a map of the store as well as answer any of your questions. You'll quickly discover one of the great strengths of this department store—Myer's service. It's a big, big store, but the personnel are extremely service-oriented. Some of the major highlights of this store are the designer clothes center on the Second Level of the Bourke Street Building where you can see garments produced by several of Australia's top designers; and Australiana, souvenirs, travel center, and bookstore as you enter the store via the overhead walkway (Lonsdale Street) that links Myer with Melbourne Central shopping center. There are few department stores in the world that can match the sheer size and variety offered by this department store. The store also is attached to the large Melbourne Central shopping center by way of Lonsdale Street. This connection provides shoppers with even more opportunities to shop and dine.

❑ **David Jones Department Store** consists of two stores on the Bourke Street Pedestrian Mall. The first store is located next to the Myer Department Store and primarily offers good quality womenswear. The second building is located directly across the mall from the first building and Myer Department Store and is located between Centrepoint Mall and The Walk shopping arcade. This store primarily sells menswear and has a very nice food and deli center on its Lower Level. While not as large as the Myer Department Store, these two David Jones Department Stores offer excellent quality products.

❑ **Daimaru:** Anchoring Melbourne Central shopping center, this is Australia's first international department store. It's a huge complex offering a large variety of Australian and international products, from clothes to jewelry.

FACTORY OUTLETS

Melbourne is Australia's factory outlet center, reflecting the fact that the garment industry is centered in and around Melbourne. The combination of leading clothing designers and manufacturers producing millions of garments each year in Melbourne has given rise to numerous factory outlet shops that sell direct to the public at savings ranging from 30 to 70 percent on seconds, irregulars, and discontinued stock. This is a considerable savings given the general high costs of Australian clothes.

As we noted earlier in our discussions of shopping services and fashion clothes and accessories, groups such as Shopping Spree Tours (Tel. 9596-6600) sponsor shopping tours to Melbourne's major factory outlets. In addition, you can purchase local shopping guides that outline the what and where of shopping Melbourne's many factory outlets and warehouses. They all basically take you to the same places—the shops along **Bridge Street** in the nearby (10 minutes) suburb of Richmond. Some of the more popular places include **Satch** (#49 and #162), **JeansWest** (#52), **Eastbound Clothing** (#137), **Portmans Warehouse** (corner of Bridge Road and Lennox Street), **Nif Naf** (#184), **Paddington Coat Factory** (#194), **Thomas Cook Clothing** (#223), **Sportsgirl-Sportscraft Aywon Clearance Centre** (#236), **Unlimited Factory Outlet** (#243), **Country Road Wearhouse** (#261), and **Richmond Plaza Shopping Centre** (corner of Bridge Road and Church Street).

MARKETS

Melbourne's markets are also reputed to be the biggest and best in the country. You'll have to see for yourself. The markets here are a colorful mix of ethnic groups, art and craft products, food, and entertainment. You can easily spend a few days shopping the many markets in and around Melbourne. While many of these markets are only open on the weekends, others are open most of the week. The major markets of interest to visitors include:

❑ **Queen Victoria Market:** *Corner of Victoria and Elizabeth Streets, north of the city center. Take any tram up Elizabeth Street. Open Tuesday-Thursday 6am-2pm, Friday 6am-6pm, Saturday 6am-3pm, and Sunday 9am-4pm.* This is Melbourne's largest and most colorful market. It also is reputed to be the largest in Australia and the Southern Hemisphere. Consisting of a series of nine covered sheds (labeled as sheds A-M) with open air stalls plus a popular food court (Vic Market Place), more than 1,000 vendors sell everything from fresh fruits and vegetables to clothes, handicrafts, and pets. This is a very colorful and festive market to explore, reminiscent of many ethnic and Third World markets found in Europe and Asia. You can buy imported clothes, leather, jewelry, and crafts at one-third to one-half the price you might pay in department stores and shops downtown. You will find inexpensive sweaters, clothes, shoes, toys, textiles, real and fake leather goods, and luggage imported from several Asian countries. While the market is open every day except Monday, the best day to go is on crowded Sundays (9am to 4pm) when selections are better. While visiting this market, be sure to explore some of the nearby shops, especially along Victoria Street, which offer some interesting arts, crafts, jewelry, clothes, and Australiana. If you are interested in taking a tour of this huge market, contact Queen Victoria Market Tours (Tel. 9658-9601). They conduct a Tell and Taste Tour, Foodies Dream Tour, and Magical History Tour.

❑ **Meat Market Craft Centre:** *42 Courtney Street, North Melbourne, Tel. 9329-9966. Open Tuesday-Sunday 10am-5pm. Take trams 49 or 59 in Elizabeth Street to Stop 14 in Flemington Road.* This is one of Australia's best craft centers. Housed in the beautifully restored old Metropolitan Meat Market building, with cobblestoned floors and high arched timber ceilings, the Meat Market Craft Centre is a place where you can observe exhibits and craftsmen at work as well as attend workshops. Its award-winning **Crafts Shop** has some of the nicest selections of arts and crafts in all of Australia. This shop alone is worth the visit to the Centre.

❏ **Collins Place Craft Market:** *Collins Place, 45 Collins Street, corner of Collins and Exhibition Streets. Open Sunday 8am-4pm.* This is Melbourne's only undercover all-Australian-made arts and crafts market. The glass enclosed Collins Place shopping center, which is attached to the Hotel Sofitel, becomes transformed into a lively arts and crafts market every Sunday. Over 100 stalls offer good quality leather goods, ceramics, furniture, Aboriginal paintings, didgeridoos, boomerangs, candles, toys, flower arrangements, jewelry, souvenirs, bathroom products, handpainted greeting cards, picture frames, baskets, paintings, wood craft, sweaters, puzzles, T-shirts, and much more.

❏ **St. Kilda Esplanade Art and Craft Market:** *St. Kilda Road, in front of the Victorian Arts Center, St. Kilda, Tel. 9684-8581. Open Sunday 10am-5pm. Take the St. Kilda Light Rail along Bourke Street, trams nos. 15/16 along Swanston Street, or Nos. 10/11 along Collins Street to get here within 20 minutes.* Another popular market for those interested in handcrafted jewelry, leather, pottery, glass, toys, cottage crafts, lamps, ornaments, musical instruments, books, photography, paintings, woodcrafts, and Australiana. Located along the Upper Esplanade in the southern seaside suburb of St. Kilda—just 5 kilometers from the city—this open-air market has over 200 stalls selling good quality handmade items. This area is also famous for its food and cake shops as well as stores along nearby Acland, Therry, and Fitzroy Streets. Shops here remain open on the weekends in anticipation of lively crowds descending on St. Kilda on Saturday and Sunday. St. Kilda is a good place to shop on Sunday—especially since most shops in the city are closed.

Other arts and crafts markets in the Melbourne metropolitan area include the **Hawthorn Town Hall Craft Market** (first Sunday of the month, from March to December); **Customs Wharf** (in Williamstown, open daily except Monday); **Dingley Village Craft Market** (open the first Sunday of each month);

Red Hill Community Market (open first Saturday of each month, September-May); **Badger Creek Craft Market** (open fourth Sunday of each month); **Greville Street Market** (open every Sunday); and **Fitzroy Craft Market** (open third Sunday of the month). To experience one of the largest produce markets in the Southern Hemisphere, visit **Prahran Market** at 177 Commercial Road in Prahran (closed Monday).

CRAFT TOWNS OF GREATER MELBOURNE

Greater Melbourne and the State of Victoria abound with small craft towns and villages where you can discover hundreds of fine art galleries and craft shops. You can easily spend a couple of weeks visiting the various towns and shops tucked away along the seaside and in the valleys and hills. These are the areas where some of Victoria's master craftspeople live and work.

If you want to visit some of the best craft towns outside Melbourne, we strongly recommend picking up literature on the Greater Melbourne area at the Victoria Visitor Information Centre (Melbourne Town Hall, corner of Little Collins and Swanston Streets). You'll find several booklets and brochures on things to see and do in the five main regions that comprise the Greater Melbourne area. All are within a one- to two-hour drive east and south of Melbourne City: **Phillip Island** (intriguing fairy penguin parade and rugged coast); **Dandenong Ranges** (attractive sub-temperate rainforest and "Puffing Billy" steam train ride); **Yarra Valley** (a noted wine region); **Mornington Peninsula** (charming coastal villages with good beaches and resorts—Melbourne's "Riviera" in the summer); and **Bellarine Peninsula** (attractive bays). Along the way to these places you'll pass through small craft towns that offer an interesting range of arts and crafts. For example, when visiting the Dandenong Ranges, be sure to stop at the quaint village of **Olinda** which has several craft shops and galleries. The **Touchstone Craft Gallery** (31 Monash Avenue, Olinda, opposite The Mill, Tel. 9751-1715), with its four rooms of top quality crafts produced by several leading Australian craftspeople, is well worth a stop. The village of **Sassafras** also has many quaint shops selling arts, crafts, antiques, and bric-a-brac. In **Mount Eliza** (Mornington Peninsula), be sure to visit the popular **Omell Manyung Gallery** (1408 Nepan Highway, Tel. 9787-2953) which represents many of Australia's most promising artists. In **Geelong** (Bellarine Peninsula) be sure to stop at the **Brim-Brim Gallery** (560a Latrobe Boulevard, Newtown, Tel. 5221-8874) and **Geelong Art Gallery** (Little Malop Street,

Geelong, Tel. 5229-3645).

Further west of Melbourne (112 kilometers), is the charming town of Ballarat which boasts Australia's fifth largest art gallery and the largest regional gallery, the **Ballarat Fine Art Gallery**. The adjacent art and craft shops (40 Lydiard Street, North Ballarat, Tel. 5331-6361) with its quality selections is well worth visiting.

If you have the time, these regions and towns make wonderful trips in and of themselves as you immerse yourself in the arts and crafts of Victoria, meet some of Australia's leading craftspeople, and make some memorable, quality purchases. We suggest renting a car to drive to these areas. For more information on the regional art galleries, visit this useful Web site: *www.art-almanac.com.au*.

BEST OF THE BEST

While there is a lot of shopping in and around Melbourne, much of it is nondescript and dominated by trendy clothing shops of little interest to visitors. Amidst all the shops are some very special places that may warrant the attention of those who have limited time to shop while visiting Melbourne. We found these shops to be of particular interest because of their quality and unique selections.

CLOTHES AND ACCESSORIES

❑ **Collette Dinnigan:** *553 Chapel Street, South Yarra, Tel. 9827-2111.* This is the shop of Australia's most famous designer. Includes everything from sarong skirts and hand-embroidered dresses to beaded knitwear and lingerie.

❑ **Teena Varigos:** *182 Collins Street, Tel. 9650-5656, and 67 Toorak Road, South Yarra, Tel. 9866-4714.* Another one of Australia's famous award-winning designers offers elegant women's apparel for all occasions.

❑ **Le Louvre:** *74 Collins Street, Tel. 9650-1300.* This is more than just a boutique or clothing shop. Designed as a dressing salon, this well appointed shop with leopard-print carpet is for those who wish to put together a classy wardrobe from quality selections found behind the large mirrored doors.

❑ **Digbys:** *57 Toorak Road, South Yarra, Tel. 9328-2903.* For nearly 25 years this multi-branch shop (7 locations) has offered good quality coats, blouses, and slacks. Similar to some of the bridge lines found in North America in terms of pricing and quality. Everything here is made in Melbourne using imported fabrics.

❑ **Coogi Connections:** *86 Collins Street, Tel. 9650-4407.* This concept store showcases the colorful and distinctive knitwear that has found its way in shops throughout the world. Includes everything from sweaters to jackets.

❑ **Aboriginal Creations:** *Shop 3, 50 Bourke Street, Tel. 9662-9400.* Offers quality fashion, textiles, and accessories using Aboriginal designs. Includes hand-painted silk scarves, hat boxes, earthenware, T-shirts, swimwear, hats, blouses, ties, shirts, vests, childrenwear, and artifacts from Aboriginal communities.

JEWELRY AND OPALS

❑ **Makers Mark:** *101 Collins Street, Tel. 9654-8388, www.makersmark.com.au.* This is no longer the trend-setting arts and crafts shop it started out to be nearly 15 years ago. Today Makers Mark has definitely gone upmarket with its fabulous collection of jewelry. Showcases some of Australia's most unique silver and gold jewelry, as well as Argyle diamonds and Broome and South Sea pearls, crafted by some of Australia's leading designers and jewelers. Look for beautiful jewelry designed by Sandy Kilpatrick, with some stunning pieces (gold and opal necklace) going for over $25,000.

❑ **MDT Design:** *166 Swanston Walk, Tel. 9654-7235, www.mdtdesign.com.* Produces unique and award-winning jewelry designs. Will custom-make jewelry to your specifications.

❑ **Costello's:** *Shop 205, Melbourne Central, 300 Lonsdale Street, Tel. 9639-2233. www.costellos.com.au.* Specializes in Australian opals, Argyle diamonds (pink and champagne), and South Sea pearls, including black pearls. Also has similar shops in Perth and Sydney.

❑ **Schlager Antique Jewellery:** *308 Little Collins Street, Tel. 9650-4391.* This long established shop offers beautiful antique jewelry along with new pieces.

❑ **Altmann and Cherny:** *120 Exhibition Street, Tel. 9650-9685)*. One of Melbourne's major opal dealers.

❑ **Johnson Opals:** *124 Exhibition Street, Tel. 9650-7434; 65 Queens Road, Tel. 9510-6393; and 111 Little Collins Street, Tel. 9650-7744. www.sofcom.com.au/johnstonopals.* One of Australia's oldest (since 1901) opal dealers.

ABORIGINAL AND TRIBAL ARTS

❑ **Aboriginal Gallery of Dreamings:** *73-77 Bourke Street, Tel. 9650-3277, open Monday-Saturday 10am-5:30pm and Sunday 12noon-5pm.* This is Australia's largest and most influential Aboriginal art gallery. Operated by the energetic and entrepreneurial Hank Ebes, the gallery includes over 5,000 Aboriginal paintings displayed, as well as stored, on three floors. Represents top Aboriginal artists. Also includes galleries, demonstration areas, and lecture rooms along with many handcrafted artifacts, such as the ubiquitous Aboriginal jewelry, pottery, didgeridoos, and boomerangs. Excellent selection of books on Aboriginal art as well as music and prints.

❑ **Aboriginal and Pacific Art Gallery:** *42 Hardy Terrace, Ivanhoe, Tel. 9499-4699 (call ahead for an appointment).* Located in the suburb of Ivanhoe (A$20 cab ride—15-20 minutes from downtown) and operated from the home of Rene and Mal Davidson, this is one of the best places in Australia for top quality tribal art from Papua New Guinea and Australia's Aboriginal tribes. Serious collectors will find a treasure-trove of quality shopping here.

❑ **Aboriginal Desert Art Gallery:** *31 Flinders Lane, Tel. 9654-2516.* A very nice gallery showcasing paintings, didgeridoos, and carvings as well as offering a good selection of books and music. Continuously plays an informative video on Aboriginal art which is worth seeing if you know little about the various art forms.

❑ **Kimberley Australian Aboriginal Art:** *76 Flinders Lane, Tel. 9654-5890.* Very fine quality Aboriginal paintings from the Kimberley region which are very different in color and style from other Aboriginal areas of Australia. Maintains a large inventory of paintings in the back room.

- ❑ **Gallery Gabrielle Pizzi:** *141 Flinders Lane, Tel. 9654-2944.* Offers an excellent collection of quality Aboriginal art from central and northern Australia. Includes paintings to sculptures.

AUSTRALIAN ARTS, CRAFTS, AND GIFTS

- ❑ **Craft Shop:** *Meat Market Craft Centre, 42 Courtney Street, North Melbourne, Tel. 9329-9966. Closed Monday.* This award-winning craft shop offers the works of Victoria's top craftspeople. Includes a terrific collection of ceramics, jewelry, glassware, wood turned bowls, and cards. Check out the **Gallery of Handweavers and Spinners Guild of Victoria** (Tel. 9329-6191), which is located nearby, for nice handwoven and handspun items.

- ❑ **Potoroo Fine Craft Gallery:** *Shop U10, St. Kilda Road Level, Southgate Arts and Leisure Precinct, Tel. 9690-9859. Open daily 10am-6pm and Saturday until midnight.* Another award-winning crafts shop that showcases some of Australia's best quality handcrafted ceramics, studio glass, jewelry, textiles, and timber and artworks of selected local artists.

- ❑ **Makers Mark:** *101 Collins Street, Tel. 9654-8388, www.makersmark.com.au.* In addition to offering top quality silver and gold crafted jewelry, this is one of Australia's finest craft shops. Represents the handcrafted works of Australia's top craftspeople and artisans. Look for sculptures. However, most of this shop is devoted to unique handcrafted jewelry. Their Sydney shop (Chifley Plaza) has additional handcrafted items.

- ❑ **Arts Centre Shop:** *National Gallery of Victoria, 180 St. Kilda Road, Tel. 9208-0220.* Includes lots of handcrafted jewelry (look for replica jewelry from the world's leading collections), porcelain, glassware, woodcraft, and art books.

- ❑ **Sheil Abbey and Gallery:** *53 Toorak Road, Tel. 9866-6886; also at 21 Carpenter Street in Brighton, Tel. 9592-8192.* This is one of Melbourne's most unique shops because of the beautiful silver work produced by noted craftsman Don Sheil who turns out lovely silver plates, bowls, and goblets in unique designs using a special aluminum-based alloy metal called "Sheil Silver."

FINE ARTS AND ANTIQUES

❑ **Sandilands Antique Prints:** *546 High Street, Prahran, Tel. 9529-8011.* Offers a nice collection of rare prints and antique maps.

❑ **Graham Cornall Antiques:** *731-735 High Street, Armadale, Tel. 9576-1151.* Includes a very good collection of 17th and 18th century period and provincial furniture and decorative art from England, France, Spain, and Italy. Also includes several pieces from Australia.

❑ **Christine Abrahams Gallery:** *27 Gipps Street, Richmond, Tel. 9428-6099.* Specializes in contemporary Australian art with a strong emphasis on the primitive ceramic sculptures of Melbourne's noted Deborah Halpern.

❑ **Kozminsky:** *421 Bourke Street, Tel. 9670-1277.* Offers fine antique and estate jewelry, silver, and objects d'art.

❑ **Kazari:** *290 Malvern Road, Prahran, Tel. 9521-1107.* A very nice quality Japanese antique furniture and home decorative shop. Includes screens, paintings, lacquerware, and decorative pieces. Also has a warehouse on Hill Street.

❑ **Soo Tze Oriental Antiques:** *46 Commercial Road, Prahran, Tel. 9521-2892.* Showcases an excellent collection of quality Burmese, Thai, Indian, Tibetan, and Nepalese arts, antiques, and home decorative items. Includes many unique textiles, carvings, bronzes, and chests.

ACCOMMODATIONS

Melbourne offers a good range of accommodations both within the city and outlying areas ranging from deluxe to budget. Similar to Sydney, deluxe and first-class hotels are very expensive. Melbourne's best properties include:

❑ **Grand Hyatt Melbourne:** *123 Collins Street, Melbourne, Victoria 3000, Australia, Tel. (61 3) 9657-1234, Fax (61 3) 9650-3491.* Located in the heart of the city at the very top of Melbourne's business district is the Grand Hyatt—formerly known as Hyatt on Collins—winner of numerous industry awards. The public areas are a spectacular combination of art deco set against Veronese marble highlighted by sculpture and art commissioned from around the world. Set around the atrium public space are two promenades featuring chic boutiques and galleries. The 547 spacious guestrooms feature king sized beds with fluffy coverlets and plenty of light for reading. The luxury marble and mirrored bathrooms feature all expected amenities and provide a separate bathtub and shower enclosure. Regency Club floors offer additional amenities and services including buffet breakfast, all day refreshments and evening cocktails and hors d'oeuvres. Max's Restaurant, reached by private elevator, offers an eclectic menu; Plane Tree Café offers an a la carte international menu day and night. Fitness Center; Business Center; Convention and Banquet Facilities.

❏ **Park Hyatt Melbourne:** *1 Parliament Square, Melbourne, Victoria 3002, Australia, Tel. (61 3) 9224-1234, Fax (61 3) 9224-1200.* Conveniently located near the state houses of Parliament and city center in a park-like setting, the smaller Park Hyatt is designed to provide an intimate, club-like atmosphere for its guests. Spacious guestrooms, luxurious suites—some even have fireplaces—await the guest. A walk-in wardrobe area and spacious bathroom featuring a deep bathtub with television set in the wall, separate shower enclosure, and vanity with double sinks are standard features. Every room is equipped with four direct dial phones, data ports, modem port and interactive television. Regency Club rooms offer extra amenities. Radii Restaurant offers an open kitchen and makes extensive use of its wood-fired oven and its grill. Trilogy Bistro and Lounge features French bistro-style cuisine. Fitness Facilities; Business Center; Conference and Banquet Facilities.

❏ **Grand Mercure Hotel Melbourne:** *321 Flinders Lane, Melbourne, Victoria 3000, Australia, Tel. (61 3) 9629-4088, Fax (61 3) 9629-4066.* Located in the heart of Melbourne's business and art centers, the Grand Mercure (formerly The Sebel) is an elegant boutique hotel set around a garden courtyard. 58 elegantly appointed suites include 35 Flinders suites, 15 executive suites and 4 deluxe one or two-bedroom suites. Bathrooms provide expected amenities. Matthew's Restaurant and Bar provides the ambience of a private dining room. The menu is more a list of suggestions—the chef is happy to accommodate requests from guests. Fitness Facilities; Business Services; Meeting Facilities.

❑ **Stamford Plaza Melbourne:** *111 Little Collins Street, Melbourne, Victoria 3000, Australia, Tel. (61 3) 9659-1000, Fax (61 3) 9659-0999.* Located in the heart of the city at the "Paris end" of Little Collins Street surrounded by boutiques, theaters and restaurants. The Stamford Plaza is an all-suite hotel with 239 one-bedroom suites, 41 two-bedroom suites, 2 penthouse suites and the Hermitage suite. All suites include a well-equipped kitchen with microwave oven and dishwasher, dining and lounge area plus spa bath and separate shower enclosure. Harry's Restaurant offers a contemporary, eclectic menu for all-day dining; Harry's Café offers a selection of hot foods, gourmet sandwiches and salads. Harry's Noodle Bar offers freshly prepared noodle dishes. Fitness Facilities; Business Center; Conference & Banquet Facilities.

❑ **Windsor Hotel:** *103 Spring Street, Melbourne, Victoria 3000, Australia, Tel. (61 3) 9653-0653, Fax (61 3) 9650-3233.* Located in the city center across from the state Parliament building, The Windsor combines the architecture of the Victorian era—lovingly restored to its original splendor by the Oberoi chain—with the modern comforts and amenities expected by today's traveler. The 180 guestrooms and suites are decorated with Laura Ashley style small floral prints and rosewood furniture. The marble bathrooms carry out the Victorian theme with period reproduction fixtures. The Deluxe rooms are twice the size of the standard rooms. One Eleven Spring Street, the hotel's signature restaurant, is a leading venue for business lunches and special occasion dining. Fitness Center; Business Services; Conference and Banquet Facilities.

❑ **Duxton Hotel Melbourne:** *328 Flinders Street, Melbourne, Victoria 3000, Australia, Tel. (61 3) 9250-1888, Fax (61 3) 9250-1877. Web site: www.duxtonhotels.com.sg.* Located in the heart of Melbourne's central business district, the Duxton's 350 guestrooms include 316 deluxe rooms, 27 Club rooms, 6 executive suites and the presidential suite. Rooms are tastefully decorated. Club rooms offer additional services including Continental breakfast and exclusive use of the cardiovascular gym. Club rooms feature Edwardian Baroque design ornate ceilings, columns, and leaded glass windows. The Duxton Grill offers a range of local Victorian products. Business Services; Meeting Facilities.

❑ **Hotel Como:** *630 Chapel Street, South Yarra, Melbourne, Victoria 3141, Australia, Tel. (61 3) 9825-2222, Fax (61 3) 9824-1263. Web site: www.hotelcomo.com.au.* Located in the Melbourne suburb of South Yarra a few kilometers from the city center, the Hotel Como has just completed (June 2000) a refurbishment. Winner of travel industry awards for innovative style, luxury and service, its 107 guestrooms provide exceptional space and understated elegance. Most suites have a spa or deep tub and some have their own office, kitchen, balcony or courtyard. Penthouse suites offer two levels, complete with a spiral staircase leading to a private sauna and spa. Complimentary transfers to the central business district each weekday morning. The Brasserie Restaurant. Fitness Facilities; Business Services.

RESTAURANTS

From the ubiquitous food courts of shopping centers, markets, and hotels (Grand Hyatt) to the outdoor dining at Southgate and the ethnic eateries found in Richmond, Fitzroy, Carlton, and Chinatown, Melbourne is an international gastronomic delight. Catering to all budgets and dining styles, the city and suburbs are filled with take-away shops, cafes, and restaurants. Dining here is generally casual; reservations are recommended at most major restaurants, especially on weekends.

Given this area's distinctive ethnic makeup, you can find just about any cuisine in Melbourne. Indeed, the multi-cultural make-up of this city, with its many villages and ethnic enclaves, is a delightful adventure in dining. Little Bourke Street in the central business district, for example, is Melbourne's **China-town** with several popular Chinese, Malay, and Thai restaurants; Victoria Street in Richmond is the area's **Little Saigon** with its many Vietnamese restaurants; Richmond also is the center for **Greek** restaurants; Carlton is **Little Italy** with lots of inexpensive and fun Italian eateries; Fitzroy is the center for the city's Spanish community, and its Brunswick and Johnston Streets are known for their **Middle Eastern**, **Asian**, **Turkish**, **Indian**, **Mediterranean**, and **vegetarian** restaurants; Toorak Road is a center for **chic bistros**; and Southgate pulls them altogether with it 35 delightful indoor and outdoor restaurants facing the city skyline. As you'll quickly discover, the best restaurants in Melbourne are spread throughout the city and suburbs. Be sure to enlarge the scope of your dining plans to include marvelous suburban dining. Try these for starters:

MODERN AUSTRALIAN

❏ **Est Est Est:** *440 Clarendon Street, South Melbourne, Tel. 9682-5688.* Two of Melbourne's top international chefs lay claim to some of the city's best dishes. Try the scallops and roasted calamari and finish off with chocolate desserts.

❏ **The Brasserie:** *Georges, 162 Collins Street, Tel. 9929-9900. Closed Sunday. No lunch on Saturday.* This elegant restaurant in the city's most elegant department store (Georges) turns out many inventive international dishes. Try the seafood dishes, especially the tuna and barramundi.

❏ **Walter's Wine Bar:** *Southgate, Upper Level, South Melbourne, Tel. 9690-9211.* Offering both indoor and outdoor dining options and great ambience, this busy restaurant serves a good range of inventive dishes, from smoked salmon to classy hamburgers.

❏ **Jacques Reymond's:** *78 Williams Road, Windsor, Tel. 9525-2178. Closed Sunday and Monday. No lunch on Saturday.* Always dependable, this inventive restaurant with open fireplaces and candlelight dining serves terrific dishes that combine the best of French and Asian cuisine. Try the kangaroo with beetroot and the barramundi.

❏ **Guernica:** *257 Brunswick Street, Fitzroy, Tel. 9416-0969.* This chic restaurant with Chef Teage Ezard at the helm turns out many interesting dishes that combine Asian and Mediterranean foods. Try the coconut-fried garfish with Vietnamese noodles.

❏ **O'Connell's:** *Montague and Covertry Streets, South Melbourne, Tel. 9699-9600. Closed Sunday. No lunch on Saturday.* Go here for the interesting dishes—not the ambience. Combines European and Middle Eastern cuisines. Try Moroccan flavored lamb pot roast and the mezza platter.

ITALIAN

❏ **Café di Stasio:** *31 Fitzroy Street, St. Kilda, Tel. 9525-3999.* Elegant Italian dining with flamboyant service and a great wine list. Try the crisply roasted duck, char-grilled baby squid, and any of the tempting pasta dishes.

❏ **Melbourne Wine Room Restaurant:** *25 Fitzroy Street, St. Kilda, Tel. 9525-5599. No lunch.* This popular restaurant is under the reliable hand of Chef Karen Martini-King. Try any of the risottos, pastas, or grill dishes.

❏ **Caffè e Cucina:** *581 Chapel Street, South Yarra, Tel. 9827-4139.* This popular cafe/restaurant is always crowded, even on weekdays and especially for lunch. A great place for cappuccino and people-watching. Also serves excellent Italian dishes. Upstairs dining room requires reservations. Outdoor dining is very popular.

FRENCH

❏ **Pomme:** *37 Toorak Road, South Yarra, Tel. 9820-9606.* Everything here is excellent. But be sure to try the white sausage with French black truffles and the pot-roasted pigeon with potatoes.

❏ **France-Soir:** *11 Toorak Road, South Yarra, Tel. 9866-8569.* Authentic French dining in a crowded setting.

❏ **Republique Brasserie:** *23 Bourke Street, Tel. 9654-6699.* A very stylish dining setting for excellent French/Italian cuisine.

SEAFOOD

❏ **Toofey's:** *162 Elgin Street, Carlton, Tel. 9347-9838. No lunch on Saturday and Sunday.* Still the best seafood restaurant around for the past ten years. Serves the freshest catch daily. Try the spaghetti marinara, grilled tuna, and seafood risotto.

CHINESE

❏ **Mask of China:** *115-117 Little Bourke Street, Tel. 9662-2116.* This elegant Chiu Chow restaurant is especially noted for its seafood dishes. Try the abalone, sweet and salty prawns, and chicken with deep-fried pearl leaves.

❑ **Flower Drum:** *17 Market Lane, Tel. 9662-3655. Closed Sunday.* Offers outstanding Cantonese and Szechuan cuisine. Try the specials for the day which are always excellent.

❑ **Fortuna Village:** *235 Little Bourke Street, Tel. 9663-3044.* Very popular for its many delicious seafood dishes.

JAPANESE

❑ **Akita:** *Courtney and Blackwood Streets, North Melbourne, Tel. 9326-5766. Closed Sunday. No lunch on Saturday.* Arguably the best Japanese restaurant in town. Nothing fancy—just great dishes.

INDIAN

❑ **Jewel of India:** *373 Chapel Street, Prahran, Tel. 9824-1822. Closed Monday. No lunch on Saturday or Sunday.* This opulent restaurant serves excellent dishes from all regions of India. Try the special Goan dishes and the spicy fish curry from Kerala.

ENJOYING YOUR STAY

Melbourne abounds with many things to see and do in addition to shopping. It has many attractive historical sites, first-class museums, cultural events, and numerous sports activities and sporting events to keep you busy for several days during your stay.

Melbourne is famous for its architecture, parks, arts, museums, and shopping events. It's a great walking and tram-riding city. One of the best ways to see this city's major attractions is to take a self-guided or sponsored walking tour. When you visit the Victoria Visitor Information Centre in the Melbourne Town Hall, look for a booklet entitled *Walking Melbourne.* It outlines four major self-guided walks that emphasize various dimensions of Melbourne: Marvelous Melbourne, Mercantile Melbourne, Commercial Melbourne, and Traditional Melbourne. Each walk takes from 1.5 to 2.5 hours and covers anywhere from 10 to 40 buildings. If you follow all four walks, you'll visit over 160 sites. You'll get an excellent overview of Melbourne's history, architecture, art, culture, and commercial scenes.

Many visitors prefer joining city tours, shopping tours, and several of the art walks. For a guided city tour by bus, contact **City Sightseeing** (9563-9788). It offers several tours: City Explorer (Shopping Tours with 16 stops); City Wanderer (Oriental Tour with 18 stops); Half Day, Day and Heritage Tours; and Citilights Melbourne Explorer (Night Tours). The buses depart hourly from the Melbourne Town Hall on Swanston Street. You can purchase tickets from the driver and hop on and off the buses all day. **Shopping Spree Tours** (Tel. 9596-6600) will take you to 8-10 of Melbourne's best factories and warehouses as well as include lunch and a stop at the Rialto Observation Deck.

Some of the best walks of the city are conducted by **Art and About** (Tel. 9696-0591). Led by leading experts on art, galleries, aboriginal art, architecture, and performing arts, each walking tour takes 1.5 hours and is scheduled on specific dates: Fabulous Fitzroy–The Cutting Edge of Australian Art, Aboriginal Art Discovery, Arts City Backstage, Fine Art in Flinders Lane, and Melbourne Treasures (architecture). Participants have a chance to go behind the scenes, meet artists, and learn about what makes the art and culture scene in Melbourne really tick. A variety of other interesting walking tours are sponsored by **SaveTime** (Tel. 9654-2535): Booklovers Walk, Wine Lovers Walk, Magic of Theatre Walk, Chocolate Indulgence Walk, Just Desserts Walk, and Bridal Waltz.

Other interesting tours of Melbourne include **Old Melbourne Gaol Tours** (Tel. 9663-7228), **Tram Tours** (Tel. 9531-3114), **Scenic Air Tours** (Tel. 9379-6099), **Food and Wine Tours** (Tel. 9621-2089), and **Melbourne River Cruises** (Tel. 9614-1215).

While shopping you may also want to visit some of Melbourne's major landmarks:

❑ **Rialto Towers Observation Deck:** *525 Collins Street, Tel. 9629-8222. Open Monday-Friday 11am-11:30pm and Saturday and Sunday 10am-11:30pm.* This is the tallest building in the Southern Hemisphere and Melbourne's number one tourist attraction. Go to the 55th floor where you can get a panoramic view of the city. On a clear day you can see as far as the Dandenong Ranges in the northeast and Port Phillip Bay in the south.

❑ **Victorian Arts Centre:** *100 St. Kilda Road, Tel. 9281-8000.* This is Melbourne's attempt to provide its own alternative to Sydney's Opera House. Located on St. Kilda Road adjacent to the Yarra River and the downtown commercial area (walk south on Swanston Street which becomes St. Kilda Road as soon as you cross the bridge), this huge complex is topped by an uninspiring Spire (Melbourne's "Eiffel Tower") and houses a concert hall, theater, and playhouse. See the museum and take a one-hour guided tour of this building to see it thoroughly. However, you may want to call ahead as many of the scheduled tours are fully booked by large groups.

❑ **The National Gallery of Victoria**: *180 St. Kilda Road, Tel. 9208-0222.* Located next to the Victorian Arts Centre, the Gallery houses Australia's largest collection of paintings by traditional masters (Rembrandt) and noted Australian artists, including Aborigines.

❑ **Melbourne Town Hall**: *Corner of Collins and Swanston Streets.* The beautiful Council Chambers and function rooms are worth visiting.

❑ **Parliament House**: *Spring Street, Tel. 9651-8911.* Located at the east end of Bourke Street and across from the Windsor Hotel. This beautiful Victorian building which was built in 1856 now houses the Victorian Parliament. Guided tours available when parliament is not in session (avoid Wednesdays and Thursdays from March to July and August to November).

❑ **Royal Botanic Gardens**: *King's Domain South, Birdwood Avenue, Tel. 9650-9424, www.rbgmelb.org.au.* Located between Alexandria Avenue and Domain Road in South Yarra (use the Birdwood Avenue entrance). Considered by many observers to be one of the best botanic gardens in the world with 35 hectares of beautifully landscaped gardens displaying more than 60,000 plants. Free guided walks daily at 10am and 11am. Look for special outdoor theatrical performances during the summer evenings. Includes exclusive gift shops and lakeside Tea Rooms.

❑ **Melbourne Zoo**: *Elliott Avenue, Parkville, Tel. 9285-9300. Open daily 9am-5pm.* Covers 22 hectares of gardens. Considered by many experts to be one of the world's best zoos with animals living in natural habitats. Includes nearly 400 Australian and exotic animals from around the world. Be sure to visit the intriguing Gorilla Rainforest.

❑ **MCG Sports Museum:** *Brunton Avenue, Yarra Park, Tel. 9654-5511.* If you want to understand why the locals are so fascinated with sports, just visit this museum and you'll discover why. Very interesting Olympic exhibits. MCG stands for the Melbourne Cricket Ground, one of Australia's most important sports arenas.

❑ **Old Melbourne Gaol:** *Russell Street, Tel. 9651-2233.* Captures the essence of a 19th century prison. Includes scenes from the last hanging in Victoria. The place where the notorious bushranger, Ned Kelly, was hanged in 1880.

❑ **Architectural masterpieces:** Melbourne is well noted for its Victorian architecture. Indeed, it has numerous interesting buildings that are included on various walking tours of the city. Be sure to view the **ANZ Gothic Bank** (corner of Collins and Queen Streets) for an example of Gothic revival architecture, both the interior and exterior; **Princess Theatre**; old dining room in the **Windsor Hotel**; Legislative Council Camber at **Parliament House**; interior of the **State Library**; **Block Arcade**; **Old Treasury Building**; **Queen Victoria Market**; and the **Shrine of Remembrance** (St. Kilda Road). Just viewing these buildings will give you a good sense of the importance of history, art, and culture in Melbourne.

Two of Melbourne's **ethnic groups** also have their own museums. If you are interested in the Australian Jewish community, consider visiting **The Jewish Museum of Australia** (corner of Toorak Road and Arnold Street; open Wednesday and Thursday, 10am to 4pm) and the **Jewish Holocaust Centre** (13 Selwyen Street, Elsternwich; open Monday to Thursday, 10am to 2pm). The Chinese also have their own museum depicting the colorful history of the Chinese in Australia: **Museum of Chinese Australian History** (22 Cohen Place; open Monday, Wednesday, Thursday, and Friday, 10am to 5pm, and Saturday and Sunday from 12 noon to 5pm).

Sports in Melbourne play a very important role in defining the character of this city. This is a sports-minded city and a center for several national and international sporting events. It boasts superb golf courses, horse racing (Melbourne Cup), soccer, football, cricket, tennis (Australian Open), motor races, sailing, and hot-air ballooning. If you love **sports and sporting events**, be sure to pick up information on upcoming sports events at the Victoria Visitor Information Centre at the Melbourne Town Hall. You may also want to visit Melbourne's popular **Australian Gallery of Sport** (Melbourne Cricket Ground, Jolimont; open Wednesday to Sunday, 10am to 4pm) to get an excellent overview of the sporting traditions in Australia as well as the **Victorian Racing Museum** (Caufield Racecourse Station Street, Caufield; open Tuesday and Thursday, 10am to 4pm).

Several tour companies offer a variety of tours to further enjoy the city and surrounding countryside. You can choose city tours, walking tours, cruises on the river and bay, helicopter and hot air balloon flights, vintage railway tours, vineyard and Australiana tours, and adventure tours into Australia's outback. You may want to see the Penguins at the highly touristed Phillip Island Penguin Reserve south of Melbourne; head into the hills and valleys for a day of wine tasting in Victoria's many vineyards; or just lie on the beach in St. Kilda, Elwood, or Mornington Peninsula. It's all here in Melbourne. All you need is lots of time, money, and information on where to go and what to see. Again, be sure to pick up information at the Victoria Visitor Information Centre.

ENTERTAINMENT

Melbourne's nightlife is very active—24 hours a day of dining, drinking, dancing, and gambling. Most of the city's dance clubs are found in the lower numbers of King Street. Late night and all night eateries are found in South Yarra, Fitzroy, and St. Kilda. Comedy clubs are popular in Fitzroy, Carlton, and Collingwood. Numerous pubs and supper clubs offer a wide range of music, from jazz and reggae to hip-hop, grunge, and the latest music style.

Gamblers head for Melbourne's only and Australia's largest casino, the huge **Crown Casino**. Dominating four blocks along Riverside Avenue (Tel. 9685-4200) and linked by a promenade to the popular riverside Southgate shopping and dining complex, this is a very popular although somewhat controversial center for both locals and visitors. The gaming rooms are terribly smokey. Here you'll also find Australia's largest hotel with 1,000 rooms as well as numerous restaurants, bars, and entertainment venues.

Index

ADELAIDE

ALICE SPRINGS

BRISBANE

BROOME

CAIRNS

DARWIN

FREMANTLE

MELBOURNE

PERTH

SYDNEY

The Authors

WINSTON CHURCHILL PUT IT BEST—*"My needs are very simple—I simply want the best of everything."* Indeed, his attitude on life is well and alive amongst many of today's travelers. With limited time, careful budgeting, and a sense of adventure, many people seek both quality and value as they search for the best of the best.

Ron and Caryl Krannich, Ph.Ds, discovered this fact of travel life 17 years ago when they were living and working in Thailand as consultants with the Office of the Prime Minister. Former university professors and specialists on Southeast Asia, they discovered what they really loved to do—shop for quality arts, antiques, and home decorative items—was not well represented in most travel guides that primarily focused on sightseeing, hotels, and restaurants. While some guidebooks included a small section on shopping, they only listed types of products and names and addresses of shops, many of which were of questionable quality. And budget guides simply avoided quality shopping altogether, as if shopping was a travel sin!

The Krannichs knew there was much more to travel than what was represented in most travel guides. Avid collectors of Thai, Myanmar, Indonesian, and South Pacific arts, antiques, and home decorative items, they learned long ago that one of the best ways to experience another culture and meet its talented artists and craftspeople was by shopping for local products. Not only would they learn a great deal about the culture and society, they also acquired some wonderful products, met many interesting and talented individuals, and helped support the continuing development of local arts and crafts.

But they quickly learned shopping in Asia was very different from shopping in North America and Europe. In the West, merchants nicely display items, identify prices, and periodically run sales. At the same time, shoppers in the West can easily do comparative shopping, watch for sales, and trust quality and delivery; they even have consumer protection! Americans and Europeans in Asia face a shopping culture based on different principles. Like a fish out of water, they make many mistakes: don't know how to bargain, fail to communicate effectively with tailors, avoid purchasing large items because they don't understand shipping, and are frequent victims of scams and rip-offs, especially in the case of gems and jewelry. To shop a country right, travelers need to know how to find quality products, bargain for the best prices, avoid scams, and ship their purchases with ease. What they most need is a combination travel and how-to book that focuses on the best of the best.

In 1987 the Krannichs inaugurated their first shopping guide to Asia—*Shopping in Exotic Places*—a guide to quality shopping in Hong Kong, South Korea, Thailand, Indonesia, and Singapore. Receiving rave reviews from leading travel publications and professionals, the book quickly found an enthusiastic audience amongst other avid travelers and shoppers. It broke new ground as a combination travel and how-to book. No longer would shopping be confined to just naming products and identifying names and addresses of shops. It also included advice on how to pack for a shopping trip (take two suitcases, one filled with bubble-wrap), comparative shopping, bargaining skills, and communicating with tailors. Shopping was serious stuff requiring serious treatment of the subject by individuals who understood what they were doing. The Krannichs subsequently expanded the series to include separate volumes on Hong Kong, Thailand, Indonesia, Singapore and Malaysia, Australia and Papua New Guinea, the South Pacific, and the Caribbean.

Beginning in 1996, the series took on a new look as well as an expanded focus. Known as the Impact Guides and appropriately titled *The Treasures and Pleasures . . . Best of the Best*, new editions covered Hong Kong, Thailand, Indonesia, Singapore, Malaysia, Paris and the French Riviera, and the Caribbean. In 1997 and 1999 new volumes appeared on Italy, Hong Kong, and China. New volumes for 2000 cover India, Australia, Thailand, Hong Kong, Egypt, Singapore and Bali, Israel and Jordan, and Rio and São Paulo.

Beginning in June 2000, the Impact Guides became the major content for launching the new *i*ShopAroundTheWorld Web site:

www.ishoparoundtheworld.com

While the primary focus remains shopping for quality products, the books and Web site also include useful information on the best hotels, restaurants, and sightseeing. As the authors note, *"Our users are discerning travelers who seek the best of the best. They are looking for a very special travel experience which is not well represented in other travel guides."*

The Krannichs passion for traveling and shopping is well represented in their home which is uniquely designed around their Asian, South Pacific, Middle East, North African, and Latin American art collections. *"We're fortunate in being able to create a living environment which pulls together so many wonderful travel memories and quality products,"* say the Krannichs. *"We learned long ago to seek out quality products and buy the best we could afford at the time. Quality lasts and is appreciated for years to come. Many of our readers share our passion for quality shopping abroad."* Their books also are popular with designers, antique dealers, and importers who use them for sourcing products and suppliers.

While the Impact Guides keep the Krannichs busy traveling to exotic places, their travel series is an avocation rather than a vocation. The Krannichs also are noted authors of more than 30 career books, some of which deal with how to find international and travel jobs. The Krannichs also operate one of the world's largest career resource centers. Their works are available in most bookstores or through the publisher's online bookstore: *www.impactpublications.com*

If you have any questions or comments for the authors, please direct them to the publisher:

Drs. Ron and Caryl Krannich
IMPACT PUBLICATIONS
9104 Manassas Drive, Suite N
Manassas Park, VA 20111-5211
Fax 703-335-9486
E-mail: *krannich@impactpublications.com*

More Treasures
and Pleasures

T HE FOLLOWING TRAVEL GUIDES CAN BE ordered directly from the publisher. Complete the following form (or list the titles), include your name and address, enclose payment, and send your order to:

IMPACT PUBLICATIONS
9104 Manassas Drive, Suite N
Manassas Park, VA 20111-5211 (USA)
Tel. 1-800-361-1055 (orders only)
703/361-7300 (information) Fax 703/335-9486
E-mail: *singapore@impactpublications.com*
Online bookstores: ***www.impactpublications.com*** or
www.ishoparoundtheworld.com

All prices are in U.S. dollars. Orders from individuals should be prepaid by check, moneyorder, or credit card (we accept Visa, MasterCard, American Express, and Discover). We accept credit card orders by telephone, fax, e-mail, and online (visit Impact's two online travel bookstores). If your order must be shipped outside the U.S., please include an additional US$1.50 per title for surface mail or the appropriate air mail rate for books weighting 24 ounces each. Orders usually ship within 48 hours. For more information on the authors, travel resources, and international shopping, visit ***www.impactpublications.com*** and ***www.ishoparoundtheworld.com*** on the World Wide Web.

Qty.	TITLES	Price	TOTAL
__	Travel Planning on the Internet	$19.95	_____
__	Treasures and Pleasures of Australia	$17.95	_____
__	Treasures and Pleasures of the Caribbean	$16.95	_____
__	Treasures and Pleasures of China	$14.95	_____
__	Treasures and Pleasures of Egypt	$16.95	_____
__	Treasures and Pleasures of Hong Kong	$16.95	_____

__ Treasures and Pleasures of India	$16.95	_____
__ Treasures and Pleasures of Indonesia	$14.95	_____
__ Treasures and Pleasures of Israel & Jordan	$16.95	_____
__ Treasures and Pleasures of Italy	$14.95	_____
__ Treasures and Pleasures of Paris and the French Riviera	$14.95	_____
__ Treasures and Pleasures of Rio and São Paulo (Brazil)	$13.95	_____
__ Treasures and Pleasures of Singapore and Bali	$16.95	_____
__ Treasures and Pleasures of Thailand	$16.95	_____

SUBTOTAL ------------ $ _____

- Virginia residents add 4.5% sales tax $ _____

- Shipping/handling ($5.00 for the first title and $1.50 for each additional book) $ _____

- Additional amount if shipping outside U.S. $ _____

TOTAL ENCLOSED ---------- $ _____

SHIP TO:

Name _____

Address _____

_____

_____

Phone Number: _____

PAYMENT METHOD:

❏ I enclose check/moneyorder for $ _____ made payable to IMPACT PUBLICATIONS.

❏ Please charge $ _____ to my credit card:

❏ Visa ❏ MasterCard ❏ American Express ❏ Discover

Card # _____

Expiration date: _____/_____

Signature _____

Experience the "best of the best" in travel Treasures and Pleasures!

Emphasizing the "best of the best" in travel and shopping, the unique Impact Guides take today's discerning travelers into the fascinating worlds of artists, craftspeople, and shopkeepers where they can have a wonderful time discovering quality products and meeting talented, interesting, and friendly people. Each guide is jam-packed with practical travel tips, bargaining strategies, key shopping rules, and recommended shops, hotels, restaurants, and sightseeing. The only guides that show how to have a five-star travel and shopping adventure on a less than stellar budget!

New for 2000!

▶ *The Treasures and Pleasures of Australia: Best of the Best.* April 2000. ISBN 1-57023-060-9

▶ *The Treasures and Pleasures of Hong Kong: Best of the Best.* April 2000. ISBN 1-57023-115-X

▶ *The Treasures and Pleasures of Singapore and Bali: Best of the Best.* April 2000. ISBN 1-57023-133-8

▶ *The Treasures and Pleasures of Thailand: Best of the Best.* April 2000. ISBN 1-57023-076-5

▶ *The Treasures and Pleasures of India: Best of the Best.* January 2000. ISBN 1-57023-056-0

Order Online! www.impactpublications.com

Rave Reviews About The Impact Guides:

Travel and Leisure: *"An excellent, exhaustive and fascinating look at shopping."*

Travel-Holiday: *"Books in the series help travelers recognize quality and gain insight to local customs."*

Washington Post: *"You learn more about a place you are visiting when Impact is pointing the way. The Impact Guides are particularly good in evaluating local arts and handicrafts while providing a historical or cultural context."*

▶ *The Treasures and Pleasures of China: Best of the Best.* 1999. 317 pages. ISBN 1-57023-077-3

▶ *The Treasures and Pleasures of the Caribbean.* 1996. 371 pages. ISBN 1-57023-046-3

▶ *The Treasures and Pleasures of Indonesia.* 1996. 243 pages. ISBN 1-57023-045-5

▶ *The Treasures and Pleasures of Italy.* 1997. 271 pages. ISBN 1-57023-058-7

▶ *The Treasures and Pleasures of Paris and the French Riviera.* 1996. 263 pages. ISBN 1-57023-057-9

▶ *The Treasures and Pleasures of Singapore and Malaysia.* 1996. 282 pages. ISBN 1-57023-044-7

Authors: Drs. Ron and Caryl Krannich are two of America's leading travel and career writers with more than 40 books to their credit. They have authored 10 books in the Impact Guides series, including volumes on Hong Kong, Singapore, Malaysia, Indonesia, Italy, and France.

Order Toll-free! 1-800/361-1055

Plan Your Next Trip On the Internet!

Travel Planning On the Internet:
The Click and Easy™ Guide
Ron and Caryl Krannich, Ph.Ds

The Internet has fast become an invaluable resource for savvy travelers. You can quickly go online for airline tickets, hotel and cruise reservations, car rentals, restaurants, shopping, visa applications, tours, newspapers, translations, travel gear, tips, and information on your favorite destinations—nearly everything you ever wanted to know about the wonderful world of travel. Here's the book that pulls it all together. Identifying over 1,000 key Web sites dealing with all aspects of travel, the new Click and Easy™ *Travel Planning on the Internet* is your passport to a whole new world of travel planning in cyberspace. Along with *www.ishoparoundtheworld.com*, use this invaluable guide to plan your next trip or explore new travel options 24-hours a day. Even use it while traveling for locating restaurants, shops, tours, travel tips, and more! October 2000. $19.95 plus shipping.

TO ORDER: Use the form on pages 377-378 or order online: *www.impactpublications.com* or *www.ishoparoundtheworld.com*

Travel the World for Treasures!

Welcome to *iShopAroundTheWorld*, an Internet site that brings together the best of the best in shopping and traveling around the world. If you enjoy shopping, be sure to visit our one-stop-shop for great advice, resources, discussion, and linkages to make your next trip a very special adventure. Discover how to:

- Prepare for a shopping adventure
- Find quality shops and products
- Bargain for the best prices
- Identify local shopping rules
- Order custom-made goods
- Handle touts and tour guides
- Avoid shopping and travel scams
- Pack and ship goods with ease
- Select the best hotels and restaurants
- Use the Internet to travel and shop
- Find inexpensive airfares and cruises
- Travel independently or with tours
- Hire cars, drivers, and guides
- Schedule times and places
- Choose the best sightseeing
- Enjoy terrific entertainment

…and meet talented, interesting, and friendly people in some of the world's most fascinating destinations. Join our community as we travel to the intriguing worlds of artisans, craftspeople, and shopkeepers in search of fine jewelry, clothing, antiques, furniture, arts, handicrafts, textiles, and numerous other treasures to grace your home and enhance your wardrobe. Best of all, shop and travel online before and after your next trip!

www.ishoparoundtheworld.com